The book from which the above was reproduced was published in 1816 and was dedicated "To the officers of the United States Navy who by their bravery and skill have exalted the American character, secured the applause of their country, and excited the admiration of the world." (Frontispiece of *The Naval Monument*)

NAVAL CUSTOMS

TRADITIONS AND USAGE

BY

LIEUTENANT COMMANDER LELAND P. LOVETTE

U. S. NAVY

$2.00 Postpaid

UNITED STATES NAVAL INSTITUTE

ANNAPOLIS, MARYLAND

1939

GEORGE BANTA PUBLISHING COMPANY, MENASHA, WISCONSIN
PRINTED IN THE UNITED STATES OF AMERICA

TO MY COMRADES OF THE NAVY

Past, Present, and Future

PREFACE TO FIRST EDITION

THE major portion of the contents of this book was presented in a series of lectures to a group of student officers at the Postgraduate School, Annapolis, Maryland. The lectures comprised the directives of a specific course in customs, traditions, social usage, and regulations pertaining to honors and ceremonies. Attention was directed to actual mistakes in honors and ceremonies that have been made in the past, and general discussions were centered on those debatable, perplexing situations where only precedent and good judgment may guide. Sufficient rearrangement was made of the lectures in order that the following pages might answer some of the questions asked by those interested in the Navy.

The ample purpose that served to inaugurate the course needs no justification. It appeared most desirable that the course should not only cover the existing regulations and usage, but go a step further and examine the origin of our well established customs and language of the sea. A brief excursion was made also in the field of tradition—the binding force of the Service.

And so, in conformance with the conception of the course desired, the following mission was formulated:

To learn existing regulations of ceremonies, salutes, and honors, and by student research and lecture presentation to lay emphasis upon outstanding customs, traditions, nautical phraseology, usage, and courtesies of the Navy in order to develop in students a finer recognition of their worth and effectiveness.

The mission was approached from several directions, each more or less independent. Not only was it hoped that by this method the subject would be encompassed, but also that by an examination of each direction the student officer would be stimulated to further thought along the line pursued. For example, it was considered that the well-rounded officer should not only know and observe "sea manners" and the customs of the Service, but also be thoroughly familiar with the best social usage of his time. The matter of precedence among our own as well as foreign officials was touched upon. It was an aim in the social customs phase of the course to impress the necessity of knowing at any time—what to do, when to do it, and how.

There was another phase that could not be neglected. That was, inquiry into the salutary effect on *ésprit de corps* of dignified ceremony, and the value of the correct observance of well established naval conventions. As the Japanese phrase it, "Both land and sea forces must observe the etiquette of discipline. The Commander-in-Chief and the lowest soldier have their functions one toward the other."[1]

The fact that our finer customs, ceremonies, and courtesies comprise a splendid heritage; that upon their practical application and observance depend so much that is vital to the Navy, all in all, made every phase of the work one of absorbing interest. And such studies, if they taught nothing else, taught (if the past is a reliable guide) that it takes something more than an education, a uniform, and a commission to effect a love for the Service. In this connection, due to the recent minority recommendation of one of the Board of Visitors of the Naval Academy as to the advisability of a more advanced curriculum, with older and more highly educated admissions, the New York *Times* of 19 July, 1933, said in an editorial, "Besides could comradeship, loyalty to the Service, and emulation which now make the corps so homogeneous and efficient, be inculcated in so short a time?" I do not believe that it can.

I found after the initial research that the mission embraced a study of formidable proportions. For, it was soon apparent that the research ran in divers channels, that the authorities were many, and that some matters I wanted to investigate thoroughly were shrouded in the mists of hearsay and tradition. Also, slight differences of opinion in the Service were found in the realm of the *lex non scripta* of our own usage. For example, is it correct while in uniform to take off one's cap to ladies? Are you "on" a ship or "in" a ship? Do you hoist a flag or break a flag on relief of a flag officer? So, should readers discover omissions which they

[1] The Japanese Rescript to the Army and Navy, January 4, 1882.

regard as serious, an opinion or interpretation in which they do not concur, please consider the compilation as an outline of facts, definitions, regulations, and traditions, as well as an attempt to set forth the best accepted usage that could be gained from the information known and obtainable. Some areas had to be navigated partly by "dead reckoning." Accordingly, the study makes no pretension to completeness; but it may adumbrate in a restricted compass the general nature of a broad subject.

I have done my best to make the book one of convenient reference by collating under the appendixes a part of the useful information that at one time or another the officer will have occasion to use. The nautical phraseology and terms are included in a separate chapter. Most of the definitions of our every-day sea language are well known, but their origins and derivations may prove of interest. It would have been a useless repetition to quote naval regulations relating to honors and ceremonies; nevertheless there has been included in the third chapter a useful table covering the salient features of all honors and ceremonies. This table was compiled in the Fleet, and slight changes were made to bring it to date. The bibliography may be useful to those who care to go further into the study of sea life, customs, and usage.

I desire to express my sincere thanks to Captain F. H. Sadler, U.S.N., who as Head of the Postgraduate School was mainly instrumental in launching the course on the advice and with the approval of Rear Admiral F. B. Upham, U.S.N., then Chief of Bureau of Navigation. Captain Sadler not only sponsored the craft at launching, but also helped get the course under way by encouragement and friendly counsel. To Commander T. E. Van Metre, Executive Officer of the Postgraduate School, my thanks for his assistance and interest in the course. I thank the Librarian and Assistant Librarians of the Naval Academy Library; they gave me all possible aid. I must acknowledge my debt to the student officers of the Postgraduate School classes of 1933 and 1934. Their keen interest in the course was at all times apparent, and to that source I ascribe much of the incentive that I felt to extend the research and to trace some of the regulations to and from their inception.

It is a subject that, so far as I could learn, had never been investigated by an officer of our active list. There is much to be uncovered, and I hope at a later date to add to this collection of naval customs and usage. The source material of nautical terms and customs is usually found in biographies of officers, old naval histories, narratives and logs of voyages, and in particular the accounts of civilian passengers and guests aboard men-of-war. The man of the sea takes much of the customs of life afloat for granted; the landsman is ofttimes inquisitive as to the origin of customs, and describes sea life as it impresses him on first view. For example, one of the most interesting descriptions of honors and ceremonies to be found in our naval history is a description of Farragut's triumphal cruise to Europe after the Civil War. The book was written by a university graduate who went as private secretary to the Admiral.

Aside from the assistance at the Postgraduate School, I thank Admiral Albert Gleaves, U.S.N. (Retired), for his seasoned advice and criticism. My sincere thanks to Commander H. H. Frost, U.S.N., for the inspiration derived and quotations used from his excellent work *We Build a Navy*. To go further afield, I am greatly indebted to Admiral Sir Vernon Haggard, K.C.B. (Retired), for his kindness in sending me most valuable material from England. Rear Admiral Gerald Hall, R.N., Commander W. N. T. Beckett, M.V.O., D.S.C., R.N., and Lieutenant Commander R. G. Lowry, R.N., gave me courteous permission to use excerpts and pertinent matter from their respective books on similar subjects. I am grateful to these officers from over the sea. I thank Professor Allan Westcott, of the Department of English and History, U. S. Naval Academy, for general editing.

Although I have long been of the opinion that the Naval War of 1812 was our "golden age," it was particularly after reading *We Build a Navy*, by Commander H. H. Frost, that I received the incentive to treat that phase of our history as an ideal one for a lecture. My chapter is short and fragmentary, but it may serve as a source of inspiration in its enumeration of the outstanding battles and the makers of naval tradition of that period.

It was necessary to go to British source material for much that is of value and interest to those of our Service, for it was with a common speech and stock that our Navy was founded. Although in many respects our ways have widely diverged, our oldest customs, nautical phraseology, and ceremonies and honors came mainly from the Navy of Britain.

In conclusion, I must say that the research became a work of affection. Possibly the thought of the age we live in gave rise to the feeling. For, when chicanery and corruption have been revealed in high places, when selfish interests and petty politics strive for the "spoils," it is inspiring to inspect the beginnings of our naval heritage and the splendid manner in which it has been transmitted to us. The record of the Navy is clear to date.

The naval heritage, after all is said, should clearly indicate that *honor* and *loyalty* comprise its essence; that will be true as long as a service worthy of the name exists. The midshipman is taught at the beginning of his naval career that *"Honor* is the fundamental essential in a naval officer's character." That tradition has lived, and it must live on or the prestige of the Service dies. By their records and traditions ye shall know them.

L.P.L.

Postgraduate School,
United States Naval Academy, Annapolis, Md.,
July, 1934.

PREFACE TO SECOND EDITION

THE first virtue of a work such as *Naval Customs, Traditions, and Usage* is to be accurate and the second, to be interesting. The first was attained to an unanticipated degree; the second was satisfactorily gained if criticism, reviews, and the reception of the book by readers may be accepted as criteria.

The few slight errors in the first edition were corrected before the second printing of that edition. In the present edition, some matter has been added, such as more detailed information pertinent to official calls in Washington; a short history of the

Marine Corps and of the Coast Guard with a much too brief mention of their splendid traditions; and the expansion and amplification of Chapter IX, "Nautical Words and Naval Expressions."

The author acknowledges, with gratitude and appreciation, his indebtedness to the officers of the Navy, Marine Corps, and Coast Guard, and to the keen critics of things literary and maritime outside the Service, who have carefully read the first edition. Their suggestions have resulted in an improved second edition.

L.P.L.

Chefoo, China
   March 1, 1936.

PREFACE TO THIRD EDITION

The writer is greatly indebted to several research students of sea lore for their meticulous inspection of the second edition of this work. The errors that were found have been corrected in this edition. The appendices have been extended to cover wedding ceremonies, toasts, and a recent opinion on the yacht ensign. An up-to-date precedence list of official Washington has been added along with other new material.

The author has been gratified to receive considerable correspondence to the general effect that this collection of naval customs and traditions has proved useful to the regular and reserve personnel of the Navy. Some went so far as to state that they had gained an enhanced appreciation of the value of our traditions. May that trend continue at this time when all emphasis should be placed on the past defenders of American institutions.

To add the best of the old; to keep alive the most pertinent of the new; and to emphasize the importance of our naval and sea heritage will be guiding factors in all future editions.

L. P. L.

Navy Department
   Washington, D.C.
     April 30, 1939

ACKNOWLEDGMENTS

It is of course impossible to give proper credit to all who by their writings have greatly facilitated the preparation of this book. The occasional footnotes scattered throughout the volume indicate from what sources most of the material has been drawn. The bibliography was not added with a design to impress the reader; all books listed have been consulted, and are recommended for further inquiry into the many phases of a study of this nature. The views expressed are solely those of the author, and therefore do not necessarily reflect the Navy Department or any other government department, unless text is specifically designated as official.

I wish to express my appreciation for the use of copyrighted material by the following:

Harper and Brothers. For permission to reproduce from *All Hands*, by R. F. Zogbaum, drawings of the "Old Navy."

Gieves, Ltd., London. For permission to use material from *A Few Naval Customs, Expressions, Traditions, and Superstitions*, by Commander W. N. T. Beckett, M.V.O., D.S.C., Royal Navy.

The Macmillan Company, New York. For permission to use material from *The Secretary's Handbook*, by Taintor and Munro.

Naval Institute, Annapolis, Md. For permission to make liberal use of various articles of contributors. Also my appreciation for the permission to use excerpts from Commander H. H. Frost's book, *We Build a Navy*.

Funk and Wagnalls, New York.

Alfred A. Knopf, New York.

American Lithograph Company, Inc., New York.

Houghton Mifflin Co., Boston.

OBSERVATIONS AND REFLECTIONS

"In the Navy, after you have been in it a certain number of years, everyone knows you, has you labeled, sized up, and catalogued. If you have gotten into trouble, it is lovingly remembered and fixed to your name."

* * *

"However, line officers of the Navy are the only class of people who have actually and continuously to demonstrate their fitness to hold their jobs, and the only ones who have to take a chance on being 'smirched' after making good on all the requirements. Meanwhile, from year to year the great uplift movement goes on, always new schemes to improve the efficiency of line officers, physically, mentally, and morally. Examinations become more rigid. New tests are exacted. Inspections are made to test the efficiency of commanding officers, and every year the plucking knife sinks deeper and deeper.

"Meanwhile nobody else under the government has necessarily to know much of anything, except to be geographically and politically well located. There is no examination for ambassador, collector of internal revenue, postmaster-general, marshal, district attorney, interstate commerce commissioner, etc. It is merely a question of getting the appointment, and being confirmed by the Senate.

"It is therefore some achievement, after all, to survive the slings and sorrows of outrageous fortune, and retire for age on attaining the age of 62 as a rear admiral, U. S. Navy."

* * *

"So cheer up, my son. Play the game. Take your medicine. Don't squeal. Watch your step. After all, it is a splendid profession and an honorable career."

* * *

"Personally, I would rather be a commissioned officer in the Navy than hold any other position under the government. It is an honor; it is a career; it is one of the most exacting and difficult of all professions. Otherwise, I would not have urged you to enter the Navy."

* * *

"You ask me if I think it pays to be a naval officer. It depends. It depends on whether or not you are prepared to play the game. 'Obedience to the law is liberty.' If you keep the law, it pays. If you have the courage of your convictions, it may not pay. If you play the game; if you always keep a month's pay on the books; if you put nothing else ahead of your profession; if you pocket your opinions, it pays. Otherwise it may not. . . .

"The naval profession is much like the ministry. You dedicate your life to a purpose. You wear the garb of an organized profession. Your life is governed by rules laid down by the organization. You renounce the pursuit of wealth. In a large measure you surrender your citizenship; renounce politics; and work for the highest good of the organization. In the final analysis your aims and objects are quite as moral as any minister's, because morality consists in the conservation of the best interests of civilization, and you are not seeking your own good, but the ultimate good of your country. You train the men under you to be good and useful citizens, and, like the minister, what you say must conform to the rules of the organization."

Naval Institute PROCEEDINGS, XLI, No. 157, "Letters of a Retired Rear Admiral to his Son," written by Captain A. P. Niblack, U. S. Navy, 30 May, 1913.

CONTENTS

LIST OF ILLUSTRATIONS

PART I

TRADITIONS, CEREMONIES, AND CUSTOMS

PERRY TRANSFERS HIS FLAG AT LAKE ERIE—"If a victory is to be gained, I'll gain it." (Painting by W. H. Powell, in Capitol of U. S.)

CHAPTER I

TRADITIONS, CEREMONIES, AND CUSTOMS OF THE SERVICE

"What men will fight for seems to be worth looking into."
                                             H. L. MENCKEN[1]

"May we not who are of their brotherhood claim that in a small way at least we are partakers of their glory? Certainly it is our duty to keep these traditions alive and in our memory, and to pass them on untarnished to those who come after us."
                    REAR ADMIRAL ALBERT GLEAVES, U. S. Navy[2]

"It is the soul of the Navy [ésprit de corps] and ours from the junior cadet to the senior admiral, the charge to 'save that soul alive.'"
      CAPTAIN [later Rear Admiral] CASPAR F. GOODRICH, U. S. Navy[3]

"It should be the first duty and pride of a midshipman to learn and to conform to the customs and traditions of the Naval Service. The rules for military etiquette are founded on custom and tradition, and their strict observance forms an important factor in the maintenance of discipline. It must be thoroughly understood at the outset that these evidences of respect and courtesy are to be observed equally by all officers and men in the Naval Service, the junior to be the one to take the initiative."

                    Regulations, United States Naval Academy[4]

TRADITIONS, ceremonies, and customs exert a profound influence upon human behavior throughout life. The effect is particularly marked in such professions as the military and naval, organizations that lend themselves to passing on and perpetuating the more venerated customs, heroic traditions, and dignified ceremonies. Such stimuli when understood and properly directed effect a discipline, a distinction, and a service *ésprit de corps* of incalculable value.

It is unfortunate that in the last few decades we have witnessed a dethronement of important ethical postulates and criteria that were once part and parcel of certain honorable professions. The naval service has suffered very little in this respect. Never-

[1] *Prejudices* (3d series) "Traditions," 31 May, 1924 [2] Response to the toast "Naval History and Traditions," 31 May, 1924 [3] *"Ésprit de Corps,"* Prize Essay, U. S. Naval Institute, 1898 [4] Art. 996

theless, a materialistic and machine age leaves its mark, and none may escape entirely the new thought and ideology incident to its existence. For example, the naval officer has been required to devote all the time and the intellect that he could muster to keeping abreast of his profession as it moved rapidly with the advance of science. There has been time for little else. Such a ferment of modernity may cause the Service to underestimate the value of its traditions, customs, and ceremonies, and with it their composite, concomitant effect. This would be a distinct loss in spite of the fact that some traditions are unreliable; some customs impractical; and some ceremonies of little apparent value; yet, in the main, the heritage is impressive.

The value of tradition to a military or naval service is recognized only by those who know something of the deeds contained in its "Golden Book." The effect that customs had in the formulation of naval regulations is a particular example of the influence of sound usage. Moreover, the worth of ceremony rests mainly upon the fact that it binds us to the past while at the same time it lends an air of dignity and respect in all official relations whether they occur at home or abroad. Ceremony is to a marked degree the cement of discipline, and upon discipline the service rests. Tradition, when coupled with courage and pride, gives to the officer corps its highest incentive to carry on. For, is it not true in any age of rapidly changing values and intellectual unrest that we are inclined to underestimate tradition's contribution to *ésprit de corps,* and particularly its significance in relation to discipline? In this age of world ferment, with the existing chaotic economic conditions, the defaulting of just debts, with sinister moves by nations on other fronts for hegemonies, domination of weaker states, and in some cases the deliberate planting of the seeds of revolution, every sound bulwark to morale is needed by the Service.

All will not hold that "Indeed it is self-evident that were it not for the Navy the independence of the United States would long ago have ceased to exist."[1] But thrilling and inspiring naval

[1] Joseph Gurn, *Commodore John Barry, Father of the American Navy* (1933), p. 3.

history records that the policies of the Continental Congress were fought for by John Paul Jones and John Barry. The policies of Jefferson, Adams, and Madison were defended on the seas by Hull, Macdonough, Lawrence, and Perry. The policies for the maintenance of the Union as promulgated by Lincoln were defended by Farragut. The Service has ever been the strong right arm of government. In reality, it is in the face of public apathy that the Service most needs its worthy traditions. The faithful and sincere performance of monotonous detail constitutes commendatory tradition.

To maintain the high ideals of profession, of character, and of belief in their cause that were characteristic of our greater sea leaders, requires sturdy idealism. Ideals play a prominent part in the time-honored criteria for the gauging of the true officer. The late John Grier Hibben, former President of Princeton University, recently wrote, "We need a renaissance of idealism." He follows this with a plea for higher values in life, a recapitulation, as it were, and an estimate of the situation, with the question as to what are "those thoughts and feelings which transcend this material world." Who doubts the existence of such thoughts? An examination of the honor, the loyalty, and the creditable performance of duty, both individually and *en masse,* of the brotherhood that have passed on, tends to impress one with the worth of the traditional, professional ethics of the naval code.

The Service must ever guard against becoming soft and permitting the material comforts of the age to weaken its fiber. Privations and a "hard school" have produced our outstanding sailors. The officers corps should appreciate world history to the extent that their sword edge will not be dulled by the idle talk that universal peace and brotherhood have reached such an advanced stage that the naval profession has no place in the organization of strong government. The maintenance of all law depends upon force in the last resort. We need less internationalism and more enlightened nationalism. Who will respect defenselessness?

Let us examine custom. Custom is defined as "habitual repeti-

tion of the same act or procedure, established manner or way."
Woolsey, in his introduction to international law, wrote, "Customs within each country existed before statutes, and so observances come imperceptibly, and control the conduct of a circle of nations." Emerson once remarked, "We all live according to custom." Bacon, in recognition of the influence of customs in the Elizabethan age, wrote, "since custom is the principal magistrate of men's lives, let men by all means obtain good customs." Customs have played an important rôle in the administration of a naval or military organization. The conservatism of the Navy has enabled the Service, in much the same manner as royalty, nobility, and the priest-craft in the hierarchy of religions, to pass on to future members the established customs and definite traditions.

Customs of the Service have the full effect of law when they fulfill the naval legal definition. It has been held that "Customs of the Service can only be taken as precedents to follow when intrinsically proper in themselves and supplementary of the written law and regulations on points on which the latter are silent."[1] Moreover, "Customs of the Service" are again legally acknowledged in that "specifications of naval courts-martial must on their face allege facts which constitute a violation of some law, regulation, or custom of the Service. . . ."[2]

As a rule, customs of the Service when established by long usage have led to definitive regulations. This fact is noted in the *Naval Digest,* wherein it is stated: "Customs and usages of the Service, whether originating in traditions or in specific orders or rulings, are now, as such, not numerous in the Army (or Navy), a large proportion, in obedience to a natural law, having changed their form by becoming merged in written regulations." It is apparent that regulations are merely customs that have crystallized because of long usage.

Customs have a legal definition. The *Naval Digest,* 1921, states:

[1] *Court-Martial Orders,* 43 (1906), 3.
[2] *Court-Martial Orders,* 33 (1914), 6.

GERMAN SUBMARINE *U-103* RAMMED BY H.M.S. *Olympic*—This incident took place off the south coast of Ireland 3:50 A.M., 12 May, 1918. The U.S.S. *Davis*, Commander W. V. Tomb, U. S. Navy, rescued 35 of the crew, 9 perished. (Courtesy Navy Department. From a painting by Pointer, QM3c, U.S.S. *Davis*, copy by Replogle Navy Yard, Philadelphia)

FARRAGUT AT MOBILE BAY.—The *Hartford* and *Tennessee* at close quarters, Mobile Bay, 5 August, 1864. (Courtesy Naval Records and Library, Navy Department. From a painting by W. H. Overend)

Elements necessary to establish the principal conditions to be fulfilled in order to constitute a valid custom are: (a) It must be long continued; (b) it must be certain and uniform; (c) it must be compulsory; (d) it must be consistent; (e) it must be general; (f) it must be known; (g) it must not be in opposition to the terms and provisions of a statute or lawful regulation or order.[1]

Foreign customs have a legal status. "The religious institutions and customs of foreign countries visited by ships of the Navy must be respected."[2]

In general, any research that concerns the development of regulations and law clearly indicates that usage has led to custom, and custom to laws, regulations, and established ceremony. The *New Century Dictionary* defines *usage* as,

Long continued use or practice, customary way of acting, custom, practice; as, the ancient *usage* of Parliament. Technically in English law *usage* has a different signification from *custom,* in not implying immemorial existence or general prevalence. In earlier times *custom* was defined as a law created or evidenced by immemorial usage. Some American writers use the terms as practically equivalent, except in regarding *usage* as the facts by which the existence of *custom* is proved; others treat usage as the habit of individual classes. . . . "

One of the most interesting subjects of sociology is the history of ceremonies and forms.[3] Whether the research be confined to ceremonies, ecclesiastical, legal, military, or naval, the student will find a wealth of source material, and throughout such an investigation he will be impressed with the continuity of tradition and custom. We are of course concerned particularly with ceremony, usage, and customs from the point of view of the naval service. Although it is beyond the scope of this

[1] *Naval Courts and Boards* (1917), p. 9. File 26251, 25288, 2 Nov., 1920. *Court-Martial Orders* 133 (1920), 11.
[2] *U. S. Navy Regulations* (1920), art. 117.
[3] Ceremony is defined as "formalities observed on some solemn or important public or state occasion in order to render it more imposing or impressive; as the ceremony of crowning a king, or laying a foundation stone; the ceremony of inaugurating a President of the United States . . . , " and again it is "a usage of politeness, or such usages collectively; formality."

study to treat ceremony and form from a sociological point of view, it is fitting that this historical aspect be mentioned. Thorstein Veblen, in his erudite study entitled *Theory of the Leisure Class,* discusses ceremonial institutions from their inception, with comment on their ethnological bearing. Although ceremony has a different connotation today from that understood in its early practice, it is interesting to read Veblen's comments on the slow change in definition. He writes of the history of ceremonial rule:

We have seen how ceremony originates from fear: on the one side supremacy of a victor or master, on the other side dread of death or punishment felt by the vanquished or the slave. And under the régime of compulsory co-operation thus initiated, fear develops and maintains in strength all forms of propitiation. But with the rise of a social type based on voluntary co-operation, fear decreases. The subordinate ruler or officer is no longer wholly at the mercy of his superior; the trader, not liable to be robbed or tortured by the noble, has a remedy against him for non-payment; the laborer in receipt of wages cannot be beaten like the slave. In proportion as the system of exchanging services under contract spreads and the rendering of services under compulsion diminishes, men dread one another less; and, consequently, become less scrupulous in fulfilling propitiatory forms.

Ceremonies, in their transition from the servility that originated in fear and awe, are accepted today in military organizations as regulations of dignified respect to the symbols of the state and the state's officials. Those in the Service entered voluntarily, and thereby embraced a system of ceremonial institutions. Ceremonies are a function of discipline; definitive regulations for important occasions. In a sense, they are tributes to worthy tradition. If the respect for lawful authority and the symbolism of the flag are worthy of preservation, they must be revered by their defenders.

A man may be taught to feel pride in uniform, pride in service, and pride in his respect to the flag. Of Lord Jervis, the Earl of St. Vincent, a master seaman and great disciplinarian, Mahan writes:

He wisely believed in the value of forms, and was careful to employ them, in this crisis of the mutinies, to enforce the habit of reverence for the insignia of the state and the emblems of military authority. The discipline of the cabin and wardroom officer is the discipline of the fleet said the admiral [St. Vincent]; and savage almost were the punishments that fell upon officers who disgraced their cloth. The hoisting of the colors, the symbol of power of the nation, from which depended his own and that of all the naval hierarchy, was made an august and imposing ceremony. . . . Lord St. Vincent made a point of attending always, and in full uniform; a detail he did not require of other officers . . . the very atmosphere the seamen breathed was saturated with reverence.

Mahan again relates how Jervis adhered strictly to custom and ceremony

to pay outward reverence to the national flag, to salute the quarter-deck as the seat of authority, were no vain show under him. "Discipline," he was fond of quoting, "is summed up in the one word obedience," and these customs were charged with the observance which is obedience in spirit. They conduce to discipline as conventional good manners, by rendering the due of each to each, knit together the social fabric and maintain the regularity and efficiency of common life; removing friction, suppressing jars, and ministering constantly to the smooth and even working of the social machinery.

It was thus that Jervis by inculcation of spirit, regular drill, and observance of ceremony wielded the weapon that won for him the decisive victory of Cape St. Vincent, and passed on to Nelson the fleet that the hero of Trafalgar commanded with incomparable genius.

Tradition, as a word, is often loosely used. The original Latin *traditio* meant a giving up, surrender, or delivery. The *Century Dictionary* gives as a definition for our restricted purpose,

The handing down of opinions; doctrines, rites, and customs from ancestors to posterity; the transmission of any opinion or practice from forefathers to descendants or from one generation to another, by oral communication, without written memorials.

In every phase of human behavior as well as in the fields of knowledge, we encounter tradition; sometimes traditions that are good and frequently those that are bad. "Say what you will against tradition; we know the Signification of Words by nothing but Tradition."[1] Or again in the realm of manners and of law, Herbert Spencer observes, "While in the course of civilization written law tends to replace *traditional* usages, the replacement never becomes complete."

It is granted that the years add a glamor to the courageous or heroic acts of those who have gone. Mankind tends to weave some embroidery on the fabric of the actual event. Most romantic and many sentimental traditions hold little truth.

There is also a most practical justification for the fostering of traditional customs. Think of the difficulty should the officer be compelled to decide whether the starboard or port side would be the ceremonial side of a ship, or whether it may or may not be well to "sound taps" at a funeral, or what side of the quarter-deck should be the captain's.

Tradition justifies itself because it leads to economy of effort; the individual is released from the burden of having to learn everything from the ground upward, and is able to make use of the experience of others.[2]

A reactionary spirit is only to be commended when it clings to an old tradition, custom, or usage, certain that a change will effect neither enlightenment nor improvement.

It is difficult to estimate the value of tradition to a military or naval service. Mahan in his essay, "Military Rule of Obedience," wrote:

The value of tradition to the social body is immense. The veneration for practices, or for authority, consecrated by long acceptance, has a reserve of strength which cannot be obtained by any novel device. Respect for the old customs is planted deep in the hearts, as well as in the intelligence, of all inheritors of English speaking polity.

The outstanding officers of the Service have ever recognized the power of tradition. In a desire to emulate their progenitors,

[1] Selden, *Table Talk*, p. iii.
[2] W. A. Edwards, "Plagiarism," Le Bas Prize Essay, 1932, Cambridge University.

one becomes imbued with some of the spirit that prompted a tradition's birth. In fact, the greatest thing that can ever be said of an officer after he passes into civil life, retired status, or to the Great Beyond, is that he lived and acted according to the best traditions of the Service. In order that one may live up to traditions one must know them; one must appreciate them.

It is of interest to consider the marked continuity of naval tradition. John Paul Jones probably gave us the great tradition of engaging and defeating the first frigate of the then "Invincible Royal Navy." This action gave hope to the American cause, and inspired our infant Navy with the possibility of rendering real aid to the struggling Colonies. We gained from Jones another tradition of which historians seldom speak, namely, that of magnanimity to foe when our arms are victorious. After the *Bon Homme Richard-Serapis* action when the gallant Pearson presented his sword to Jones, tradition relates that this Captain of the Royal Navy said: "I cannot, Sir, but feel much mortification at the idea of surrendering my sword to a man who fought me with a rope around his neck."

Jones received his sword but returned it at once saying: "You have fought gallantly, Sir, and I hope your king will give you a better ship."

In the War of 1812 after the battle of Lake Erie, Perry returned the swords of the British captains as a mark of recognition for the stubborn resistance that they had made.

The little Navy of the War of the Revolution was finally disbanded, leaving nothing behind it except "the recollection of its service and sufferings," but traditions lived on. When the famous frigates, the *Constitution,* the *President,* the *United States,* the *Chesapeake,* the *Constellation,* and the *Congress* were completed, the heroes of the Revolution—Barry, Nicholson, Barney, Dale, and Truxtun—were chosen to command. Truxtun gave a glorious account of himself in the *Constellation* when he captured the *Insurgente,* and crippled the *Vengeance,* in the short maritime war with France.

Our naval activities then turned to another part of the world. Preble attacked the forts of Tripoli. Captain Somers with Wadsworth and Israel went to their death in the daring explosive boat attack. Their deeds are commemorated by the Tripoli Monument at the Naval Academy. Before Preble's attack on Tripoli, the *Philadelphia* commanded by Bainbridge was lost to the Tripolitan pirates. The ship went aground in shoal water before the surrender. The resistance, to say the least, was faint-hearted. Frost writes,

It is true that then we had no naval tradition—but Germans also had none when they entered the World War. Yet they knew how to die! True, for Bainbridge there are many good excuses. But how we wish that he had stood forth there and spoken to his comrades, in the words of Beowulf:

> "Each of us must his end abide
> in the ways of the world; so win who may
> glory ere death! When his days are told,
> that is the warrior's worthiest doom."

Stephen Decatur afterwards attacked and burned the captured *Philadelphia* that his father had once commanded. Even Nelson in his cabin in the *Victory* off Toulon said the feat was "the most bold and daring act of the age." A great tradition that will never die! With but few exceptions, it was a brilliant naval campaign and resulted in eliminating forever the tribute that had been paid to the Barbary Coast "racketeers."

Next came the "second war for independence," the War of 1812. Hull's victory in the *Constitution* against the *Guerrière* astonished both sides of the Atlantic. Congress thanked Hull in the name of the nation and gave the officers and crew $50,000 in prize money. This victory was far-reaching in that it gave our new Navy confidence, and disspelled the prevailing idea that the British Navy was omnipotent. Our Navy was slowly but surely making tradition.

Great Britain's attention was emphatically called to the exploits of the "Yankee sailors" and their frigates. The London *Times* wrote:

It is not merely that an English frigate has been taken, after what, we are free to confess, may be called a brave resistance, but that it has been taken by a new enemy, an enemy unaccustomed to such triumphs, and likely to be rendered insolent and confident by them. . . . Never before in the history of the world did an English frigate strike to an American; and though we cannot say that Captain Dacres, under all circumstances, is punishable for this act, yet we do say that there are commanders in the English Navy who would a thousand times rather have gone down with their colors flying than have set their brother officers so fatal an example.

The London *Times* was correct as to the confidence engendered, for the American Navy had achieved the first of the victories that astounded our own people. Decatur in the *United States* captured the *Macedonian;* the *Constitution* shot every spar out of the frigate *Java,* and shortly afterwards captured both the *Cyane* and *Levant* in the same action.

It was an era when fighting slogans were coined, such as Lawrence's dying words in the *Chesapeake,* "Fight her till she sinks and don't give up the ship." There follows again the continuity of tradition, for Perry carried the watchword on to Lake Erie, when he hoisted at the main royal masthead of the *Lawrence* the flag upon which were sewed Lawrence's last words, "Don't give up the ship." Then came Perry's dispatch which has been so often quoted, "We have met the enemy and they are ours, two ships, two brigs, one schooner, and one sloop"—a regrettable war, but one that gave impetus to American sea power, for it was a test of American shipbuilding and seamen.

Greek met Greek in the 1812-1815 naval war. The Yankee sailors demonstrated a coolness that was inherent in their native English stock, and a daring that derived from their pioneer spirit. Due to the constant gun drills, American marksmanship was unexcelled. American sea power dealt powerful blows in this second war of Independence; *they believed in their cause.*

The continuity of the great sea tradition was passed on to Farragut. Farragut at the age of twelve, and trained by David Porter, was appointed prize master of the *Barclay.* It was half a century before Farragut won the battle of New Orleans. Dewey was with Farragut at New Orleans as a young lieutenant. The late Admiral of the Navy said that at Manila Bay he thought "What would Farragut do?" There are officers at the top of the Navy list today who were with Dewey and will insure that the continuity of great tradition will be maintained.

This brief recital of a few of the outstanding makers of tradition should emphasize their priceless gifts to the Country and the Service. The traditions of the military and naval service evolve by hard work, prompt action, accurate decisions, acts of self-sacrifice, and if necessary the giving up of life itself. Should not the memories of our finest traditions toughen the fibre and strengthen the character of officers and men?

It is the privilege of the Navy to maintain not only the traditions of the Service but also the traditions of the sea. Those who follow the sea feel a brotherhood with the seamen of all nations. For, as Conrad wrote,

The mysteriously born tradition of sea craft commands unity in an occupation in which men have to depend on each other. It raises them so to speak above the frailties of their dead selves.

Such mutual help has from mankind's first venture upon great waters been characteristic of men of the sea. This aspect has been the theme of some great literature—tragedy, romance, and adventure.

It is natural that the Service will ever hold nearest the deeds of its own, but it is most profitable for the sea officer to turn to other navies and to learn something of their great seamen. Nelson, Rodney, and Suffren, all impressed their genius on the saga of naval warfare. The daring of Von Müller in the *Emden* as he roamed the Pacific and Goodenough's work in command of the Fifth Light Cruiser Squadron at Jutland will give the officer of any Navy accounts of courage and daring that are worthy of remembrance.

Who are the most outstanding officers in the Navy? Carved on the amphitheater at Arlington are the following names: John Paul Jones, Thomas Truxtun, Edward Preble, Isaac Hull, Stephen Decatur, Oliver Hazard Perry, Thomas Macdonough, Charles Stewart, David Glasgow Farragut, David Dixon Porter, Andrew Hull Foote, John Lorimer Worden, George Dewey, and William Thomas Sampson. These names were selected a few years ago as the most distinguished American naval offi-

"ENGLAND EXPECTS EVERY MAN TO DO HIS DUTY" (Reproduced from old engravings)

cers, by a committee of admirals, captains, and college presidents. The names comprise a great composite tradition. All of these officers reached an eminence in the Service that few will attain. The best traditions of the Service will be served if their careers are patterned after.

It would be a matter of profitable professional research to select a composite group from the galaxy of great sea officers of other services. When it comes to Britain, there is one officer who stands alone—Nelson. Mahan did not include him in his types, for in the words of St. Vincent there was but one Nelson. British officers are unanimous in their opinion that the most inspiring, living, outstanding tradition of the Royal Navy is the Nelsonian one. Conrad expressed the power of this tradition in his inimitable style when he wrote, "Like a subtle and mysterious elixir poured into the perishable clay of successive generations, it [Nelsonian tradition] grows in truth, splendor, and potency with the march of ages." Who will deny the strength of the supreme sea tradition of Britain?

In France, one of the most impressive of all military traditions is observed. By a decree of Napoleon, it was ordered that the name of the gallant La Tour d'Auvergne should be forever carried on the company's rolls. During the World War, an officer of our Marine Corps witnessed this ceremony. As the name was called, "La Tour d'Auvergne," the color sergeant stepped forward and answered to the call, "Dead on the Field of Honor." Bravery lives again by the enacting of this solemn ceremony, and it deserves its place in distinguished military tradition alongside the alleged French saying, "The Old Guard dies but never surrenders."

Admiral Jedina of the old Austrian Navy once said that all sailors belong to one great international brotherhood of the sea; that they speak a common language, live the same life, and expect the same death. For this reason, those who follow the sea; those who are sensible to the caprices and ever changing moods of oceans; those who know the type of men best fitted to combat the elements find great traditions among seafarers of all races. There is Lieutenant Sakuma of the Japanese

Navy, who, imprisoned in a submarine that sank in maneuvers, died at his desk while writing a detailed report of the disaster. Those who met death in the U.S.S. *S-4* left a record of courage that is unsurpassed. The gallant Scott of the Royal Navy wrote until his fingers were too frozen to hold a pen. His last words, written before his death in the wastes of the Antarctic were, "We are very near the end, we did intend to finish ourselves when things proved like this, but we decided to die naturally without . . ." Years before Scott's death, De Long of the United States Navy died in the Arctic from starvation and exposure. He met death with that calmness characteristic of brave men. His journal was kept to the last. Admiral Tryon of the British Navy stood on the bridge of his ship with folded arms after the *Camperdown* rammed the *Victoria,* and with no visible emotion went to a sailor's grave. In our Navy, Captain William L. Herndon, when he realized that his command, the *Central America,* could not be saved, went to his cabin and donned his frock coat, removed his cap cover to show the distinctive braid of a captain, waved off a rescue boat to keep it from being swamped by the sinking ship; uncovered, and in plain view of his crew in the boats went down in his ship.

There are many brave and heroic deeds of the sea that will never be generally known. This is of course true for the Merchant Marine as well as the Navy. Every man who follows the sea knows some of these "untitled knights of the blue ocean." But after all are they not carrying on the traditions of the sea, and striving to live up to the courage, the stamina, and the seamanship that have characterized their predecessors? Such men have a pride of profession and a pride of service that are unsurpassed in any walk of life. They have a kinship with Nelson in that they understand how he felt at Copenhagen when a shot knocked splinters off the mainmast near where he was standing, and he observed with a smile, "It is warm work, and this may be the last of us at any moment," and then with great emotion he added, "But, mark you—I would not be elsewhere for thousands." Men of this ilk are not pacifists; they comprise the bulwark of a nation in arms.

Unflinching courage in the face of disaster and adversity constitutes the essence of the tales that thrill all races. The sea has been the scene both in fact and fiction of some of the most daring and noble acts of mankind.

Down the years from the Scandinavian sagas to the most recent rescue in great storms, there is a quickening of interest in accounts of "men against the sea." These heroic deeds become the precious stuff of tradition. They live because of their worth.

It may be the priest Zosima of the torpedoed *Proot* of the old Russian Navy, who, in clerical vestments and with silver crucifix, blessed many of those struggling in the water. Or it may be Admiral Koltchak, the last Commander in Chief of the Imperial Russian Black Sea Fleet, who threw his gold ceremonial sword overboard rather than surrender it to the revolting crew. Or it may be Captain Weniger who, until he and his officers fell, resisted any attempt of the mutineers to haul down the naval flag of Prussian cross and Imperial eagle.

There is Admiral Beatty at Jutland who, after witnessing great losses and suffering heavy gunfire, turned towards his Flag Captain and said: "Chatfield, there seems to be something wrong with our bloody ships today, turn two points to port." (Towards the enemy.) Or on the night of Jutland, it is recalled that the survivors of the last *Tipperary*, although crowded upon a raft and suffering from exposure, were recognized afar off by the tune they were singing—"It's a long, long way to Tipperary."

It is well that we should read our own sea annals with care, for in them we will find heroic traditions second to none, traditions that bespeak the iron will of "Surrender be damned, I have not yet begun to fight," that reflect the fighting spirit of "Don't give up the ship," and the preparation and planning implied by "We are ready now." Their preservation and perpetuation rests with the officers and men of the Navy.

CHAPTER II

SOME TRADITIONS, CEREMONIES, AND CUSTOMS OF THE SERVICE

"Customs may not be as wise as laws, but they are always more popular."

DISRAELI

"Let me premise here that the bedrock of a naval service is organization; its soul, honor; its necessity, subordination; its demand, courage; its inspiration, love of country; its crown, honor."

ADMIRAL G. E. BELKNAP, U. S. Navy[1]

"The worth of a sentiment lies in the sacrifices men will make for its sake. All ideals are built on the ground of solid achievement, which in a given profession creates in the course of time a certain tradition, or in other words, a standard of conduct."

JOSEPH CONRAD

WE EVER pay an unthinking tribute to tradition. Some of our best known customs and ceremonies may be traced in origin to antiquity, while others grew from practices of the Middle Ages. It is definitely known that the ceremonies connected with the launching of ships, with the rendering of salutes, and with military funerals antedate the Christian Era. Boisterous ceremonies comparable to "crossing the line" may be traced to the Vikings most adventurous age, and possibly existed with other mariners prior to the Norsemen's distant ventures. Xenophon refers in his *Hellenica* to certain duties of the boatswain, while on a voyage of triremes of war from the Piraeus to Corfu in 373 B.C. Marines or sea soldiers were in this fleet. Livy employs the expression *"praetoria navis"* to refer to the admiral's ship or the flagship, *"praetor,"* meaning "he who leads the Navy into battle." *Praetor* was used in the Roman Army to designate the commander in chief. Cargo ships in the Punic Wars were commanded by *magestis navis* or master of ships; hence the modern expression "ship's master. '

In the time of St. Paul, so relates the Greek Testament, sound-

---

[1] Lecture delivered Naval War College, 30 July, 1897.

ings were taken after a gale, and the ship was found to be in twenty fathoms of water. The Greek word *orgina* was used for fathom, and comes from the verb *orego,* which means to stretch or reach out with the arms. Today, the modern sailor stretches out both arms and thereby measures from finger tips to finger tips an approximate fathom.

Traditions, ceremonies, and customs play prominent rôles in all occupations and professions. All in all, they comprise the soul of a military or naval service. It is true that ceremonies by their very nature may tend in time to become a hollow show should the reason for their existence terminate or their traditional effect become nil. On the other hand, it seems to be a way of the world to commence an organization with little ceremony and then add with time. Christ employed little or no ceremony in his conduct of religious worship. Men decreed otherwise. Lenin abolished all the traditional decorations of Imperial Russia, but today the Order of Lenin is the highest decoration in Sovietdom, while the Order of the Red Star has been recently decreed by Stalin. The impressive procession that files by the embalmed remains of the Grand Master of Communism is in essence a ceremony.

A correspondent of the Manchester *Guardian,* after describing the physical appearance of Lenin in his glass bier, says, Here, then, is the single retrospective gesture encouraged in Soviet Russia. Everything except Lenin is in the future. To pause and look backward is permissible only in the one case. Apart from Lenin the past has no existence.

It is Lenin, the great Communist tradition, that is ever kept by appropriate ceremony before the people. If there were no God, Voltaire said that mankind would invent one.

Ceremonies, customs, and taboos have influenced so profoundly the religions, superstitions, and manners of tribes, races, and states, that their treatment comprises the greater part of most sociological and ethical works. The seafaring man will gain a clearer conception of why he is what he is after an inspection and examination of the derivation of customs, ceremonies, and the language of the sea. The sailor of ancient Greece, four hundred years before the Christian Era, was considered by some to be of a curious breed. The modern sailor is considered so today by many landsmen. The steamship sailor cannot in many respects be compared with the seaman of sail, but the two types have a common cast of thought that has characterized mariners since they first ventured upon great waters. Men who brave the elements in hazardous callings understand this.

The record of the Navy has been to date one of very good fortune, for neither has the United States lost a war, nor the Navy a fleet action. The record is a work of collective effort; teamwork it is called today. It is not to be gainsaid that stupid mistakes have been made; some over-weening ambition has cropped out; some professional jealously has gone beyond conventional bounds. Nevertheless, morale has been uniformly high, the record is clear of mutinies, and officers and men of today are certainly ready to strive to emulate the heroic traditions of the golden age. In short, it is a consistently high and compositely fine textured tradition that has been left to the modern Navy to maintain; whether or not it will be a stimulus to the imagination of the sailors of the future and a symbol of pride to officers yet unborn, *rests with the officers and men of today.*

The legislative and executive departments of our government are charged by the Constitution with furnishing the tools. The acquisition of high morale, prompt obedience, unswerving and loyal devotion to duty, with effective training comprise the task.

From the British Navy came the greater share of the American Navy's first usages and written regulations. This was particularly true in the early regulations, articles for the government of the Navy, and ship organization. John Adams in drafting the first regulations was influenced by the logic of modeling his draft on the instructions and tried regulations of the largest, most successful Navy in the world at the time; for it would have been unnatural for him to have sought elsewhere, considering the common speech, common traditions, and common law that composed the Anglo-Saxon heritage. In a study of American traditions and customs of the sea, one must turn to the archives of maritime Britain for much source material.

John Paul Jones, who gave considerable thought to matters maritime and proffered constructive criticism at the founding of our Navy, wrote in 1776,

I propose not our enemies as an example for our general imitation, yet, as their Navy is the best regulated of any in the world, we must in some degree imitate them, and aim at such further improvement as may one day make ours vie with, and exceed theirs.

Again, in 1782 Jones wrote to the United States Minister of Marine, "We are a young people, and need not be ashamed to ask advice from nations older and more experienced in marine matters than ourselves." The letter was prompted by Jones's strong plea that the *Navy Regulations* of 1775 be modified. He strongly urged that all captains of the line should be tacticians, with emphasis on what could be learned at the time from the French Navy.

In the brief history of some of the customs, honors, and ceremonies that will be considered hereafter, it is hoped that their venerable antiquity, their unbroken continuity, and their general use by the profession of arms will give a clearer picture of their origin, as well as direct attention to their distinctive place in naval life. They are after all part and parcel of the naval profession; to overemphasize them is a mistake, to underestimate them displays a lack of perspective. For, as Bacon said in regard to ceremonies,

not to use ceremonies at all is to teach others not to use them again, and so diminish the respect to himself; especially, they ought not to be omitted to strangers and formal natures; but the dwelling upon them, and exalting them above the moon, is not only tedious, but doth diminish the faith and credit of him that speaks.

It is by the proper employment of dignified ceremony that discipline and order gain a buttress that is not to be underestimated.

SALUTING THE QUARTER-DECK

It is general belief that the salute to the quarter-deck is derived from the very early seagoing custom of the respect and obeisance that all paid to the pagan altar on board ship—and later to the crucifix and shrine. There are competent authorities on customs and traditions who do not fully support this belief, and base their reasons on the fact that from the early days of the British Navy all officers who were present on the quarter-deck returned the first salute of the individual by uncovering. (The original personal salute consists in uncovering.) Nevertheless, it is reasonable to agree with the majority opinion that it was a salute to the seat of authority, the quarter-deck, the place nearest the colors. At any rate, it is definitely established that genuflections and obeisances were made to pagan shrines aboard ship in the days of Greek, Roman, and Carthaginian sea power. The gods of the sea were propitiated. With the advent of Christianity, the same respect was paid the shrine of the Virgin. The flags of the suzerain or sovereign became in time symbolical of the religion of the state and emblematical of the house of the ruler. In time the colors had a twofold significance —religion and state. The custom of obeisance or marks of respect survived after the shrines were removed. Or to put it another way, kings for a long time ruled by the now out-moded theory of "divine right," and as eventually the "king's colors" were symbols of church and state combined, the colors became the central object of respect. In this connection it is interesting to note that today most European Catholics raise their hats on passing Catholic churches or shrines. Europeans uncover or salute when passing the tombs of their respective Unknown Soldiers. All, forms of respect.

The quarter-deck has been a dignified and sacred area from the earliest days. Captain Basil Hall, R.N., writing in 1831 of his days as a midshipman, said:

Every person, not excepting the captain, when he puts his foot on this sacred spot, touches his hat; and as this salutation is supposed to be paid to the privileged region itself, all those who at the moment have the honor to be upon it are bound to acknowledge the compliment. Thus even when a midshipman comes up and takes off his hat, all the officers on deck (the admiral included, if he happens to be of the number) return the salute.

So completely does this form grow into a habit, that in the darkest night, and when there may not be a single person near the hatchway, it is invariably attended to with the same precision.

It seems sufficient to say that it is an old and impressive tradition; a short, dignified, personal recognition of the colors, the symbol of the state, the seat of authority.

THE HAND SALUTE

The hand salute in the American Navy came to us by way of the British Navy. The gesture of the hand salute was borrowed by the British Navy from the British Army. The tradition of its origin is of interest; but, as in the derivation of saluting the quarter-deck, it has several explanations. That it is the first part of the movements of the uncovering is generally agreed. That there was nothing in the hand is a possible explanation of the British and French Army salute with the palm turned out.

From the earliest days of organized military units, the junior has uncovered in addressing or meeting the senior. A survival of this custom is noted in the Guard Regiments today in that they remove their caps when salutes are rendered in fatigue dress. Lord St. Vincent, in 1796, promulgated an order to the effect that all officers were to take off their hats when receiving orders from superiors, "and not to touch them with an air of negligence." Although we see that touching the cap was considered slovenly, the custom was creeping into the British Service. One finds in Jones's *Sketches of Naval Life,* written on board the U.S.S. *Constitution,* in 1826, an account of Sunday inspection on board that describes the salute of the day as follows:

The Captain and First Lieutenant, Mr. Vallette, are now on the deck; they pass around and examine every part of it, each man lifting his hat, as they pass, or, in default of one, catching hold of a lock of hair.

In 1849, an officer records:

Some very good officers to show a marked distinction between the petty officers and the other part of the crew, have given instructions that on those occasions on which the seamen generally pull off their hats as a mark of respect, such as divisions, muster by the open list, etc., that the petty officers shall then only touch their caps.[1]

[1] Captain Liandet, R.N.

In his book on naval customs and traditions, Commander Beckett, R.N.,[1] states that during the World War some of the retired officers called back to active duty always doffed their hats as a salute. It was to them proper, for it was a custom that they had known throughout their careers.

There is a certain plausibility in placing the origin of the salute in the days of chivalry. It was customary for the knights in mail to raise their visors, in order that those of the same order as well as friendly orders, could see the face. In time, the gesture denoted membership in the same order or another friendly organization. Because of the strict gradations of rank in the days of chivalry it is believed that the junior was required to make the first gesture, and that distinction in class and grade entered into the beginnings of this custom.

Today, the personal salute is a dignified and military gesture. It is the act of the military and naval men looking another companion in arms in the eye and, by proper salute, paying due respect to the uniform and to the authority of another servant of the state. On through the scale, from the "jack of the dust" to the commander in chief, the junior salutes first; but humble and high meet on common ground when the circle is completed by the respect that all pay the flag, the symbol of the state, and their symbol of duty.

The *Bluejackets' Manual* (1939) states in regard to salutes,

Salutes: Nothing gives a better indication of the state of discipline than the observance of the forms of military courtesy.

From time immemorial the salute has been a form of military courtesy that has been strictly and conscientiously observed by men of every nationality, who follow the profession of arms.

As to the regulation manner of rendering the hand salute,

All salutes in passing or approaching are begun first by the junior at six paces distant or at six paces from the nearest point of passing.

Although the U. S. Army salute is the same as that of the U. S. Navy, such is not the case in the other armies of the world. A good explanation of this is made by Lieutenant Commander

[1] W. N. T. Beckett, Commander, R.N., *A Few Naval Customs, Expressions, Traditions, and Superstitions.*

Lowry, R.N. He sets forth the training ship regulations of 1882, in which the salute is defined as follows:

The Naval Salute is made by touching the hat or cap or by taking it off, always looking the person saluted in the face. By touching the hat is meant holding the edge with the forefinger and thumb.

We see that the naval salute evolved from the palm "inboard." In 1888 this British order was amended to read:

The Naval Salute is made by touching the hat or cap, or taking it off and looking the officer saluted in the face. Admirals, Captains, Officers of the same relative rank and the Officers commanding the saluter's ship of whatever rank, are on all occasions saluted by the hat being taken off.

There was a great divergence of practice, and so in January, 1890, the hand salute only was decreed by Queen Victoria because of her displeasure at seeing officers and men stand uncovered when they appeared for royal commendation at Osborne.

In the United States Navy, officers in the open uncover only for divine services. Men uncover when at "mast" for reports and requests, and in officers' country when not in leggings and belt.

Sword Salute

Again authorities differ when it comes to the derivation of the sword salute. The Royal Military Training College taught for some years that it was derived from the oriental custom of the junior raising the sword and shading his eyes from the magnificence of the superior. The first etiquette or "school of the sword" was most probably of oriental origin. But all that can be found tends to indicate that the salute as we know it is probably of crusader origin.

The crucifix, symbolical of the cross, was in the days of chivalry symbolized on the sword by the handle and the guard. It was customary, in that chivalric era of religious fervor, to kiss the sword hilt before entering battle and, of course, for vows and oaths. The cross on the sword survives in the British midshipmen's dirk, the swords of the Scottish archers, and the undress swords of the Highland regiments, as well as the dress swords of diplomatic officers of several foreign countries.

Most of the ancient history of the sword salute is displayed in the present day salute. The sword held at arm's length was originally the hail or initial salute to the superior. The act of permitting the point to descend to the ground is the ancient act of submission or juniority. The start of both these movements, namely, bringing the sword hilt to the mouth or chin, is a survival of the custom of kissing the cross on the sword.

The British Navy has an interesting sword custom. When an officer is tried by court-martial and found guilty, his sword is placed on the table with the point towards the accused, while the hilt is placed towards him if he is found not guilty. This is a survival of the custom in old England when the executioner preceded a prisoner on the route from the court to the prison, informing the populace by the direction of the blade of the headsman's axe whether or not the prisoner had received the death sentence.

The only distinctive accouterment of the old Imperial German Navy that was left to the Navy of the German Republic before Hitler's régime was the undress dirk or short sword that the German officer wears ashore. This weapon has particular historic significance in that its original presentation was made as a friendly gesture by Nicholas II, the last Czar of the Russias, to the Imperial Navy of Wilhelm II.

The sword salute on the march is a survival of the fancy turns and flourishes that were made by military officers in the reviews of the seventeenth century. Halberds and short swords were used in those days, and apparently the fancier the flourishes the better the show on parade and the more effective the salute. The fancy flourish of the drum major is a survival of this.

GUN SALUTES

All salutes were in theory originally the act of the one who first saluted, rendering himself or the ship powerless for the time of the rendition of the honors. Guns in olden days were kept shotted, and after firing a salute an appreciable time was required before the guns could be fired again. In Henry VII's

John Paul Jones

Commodore au Service des Etats-Unis de l'Amerique

et qui'l étoit dans le combat du 23. 7bre 1779 contre le Commodore Pearson
Son Vaisseau le bon homme Richard montoit 40. canons le Vaisseau Anglois le
Serapis 44. nonobstant l'avantage du calibre, et la légéreté Le Commodore P. Jones
par sa manœuvre engagea le Bonefrre de terre à terre et s'empara du Serapis en le
combattant bord a bord pendant 2 heures ¼ l'action dura 3h. ¼. Le Bon homme
Richard coula le lendemain.

(From an old French etching owned by the author)

period, to fire a gun twice in an hour was average time. The point of the sword on the ground at the finish of the sword salute rendered the saluter powerless for the time being. The salute executed today by "present arms" originally meant to present for taking.

The salutes to vessels flying the English flag started when the waters from the coast of Norway to Cape Finisterre were claimed as "English seas." It is known that before Norman days, sails of foreign vessels were lowered in these waters as a mark of respect to English sovereignty. This "mark of respect" rendered the vessel powerless for a time. The ship had no appreciable way on after sails were lowered, and with decks clattered with rigging and sail, the one saluted feared no attack. From this old custom grew the present regulations of tossing oars, "lying on oars," "stopping engines," and in sail boats "letting fly the sheets" in order to render honors to superiors.

It is a very ancient superstition that gun salutes should be of odd number. In Boteler's *Dialogues* of 1685, published by the British Naval Records Society, the captain referring to a very distinguished visitor aboard states, "Have his farewell given him with so many guns as the ship is able to give; provided that they always be of an odd number."

Admiral: "And why odd?"*

Captain: "The odd number in ways of salute and ceremony is so observable at sea that, whensoever guns be given otherwise, it is taken for an expression that either the Captain, or Master, or Master Gunner is dead in the voyage."

"And this ceremony of giving of guns is also in use whensoever any prime passenger, or the Captain of the ship, is to leave the ship and go to the shore."

---

* In the Coronation Program of George VI, a royal salute of 41 guns, one for each completed year of his Majesty's age, was fired at St. James Park. At the actual moment of coronation a 62-gun royal salute, the age salute with 21 guns added, was fired at the Tower of London. A British army officer in a letter to the London *Times* recalled the ancient custom of odd and even guns, and continued:

"It may be a foolish superstition to regard the firing of an even number of rounds in a salute to a live person as ominous, but it is a pity that old custom should be neglected in such an important ceremony."

Sir William Monson in his *Naval Tracts,* written prior to 1600, remarks:

The saluting of ships by another at sea is both ancient and decent, though in this latter time much abused, for whereas 3, 5, or 7 pieces may have been the ordinary use for an Admiral, and never to exceed that proportion, and an Admiral not to answer with above 1 or 3, now they strive to exceed the number, thinking that many pieces add honor to the salutation; but the owners of merchant ships would be gladden it might be done with less cost and more courtesy in another kind. But tho the Admiral cannot restrain this compliment in the ship that salutes, yet he may command his gunner not to return above 1 or 3 pieces according to the old manner.

It seems that it was customary at dinners on board, to fire a salute when toasts were drunk to high ranking officers; for Monson continues,

The excessive banqueting on board is a great consuming of powder, for as men's brains are heated with wine, so they heat their ordnance with ostentation and professed kindness at that instant, and many times not without danger. . . . (It must be remembered that shot was fired with the salutes.)

"No jocund health that Denmark drinks today,
But the great cannon to the clouds shall tell, . . . "
Hamlet, Act I, Sc. ii.

Monson was a very practical man, for in his command it was ordered that musketry be fired for toasts and leave taking. He utilized these honors as drills and directed that the muskets always be fired at a mark in the shape of a man. The Turkish Navy fired shotted salutes until 1910.

The custom of returning gun for gun is very old. In 1688 Sir Cloudesly Shovel, writing on board the *James Galley* to Sir Martin Wescomb, said,

I shall ever be careful in keeping especially my Royal orders, which positively command me to salute neither garrison nor flagge of any forrainer except I am certaine to receave gunne for gunne.

The history of salutes comprises much ancient usage. Today for a revolutionary or *de facto* government to secure a salute from a foreign state is tantamount to recognition. At one time, when England maintained by force her proud title of "mistress of the seas," it was customary for kings of foreign states to salute the British flag on the seas. This, of course, held particularly in the Narrow Seas, for it was asserted for a long period after Edward I that England had claim to both sides of the Channel. In fact, one of King John's titles was Duke of Normandy. Sovereigns who were compelled to salute by cannon the English flag were King Philip of Spain, on his visit to Queen Mary in 1554; and the King of Denmark, on his return from an official visit to King James I in London. Also foreign ambassadors and foreign captains were in cases held accountable before a Court of Admiralty for failure to salute.

The most important salute in U. S. naval history is the first one to the Stars and Stripes by a sea power in recognition of our status as a sovereign state. On 13 February, 1778, John Paul Jones arrived in the *Ranger* at Quiberon Bay, France, and after learning that his salute would be returned fired thirteen guns to Admiral La Motte Picquet, which salute was returned with nine. At Brest he also received a salute in reply to his own, for he reports, "I also demanded and obtained a salute from the flag of France, both at Quiberon and at Brest before the treaty of alliance was announced." In this salute Jones gave one gun for each American state (former colony); the nine-gun reply was based on the custom of saluting Holland, a republic, with fewer guns than France, a monarchy.

CHEERING

U. S. Navy Regulations (1920), art. 292, reads: "Cheers shall not be given any officer." Cheering was a generally accepted personal honor in the early days of our Service. In exceptional circumstances it is possible that organized cheering might be given to foreign ships, such as the cheering led by Admiral Beatty in welcoming the arrival of the United States battleships that afterward comprised the Sixth Battle Squadron, when they entered Scapa Flow. In instructions printed in 1824 in the United States, directions are given for standing by to salute or cheer on entering port.

In manning the rigging for cheering, the people should be chosen for their size, to stand together or on the same ratlines, observing the space of two or three ratlines between each. The men should be drest alike, the marines at the time drawn up on the gangway without their arms. After the three cheers have been given, if the Commodore returns the same number, it must be answered by one; if he returns but one no further notice to be taken, and the people called down.

Cheering was given also when distinguished passengers left the ship, and for shifts of commands. Research shows that it has long been a maritime custom of respect. In *Sketches of Naval Life,* by Jones, a description is given of Lafayette's departure from the U.S.S. *Brandywine,* as he went ashore in France after his last visit to the United States. A description is also given of the turning over of naval command in 1826. Jones writes in his log,

Tuesday, 21 (January, 1826). The Commodore visited and inspected her, on the 19th; and today Captain Read went on board to take the command. He was received by Captain Patterson; the men had been ordered to clean themselves, and all hands were piped; the officers were summoned to the quarter-deck, where the orders of the Secretary for the exchange were read by one of the lieutenants, and the two captains then saluted each other, and bowed to the officers. The shrouds were next manned, and three cheers given. The cheers were repeated, when Captain Patterson left the ship; and in this manner he was also received by the *Constitution.*

The evolution was called "Manning the Yards and Cheering."

When advance notice could be had of the visit of a distinguished personage, on his passing close aboard all hands were ordered "to clean themselves." Then at the words "lay aloft," all hands would spring upon the rigging and cluster on to the tops around the topmast crosstrees and the top-gallant masthead. The second command was "Lay out upon the yards." The men spread each way and supported themselves by means of life lines that were fastened to the lifts and masts. Next, when the order came from deck "To cheer," the men took off their hats and waved them during the three cheers.

Manning the rail and cheering ship is a very old custom. A manuscript written by Dr. Roger Marbecke in 1596, at the time of the English Cadiz Exposition, states,

These hailings then are in this order. When after a day's absence or more, as occasion serveth, they come near to the Lord Admiral, and yet not too near, but of such seasonable distance as they may not endanger themselves of going foul of one another; they presently man the ship and place every one of their companies both upon the upper and middle deck and also upon the waist and shrouds and elsewhere to the most advantage they can to make the bravest show and appear the greater number. Then the masters and mates of the ships immediately join upon the sounding of their whistles in a pretty loud tunable manner, all the company shaking their hands hats and caps, give a marvelous shout, with as much mirth and re-joicing as they can, which consisting of so many loud, strong and variable voices maketh such a sounding echo and pleasant report in the air, as delighteth very much, and this ceremony is done three times by them and three times interchangeably answered by the Lord Admiral.

Salutes before standardization were often matters of contro-versy, and to this day mistakes are made. National salutes are today based upon the equality of sovereign states; but in olden days the weak saluted the strong, and the stranger usually sa-luted the country which claimed jurisdiction over the waters he entered. In 1594 one of the Fugger correspondents from Rome wrote:

The disputes, which have so long prevailed among Christian powers about procedure at sea, have now been settled. Only the Pope and the King of Spain can sail their galleys with colors flying. If they meet, they must salute each other. All other nations must yield precedence to these two.

The old English Navy insisted on respect by foreigners and English merchantmen. It is recorded that Richard Bullen, cap-tain of H.M.S. *Nicodemus,* was in 1638 given a severe punish-ment for not having enforced a French ship of war to salute him.

An English merchant ship was fined £500 for not lowering topsails to Charles' fleet. In 1643 instructions to the Navy read,

If you chance to meet in his Majesties seas any shipps or fleet belonging to any foreign power or State and if they do not strike flaggs or take in topsail you are to force them thereunto.

TENDING THE SIDE

The boatswain's pipe is one of the oldest and most distinctive pieces of personal nautical equipment. A pipe or flute was used in the days of antiquity, by which the galley slaves of Greece and Rome kept stroke. There is a record that the pipe was used in the Crusade of 1248 when the English crossbowmen were called on deck to attack by its signal. The pipe is mentioned by Shakespeare in the *Tempest,* and Pepys refers to its use in his *Naval Notes.*

In time, the pipe came to be used as a badge of office; it was also in some cases a badge of honor. The Lord High Admiral carried a gold pipe on a chain around his neck. A silver one was used by high commanders as a badge of office, or "whistle of command," in addition to the gold whistle of honor. The whistle was used for salutes to distinguished personages, as well as to pass orders, and the old instructions read that on most occasions it was to be blown "three several times." In the action off Brest on 25 April, 1513, between Sir Edward Howard, Lord High Admiral and son of the Earl of Surrey, and the Chevalier Pregant de Bidoux, it is related that when the Lord High Admiral was certain that he would be captured, he threw his gold whistle into the sea. The silver whistle of command was afterwards found on his body. The weight of a standard whistle of honor and names for its part were designated by Henry VIII. The monarch decreed that it should weigh 12 "oons" of gold, an oon being the original ounce. The chain was also to be of gold and to have an equivalent in gold ducats.

Aside from the symbol of the pipe as a badge of office and its use by officers for piping evolutions, it was used at the reception of high personages. Boteler, in his *Dialogues* of 1645, describes the correct procedure. "In receiving, the Prince himself or his Admiral. . . . They were to be received publicly with ceremonies." He adds:

AN OFFICIAL VISIT—Note the custom of holding the bill of the cap as a salute, or raising the cap. (From *All Hands,* by R. F. Zogbaum. Courtesy Harper and Bros.)

THE COMMANDER IN CHIEF OF THE ARMY AND NAVY LEAVES THE FLAGSHIP OF THE COMMANDER IN CHIEF OF THE FLEET. (See footnote, opposite page)

The ship's barge to be sent to fetch the visitor having the cockson with his silver whistle in the stern. . . . Upon the near approach of the barge the noise of the trumpets are to sound and so to hold on until the barge comes within less than musket shot, and that time the trumpets are to cease and all such as carry whistles are to whistle a welcome three several times.

Tending the side with side boys, as we know it in modern practice, originated at a later date. Piping as a ceremony with side boys became the custom. It was customary in the days of sail to hold conferences on the flagships, and to invite officers to dinner while at sea, weather permitting. Sometimes the weather necessitated hoisting the visitors aboard in boatswain's chairs. The pipe was, of course, used for "hoist away" and "avast heaving." Members of the crew did the hoisting; and it is from the aid they rendered in tending the side that the custom originated of having a certain number of men in attendance. In time, it became a nautical gesture of courtesy. In the British Navy today when the captain is reported coming alongside, the officer of the deck gives the order, "hoist him in," even though the accommodation ladder is in use. Tending the side is not to be confused with a guard of honor.

The piping of the side is a distinct nautical courtesy, but the United States Navy has extended it to military, diplomatic, and consular officers, as well as to others of the legislative and executive departments of the government. In the British Navy, Commander Beckett writes that by Admiralty regulations,

No Military Officer, Consular Officer, or other civilian is entitled to this form of salute. By the Custom of the Service a corpse of any Naval officer or man is piped over the side, if sent ashore for burial.

It is of interest that at the funerals of both Queen Victoria and King Edward the venerable custom of piping was carried

FOOTNOTE.—Note President Harding and Admiral H. B. Wilson aft; the captain of the ship and the flag lieutenant at the gangway; the officer of the deck, full marine guard and band, and boatswain at the rail in readiness to pipe the side. The rail is manned. The seamen at salute on the left face outboard when the President leaves the ship. It is exceptional that service uniform is worn, as illustrated; full-dress uniform is prescribed for the reception and departure of Presidents and Sovereigns.

out as the coffins were lowered. In this manner the Royal Navy paid distinct nautical respects to two sovereigns who ever held the "Senior Service" of their empire close to their hearts.

There is a tradition that the present form of the whistle of the boatswain was adopted in commemoration of the defeat and capture of the body of the notorious Scotch pirate, Andrew Barton. Lord Edward Howard, in command of the *Lieon* and the *Jenny Perwin,* made the capture after a severe battle. It is related that Howard took the whistle from the body of Barton. When Howard in time became Lord High Admiral, he caused its adoption. Whistles of other kinds had been in use prior to this date, but it is believed that the design and probably the idea of a more elaborate and costly model as a badge of office sprang from this capture.

In the seventeenth century, it is recorded the master, the boatswain, and the coxswain rated the whistle. The coxswain had charge of the barge and shallop and was at all times to be in readiness to take the captain or admiral ashore. The orders were that the coxswain

is to see her [the barge] trimmed with her carpets and cushions, and to be the person himself in her stern with his silver whistle to cheer up his gang. . . . And this is the lowest officer on the ship that wears a whistle.

Launching Ship Ceremonies[1]

From the earliest days of sea-borne craft, launching ceremonies have had a religious significance. There is a record of a christening ceremony of date 2100 B.C. Christening originated as a propitiation to the gods of the elements. In Tahiti it was once the custom to shed human blood at the launching ceremonies. The Chinese have not changed in centuries their elaborate launching ceremonies, and today all the large junks carry a shrine in respect and propitiation to the Mother of the Dragon.

Wine was used in the rituals in the early days, but the Greeks

[1] Acknowledgment to Robert G. Skerrett for use of material from his comprehensive treatment of the subject: *"The Baptism of Ships,"* U. S. Naval Institute PROCEEDINGS, XXXV, No. 130.

introduced water in the ceremony of lustration. Later, the Romans used water as a token of purification in the solemn priestly blessing. Christian ceremonials as in pagan ceremonials used wine as the sacrament, and water as the token of purification.

The religious zeal of the Middle Ages was extended to things maritime. Ships were named after saints; shrines were placed aboard; and religious effigies found their way on figureheads and in the elaborate niches in the gilded stern galleries. The altars or shrines were placed aft in the same location as the image altars of the Greeks and Romans. The name "poop deck" survives the custom. This nautical word is derived from the Latin word *puppis,* a name the ancients gave to that ceremonial, sacred, honored deck where was kept the *pupi* or doll images of the dieties. Here sacrifice was offered. One is impressed with the thought that the quarter-deck in reality has always been the honored part of the ship.

In Catholic France throughout the eighteenth century and well into the nineteenth there was a launching ceremony that in most respects was analogous to the baptismal ceremony. This was performed by priests at the launching of merchant vessels and fishing craft in Brittany and Normandy. No wine was used in the ceremony of launching, but *vin d'honneur* was always served to those present.

It was only in the early part of the nineteenth century that women and those other than the clergy and high officials took any part in the ceremony of launching British ships. The Canadian Pacific Liner *Empress of Britain* was christened recently by the Prince of Wales. It is written that Victoria desired and inaugurated the religious part of the ceremony that is now used in the launching of British warships. The civil ceremony usually consists in the naming of the vessel by a sponsor, at the same time breaking a bottle of wine against the bows of the ship as she slips down the ways. Of late, due to the "noble experiment" in the United States this custom has been held in abeyance.

Champagne has again taken its place as the liquid for launching ceremonies. The first time wine was used after the repeal of the Eighteenth Amendment was on 21 November, 1933, at the launching of the U.S.S. *Cuttlefish*, built by the Electric Boat Company. Mrs. B. Saunders Bullard, wife of Commander Bullard (C.C.), U. S. Navy, cracked a bottle of champagne against the ship's bow as she left the ways.

The first record that can be found of a woman sponsor in the American Navy is that of a "Miss Watson of Philadelphia," who used a mixture of water and wine when she christened the *Germantown*, a ship of war, on 22 October, 1846. The Philadelphia *North American* in describing the ceremony said, "Miss Watson was attired in pure white and wore in her girdle a neat bouquet of freshly culled flowers."

When the *Chicago* was sponsored in 1885, Mrs. Henry W. B. Glover released three doves from red, white, and blue ribbons. Mrs. Herbert Hoover released a flock of white pigeons when the ill-fated airship *Akron* was christened. The Japanese were the first to use birds in connection with launchings.

So many prominent women of the United States have launched ships that in order to preserve the records, Edith Wallace Benham and Anne Martin Hall wrote a book called, *Ships of the United States Navy and Their Sponsors*. There is also the Society of Sponsors of the United States Navy that holds periodic meetings.

Tradition has it that water was used in the first attempt to launch the *Constitution;* but we do know that "Old Ironsides" would not move. It took three efforts to launch the ship. Admiral George Preble notes that the interesting story of her launching after two attempts may be found in the history of the Boston Navy Yard. The record reads:

Commodore James Sever stood at the heel of the bowsprit and according to time honored usage baptised the ship with a bottle of choice old Madeira, from the cellar of the Honorable Thomas Russell, a leading Boston merchant.

In 1858, the U.S.S. *Hartford* was launched with three sponsors. Commodore Downes's daughter smashed a bottle of Hartford Springs water across the bows; Commodore Stringham's daughter broke a bottle of Connecticut River water across the

ship's figurehead; Lieutenant Preble emptied a bottle of sea
water on the bow. This was a "triple-barreled" water ceremony.[1]

COINS AT STEP OF MAST

The ancient custom of placing coins under the step of a mast
when building the vessel dates from antiquity. Some years ago,
a naval officer stated that he placed a coin under the "step" of
the mast of one of our gunboats.[2] This is a very old superstition.
One explanation, given by Commander Beckett, R.N., is that
possibly it is a survival of the old Roman custom of placing coins
in the mouths of the dead to pay their way to Charon for transportation across the River Styx. If a ship met with mishap at sea,
this ensured that the way of all was paid.

All these customs tend to show that seafaring men subscribe
most cheerfully to superstition, and that sea services unwittingly
maintain many ancient traditions that have no particular bearing on modern sea life.

FUNERAL CEREMONIES

At military and naval funerals, there survives an ancient symbolism of traditional and religious significance. The reversal of
rank at funerals is an acknowledgment that at death all men
are equal. Seniors take their proper precedence in the procession after burial. This form of "the last shall be first and the
first shall be last" is carried out in the recessional and proces-
sional of churches. There was a Roman custom of reversing all
rank and position when celebrating the feast of Saturn. Today
in the British Navy the youngest officer strikes sixteen bells as
the New Year comes in.

The superstitions and significance of military funeral customs were set forth by one Stephen Graham, a private in the
Guards. This soldier wrote before the American Revolution,

[1] Mrs. Franklin D. Roosevelt christened the huge flying boat *Yankee Clipper*
on 3 March, 1939, at U. S. Naval Air Station, Anacostia, D.C., with a bottle of
water mixed from the Seven Seas.
[2] The officers of the U.S.S. *New Orleans* (commissioned 1934) placed during construction 10 pennies beneath the foremast and 2 dimes, 3 nickles, and 28 pennies
at the heel of the mainmast. All coins were placed "heads up."
An old Spanish wreck found in the Orkneys had under the mast and on the
keel a coin dated 1618.

When a soldier dies, the Union Jack is laid upon his body in token that he died in the Service of the State, and that the State takes the responsibility of what it ordered him to do as a soldier.

The reversed arms are an acknowledgment of the shame of killing. Death puts the rifle to shame, and the reversal of the barrel is a fitting sign of reverence.

The three volleys fired into the air are fired at imaginary devils which might get into men's hearts at such a moment as the burial of a comrade-in-arms. An old superstition has it that the doors of men's hearts stand ajar at such times and devils might easily get in.

The last post is the *Nunc Dimittis* of the dead soldier. It is the last bugle call . . . but it gives promise of reveille . . . of the greatest reveille which ultimately the Archangel Gabriel will blow.

At the funeral of George Washington the troops came first, then the clergy, and next the General's horse with the two colored grooms. After the body, came the mourners with Lord Fairfax as the last mourner. Only recently, at the funeral of one of our most distinguished and beloved admirals, two old colored former servitors of the family accompanied the immediate bereaved and preceded the honorary pallbearers chosen from the highest ranking officers of the Navy. There is something most compelling in the ancient ceremony that brings to man the stern realization of the mystery that envelops the great leveler Death.

BURIAL AT SEA*

The most awesome ceremony of the sea is the one which consigns mortal remains to the deep. It antedates all other ceremonies. Pagan burial rites were conducted at sea in the days of Greece and Rome; gods were propitiated; coins were placed in the mouths of the deceased for payment of fare to Charon for transportation over the River Styx.

According to a very old custom in preparing a body for burial at sea, the sailmaker in sewing the canvas shroud takes the last stitch through the nose of the deceased. Research has disclosed considerable instances of this custom. Herman Mel-

* "Gone West" dates to the Norsemen. When a Viking chief died, his body was placed in a special bier aboard a Viking war boat, steering oar was lashed, and sails set with the intent that the body would sail on alone toward the setting sun. Chiefs were occasionally buried in their boats.

ville, in *White Jacket,* speaks of this custom in his writing of the conversation of an old sailmaker with a seaman as to whether or not it should be done. Commander Beckett, in his work *Customs and Superstitions,* reports that twenty-three guineas from government funds were paid to the rating that sewed up the twenty-three bodies on a British man-of-war after the battle of Jutland. It is an ancient custom in the British Navy that a guinea will be paid from the public funds for each corpse placed in the canvas shroud. This duty is usually performed by a sailmaker, or by one of his mates.

In this day it will seldom be necessary to commit a body to the deep; nevertheless, the ceremony of time-honored tradition should be known by all. No matter what time of day or night that a death occurs aboard, it should be reported to the captain. Old custom decrees that the doctor make this report to the officer of the watch who, in turn, will log it and make immediate report to the captain.

If for any reason the deceased is buried at sea, the body is placed in canvas or coffin with weights to insure sinking. An American flag is placed over the body and gently pulled off as the body is released over the side.

It has ever been customary for all officers and men not on duty to attend the services of a late shipmate. The chaplain or, in his absence, the captain, or an officer detailed by the captain, reads the burial service at sea. In most cases the Episcopal prayer-book service is used. The ritual ends with the very beautiful and time-honored words,

. . . we therefore commit this body to the deep, to be turned into corruption, looking for the resurrection of the body, when the sea shall give up her dead, and the life of the world to come. . . .

At the point in the service "we commit this body to the deep," a seaman tilts the grating or wooden platform, slips off the flag, and the body is projected into the ocean.

In order to show the superstitions of the olden days, and at the same time to describe a funeral at sea under circumstances of sea life that will never come again, there follows a descrip-

tion written by Captain Basil Hall, R.N., in 1831. The funeral
was that of one of his dear friends, a young and much beloved midshipman of his mess who was buried off the shores of
the United States during the War of 1812. As Hall records it,

The peculiar circumstances connected with the funeral which I am
about to describe, and the fanciful superstitions of the sailors upon
the occasion, have combined to fix the whole scene in my memory.
Something occurred during the day to prevent the funeral taking
place at the usual hour and the ceremony was deferred until long
after sunset. The evening was extremely dark, and it was blowing a
treble-reefed topsail breeze. We had just sent down the top-gallant
yards, and made all safe for a boisterous winter's night. As it became
necessary to have lights to see what was done, several signal lanterns
were placed on the break of the quarter-deck and others along the
hammock railings on the lee gangway. The whole ship's company
and officers were assembled, some on the booms, others in the boats;
while the main rigging was crowded halfway up to the cat harpings.
Overhead, the mainsail, illuminated as high as the yard by the lamps,
was bulging forwards under the gale, which was rising every minute
and straining so violently at the main sheet, that there was some
doubt whether it might not be necessary to interrupt the funeral
in order to take sail off the ship. The lower deck ports lay completely under water, and several times the muzzles of the main deck guns
were plunged into the sea; so that the end of the grating on which
the remains of poor Dolly were laid once or twice nearly touched the
tops of the waves, as they foamed and hissed past. The rain fell fast
on the bare heads of the crew, dropping also on the officers, during
all the ceremony, from the foot of the mainsail, and wetting the
leaves of the prayer-book. The wind sighed over us amongst the wet
shrouds, with a note so mournful, that there could not have been a
more appropriate dirge.

The ship, pitching violently, strained and cracked from end to
end; so that, what with the noise of the sea, the rattling of the ropes,
and the whistling of the wind, hardly one word of the service could
be distinguished. The men, however, understood, by a motion of
the captain's hand, when the time came, and the body of our dear
little brother was committed to the deep.

So violent a squall was sweeping past the ship at this moment,
that no sound was heard of the usual splash, which made the sailors

"ALL HANDS TO BURY THE DEAD" (From *All Hands,* by R. F. Zogbaum. Courtesy Harper and Bros.)

allege that their young favorite never touched the water at all, but was at once carried off in the gale to his final resting place!

In connection with funeral services and ceremonies, it should be mentioned that in the early days of the Navy the colors were only half-masted for captains. Jones, in *Sketches of Naval Life*, written on board the frigate *Constitution* at Port Mahon, 30 October, 1826, relates,

We buried one of the officers, a surgeon's mate, and a member of our mess; application was made to have him interred in the officers' burying grounds, within the walls; but his disease, the typhus fever, alarmed them, and it was refused. I expected to see our colors half-masted; but, it seems, this is an honor due only to captains, and it was not done. The funeral was attended by nearly all the officers of the squadron.

In the seventeenth and early eighteenth centuries it is reported that French men-of-war carried the remains of those who died at sea, in the holds until the ships reached shore. We are led to believe by reports of those olden days that this was a very disagreeable practice and, of course, was executed only in the name of religion (for the purpose of burying in consecrated soil).

The deep sentiment of sailors for shipmates is proverbial. In connection with funeral exercises, it is interesting after a lapse of more than a hundred years to read the epitaphs written by messmates for their lamented shipmates. The following inscription may be found in a cemetery at Port Mahon, once the base of the old United States Mediterranean Squadron.

Sacred
to
The Memory
of
ALEXANDER GRAVES
Quarter Gunner On Board The
U. S. Frigate Brandywine
Who Departed This Life Jan. 17th
Aged 44 Years.

Here lies, beneath this consecrated sod,
A man who loved his country and his God:
True to them both, I've heard his shipmates say;
But now he's gone; and slumbers in the clay.
A better messmate never crossed the seas:
I hope he's gone to Heaven. God be pleased.
Faithful in duty; contented with his mind:
And died lamented by the Brandywines.

Another epitaph that surely compensated in sincerity and sentiment for its deficiency in composition:

Sacred
To
The Memory
Of
JAMES SMITH
Captain Of The Main Top
On Board The U. S. Frigate Brandywine
Who Departed This Life Feb. 4th
1826
Aged 30 Years

He who lays here, was much beloved,
By all his shipmates round;
But he's no more, 'twas accident,
The unfortunate man was drowned.
Alas, he's gone, the debt is paid,
He owed for a short time;
Mourn not for him, he's better off,
He sails with more divine.

CROSSING THE LINE

The boisterous ceremonies of "crossing the line" are of such ancient vintage that their derivation is lost. It is well known that ceremonies took place long ago when the ship crossed the thirtieth parallel, and also when going through the Straits of Gibraltar. These early ceremonies were of the roughest sort and were, to a great extent, supposed to try the crew to determine whether or not the novices on their first cruise could endure the hardships of a life at sea. Then, as is the custom at the present time, it was primarily a crew's "party." The Vikings were

THE OLD NAVY—Left to right: David Ireland, age 55; Gilbert H. Purdy, age 60; John T. Griffith, age 62; and John King, age 54. (See footnote, opposite page) (From a photograph, U.S.S. *Mohican* [1888], by Assistant Surgeon H. W. Whitaker, U. S. Navy)

reported at an early date to carry out these ceremonies on crossing certain parallels. It is highly probable that the present-day
ceremony was passed on to the Angles, Saxons, and Normans
from the Vikings.

At an earlier date, ceremonies of propitiation were carried
on. Neptune, the mythological god of the seas, was appeased by
the seamen, and marks of respect were paid those of his under-
water domain. It is plausible that a part of the ceremony grew
out of traditions of other days, even though sailors had come
to doubt the existence of Neptune. Nevertheless, Neptunus Rex
is today the majesty who rules in the ceremonies.

Those who have "crossed the line" are called "shellbacks."
These Sons of Neptune compose the cast for the present-day
ceremonies. It is a curious fact of human nature, but men will
suffer a very severe initiation in order to be permitted to inflict the same on other men.

Sailormen treasure the certificate which testifies that "in Latitude oo-oo and Longtitude ....," and usually addressed
to

all Mermaids, Sea Serpents, Whales, Sharks, Porpoises, Dolphins,
Skates, Eels, Suckers, Lobsters, Crabs, Pollywogs, and other living
[name]
things of the sea, ... has been found
worthy to be numbered as one of our trusty shellbacks, has been
gathered to our fold and duly initiated into the solemn mysteries of
the ancient order of the deep.

Usually the ceremonies of the modern Navy are picturesque,
and with the exception of the discomfort of a good wetting

FOOTNOTE.—"This picture, 'The Old Navy,' " wrote Captain J. K. Taussig, "de-
picts for us a rare combination of characters. We have here in Purdy the spinner
of yarns and exploiter of theories—different from the usually accepted ones—but
always of sufficient interest to guarantee an audience. In Ireland we have the
serious-minded listener—a man of sturdy character who loved his ship and who
loved to stay on board—preferring to save his money to spending it on a good
time. King typifies the sailor of the stories; one who loved rum and who spent his
money freely whenever he had the chance. He was the type who was absolutely
reliable when on board ship, but did not see that the beach was for any other use
than a place where one could get drunk. Griffith shows us the old man who has
matured in the service—the kind that acquired none of the bad traits, but all of
the good traits of the old-time sailor."—U. S. Naval Institute PROCEEDINGS, XLVII,
No. 215.

in the tank, a slight shock of electricity from the "Devil," and the shaving ceremony, the initiation cannot be called extremely rough. I am told that in merchant ships the ceremony is still severe in the physical discomforts inflicted. Officers of the United States Navy could at one time "buy off" by giving the Neptune party so many bottles of beer. Unless the ceremonies are very crude, it is a tradition that younger officers in particular undergo the initiation.

The eldest and most dignified member of the crew is usually selected as Neptunus Rex; his first assistant is Davy Jones. Her Highness Amphitrite is usually a good looking young seaman who will appear well in the déshabillé of seaweed and rope yarns. The Court in general consists of the Royal Scribe, the Royal Doctor, the Royal Dentist, the Devil, and other names that suit the fancy of the party. The Bears have the difficult task of rounding up the uninitiated, and also standing "dousing" watches in the canvas water tank.

The night before the ship crosses the line, it is the custom that Davy Jones shall appear on board with a message to the Captain from His Majesty, Neptunus Rex, stating at what time he wants the ship hove to for the reception of the Royal Party, and with particular summons for certain men to appear before him. This reception of Davy Jones usually takes place at night and may be made most impressive. The ship is stopped and, amid a glare of lights and a whirl of water, Davy Jones emerges from the hawse or is hoisted in over the bows to deliver his message. He is usually received by the Captain and Officer of the Deck on the bridge.

A part of the customary dialogue follows:

A RITUAL FOR ANCIENT ORDER OF THE DEEP
Davy Jones comes aboard and hails the bridge.
Davy Jones to Officer of the Deck: Ship Ahoy!
O.O.D.: Aye, Aye, Sir.
Davy Jones: What ship?
O.O.D.: U.S.S. ——
Davy Jones: What course?

O.O.D.: *State course*
Davy Jones: Very well, Sir, I have been waiting your arrival. You will notify the Commanding Officer that I, Davy Jones, have a message to deliver to him from His Royal Highness, Neptunus Rex.
O.D.D.: Aye, Aye, Sir.

Permit a few minutes to elapse

O.O.D.: Your Honor, the Commanding Officer awaits you.
Davy Jones (proceeding to place designated): Very well, Sir.

If the meeting takes place on the quarter-deck, all hands are permitted to follow Davy Jones aft.

Captain to Davy Jones: Greetings, Davy Jones.
Davy Jones: My congratulations to you, Captain. Some few years since I saw you.
Captain: Yes, it was aboard the U.S.S. ——.
Davy Jones: I have a summons to you from Neptunus Rex.
Captain: I will be glad to receive it.

Davy Jones reads the summons. He then shakes hands with the Captain.

Davy Jones: I will await your pleasure tomorrow, Sir, and will see you when I return with my Royal Master, Neptunus Rex. Good night, Sir.

Davy Jones walks forward.

On the next day when all is in readiness for the reception of Neptune and Party, the navigator reports the ship is on the "line." Davy Jones appears and reports to the Officer of the Deck that the Captain is to be informed that Neptunus Rex and Party have been sighted ahead. The Flag of Neptune is broken when Neptune and Court appear on deck. The bugle call "attention" is sounded; officers and crew fall in at quarters or where designated. The Royal Party then proceeds slowly aft to meet Davy Jones.

Neptune (when he meets Davy Jones) : Well, well, what a fine ship and what a cargo of landlubbers.

Officer of the Deck salutes and reports with much dignity that the Captain awaits the Royal Party. Party proceeds.

Captain: A sailor's welcome to you, Neptunus Rex; it is a great pleasure to have you with us.

Neptune: The pleasure is mine (a short speech). Allow me to present Royal Navigator Shellback who will relieve you. I am glad to be with you again, Captain, and have prepared for a busy day in order to make your landlubbers fit subjects of my great sea domain. Captain: May I invite your attention to the fact that I have several young officers and members of the crew aboard who have not been in the Service long enough to have had an opportunity to visit your domain and become shellbacks. I beg you to be as lenient with them as possible.

Neptune: Ah! Captain, I will be as severe as I can—as severe as I can.

Captain then introduces officers who have crossed the line before. These officers converse with the immediate personal staff of Neptune for a minute or so.

Captain: Neptune, I turn over my command to you for such time as you wish.

Neptune: Very well, Captain, thank you. *Turning to Royal Navigator.* Royal Navigator proceed to the bridge and direct the ship on the course assigned.

Royal Party is then escorted to the throne. They ascend. Initiation commences with officers first.

Dramatis Personæ.—Amphitrite, Neptune, Royal Baby, Davy Jones, Royal Chaplain, Royal Navigator, Neptune's Officer of the Day, Judges, Attorneys, Barbers, Doctors, Bears, Police.*

Note.—The writer is indebted to Lieutenant Commander T. R. Cooley, U. S. Navy, for an opportunity to examine the original manuscript of dialogue and ceremony used aboard the U.S.S. *Sacramento* and U.S.S. *Pruitt* when those ships "crossed the line." Much fun may be derived from charges and specifications that deal with the peculiarities and idiosyncrasies of the "victims" of the initiation. The *Sacramento* received advance dispatches and letters from Neptune much to the discomfiture of landlubbers.

* The U.S.S. *Henderson* and *Chaumont,* which make frequent cruises across the Pacific, have instituted the ritual of initiation into the Realm of the Golden Dragon, when ships cross the international date line on sailing to the westward. The neophytes, both officers and men, are subpœnaed and appear before the Court of the Grand Dragon for sentence and initiation.

A Sample Summons[1]

U.S.S. ——— ON ENTERING
DOMAIN OF NEPTUNUS REX
NOTICE AND LISTEN YE LANDLUBBER

I order and command you to appear before me and my court on the morrow to be initiated in the mysteries of my Empire. If not, you shall be given as food for sharks, whales, pollywogs, frogs, and all living things of the sea, who will devour you, head, body, and soul as a warning to landlubbers entering my Domain without warrant.

You are charged with the following offenses....................
....
THEREFORE, appear and obey or suffer the penalty.

Registered: DAVY JONES
                                   Secretary to His Majesty

Decorative certificates of distinct nautical phraseology are presented to those initiated. It is customary for the captain to sign the "diploma," also the seal of the ship is affixed thereto. No custom of the sea is better known, for to qualify as a "shellback" is a distinction desired by all sailormen.

As an example of the importance given to the ceremonies of crossing the line, the writer[2] has seen a squadron of ships sail along for days just north of the "line," awaiting a favorable time to head south and cross. . . . This ancient ceremony that we observe is most spectacular and dear to the heart of the seamen of all nations.

Captain Hall, writing a hundred years ago, said of this ceremony,

Its evil is transient, if any evil there be; while it certainly affords Jack a topic for a month beforehand and a fortnight afterwards; and if so ordered as to keep its monstrosities within the limits of strict discipline (which is easy enough) it may even be made to add to the authority of the officers, instead of weakening their influence.

---

[1] The "Summons" given is one of many forms used. They are usually folded and made up in the form of a subpoena.
[2] Chief Boatswain John D. Thompson, U. S. Navy.

Cockbilling Yards—Mourning in Days of Sail

Yards were once "cockbilled," and rigging was slacked off as a sign of mourning. The half-masting of colors is in reality a survival of the days when a slovenly appearance characterized mourning. Even in the British Merchant Service today there are recent cases of trailing rope ends, "slacking off" of rigging, and scandalizing yards as a sign of mourning. In this connection, Commander W. T. N. Beckett, R.N., writes,

I think that the last occasion that one of H.M. ships scandalized her yards as a sign of mourning, was when H.M.S. *Exmouth* carried out the procedure in 1908 while laying off Lisbon after the murder of Don Carlos King of Portugal. H.M.S. *Exmouth* was commanded by Captain Arthur Henniker-Hughan and was flying the flag of Admiral the Honorable Sir Assheton George Curzon Howe, K.C.B. H.M.S. *Arrogant* was also present and, for lack of known precedent, yards were cockbilled, mainstay down to starboard, foremast down to port, lower booms were dropped. *Arrogant* copies *Exmouth* and the condition prevailed from 0800 with a gun fired every fifteen minutes until sunset.[1]

After some research to find out whether or not this custom was observed in the United States Navy, an interesting item in the journal of Mr. George Jones, a schoolmaster on board the U.S.S. *Constitution,* was found. He wrote:

Thursday, 25 [September, 1826]. The Commodore sailed yesterday for Gibraltar and today we have been paying "honor to whom honor was due." Our flags have been at half mast all day; and at noon, twenty-one guns were fired, first by this ship, and then, by the *Porpoise.* This was for the late Ex-President Jefferson. After an interval of thirty minutes, the same number were given for his compatriot, John Adams, by a singular coincidence so closely associated with him in death as well as in life. At the first gun, each ship cockbilled its yards. I will explain the term as far as I am able. On common occasions, the yards are kept at right angles with the mast; and to a sailor's eye, nothing looks so slovenly as a different position; and nothing is noticed sooner, or sooner disgraces a ship. The slings, however, had now been loosed, and at the first gun, every

---

[1] W. N. T. Beckett, Commander R.N., *A Few Naval Customs, Expressions, Traditions, and Superstitions,* pp. 42-43.

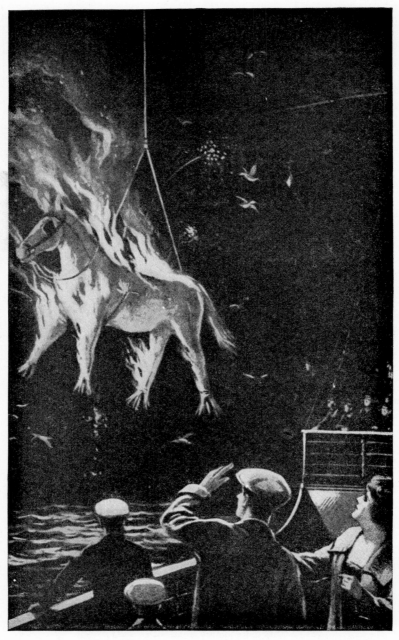

BURNING THE "DEAD HORSE"—Merchant sailors celebrating the completion of the first five weeks of a long voyage. (From *Illustrated London News*)

yard was thrown into a slanting position, so as to form an angle of about 70° with the horizon, the lower main yards inclining to starboard, the fore and mizen to larboard; while the upper yard of each mast took a direction contrary to that of the lower ones (*passis crinibus*). The operation is an unusual one in our service. The French and Austrians have their ships thus in mourning annually during the last three days of Holy Week.

This custom has no bearing upon the comment of a lady visiting a man-of-war in Villefranche Harbor some years ago, when she remarked,

Captain, I think that you have the most beautiful ship in port, for all your rigging hangs in such beautiful festoons, and it is so graceful to see rope ends waving in the breeze.

DRAWING A DEAD HORSE

Much to many a naval officer's regret, this old custom survives. A real ceremony was connected with the days when the crew "stopped working for nothing." In the days of sail, both in the Navy and particularly in the Merchant Marine, seamen were permitted to draw some money in advance. In the British Merchant Service, it was approximately a month's advance when the sailor shipped. After five weeks at sea or at whatever time the advance money had been worked off, the men made a horse out of canvas stuffed with old cordage and waste material or out of a cask with oakum tail and mane, and permission was requested to light it and hoist it out to the end of a boom or yard. This was done amid cheers, and marked the time that the crew started to accumulate wages "on the books." The advance was usually spent in high living in the port just left. Plans could now be made for the next port.

Both watches used to sing in a chorus:

> Now, old horse your time has come,
>   And we say so, for we know so!
> Altho' many a race you've won,
>   Oh! poor old man,
> You're going now to say good-bye,
>   And we say so, for we know so;
> Poor old horse, you're going to die.

DUELING AMONG THE OFFICERS OF THE NAVY

The word duel is derived from the Latin *bellum* and *duo,* with a meaning that was finally accepted as a war between two.

In the first half-century of our Navy there are recorded numerous duels. The practice of settling by duels "affairs of honor among gentlemen" was not confined to the senior officers, but was also a method of redress among juniors and midshipmen.

The history of the early Mediterranean Squadron of the U. S. Navy discloses a tragic record in this respect. One may read today on a tombstone, near Syracuse, Sicily, the following epitaph:

In memory of William R. Nicholson, a Midshipman in the Navy of the United States, who was cut off from society in the bloom of his youth and health, on the 18th day of September, A.D. 1804, aged eighteen years. His untimely death resulted from a duel fought with Midshipman Frederick C. DeKraft of the same ship.

Lieutenant William B. Finch, U. S. Navy, who afterwards changed his name to William Compton Bolton and who died as a commodore in command of the Mediterranean Squadron in 1849, killed Lieutenant Francis B. White, of the Marine Corps, in a duel fought at Boston in 1819.

Commodore Oliver Hazard Perry fought a duel with Captain John Heath of the Marine Corps. Commodore Decatur was Perry's second.

Lieutenant William Bainbridge killed the Secretary of the British admiral at Gibraltar in a duel fought over what was alleged to be an affair involving the "honor of the service." Stephen Decatur acted as Bainbridge's second.

There are many other cases. In fact, one historian alleges that more officers were killed in duels than in the naval actions of the period. But the most outstanding duel of our naval history was that between Commodore Barron and Commodore Decatur. This duel took place after a long interchange of acrimonious correspondence. The dispute centered on Barron's restoration to duty after five years' suspension of rank and pay that dated from 8 February, 1808, in consequence of the *Chesapeake-Leopard* action of the Virginia capes on 27 June, 1807.

The duel was fought on the morning of 22 March, 1820, in a valley one-half mile from Bladensburg village, and about that distance from the present Washington-Annapolis highway. Decatur had Commodore Bainbridge as a second; Barron had Captain Jesse D. Elliott.

Just before the duel Barron expressed to Decatur the hope that, "On meeting in another world they would be better friends than in this." Decatur replied, "I have never been your enemy, Sir." The firing took place on the count two. Both officers fell. Decatur was shot through the abdomen, and Barron wounded in the thigh.

The brilliant, intrepid Decatur died at the age of 41, twelve hours after he was carried to his home, Lafayette Square, Washington. Barron was subsequently restored to the active list and lived to become the senior commodore of the Navy, but never secured active sea service.

It is a civilized step forward that the custom of dueling has been relegated to the limbo of an obsolete section of the code of an officer and a gentleman.

Firing Three Volleys at Funerals

Mention has been made before of firing three volleys at funerals. By this superstitious custom it was supposed that evil spirits were driven away as they escaped from the hearts of the dead.

Before the advent of firearms, the number 3 had a mystical significance. It was utilized in the ancient Roman funeral rites. Earth was cast three times into the sepulcher; friends and relatives called the dead three times by name, and then as they departed from the tomb they pronounced the word *vale*, meaning "farewell," three times.

The numbers 3, 5, and 7 had a mystic and symbolic significance long before Roman civilization. A survival today may be found in the "Three Graces," "the Holy Trinity," "the three witches" in Macbeth, the frequent use of three in Masonic rituals, three volleys at funerals, three cheers, and it was customary in some regiments of the Army when a soldier was absent, to call his name three times at the end of roll call. We are all familiar with "once, twice, three times, and sold."

The Bureau of Navigation in 1938 made some pertinent and valuable comments as follows:

The Bureau has received advices on several occasions of the undesirable and, at times, pathetic effect of the volleys fired at military funerals upon the bereaved. It is desired that this aspect of the honors rendered at the interment be considered by commanding officers when acting upon requests for funeral escorts.

The following points are offered as a guide in this connection:

(a) That the full import of the part of the firing squad be explained to the next-of-kin or those representing the next-of-kin.

(b) That those in charge of or in command of the firing squad so place the squad that it is some distance from the grave. It is not necessary that the volleys be fired directly over the grave.

(c) That the firing squad be omitted, as a matter of expedience, in the case of funerals when the omission is expressly requested by the next-of-kin or those representing the next-of-kin.

Although not prescribed by regulations, it has become customary to hold a short religious service aboard for deceased officers and men when their remains are sent from ships on a foreign station for further transportation to the homeland. In short, crew mustered aft and a religious service. Volleys may be omitted, but taps should be sounded as the body is lowered to waiting boat, and bell tolled as customary. Flag should be half-masted in accordance with regulations.

Removing the Right Glove when Sworn as a Witness

The custom of raising hands and eyes heavenwards when taking an oath is of great antiquity. The head was bared to the deity or superior authority when taking the oath. When the Bible was collected into a tome, the right hand was placed upon the Bible during the administration of the oath, and upon completion the Bible was kissed. In fact, the kissing of the Bible continues in some localities, and was a general custom in this country until about fifty years ago, when the custom of raising the bared right hand, with head uncovered, became general.

The Bible is still used in the Navy for the swearing of the court, judge advocate, recorder, and witnesses of courts-martial.

The practice of the right hand ungloved came from the early days in England when all criminals were branded on the right hand. The hand was bared in order to ascertain whether or not the witness to be sworn was branded.

Custom of Wearing Medals on the Left Breast

Medals and decorations are, for the most part, worn on the left breast. This custom may be traced from the practice of the Crusaders in wearing the badge of honor of their order near the heart. Also, the left side was the shield side of the Crusader, for the large shield carried by the left arm, protected both the heart and the badge of honor.

The Twenty-One-Gun International Salute

All personal salutes may be traced to the prevailing usage of earlier days to insure that the saluter placed himself in an unarmed position and virtually in the power of the saluted. This is seen in the dropping of the point of the sword, presenting arms, firing cannon and small arms, lowering sails, manning the yards, removal of the headdress, laying on oars, etc.

Salute by gunfire is a most ancient ceremony. The British for years compelled weaker nations to make the first salute; but in time international practice compelled "gun for gun" on the principle of equality of nations. In the earliest days seven guns was the recognized British national salute. Here again we see that the number seven had a mystical significance, for in the Eastern civilization, seven was a sacred number; hence, astronomy listed the seven planets, the moon changed every seven days, the earth was created in seven days, every seventh year was a sabbatical year, and the seven times seventh year was a jubilee year. Those early regulations stated that although a ship could fire only seven guns, the forts could fire for honors three shots (again the mystical three) to one shot afloat. In that day, powder of sodium nitrate was easier to keep on shore than at sea. In time, when the quality of gunpowder improved by the use of potassium nitrate, the sea salute was made equal to the shore salute—twenty-one guns as the highest national honor. Although for a period of time monarchies received more guns than republics, eventually republics claimed equality. There was much confusion, due to the varying customs of maritime states, but finally the British government proposed to the United States a regulation that provided for "salutes to be returned gun for gun." The British at that time officially considered the international salute to be twenty-one guns, and the United States adopted the twenty-one guns and "gun for gun" return, 18 August, 1875.

Previous to this time our national salute was one gun for each state. This practice was also a result of usage, for John Paul Jones saluted France with thirteen guns (one for each state) at Quiberon Bay, when the Stars and Stripes received its first salute. This practice was not authorized until 1810. By the admission of states to the Union, the salute reached twenty-one guns in 1818. In 1841, the national salute was reduced to twenty-one guns. In fact, the 1875 adoption of the British suggestion was a formal announcement that the United States recognized twenty-one guns as an international salute.

The *National Geographic* says:

This country has also an extra-special ceremony known as the "salute to the nation," which consists of one gun for each of the forty-eight states. This mimic war is staged only at noon on July 4 at American military ports, although it has been given on a few other occasions, such as the death of a President.

The Navy full dresses ship and fires twenty-one guns at noon on the Fourth of July.

"Sounding Off" at Parade and Guard Mount

At parades and guard mounts in military and naval service, when the adjutant commands "sound off," the band plays three chords of flourishes which are called the "Three Cheers," before marching up and then down in front of the men under arms.

When the band returns to its position, "Three Cheers" are again played.

This custom is of crusade days origin. The soldiers designated for the crusades were set apart but formed in line with the other troops, and the music of the organization would march and then counter-march in front of those selected. This was a form of dedication ceremony. It is thought by authorities that the populace would give cheers throughout the ceremony, and that the three flourishes have remained symbolical of the applause accorded by the populace.

The dress parade is a survival of the days when visiting celebrities in all countries were shown the King's troops in impressive parade. The original intent was to render the display formidable and to impress the visitor with the strength of the state visited, rather than the present idea of a parade as a distinctive honor rendered the visitor.

WAR INSTRUCTIONS IN THE SIXTEENTH CENTURY[1]

Before ships and fleets encounter, or enter upon action, these things following are necessary to be done: to divide the company into three parts; the one appointed to tack the ship, the second to ply the small shot, and the third to attend the ordnance; but not so precisely, but that one may be assisting to the other in the three several places. The ship is to be brought into its short and fighting sails (viz), foresail, main-topsail, and fore-topsail; for the other sails are troublesome to handle, and make the ship heel so, that her ordnance cannot be used, besides the danger of firing her sails with arrows and other wild-fire from the enemy.

The master is to appoint a valiant and sufficient man at helm; and to receive his directions from the captain how to order the fight, and where to board; which must be done with most advantage, and according to the placing of the enemy's ordnance; and therefore it is requisite to have a captain of experience.

Every officer is to do his part; the boatswain to sling their yards, to put forth the flag, ancient and streamers, to arm the tops and waste-cloths; to spread the nettings, to provide tubs and to command the company to make urine in them, for the gunners to use

[1] Sir. Wm. Monson, *Naval Tracts.*

in their spunges to cool their ordnance in the fight, and all other things that belong to his charge.

The gunner is to appoint his officers to their quarters, to have care to their files, budge barrels, tin case used to protect powder when carrying from hold to guns and cartridges; to have his shot in a locker near every piece, and the yeoman of the powder to keep his room and to be watchful of it, and to have his eye upon any leak that shall happen in the hold.

The carpenters are to be vigilant, and to have their oakham, lead nails and what else belongs to the stopping of leaks in readiness. He must have a man always ready to sling overboard, if there chance a leak. Or if there be cause to take in the lower tier of ordnance, by the sudden growing and working of the sea, he must have all things ready to caulk the ports.

BOARDING IN 1653

[1]The captain gives the command: "Make fast your grapplings," whereupon one reports to him:

"Captain, we are fowl on each other, and the ship is on fire."
"Cut anything to get clear, and smother the fire with wet clothes." In such case they will presently be such friends as to help one the other all they can to get clear, lest they both should burn together and sink; and if they be generous, the fire quenched, drink kindely one to another; heave their cans over boord, and then begin again as before.

DIVINE SERVICE AT SEA

The following description of divine service at sea is taken from the *Cruise of the Frigate "Columbia,"* by William Murrell. The U.S.S. *Columbia* made a typical around-the-world cruise in 1838-41, visiting 18 ports, spending 459 days at sea, and 313 days in port. The total mileage was 54,796.

Murrell writes:

"On Sunday mornings, immediately after quarters, should the weather permit, all hands are called to muster. The summons is instantly obeyed, by every one proceeding to the quarter-deck (the sick alone exempted) where the minister stands in readiness, arrayed in his clerical robes, and the capstern covered with the national

[1]Captain John Smith, *The Sea-Man's Grammer* (London: 1653).

MORNING QUARTERS—THE LORD'S PRAYER (From *All Hands*, by R. F. Zogbaum. Courtesy Harper and Bros.)

flag, to answer the purpose of a pulpit. The commodore takes his station on the weather side of the chaplain; the lieutenants, and all other commissioned and warrant officers on the weather side of the deck; the forward officers at the fife-rail, and petty officers at the fore-part of the main-mast. The blue-jackets take up their position abaft the mizzen-mast, clad in white frocks with blue collars, white trowsers, and straw hats, looking the picture of cleanliness; whilst the marines are stationed and drawn up in rank, on the lee side of the deck, headed by their commanding officer, all in blue uniform. . . . After the usual routine of divine services had been performed, every monthly Sunday the articles of war are read. Punishments were always read, that is to say, death, or *worse* punishment as the sailor says. By worse punishment, he alludes to his grog being stopped, which article constitutes his principal creed.

THE SOUNDING OF TAPS

The original word "taps" is derived from the Dutch word *taptoe,* or time to close up all the taps and taverns in the garrisoned towns. In a quaint volume entitled, *The Military Guide for Young Officers,* by Thomas Simes, Esq., reprinted in Philadelphia, in 1776, there are instructions for the officer of the guard:

The tat-too is generally best at nine o'clock at night in the summer and eight in the winter. It is performed by the Drum-Major, and all the drummers and fifers of that regiment which gave a captain of the main guard that day.

The tat-too is the signal given for the soldiers to retire to their barracks or quarters, to put out their fire and candle, and go to bed. The public houses are at the same time, to shut their doors, and sell no more liquor that night.

Colonel H. L. Scott, Inspector General, U. S. Army, in the *Military Dictionary* which he published in 1861, defined "tattoo" and "taptoo" as equivalent terms meaning "drum-beat and a roll call at night."

In time, trumpets were used for tattoo. The *Century Dictionary* defines the word as a beat of drum or bugle call at night; while "taps" is defined as a signal upon a drum or trumpet at about a quarter of an hour after tattoo. The British use the

term "post" for this call. Major General G. E. Voyle, Royal
Bengal Artillery, defined the term in his military dictionary
published in 1876 as "The term Post is given to the bugling
which precedes the tattoo. This is the first part, the last part
that which follows it is the last Post." The last post is sounded
on the trumpet or bugle at British military funerals.

Stephen Graham wrote two centuries ago, "The Last Post is
the *Nunc Dimittis* of the dead soldier. It is the last bugle call
. . . but it gives promise of reveillé. . . ."

Just when the American Navy adopted the custom of sounding "taps" at funerals seems to be unknown. The "Dead March
from Saul" comprised all the music rendered by the musicians
on board the *Constitution* at a buriel at sea in 1846. Commodore
Claxton was buried at Valparaiso in 1841, and at the same time
mention, was made of the "Dead March" and the muffled drums,
but no mention of "taps."

There was a melody for "taps" as early as the American Revolution: it was probably that of the "last post" of the British
Army. "Taps" of the United States Army and Navy, and the
"last post" have a few identical notes. The St. Louis *Globe
Democrat* wrote in September, 1933:

The American Army's heart-touching salute to the dead, the "song
of truce to pain," the final bugle call of the night, as soldiers in field
and barracks roll into their blankets, arose anew last fall. It was
announced in Paris that the French Army had adopted the bugle
call for its own and that it would be used in France as it is used
in America, to end the day and to mark the burial of the dead.

Vincent Norton, of Bloomfield Hills, Michigan, writes to the
New York *Times* that the call was composed by General Daniel
Butterfield, commander of a brigade in the Army of the Potomac,
and that it was first sounded by the writer's father, Oliver W. Norton, brigade bugler, in July, 1862, at Harrison's Landing, on the
lower James River in Virginia, where the Butterfield brigade was
encamped.

The son says that he often heard his father tell how General Butterfield scribbled the notes on the back of an old envelope, summoned Bugler Norton and directed him to sound the notes. After

a few trials and changes, the now world-famous call was finally arranged to suit General Butterfield and ordered substituted that night for regulation "taps" or "extinguish lights," which up to that time had been used by the United States Army.

Bugler Norton was then a young soldier assigned to brigade duty from the Eighty-third Regiment of Pennsylvania Volunteers. He later wrote a full account of the episode for his post in the Loyal Legion of the United States and included it in a volume of war letters privately published.

This contribution to the history of bugle calls used in the American Army casts light in dark places, as little has been written on the subject, it being assumed in many quarters that we got many of our bugle calls from the same source of our older and most stirring martial music—from older countries across the sea. And it is well, as we have borrowed from our over-seas neighbors, that they now borrow from us. France, of course, grew familiar with our beautiful and soothing "taps" as it was sounded in American camps and over American graves in French soil during the World War.

The chief proponent in having it adopted for use in the French Army was General Henri Gouraud, whose support for it was especially urgent after he had visited America in connection with the Yorktown Sesquicentennial in the fall of 1931. May "taps" come to be to the French the call of comfort and peace that it is now to us.

CHAPTER III

AN ACCOUNT OF THE DEVELOPMENT OF THE LAWS OF THE SERVICE

"Herein are the good ordinances of the sea, which wise men, who voyaged round the world, gave to our ancestors, and which constitute the books of the science of good customs"—

The Consulate of the Sea.

"The law is the last result of human wisdom acting upon human experience for the benefit of the public."

DR. SAMUEL JOHNSON

"Uncharted the rocks that surround thee,
Take heed that the channels thou learn
Lest thy name serve to buoy for another
That shoal, the Courts-Martial Return.
Though armour the belt that protects her,
The ship bears the scar on her side;
It is well if the court will acquit thee;
It were best hadst thou never been tried."

CAPTAIN HOPWOOD, R.N.[1]

"It ought to give any young man entering the Naval Service a certain thrill of elation that he became the heir of a long and glorious tradition, and that, studying the Articles controlling that Service, he is familiarizing himself with regulations, some of which, couched in almost exactly the same words, were obeyed by John Paul Jones and were read to the ship's company of the 'Bon Homme Richard'."

CHARLES RICHARD WILLIAMS

ALL the discipline of the Navy rests upon the basic laws that comprise the "Articles for the Government of the Navy." These articles of war and peace compose the "constitution" of the Navy, and from them have naval regulations and instructions been derived. It will be observed in tracing the history of our articles that part of the code that was embraced in our early rules and regulations has been retained, even some of the exact verbiage is effective today.

The first American naval articles were adopted by the Continental Congress, 28 November, 1775. This first "Blue Book"

[1] *The Laws of the Navy.*

was called *Rules for the Regulation of the Navy of the United Colonies.* The old English custom prevailed to the extent that it was decreed that the *Rules* were to be posted in "public places of the Ship." The infant Navy of the New World was administrated by a Committee of Congress, called the Marine Committee, and to John Adams of this committee was the task given of drafting the first rules of the Navy. As shall be later shown they were modeled after existing British regulations. John Paul Jones considered them inadequate; nevertheless, they served for the period of the War for Independence. On 2 March, 1779, a code of fifty articles was made effective.

Eleven of the original thirteen states fitted out armed vessels. Various state laws were promulgated relative to discipline, prizes, and general administration. Each of the thirteen states, with the exception of New Jersey and Delaware, had one or more armed vessels. The largest forces were maintained by Massachusetts, Connecticut, Pennsylvania, Maryland, Virginia, and South Carolina. New Hampshire had only one ship, and Georgia commissioned four galleys. No state Navy was so large as that of the Navy authorized by Congress, but their work was in most cases effective and their deeds belong to the common naval tradition. In any consideration of the naval force of the War for Independence, one must differentiate between letters of marque, privateers, state vessels, and Continental vessels.

After the excellent performance of the American Navy in the War of the Revolution, public interest and Congressional sympathy ebbed low to the needs of a naval service, and by 1785 the last ship of the fleet had been disposed of. In fact, it was in 1798 that our Navy was truly "born again."

In the establishment of the new federal government no provisions in the way of laws or regulations were made for the Navy. It was in 1798 that a Naval Department was formed, and we may consider that this year marks the beginning of the permanent service that has been maintained. Moreover, it marked the original drafts of the "Articles for the Government of the Navy." The articles grew from the 1775 *Rules and Regulations,* just as our present articles grew from those of 1798.

In order to secure a historic background for our present naval law, it is necessary to investigate the development of customs and laws of the sea, that merged in the British naval regulations in force at the time of the American Revolution.

Although no definite organization that could properly be called an English Navy existed until the latter part of the Middle Ages, an organization existed known as the "King's Ships." The quaint title "Keeper of the King's Ships" appears upon an appointment made by King John of England. In time, Lords of the Admiralty were created to carry on the duties of the Keeper. The titles "Keeper and Governor of the King's Ships" and "Clerk of the King's Ships" survived until past the middle of the sixteenth century. This early English sea power was in reality a fleet of private donations. The King owned a few ships but the towns of the Cinque Ports (Hythe, Romney, Hastings, Dover, and Sandwich) were obliged in return for royal favors to furnish the King with fifty-seven vessels upon request.

This maritime power of England was governed for many years by the general tenets of the Code of Oléron. The Laws of Oléron were based upon the sea law of the Republic of Rhodes, derived from Roman law long before and codified just as it had been also by other Mediterranean cities and states. Although this code was one of the five or six existing codes of the time, it is recorded that Richard Coeur de Lion used it at Marseilles in 1190 while awaiting transport for his Crusade to the Holy Land. William de Forz of Oléron, who was one of the five commanders of Richard I on this expedition, and afterwards became one of the justiciaries of the English Navy, was probably instrumental in urging its adoption. Alphonso X introduced and adopted the same code in Castile in the thirteenth century. Richard I after his return from the Crusades introduced the Code of Oléron with additions in England. It is of interest to note that the Code of Oléron was originally compiled and put on record by Eleanor, Duchess of Guinne, mother of Richard I of England. Parts of the Code were embraced in manuscripts of the fifteenth century, collectively called the *Black Book of the Admiralty.*

This *Black Book* was lost at the end of the eighteenth century but fortunately was found in 1874 in an old chest. Inasmuch as it was the basis of British sea law, a brief description of this rare book may be of interest. It was written in Norman-French, which at that time was the language of Court as well as the language of judicial and legal proceedings. The book measured 9½ inches high, 6¼ inches wide, and 2 inches thick. The first part of the book dates from Edward III, the latter belongs to the reigns of Henry IV, Henry V, and Henry VI. E. Keble Chatterton in his book, *Sailing the Seas,* writes in regard to the *Black Book,* "What immediately interests us is that we see order emerging out of chaos."

A few of the laws of the Code of Oléron are set forth to illustrate the punishments of that day.

Anyone that should kill another on board ship should be tied to the dead body and thrown into the sea.

Anyone that should kill another on land should be tied to the dead body and buried with it in the earth.

Anyone lawfully convicted of drawing a knife or other weapon with intent to strike another, or of striking another so as to draw blood, should lose his hand.

Anyone lawfully convicted of theft should have his head shaved and boiling pitch poured upon it and feathers or down should then be strewn upon it for the distinguishing of the offender; and upon the first occasion he should be put ashore.

The duties of an admiral in the fifteenth century were manifold and he exercised wide authority. The very power of creating a navy was delegated to him, as well as to appoint lieutenants to impress ships and men of the kingdom, and to administer justice "according to the law and ancient customs of the sea."

These beginnings of definitive rules and punishments led to "orders for war." They in time were merged with maritime law such as embraced in the Code of Oléron and Laws of Wisby.[1]

Although British authorities trace the descent of English

---

[1] The sea law of the northern maritime countries of Europe as adopted in the island of Gothland in the Baltic. Some writers claim these laws antedate the Code of Oléron.

men-o'-war and men-o'-war's men from the "buscarles" or sea police of nine centuries ago, it was not until the time of Henry VIII and his queen daughter Elizabeth that the Royal Navy was shaped as an administrative entity with a book of *Orders for War*. It is recorded that Sir Thomas Dudley, an aide to Henry VIII, framed the first book of *Orders for War* to be used both on land and sea. One of the instructions was:

First, the laws which be written what every man ought to do in the ship towards his Captain to be set in the main mast in parchment to be read as occasion shall serve.

On the fourth offense of a man sleeping on watch the following "mild" punishment was ordered:

Being taken asleep he shall be hanged to the bowsprit end of the ship in a basket, with a can of beer, a loaf of bread, and a sharp knife, and choose to hang there until he starve or cut himself into the sea.

There are to be found during this period certain special instructions such as those issued by the Earl of Essex and Lord Howard of Effingham during the Cadiz Expedition. These instructions consisted of twenty-nine articles. They were to be "openly read" twice each week. The first article ordered that religious exercises take place twice each day. Another quaint article is that the watch was "to be set every night by eight of the clock, either by trumpets or drum and singing the Lord's Prayer, some of the Psalms of David, or clearing the glass."

Punishments have in no measure been uniform throughout the years. Although crude and drastic were the punishments of early years, it was as late as 1750 that more death sentence offenses were added, while the inhuman practice of flogging was exercised on the slightest pretext. For example, for blasphemy, by the Code of Oléron, the offender was fined in silver. In the early seventeenth century, the offender was gagged and his tongue scraped; in 1644, there was an order to the effect that blasphemy was to be punished by burning the tongue of the offender with a red-hot iron. The strong religious instinct may be clearly followed through the Elizabethan and post-Elizabethan age in the respect displayed for the Psalms and Holy Writ,

The Point of Honor.

FLOGGING A SEAMAN—Note the grating to which the seaman is lashed and the petty officer with the cat-of-nine tails to the left under the break of the poop deck. (From an etching by George Cruikshank, 1825. From *Old Ship Prints*, by E. Keble Chatterton)

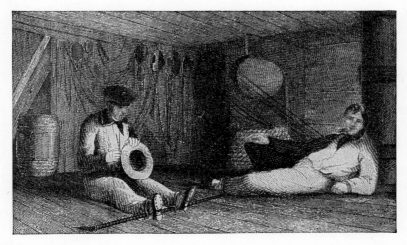

THE BRIG—Note the leg irons of the two men are attached to one iron rod. (From *Heck's Iconographic Encyclopedia*)

A Court-martial on Deck (From *Heck's Iconographic Encyclopedia*)

Keelhauling—Note that in this most cruel punishment a gun is fired to add to the misery of the culprit before he is hauled beneath the ship and brought aboard on the port side. (From *Heck's Iconographic Encyclopedia*)

and in the severe sentences for impiety and blasphemy. But in the seventeenth and eighteenth centuries the religious fervor of former days was disappearing.

The Elizabethan period of maritime history gives the first inkling of some system of standardized discipline as well as a tendency to prescribe some manner of uniform. Cabot ordered Sir Hugh Willoughby, when the latter was fitting out for a voyage to Cathay, to permit his men to wear "liveries" at the captain's discretion, "when he shall see cause to muster or show them in good array."

The Elizabethan mariners were a sturdy breed, and thanks to Hakluyt there is an excellent record of their voyages, discoveries, and the intense zeal they displayed in things maritime.

By courts-martial, offenders against the "Articles for the Government of the Navy" are tried. The court-martial is the present-day heir of the *Curia Militaris,* or Court of Chivalry, called also the Marshal's Court. This was originally the only military court that was established by the laws of England.

Originally this court was held before the Lord High Constable and the Earl Marshal jointly. In the reign of Henry VIII, the office of Lord High Constable was made extinct and all cases regarding civil matters of the military were held before the Earl Marshal.

The court by statute (13 Richard II, c. 2) had jurisdiction over "contracts and other matters touching deeds of arms and war" both in the kingdom and without. Originally it was purely a military court, or court of honor, when held before the Earl Marshal, and a criminal court when held before the Lord High Constable. Due to the weak jurisdiction and lack of power to enjoin its judgments as well as not being a court of record, both courts fell into disuse.

The constitution of military courts as we know them was adopted by ordinance in the reign of Charles I, and was in a great measure borrowed from the "Articles of War" of Gustavus Adolphus. Their adoption was expedited by the mutiny of a number of English and Scotch dragoons that had been ordered to Holland for replacement of certain Dutch troops ordered to England.

The first statutes setting forth the courts-martial (as derived from the Court of Chivalry) are found in the original Mutiny Act, 1689 (1 William and Mary, c. 5). This act was annually renewed "for the regulation of the Army." By this act the sovereign was authorized to grant, when he desired, "a commission, under his royal sign manual," giving to any officer not under the rank of a field-officer authorization for holding a general court-martial. It further provided that he could by warrant give the lord lieutenant of Ireland; the governor of Gibraltar, or governors of "any of the dominions beyond the sea" necessary authority to appoint courts-martial.

Although it has been nearly two hundred and fifty years since the above was enacted, it is still the source of military law of the English-speaking peoples. It exists in modified form in the United States, and many striking similarities will be found in a comparison of these statutes of 1689 and our own courts-martial system of precepts and jurisdiction.

Naval law and military law in England had originally many wide divergences. In the early days of the Lord High Admiral he issued the instructions and regulations of both the Royal and the Merchant Navy. Commanders administered at their discretion naval law under the instructions of the Lord High Admiral. Sentences at times were excessive. Death sentences were given in peace at the discretion of the commanders.[1]

The first regular naval tribunal was instituted by the leaders of the Long Parliament in 1645. They passed a measure called "An Ordinance and Article of Martial Law for the Government of the Navy." It was this act that for the first time authorized "general and ships' courts-martial with written records"; the former for captains and commanders, and the latter for subordinate officers and men. It was in a later law (Art. 13, Charles II, c. 9) that the Lord High Admiral was given the power to issue commissions (precepts) to officers to hold courts-martial. The first "Articles of War" for the Royal Navy were promulgated in the rule of Cromwell, although gathered from a col-

---

[1] Blackstone says, "If anyone that hath commission of martial authority doth, in time of peace, hang, or otherwise execute any man by colour of martial law, this is murder; for it is against Magna Charta."

lation of pertinent instructions issued by admirals in command, and approved about 1661 during the reign of Charles II. In 1749 Parliament enacted new "Articles of War," mainly through the efforts of Lord Anson. It was in these articles that so many death penalties were incorporated, and without doubt this accounts for the numerous death penalties in our "Articles for the Government of the Navy."

The Cromwellian "Articles for War" were not sufficient for naval administration. Commanders of the fleet and their immediate subordinates found it necessary from time to time to issue instructions and "details of service and discipline." With these instructions as a foundation, and guided by the best usage and customs of the sea, there appeared in 1731 the first issue of the *King's Regulations and Admiralty Instructions.*

John Adams was the staunchest supporter of the new-born Navy in the Continental Congress. As stated heretofore, Adams compiled the *Rules for the Regulation of the Navy of the United Colonies,* which rules were adopted by the Continental Congress on 28 November, 1775. These *Rules* formed the basic articles of the government of the Navy. They were inadequate, but served during the period of the Revolution. John Adams always evinced a great interest in matters maritime, and although he had no experience as a sea officer, he was undoubtedly acquainted as a lawyer with the legal aspects of military and naval discipline as well as with the Admiralty Law of England.

At this point it must be emphasized that British naval law, maritime history, and general sea traditions were common knowledge to the educated and well informed of the seaboard colonies. In fact, British maritime law as well as common law was the existing law of the Colonies; furthermore, there had been Colonials, both officers and men, in the British Navy. John Adams used the British Admiralty regulations as his guide for the first *Rules* of our Service. In some places the regulations were quoted verbatim, while in other cases slight modifications were necessary. The *King's Regulations* were comparatively new as to compilation (1731).

To augment the *Rules and Regulations* individual letters

of instruction were issued to commanding officers, with directions such as "Use your people well, but preserve strict discipline; treat prisoners if any you make with humanity; and in all things be duly attentive to the honor and interest of America." The above is an extract of a letter of 23 August, 1776, now preserved in the Library of Congress and written to Lieutenant John Baldwin, commander of the schooner *Wasp*.

In a letter of 1 November, 1776, it was urged upon Captain Elisha Warren of the Continental sloop *Fly* that,

Although we recommend your taking good care of your vessel and people, yet we should deem it more praiseworthy in an officer to lose his vessel in a bold enterprise than to lose a good prize by too timid a conduct.

The 1775 articles or *Rules* as they were called comprised about forty paragraphs. They sketchily defined the rights and the duties of officers, the reports required, and certain punishments for infractions of the rules. Flogging was sanctioned, and the issue of rum was authorized. The crew was allowed one half-pint of rum a day.

There were some quaint regulations in the Colonial *Naval Rules* of 1775. The third article reads:

If any shall be heard to swear, curse, or blaspheme the name of God, the Commander is strictly enjoined to punish them for every offense by causing them to wear a wooden collar or some shameful badge, for so long a time as he shall judge proper.

In the fourth article regarding punishments, it is stated:

No Commander shall inflict any punishments upon a seaman beyond twelve lashes upon his bare back with a cat-o'-nine-tails; if the fault shall deserve a greater punishment, he is to apply to the Commander-in-Chief of the Navy in order to the trying of him by a Court-Martial, and in the meantime, he may put him under confinement.

An inspection of the present "Articles for the Government of the Navy" discloses that a court-martial is authorized to adjudge the death penalty for twenty-two distinct offenses, although various other sentences may be adjudged for these offenses.

The 1775 articles had a general declaration that covered extraordinary offenses as well as those not otherwise covered. This regulation reads:

All other faults, disorders, and misdemeanors which shall be committed on any ship belonging to the 13 United Colonies, and which are not herein mentioned shall be punished according to the laws and customs in such cases at sea.

The lawmakers of the United States were fervently occupied at this time with the codification of law. Penalties and offenses became definitive. British customs and usage served as a general precedent in the lawmaking of the legislative assemblies.

In the present "Articles for the Government of the Navy" we find no reference to custom or the "ancient common law of the sea." In this connection, it is noted that in keeping with the British legal system and the fact that British common law is unwritten law, the present *King's Regulations and Admiralty Instructions,* as well as the *Naval Discipline Acts* (corresponding to United States "Articles for the Government of the Navy") refer to "customs of the sea." Section 44 of *Naval Discipline Acts* states that persons shall be proceeded against and punished "according to the laws and customs used at sea." Again, in Part III of *Naval Discipline Acts* there is found the phrase, "according to the custom of the Navy." One finds a general cover-all in the *Naval Discipline Acts,* known as the "Captain's Cloak,"

Every person subject to the act who shall be guilty of any act, disorder, or neglect to the prejudice of good order and naval discipline not hereinbefore specified, shall be dismissed from His Majesty's Service with disgrace, or suffer such other punishment as is hereinafter mentioned.

There is a striking similarity in some of the original articles of our Navy and those of today. Article 25 now effective reads, "No officer who may command by accident, or in the absence of the commanding officer, except when such commanding officer is absent for a time by leave, shall inflict any other punishments than confinements." The sixth rule of 1775 states, "The officer who commands by accident of the Captain or Commander's absence (unless he be absent for a time by leave) shall not order any correction but confinement."

Similarity is further observed. The old form of the first one of the "Articles for the Government of the Navy" was as follows:

The commanders of all ships and vessels belonging to the thirteen United Colonies are strictly required to shew in themselves a good example of honor and virtue to their officers and men, and to be very vigilant in inspecting the behavior of all such as are under them, and to discountenance and suppress all dissolute, immoral, and disorderly practice, and also such as are contrary to the rules of discipline and obedience, and to correct those who are guilty of the same, according to the usage of the sea.

Today, with little change from the above,

The Commanders of all fleets, squadrons, naval stations, and vessels belonging to the Navy, are required to show in themselves a good example of virtue, honor, patriotism, and subordination; to be vigilant in inspecting the conduct of all persons who are placed under their command; to guard against and suppress all dissolute and immoral practices; and correct according to the laws and regulations of the Navy, all persons who are guilty of them, and any such commander who offends against this Article shall be punished as a court-martial may direct.[1]

Various British regulations were embodied in the 1798 *Naval Regulations*. The following quotations are compared in order to mark the similarity:

REGULATIONS AND INSTRUCTIONS
RELATING TO HIS MAJESTY'S SERVICE AT SEA
Printed in the Year 1790

The Cook[2]

Article I

The Cook is to have the charge of the Steep-Tub and to be answerable for the meat put therein, if any part thereof shall be lost through his want of care.

---

[1] R. S. Sec. 1624, art. I.
[2] Note.—The cook was an important warrant officer at that time. For many years after the above dates, the duties of the midshipmen were listed in the *Naval Regulations* after those of the cook. The "watering" of meat was an attempt to remove the salt.

II

He is to see the meat duly watered and the provisions carefully and cleanly boiled, and issued to the men according to the practice of the Navy.

* * * * *

NAVAL REGULATIONS
ISSUED BY COMMAND OF THE PRESIDENT OF THE
UNITED STATES OF AMERICA
January 25, 1802

(The following is quoted from the personal copy of
Thomas Truxtun)

Of the Duties of a Cook

1. He is to have charge of the steep tub, and is answerable to the meat put therein.

2. He is to see the meat duly watered, and the provisions carefully boiled, and delivered to the men according to the practice of the Navy.

There is at the present time a skillful and trained body of officers to execute and review courts-martial. It has not always been so. In a *Naval Encyclopaedia,* written by "officers and others of recognized authority in the branches treated by them," published in 1881, it is stated:

The important matter of administering law and justice by means of Courts-Martial in the U. S. Navy has until recently been lamely and imperfectly conducted. . . . Until 1846, except a small book by Major General Macomb, U.S.A., there was no strictly American authority on Courts-Martial. In that year Captain Wm. C. De Hart, 2d U. S. Artillery, published a work on "Military Law adapted to the United States Army and Navy," which contained much of value and is still quoted.

Books of foreign origin, generally English, were previously employed, and the practice of our Courts-Martial was often both inconsistent and contradictory. Errors were frequent; there was no settled and uniform interpretation of either the law or the mode of procedure. . . .

The Army and the Navy are governed by separate laws. The code of the Army is known as "The Articles of War," originally

101 in number, and approved 10 April, 1806. In Great Britain "The Articles of War" are embodied in the Mutiny Act which is passed every year. The code of the United States Navy is known as "The Articles for the Government of the Navy," originally "The Articles for the Better Government of the Navy." They comprised originally 25 articles (now 70 articles) approved 17 July, 1862. Both Army and Navy codes are incorporated in the *Revised Statutes*.

Thus have tradition, custom, usage, and experience given form to the basic laws of the Navy. It is a source of pride that,

The rules of the greatest and most glorious game in the world are not a thing of yesterday or the day before. They were born in the travail and the trial of ages; they are the results of centuries of experience and experiments; heated at the forge of battle, hammered into the shape on the anvil of practical knowledge; tested and approved by great heroes of the sea. Any man in the Navy that has a heart to understand and appreciate the spiritual in life must breathe freer and walk with a firmer step when he recalls that he is obeying the same laws that Rodney and Nelson and Napier obeyed; that he is under the same discipline that Decatur, Macdonough and Perry, Dahlgren and Porter, Farragut and Dewey, and a host of other patriots have honored and made illustrious.[1]

This brief summary gives merely a scant outline of the long history of definitive regulation and rules of discipline that have led to the "law" as it is written today. But in essence their use and value may be summarized by what that master disciplinarian Admiral Lord Jervis said, "Discipline is summed up in the one word obedience." To those of the Service—no comment is required.

[1] Charles R. Williams: "History of Discipline in the Navy," Naval Institute PROCEEDINGS, XLV, No. 3.

THE CAPTAIN'S GIG—Note the old-style caps and uniforms. (From *All Hands*, by R. F. Zogbaum. Courtesy Harper and Bros.)

PART II

SEA MANNERS AND SHORE MANNERS

CHAPTER IV

HONORS, SALUTES, AND CEREMONIES

"Salutes and salutations were, in their origin, marks of submission. We take off our hats because of old the conquered took off their helmets; we bow, because the vanquished were used to bend their necks to the conqueror; and salutes were fired, shot and all, that the place or ship might be thereby without the means of present defence. Thus from the bloody forms of turbulent ages are derived the ceremonies of polished life."

The Lady's Magazine (1821)

24. *"Within his Majesty's seas his ships are not, on any account, to strike their topsails nor take in their flags, nor in any way to salute any foreign ship whatever; nor are they, in any other seas, to strike their topsails, or take in their flags, to any foreign ship, unless such foreign ships shall have first struck, or shall at the same time strike their flags and topsails to his Majesty's ships."*

Robert Simmons, one of the senior gunners of the Navy (1812)
The Sea Gunner's "Vade-Mecum."

"So far as his authority extends, the officer of the deck shall see that the regulations concerning salutes, honors, and distinctions are carefully observed."

U. S. Navy Regulations, art 1065.

NOTES FOR THE OFFICER OF THE DECK

(1) Correctness, promptness, and smartness should be the aim in rendering honors.

(2) Check and recheck by regulations where there is doubt.

(3) The promptness of a man-of-war in returning the dip of merchant ships is usually a gauge of her smartness regarding honors in general. Remember that this is an honor that is paid you, so be prompt to return the courtesy.

(4) Insure that ensign, flags, and pennants fly free and are hoisted to the very top of the hoist. Learn, as in the days of sail, to cast your eyes aloft.

(5) Remember in honors that the mainmast is the "honor mast." The flags of the President of the United States and Sec-

retary of the Navy fly at the main during their visit. It is also reserved for the national flags of other states when their presidents,
sovereigns, or members of royal families come aboard. In the
case of royalty other than the sovereign, their national flag flies
at the main only during the salute. In a foreign country a former
President of the United States receives the national flag at the
main during salutes.

*Never forget that in international salutes the ensign of the
country saluted is hoisted at the mainmast.*

(6) Take care that flags are broken at the first gun of the
salute. They are hauled down promptly at the last gun, when
required to be hauled down at the end of the salute. Officers
and men remain at attention from the first gun until the
last.

(7) Although a liberal estimate must be given, honors are
rendered when ships pass within 600 yards; boats flying a flag
or pennant, at 400 yards. Do not fail to extend these limits for
foreign ships and officers when circumstances so require it.

(8) "Attention" should be sounded when the jackstaff of one
vessel passes the jackstaff or flagstaff of the other. "Carry on"
should be sounded when the quarter-deck of the passing vessel
has definitely passed the quarter-deck of the other.

(9) No guard or band shall be given on Sundays to United
States ships, officers of the United States Navy and Marine Corps.
This applies also to United States government officials who rate
honors. Only the most extraordinary circumstances permit a
deviation in this regulation.

(10) When a senior ship passes, have "attention" sounded
before she does, and insure that "carry on" is given after she
gives it.

(11) Exercise great care that honors are never rendered of
a less degree than due.

(12) In addition to the correctness and smartness that one
must show in the attention to honors, remember that the *Navy
Regulations* state, "He (the officer of the deck) shall see that all
persons coming alongside on visiting the ship are courteously
treated."

(13) Insist that the signalmen in charge of the signal watches maintain bright lookouts for boats passing with pennants and flags of senior officers flying. Inform the signal bridge when calls are expected in order that timely information may be given the quarter-deck.

(14) Remember that you have sufficient personnel detailed to assist you with all honors and salutes; it is your responsibility to see that those of the watch get the word, and that they are always near their stations of duty.

(15) As officer of the deck of flagships maintain a close liaison with flag lieutenants, but remember always to make proper reports to your commanding officer and the executive officer.

(16) Give attention to your personal appearance on watch, with particular regard to gold braid, cap, and accoutrement.

(17) Make it a regular practice to devote some time when off watch to a study of regulations and customs—all indispensable to a proper discharge of your duties and your future success.

(18) Remember that coolness and quickness are the essentials of good watch standing.

(19) Learn first the exact regulations for honors and ceremonies, then, interpretations, precedents—the fine points.

(20) In the first edition of the *Modern Officer of the Watch,* Commander R. Plunkett, R.N., said, "The traditions of the Service are worthy of honor and respect, and while you remain in the Service it is your duty to try and live up to them."

The Navy will maintain its honored position in United States history and its recognized place in the eyes of the world by the thoughtful attention to duty and efficiency of its members, and by the high standards of honor, education, and gentility of those who direct its policies and its plans.

Note.—See end of chapter for "Tables of Honors and Ceremonies" used in connection with Chap. 5, *U. S. Navy Regulations.*

The following letter is published as an official interpretation of the *Naval Regulations* pertaining to honors. It is not enough for an officer to know what honors to render; he should also know the details of correct rendering.

United States Fleet

Battle Force

U.S.S. *California,* Flagship

San Pedro, California,
23 September, 1931.

BATTLE FORCE LETTER NO. 16-31

From: Commander Battle Force.
To: Battle Force.
Subject: Uniformity in rendering of honors.
Reference: (a) *U. S. Navy Regulations,* 1920, Chapter 5.

1. In order that there may be uniformity in the rendering of honors and salutes throughout the Battle Force it is directed that the requirements of Chapter 5, *U. S. Navy Regulations,* be strictly observed.

2. For such cases where the exact meaning of certain phrases contained in the *Regulations* may not be clear, the following interpretations are made:

(a) The term, "reaches the deck" in all references to the rendering of honors to dignitaries and officers on visiting a ship will be interpreted to mean "as he steps from the upper grating of the gangway ladder to the deck." This will ordinarily be immediately after the dignitary or officer being received has saluted the national ensign while on the upper grating of the gangway ladder.

(b) The requirement that officers and men shall salute when receiving a dignitary or officer, and at the departure of such dignitary or officer, shall be interpreted to mean that the salute shall be maintained only during the sounding of the ruffles and flourishes. The guard, however, will remain at present arms until the march is completed by the band.

(c) Piping of the side shall be done as prescribed in Article 278, *U. S. Navy Regulations,* whether the guard is paraded or not. The phrase "appears over the side" as used in Article 278 shall be interpreted to mean "when his head reaches the level of the deck."

(d) When honors are rendered for a dignitary or officer on leaving a ship, the guard shall present arms and the band sound off immediately after such dignitary or officer completes his leave-taking from the senior officer on the ship, and just prior to his passing between the lines of side boys. The piping of the side will begin as the dignitary or officer starts between the lines of side boys, and will continue until his head reaches the level of the deck.

R. H. Leigh

The high standard of smartness that has characterized the United States Navy is maintained primarily by the vigilance and direction of the officers. But more specifically, that standard was attained by knowledge and observance of the laws, customs, and traditions of the Service.

Admiral R. H. Leigh, when Commander in Chief of the United States Fleet, discussed in the following letter some of the points which tend to smartness.

Cinc File No.
P15-1
1

05/By (O)

United States Fleet

U.S.S. Pennsylvania, Flagship

San Pedro, California,
1 January, 1933.

UNITED STATES FLEET LETTER NO. 1-33

From: Commander in Chief, United States Fleet,
To: Fleet.
Subject: Smartness of ships and personnel.

1. During the two and one-half years that the commander in chief has been on duty with the Fleet as Commander Battleships, Commander Battle Force, and Commander in Chief, United States Fleet, he has observed with satisfaction the steady advance made by all units of the Fleet in Gunnery, Engineering, Communications, and the other factors which determine the efficiency of the Fleet as a whole. The general high standard of the individual ships, as exemplified by the reports of the routine inspections by the flag officers of the Fleet, has been noted. Of special note have been the uniformly high marks given for "smartness."

2. Although the commander in chief agrees with the inspecting officers that the ships are smart on the day of inspection, he knows from personal observation that this degree of smartness is not maintained throughout the other days of the year when no inspections are being held.

3. For the information of the Fleet there are here discussed some of the points which to a more or less degree on individual ships have detracted from the smartness of the Fleet as a whole:

(a) *Quarter-deck procedure.* The *Navy Regulations* define the limits of the quarter-deck and provide for the ceremonies that are required for observance by naval personnel with regard to salutes and the reception of visitors. These *Regulations* are in general complied with. But the Navy's traditions and customs with respect to the "sanctity" of the quarter-deck are gradually being ignored. This is probably due, in part, to the installation of catapults on the quarter-deck, which, together with the planes habitually carried there, require a certain amount of work to be done in this part of the ship. There can be no objection, of course, to the carrying on of this necessary work. But the tendency to loaf, to smoke, and to engage in loud conversation in this part of the ship, together with the general disregard as to the amount of noise made, is not conducive to smartness, and lessens that respect for authority which is so essential in a military organization.

(b) *Outward appearance of ships.* The outward appearance of the ships is, in general, excellent. But there has been noted that some ships permit the hanging of clothes and canvas where they present an untidy and slovenly appearance. There have also been noted growing tendencies to ignore the presence of "Irish pendants," and to permit the national ensigns, personal flags, and other flags to become foul and to remain so for unduly long periods. These faults can easily be remedied by having a routine inspection service by the junior officers of the deck, and the responsible petty officers of the watch.

(c) *Boats.* The general appearance of the boats throughout the Fleet is excellent. In fact the boats present a better appearance than the crews. Some of the faults for which there is room for improvement are:

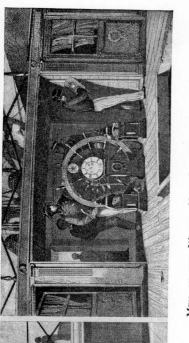

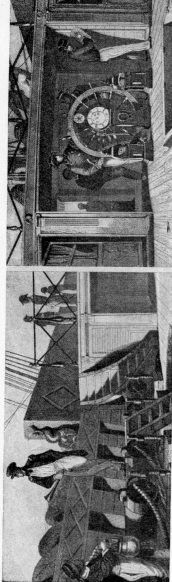

OFFICER OF THE DECK IN PORT IN THE DAYS OF SAIL

MEN AT THE WHEEL—Note lee helmsman, also quartermaster marking course on a special compass card.

FRENCH SHIP OF THE LINE FULL DRESSED

BRITISH SHIP OF THE LINE WITH YARDS MANNED DURING A SALUTE

(From *Heck's Iconographic Encyclopedia*)

(1) Carelessness with respect to fenders hanging over side, when not needed.

(2) Carelessness in uniformity and neatness of uniforms.

(3) Lounging of crews on canopies and sitting on guard rails at stern.

(4) Unnecessary standing in boats.

(5) Failure to observe *Regulations* with respect to salutes, and the provisions of art. 291 (1), *U. S. Navy Regulations*, which are quoted:

> At landings and gangway juniors shall give way to seniors and at all times juniors shall show deference to their seniors by abstaining from crossing the bows of their boats, crowding them, or ignoring their presence.

(6) Coxswains frequently overtake or cross other boats too closely. There seems to be a tendency to see how near boats can cross or pass each other without accident. The boat *not* having the right of way should give way promptly and in time.

(d) *Uniform.* At inspections the crews, as a rule, present a neat and satisfactory appearance with respect to uniforms. However, in general, the standard of the uniforms is not so high as that of the material parts of the ships. The clothing of the men at bag inspections appears to conform to the *Regulations;* but it has been noted that whenever the weather becomes cold or rainy many non-regulation sweaters, windcheckers, and other articles are worn. This situation must be well known to division officers and in some cases to heads of departments and commanding officers, and only requires suitable supervision for correction. Ashore men are seen who are not wearing neat uniforms, and in some cases non-regulation overcoats, raincoats, or other non-regulation articles of clothing.

(e) *Conduct on shore.* The commission of serious offenses on shore by enlisted personnel is an indication of laxity in discipline or indoctrination on board ship. The deliberate commission of offenses on shore is not only a reflection on the Navy uniform and the Navy as a whole, but particularly against the ships to which the offenders belong. Special efforts should be made on board each vessel by commanding officers to indoctrinate their personnel.

4. While each of these items taken individually may not seem important, taken all together they constitute a large factor in smartness and morale, both of which are essential for an efficient organization. The commander in chief desires that with the New Year all hands make an effort to correct the deficiencies to which attention is called in this letter.

R. H. LEIGH

CHANGE IN COMMAND CEREMONY

P17-1 (3297)

05/Ws (O)

United States Fleet
Battle Force
U.S.S. California, Flagship

San Pedro, California,
1 August, 1932.

From: Commander Battle Force.
To: Commander Battleships, Battle Force.
               Commander Cruisers, Battle Force.
               Commander Aircraft, Battle Force.
               Commander Destroyers, Battle Force.
               Commander Submarine Division Twelve.
Subject: Ceremony of change in command on U.S.S. *Pennsylvania,* 12 August, 1932.
Reference: (a) Cinc, U. S. Fleet file P17-1 (1174) of 28 July, 1932.

1. Reference (a) is quoted for your information and for compliance with pars. 1 and 2:

"1. Admiral R. H. Leigh, U. S. Navy, will relieve Admiral Frank H. Schofield, U. S. Navy, as commander in chief, United States Fleet, at 0900, Friday, 12 August, 1932, on board U.S.S. *Pennsylvania* at San Pedro, California. Flag officers and their aides, commanding officers and executive officers of ships present, and such officers attached to the U.S.S. *Pennsylvania* as the captain may direct, shall attend the ceremony. Flag officers and officers of the rank of captain present in San Diego are invited to attend the ceremony but such attendance is entirely optional. The uniform for officers attending the ceremony shall be 'dress blue' and the uniform for the crew of the *Pennsylvania,* 'dress blue baker.'

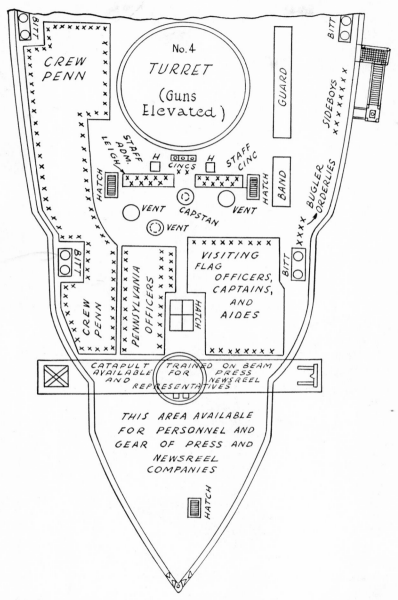

CEREMONIES, CHANGE OF COMMAND C. IN C., U. S. FLEET—Deck plan, U.S.S. *Pennsylvania*, showing parades. Reference: C. in C., U. S. Fleet File P17-1(1174) of 28 July, 1932.

"2. The staff of Admiral Schofield shall fall in on the starboard side in two ranks abreast the quarter-deck capstan, and the staff of Admiral Leigh shall fall in on the port side abreast the quarter-deck capstan, both staffs facing aft. The visiting flag officers, captains, officers, and aides shall fall in, seniors forward, on the starboard side of the quarter-deck, facing forward, and leaving a clear passage from starboard quarter-deck hatch to capstan inboard. The officers of the *Pennsylvania* shall fall in, seniors forward, on the port side of the quarter-deck, inboard, and facing forward.

"3. The guard and band shall be paraded on the starboard side of the quarter-deck forward and shall be faced inboard for the ceremony.

"4. Insofar as practicable, the crew of the *Pennsylvania* shall be massed in orderly formation on the port side of the quarter-deck outboard of *Pennsylvania* officers and forward to abreast No. 4 turret. The remainder of the crew shall be held at quarters.

"5. When the officers and crew are up and at parade, the captain of the *Pennsylvania* shall so report to the commander in chief, U. S. Fleet, who will then in company with his relief take position forward of quarter-deck capstan, facing aft.

"6. The commander in chief will step forward, make such remarks as he desires to the officers and men assembled, read his orders, and direct the commanding officer to haul down his flag. A salute of 17 guns shall be fired and the commander in chief's flag shall be hauled down at the last gun and the commission pennant broken.

"7. Admiral Leigh will step forward, make such remarks as he desires to the officers and men assembled, and read his orders. Upon the completion of the reading of his orders he will direct the commanding officer to break his flag. The flag shall be broken and a 17-gun salute fired.

"8. Upon completion of these ceremonies the crew shall be marched forward promptly and the guard and band moved into position to render honors to officers leaving the ship.

"9. The commanding officer, U.S.S. *Pennsylvania*, assisted by the flag lieutenant of the commander in chief, shall be in charge of the ceremony."

J. K. Taussig
Chief of Staff

COMMISSIONING CEREMONIES

Commissioning ceremonies are not covered by the *Naval Regulations*. Nevertheless, the precedents of custom give the outline of a uniform procedure. In general the ceremony is as follows:

(1) The officers and crew fall in aft at dress parade stations on the quarter-deck. It is customary for officers to fall in amidships and face aft. The guard and band fall in aft at stations for "colors."

(2) The captain of the yard or a delegated representative of the commandant then reads the orders for delivery of the ship.

(3) After these orders are read, "attention" is sounded on the bugle; the national anthem is played; the ensign, commission pennant, and jack are hoisted simultaneously.

(4) The officer ordered to command the ship then reads his orders from the Navy Department and orders the executive officer to "set the watch." This is particularly effective when boatswain's mates take up the piping fore and aft.

(5) The officer of the deck takes his station. All watch keepers of this first watch take stations as detailed in the watch bills.

Full dress uniform is usually worn by officers at the commissioning ceremonies of cruisers and battleships. It has been customary to invite friends of officers and others interested to attend the commissioning ceremony. The sponsor at the launching should be invited by a note from the commanding officer. Should there be a presentation of silver or other gifts to the ship by a city or state, it is fitting that this ceremony follow the commissioning. In this event it will be expected that the commanding officer will reply to the speech of presentation. In a short speech, the commanding officer expresses the thanks of the Navy Department and the officers and men of his command for the gift and the motives that prompted its presentation.

FOREIGN ENSIGNS, DISTINCTIVE FLAGS, AND PENNANTS

The following information on foreign ensigns, personal flags, special flags, and pennants has been taken from *Communication Instructions* (1929, revised 1934).

2812. On occasions indicated, the national ensign of the foreign power concerned shall be displayed,

(a) At the main, during time on board .... Visit of president of foreign republic or foreign sovereign.

(b) At the main, during salute .... Visit of members of royal family.

(c) At the main, during salute .... Whenever a ship of the Navy falls in with a friendly foreign ship of war flying the standard or flag of a president of a republic, sovereign, or member of a royal family, or passes near such standard or flag, if flying elsewhere than from a ship of war.

(d) At the main, during salute .... When firing a national salute upon entering a foreign port or when returning a salute of the same nature from a foreign ship of war.

(e) At the main, during salute .... On the occasion of celebrating foreign national anniversaries or festivals, during the salute and for such further times as the ships of such nations present may remain dressed. In case of an anniversary of a nation in whose waters a ship is lying, where no ships of that nation are present, the ensign of the nation celebrating the day shall be displayed until sunset.

(f) At the fore, during salute .... Whenever a ship of the Navy falls in with a friendly foreign man-of-war flying a flag or pennant of a foreign flag officer or commodore or while returning such a salute.

(g) At the fore, during salute .... In honor of foreign naval, military, diplomatic, or consular officials, visiting ships of the Navy.

2813. When a foreign official entitled to a gun salute visits a ship of the Navy while the ship is dressed or full-dressed, the United States ensign at the fore (or main) is to be hauled down while the ensign of the nation represented by the visitor is being saluted; the United States ensign is to be replaced at once when the ensign of the nation represented by the visitor is hauled down at the last gun of the salute.

2814. On board ships, where for want of masts the national ensign cannot be displayed as prescribed, the point of display may be modified as necessary, following the spirit of the rules herein laid down, but its display must not be omitted.

Battle Flags

2815. The use of battle flags at the fore and main has been discontinued. During battle the ensign shall be hoisted at the gaff only.

Union Jack

2816. The union jack shall be displayed on board ships of the Navy,

(a) At anchor; at 8:00 A.M., and until sunset, from the jack staff.

(b) At the mizzen or at the yardarm to denote that a general court-martial or court of inquiry is in session. It is to be hoisted (and, if in port, a gun fired) when the court meets and hauled down when the court adjourns.

2817. The union jack shall be displayed from boats belonging to naval ships,

(a) When a diplomatic official of the United States, of or above the rank of charge d'affaires, pays an official visit afloat.

(b) When the naval governor of Guam, American Samoa, or the Virgin Islands is embarked in a boat within the limits of his government for the purpose of paying visits of ceremony in his official capacity as a governor.

Personal Flags

2818. A personal flag is a distinctive mark of a ship of the Navy in commission, and at the same time a distinctive mark of command. It is also displayed as an honor to, and to indicate when an official entitled to a personal flag or pennant is embarked on board by due authority.

2819. When the personal flag of the President of the United States, or of the Secretary of the Navy, or of the Assistant Secretary of the

Navy is flying on board any ship of the Navy any other personal flag or pennant shall be hoisted at the foremast.

2820. Should any or all of the above-named officials visit a ship at the same time, the flag of the senior official only shall be displayed. With the exceptions stated in article 2819 only one personal flag or pennant shall be displayed from a ship at one time, which shall be that of the senior.

2821. No flags or pennants other than those prescribed in the *Navy Regulations* or *Visual Manual* shall be displayed on board any ship of the Navy as a personal honor to any person or for the purpose of indicating the presence of such person on board; and all flags and pennants thus displayed shall conform strictly to the patterns laid down in the *Visual Manual*.

2822. The distinctive mark of the senior on board shall be displayed, day and night, and shall be carried at the main, except the flag of an admiral, vice admiral, or rear admiral, and the pennant of the senior officer present, which shall be carried at the aftermast and starboard after yardarm, respectively.

2823. In 2-masted ships, all such flags and pennants shall be displayed from the main; in single-masted ships, from the truck; and in mastless ships from the loftiest and most conspicuous hoist.

2824. No personal flag of any official shall be displayed at the same masthead with any national ensign. Whenever such double display is required,

(*a*) In dressing ship during the visit aboard of any foreign official, the personal flag or pennant shall be displayed at the fore, while the national ensign is hoisted at the main. In dressing ship the personal flag or pennants shall be shifted to the fore during such period of dressing and no national ensign shall then be flown from the masthead. This provision shall be complied with in dressing ship in honor of our own country by shifting the personal flag or broad pennant forward and displaying our ensign at the main.

(*b*) During gun salutes, a personal flag or broad pennant at the masthead where a national flag is flown shall be lowered until clear of the national flag during salute.

2825. On board a ship where, for want of masts, the distinctive mark of command cannot be displayed as prescribed, it shall be hoisted in the most conspicuous position possible.

Commission Pennant

2826. The commission pennant is a distinctive mark of a ship of the Navy in commission, and is flown from the after masthead, except when a personal flag is displayed, in which case the personal flag displaces the commission pennant. In mastless ships it is displayed from the loftiest and most conspicuous point of hoist.

2827. It is displayed from the bow of a boat when a commanding officer, not entitled to a personal flag, is embarked on occasions of official visits.

2828. The 13-star or the 7-star commission pennant is flown by vessels in accordance with the Bureau of Construction and Repair Allowance List for vessels of the particular type concerned.

President's Flag

2829. The President's flag shall be displayed at the main at the moment the President reaches the deck and kept flying as long as he is on board. On his departure it shall be hauled down with the last gun of the salute.

2830. It shall be displayed in the bow of any boat in which he may be embarked unless otherwise requested by him.

Consular Flag

2838. When a consular representative of the United States pays an official visit afloat in a boat of the Navy, the consular flag shall be displayed on a staff in the bow.

Flag Officer's Flag

2839. The personal flag of a flag officer shall be hoisted when he assumes command. When he relinquishes command his flag shall be hauled down with the last gun of the salute.

2840. At no time shall his flag be displayed from more than one ship.

2841. When a ship is inspected by a board of inspection and survey the president of which is a flag officer, the flag of such president shall be hoisted upon his arrival and kept flying during the time he is on board. Upon his departure it shall be hauled down with the last gun of the salute.

2842. When two or more flag officers of the same grade are present, the blue flag shall be flown by the senior only; the red by all others.

THE ADMIRAL'S BARGE (From *All Hands*, by R. F. Zogbaum. Courtesy Harper and Bros.)

2843. When in a port of the United States on the occasion of the absence of a flag officer from his command afloat for a period exceeding 24 hours, his flag shall be hauled down and the command devolve upon the line officer next in rank present in the fleet, squadron, or division, subject to any direction from the flag officer.

2844. If in a foreign port the same officer shall succeed to the command and the flag shall be displayed from the ship in which the temporary commander is embarked.

2845. A flag or other officer in command afloat, or at a naval station, and any chief of staff when acting in behalf of his flag officer, shall upon official occasions and visits carry on a staff, at the bow of the boat in which he is embarked, a flag, or broad or commission pennant according to his rank.

2846. The absence of a flag officer from his flagship during the day shall be indicated by flying the alphabet flag E at the starboard main yardarm during his absence.

2847. No personal flag or pennant of any officer of the Navy shall be half-masted when displayed either from ships or boats, except upon decease of the officer.

Senior Officer's Pennant

2848. The senior officer's pennant shall be displayed as follows:

(a) By the senior ship, at the starboard yardarm in addition to the commission pennant at the main, when two or more ships of the Navy are together at anchor, with no distinctive flag of a flag officer flying.

(b) When two or more ships, each displaying a broad command pennant or burgee command pennant, are together at anchor, with no flag officer present, by the senior ship at the starboard yardarm, in addition to the broad or burgee command pennant.

(c) At the fore truck under way, by the fleet guide when in position, at the dip when not in position. When the fleet is deployed for battle it is not flown.

(d) Under a ship's call to direct that ship to take fleet guide.

(e) Under negative, under a ship's call, to direct that ship to cease being fleet guide.

(f) On the receiving ship when the senior officer in command ashore is not a flag officer; if there be no receiving ship, at some conspicuous and suitable place of hoist within the limits of his command.

Merchant Marine Naval Reserve Flag

2851. (a) The Merchant Marine Naval Reserve flag is the distinctive mark of a merchant vessel commanded by an officer of the Naval Reserve Force. It may be displayed at the main truck by seagoing merchant vessels documented under the laws of the United States which have been designated by the Secretary of the Navy as suitable for service as naval auxiliaries in time of war, provided that the master or commanding officer and not less than 50 per cent of the officers of such vessels are members of the Naval Reserve. Such flag shall not be flown in lieu of the national ensign. A house flag shall not be flown in lieu of the national ensign. A house flag may be flown immediately below the Merchant Marine Naval Reserve flag.

(b) The Merchant Marine Naval Reserve flag is authorized in three sizes: Size No. 1, 13-foot 6-inch fly; size No. 2, 10-foot 1.5-inch fly; size No. 3 6-foot 9-inch fly. Size No. 3 is the only size furnished a steamship line in accordance with existing instructions, but a vessel duly authorized to fly the Merchant Marine Naval Reserve flag may use any of the three sizes at discretion.

Naval Reserve Yacht Pennant

2852. The Naval Reserve yacht pennant may be displayed at the fore truck by such yachts and similar vessels commanded or owned by Naval Reserve officers as have been designated by the Secretary of the Navy as suitable for service as naval auxiliaries in time of war. No lettering of any kind is authorized on the Naval Reserve yacht pennant.

Naval District Pennants

2853. The naval district pennants are distinctive marks of naval district vessels and indicate that the vessels displaying them are the flagships of the force, section, or division commander. Naval district pennants shall be displayed from the after truck, and when so displayed replace the commission pennant. As naval district pennants are not displayed from boats they are furnished in one size only.

2854. The pennant of the naval district section commander has the section number surcharged in red Roman numerals, and the pennant of the division commander has the division number surcharged in red Arabic numerals.

Naval Militia Distinguishing Flag

2856. The Naval Militia distinguishing flag may be displayed at the fore masthead on vessels loaned by the Navy Department to, and actually maintained by a state, for the use of the Naval Militia when such vessels are actually under the command of a Naval Militia officer.

2857. The Naval Militia commission pennant may be displayed at the main masthead on vessels in commission loaned by the Navy Department to and actually maintained by a state for the use of the Naval Militia.

2858. In mastless ships it is displayed from the loftiest and most conspicuous point of hoist.

Red-Cross Flag

2859. The Red-Cross flag (Geneva convention) is an emblem and distinctive signal of sanitary service which shall be accompanied by the national flag of the country to whose service the sanitary establishment or formation belongs. The sanitary branch of naval encampments and naval shore establishments shall fly the Red-Cross flag, marking that part of the encampment or establishment entitled to protection under the rules of the Geneva convention. This flag may be displayed either from a separate staff or from a gaff or signal yard of the staff flying the national ensign. It shall not be flown on the same halyard as the national ensign.

2860. In time of war, hospital ships shall fly the Red-Cross flag at the main in place of the commission pennant which they shall fly in time of peace. Boats engaged in sanitary service and hospital boats of landing parties shall fly the Red-Cross flag from a staff in the bow.

The Church Pennant

2862. The church pennant shall be hoisted at the same place of hoist and over the ensign during the performance of divine services on board vessels of the Navy.

Quarantine Flag

2863. The quarantine flag (alphabet flag Q) is hoisted at the fore masthead at the most conspicuous hoist on all infected ships or ships in quarantine. It shall be kept flying day and night and be carried in the bow of all boats belonging to the ship having this flag hoisted.

2864. It should be hoisted by incoming ships, prior to entering the harbor, as a signal to the health officer of that port that pratique is desired.

Battle-Efficiency Pennant

2865. The battle-efficiency pennant shall be displayed at the fore when at anchor, on such vessels as may have been officially declared entitled to fly it for excellence in battle efficiency.

Flag of Truce

2866. The flag of truce is a square white flag and its proper use is in general in the interest of humanity. When displayed from any conspicuous place of hoist, it indicates a desire to send a communication, but the truce does not exist until the hoist has been replied to. A belligerent may decline to receive a flag of truce. On blank guns being fired while a flag of truce is displayed, the ship bearing it must stop and not approach nearer. Boats and bearers must act in a similar manner. Bearers of a flag of truce are inviolable provided they do not act improperly. Should they do so or should the flag be used improperly to obtain information, the bearers may become subject to capture and punishment as spies.

FLAGS, SALUTES, AND HONORS ABOARD YACHTS*

The following information is from the yacht routine prescribed by the New York Yacht Club, and is in general that followed by all other large yacht clubs of the United States:

Burgee .... The burgee is the official "pointed flag" of the Yacht Club. The private signal refers to personal flag or pennant of the owner.

Private signal ..... The private signal shall be displayed by yachts in commission as herein prescribed, whenever the ensign is hoisted,

(a) On a yacht with two or more masts, at the main truck.

(b) On a ketch or a yawl, at the mizzen truck.

(c) On a single-masted yacht, at the truck when under way.

(d) On a steam or power yacht with one mast and a staff at the bow, at the main truck.

* See Appendix M for decisions on status of yacht ensign and salutes thereto.

(e) On a mastless yacht, at a staff at the bow when under way.

Absent flag .... The absent flag is a rectangular blue flag. It shall be displayed during daylight at the starboard main spreader when an owner is not on board, and at the starboard main yardarm on a square-rigged yacht. An absent signal does not exempt a yacht from the observance of club routine.

Owner's meal flag The owner's meal flag is a rectangular white flag. It shall be displayed in daylight during an owner's meal hours at the starboard main spreader, or at the starboard main yardarm.

Guest flag .... A rectangular blue flag with a white stripe running diagonally across from top to fly may be displayed at the starboard main spreader or at the starboard main yardarm, when guests are on board during the absence of the owner.

Crew's meal pennant .... A red pennant shall be displayed during the crew's meal hours at the port fore spreader or the port fore yardarm of a yacht with two or more masts, and at the port spreader or the port yardarm of a single-masted yacht.

Night pennant ... A blue pennant with a length of three-quarters of an inch for each foot of height of truck from the water, and with a width one-tenth the length, may be displayed at the main truck during such times as no other flag is hoisted.

Lights

Commodore's lights .... When at anchor, the Commodore's flagship, if a steam or power yacht, shall display from sunset to sunrise two blue lights vertically on the after side of the mainmast, at and above the eyes of the lower main rigging. If, however, the flagship be a sailing yacht, then the lights shall be displayed at the starboard main spreader one-third of the distance from the mast to the topmast shrouds.

Vice-commodore's lights .... When at anchor, the vice-commodore's flagship shall display lights, as provided for the commodore, substituting red lights for blue.

Rear-commodore's lights .... When at anchor, the rear-commodore's flagship shall display lights, as provided for the commodore, substituting white lights for blue.

Absent light ...... When a yacht is at anchor and the owner is absent, a blue light shall after dark be displayed at the starboard main spreader on a fore-and-aft rigged yacht, and at the starboard main yardarm on a square-rigged yacht.

Owner's meal light .... At night, during an owner's meal hours, a white light shall be displayed at the starboard main spreader, and at the starboard main yardarm on a square-rigged yacht.

Salutes

Whistles .... Whistles shall never be used in saluting.

Gun salutes ...... Upon joining the squadron during the annual cruise, the commodore shall be saluted by all yachts present with one gun.

When the squadron is disbanded after the annual cruise, the commodore shall be saluted by all yachts present with one gun. All salutes shall be answered in kind. Yachts not carrying guns shall salute by dipping the ensign once. Guns may be used to call attention to signals, but their use otherwise shall be avoided as much as possible.

No guns shall be fired on Sunday.

Ensign salutes .... All salutes herein provided shall be made by dipping the ensign once.

Vessels of the United States and foreign navies shall be saluted.

When a flag officer comes to anchor, he shall be saluted by all yachts present, except in cases where there is a senior flag officer present.

When the commodore joins the squadron during the annual cruise, a gun salute is provided in the preceding paragraph, in which case the ensign salute shall not be made, except by yachts which do not carry guns.

When a yacht comes to anchor where a flag officer is present, such flag officer shall be saluted.

A junior flag officer anchoring in the presence of a senior shall salute.

Yachts passing shall salute, the junior saluting first.

Yachts shall salute on arriving at the home anchorage of another club.

All salutes shall be answered in kind.

Saluting quarter-deck .... When coming on board or leaving a yacht, the quarter-deck shall be saluted by touching the cap.

Procedure

Distinguished visitors .... A yacht may display the personal flag of a national, state, or municipal officer, when such an official is on board, or the national ensign of a distinguished foreign visitor. This flag should be displayed at the main for the President of the United States, and at the fore for all other officials and visitors.

Dressing ship ..... On the Fourth of July, and when ordered on other occasions, a yacht in commission shall, when at anchor and the weather permits, dress ship at 8:00 A.M. from morning to evening colors. When these days occur on Sundays, the ceremony should be postponed until the following day. In dressing ship rectangular flags should alternate with pennants. Flag officers' flags and the burgee shall not be used in dressing ship. The ensign of a foreign nation shall not be displayed except when dressing ship in compliment to such nation, in which case the ensign will be displayed at the fore truck. When a yacht is dressed, the ensign shall be displayed in lowered boats.

Table of Honors and Ceremonies[1]

Rank	Uniform	Salute Arrival	Salute Departure	Guns	Ruffles	Guard	Music	Side Honors	Flag
President	Full Dress	1	1	21	4	Full	National anthem	Yards or rail manned and 8 side boys	President's at main during visit.
President of foreign republic or a foreign sovereign	do	1	1	21	4	do	do		National, at main, during visit.
Member of a royal family	do	1	1	21	4	do	do		National, at main, during salute.
Former President	do	1	1	21	4	do	March	8 side boys	National, at main, during salute in foreign countries.
Vice-President	do		1	19	4	do	do	do	National, at fore, during salute.
Secretary of State when embarked on board a vessel of the Navy en route to a foreign country in the capacity of representative of the President	do		1	19	4	do	National anthem	do	Secretary's, at fore, during visit.
Ambassador	do	1	1	19	4	do	do	do	National, at fore, during salute.
Secretary of the Navy	do	1	1	19	4	do	March	do	Secretary's, at main, during visit.
Assistant Secretary of the Navy	Dress	1	1	17	4	do	do	do	Assistant Secretary's, at main, during visit.
Cabinet officer	do		1	19	4	do	do	do	National, at fore, during salute.
Chief Justice	do		1	17	4	do	do	do	do
Governor General, United States islands	do	1	1	19	4	do	do	do	do
Governor of state, territory or United States islands	do		1	19	4	do	do	do	do
President pro tempore of the Senate	do		1	19	4	do	do	do	do
Speaker of the House of Representatives	do		1	17	4	do	do	do	do
Committee of Congress	do		1	17	4	do	do	do	do
Envoy extraordinary	do		1	15	3	do	do	do	do
Assistant Secretary of War	do		1	15	3	do	do	do	do
Minister resident or "diplomatic representative"	do		1	13	2	do	do	6 side boys	do
Chargé d'affaires	do		1	11	1	do	do	do	do
Consul general	Of the day		1	11	1	Day	-	4 side boys	do
First secretaries of embassies or legations	do		-	-	-	do	-		None.

[1] *U. S. Navy Regulations*, Chap. 5.

Rank	Uniform					Guard	Music	Side boys	Flag
Consul	do	–	1	7	–	do	–	do	National, at fore, during salute.
Vice-consul or consular agent (where he is the only representative of the United States)	do	–	1	5	–	do	–	do	do
Admiral	Dress	–	1	17	4	Full	March	8 side boys	
Vice-admiral	do	–	1	15	3	do	do	do	
Lieutenant general									In case of foreign officers, national at fore, during salute.
Rear admiral									
Major general (Army or Marine Corps)	do	–	1	13	2	do	do	6 side boys	
Commandant of the Coast Guard									
Commodore	do	–	1	11	1	do	do	do	
Brigadier general (Army or Marine Corps)	Of the day	–	–	–	–	do	–	4 side boys	
Chief of staff, if not a flag or general officer						Day	–		
Captain								do	
Colonel									
Commander	do	–	–	–	–	do	–	2 side boys	
Lieutenant colonel									
Lieutenant commander } If commanding officers									
Major	do	–	–	–	–	do	–	do	
All other commissioned officers of the rank of lieutenant commander and major, and officers below that rank									

1. All other ships present man rail and fire national salute at official reception or departure of President, unless otherwise directed.

2. For President of the United States, president of a foreign republic, foreign sovereign, or member of royal family, officers assembled on quarter-deck in full dress, crew man rail, and others unemployed formed forward of guard.

3. For others for whom full dress or dress uniform is prescribed, all officers assembled on quarter-deck and crew formed forward of guard.

4. If a flag or commanding officer comes on board without flag or pennant flying, only side honors shall be given unless he should request full honors on departure. All persons on the quarter-deck shall stand at attention by command without bugle.

5. No officer in civilian clothes shall be saluted with guns or have a guard paraded in his honor.

6. When side honors only are rendered to a flag or commanding officer, officers and men on deck and in view from the gangway shall stand at attention facing the gangway, and salute as the officer appears over the side and shall remain at attention until the end of the pipe.

7. The officer of the deck shall attend at the gangway on the arrival or departure of any commissioned officer or distinguished visitor.

8. All honors except attendance at gangway by the officer of the deck, except as social courtesy may demand, shall be dispensed with,

(a) When officers are in plain clothes.

(b) From sunset to 0800 (except that for foreign officers side shall be piped).

(c) During meal hour of crew for officers of U. S. Navy, Marine Corps, or Coast Guard.

(d) When coaling ship or at battle stations for officers of the U. S. Navy, Marine Corps, or Coast Guard.

9. The guard and the band shall not be paraded on Sundays for U. S. Navy, Marine Corps, Army, or Coast Guard officers.

10. All sentries on the upper decks, or in view from outside, shall salute all commissioned officers passing them close aboard, in boats or otherwise.

Old Regulations

13. When a public character, high in rank, shall embark on board of any of the United States' ships of war, he may be saluted with 13 guns.

14. When a commanding officer anchors in any foreign port, he is to inform himself what salutes have been usually given or received by officers of his rank of other nations, and he is to insist on receiving the same mark of respect. Captains may salute foreign ports with such a number of guns as may have been customary, on receiving an assurance that an equal number shall be returned—but without such assurance, they are never to salute.

15. Foreigners of distinction, on visiting the United States' ships of war, are to be saluted with such a number of guns as may suit their rank and quality.

Rules, Regulations, and Instructions
for the
Naval Service of the United States,
1818

Gun Salutes—General

(1) The interval between guns in all salutes shall be five seconds, except on occasions when minute guns are prescribed.

(2) During the firing of a salute all officers and men on deck shall stand at attention and face toward the ship or person saluted.

(3) No salute shall be fired between sunset and sunrise. As a general rule, salutes shall be fired between 8:00 A.M. and sunset. Salutes shall not be fired on Sunday, unless required by international courtesy.

(4) The national ensign shall always be displayed during a salute.

(5) In the case of a salute at 8:00 A.M., the first gun shall be fired at the last note of the national anthem.

(6) Whenever a salute is fired, following the motions of the flag-ship or ship of the senior officer present, each ship shall begin its salute with the first gun from the flag or senior ship.

(7) In the official presence of the President of the United States or of the president or sovereign of any other nation, no gun salute shall be fired by vessels of the Navy to any personage of lesser degree.

(8) (a) No salutes shall be fired in the presence of a senior without his permission, except it be one in honor of such senior.

(*b*) In the presence of a senior flag officer, salutes to junior flag officers shall not be fired except in the following cases [the senior flag officer's permission must first have been obtained]:

(1) Flag officer relinquishing command.

(2) Flag officer inspecting ship of his command on arrival and again on departure if his flag is hoisted on board.

(3) On departure of flag officer visiting officially for the first time a ship of the Navy not under his command.

(4) Flag officer as president of Board of Inspection and Survey on arrival and again on departure.

(*c*) If flag officer assumes command in the presence of another flag officer his senior, the flag of former shall not be saluted, but he shall salute the flag of his senior, which salute shall be rendered according to number of guns to which junior is entitled. If flag officer assumes command in presence of one or more flag officers his junior, salute is fired by his own flagship, and in addition he is saluted by flag officer next in rank and by him only.

Falling in at Sea or Elsewhere with Ship Flying Flag

Flag	Guns	Remarks
President	21	All ships in company fire salute while passing.
Or standard of president of foreign republic, sovereign, or member of royal family	21	National ensign of foreign nation at main during salute. All ships in company fire salute while passing.
Secretary of Navy	19	Senior ship only (if two or more in company) fires salute.
Secretary of State	None	See Arts. 240 and 243, *U. S. N. Regs.* No gun salute by passing ships.
Assistant Secretary of Navy	17	Senior ship only (if two or more in company) fires salute.
Admiral	17	In case of foreign officers, national at fore during salute. (See notes below.) See Art. 298, *U. S. N. Regs.*
Vice admiral	15	
Rear admiral	13	

(1) When a ship of Navy, other than a flagship, falls in with a flag officer afloat, the latter should be saluted unless the same captain has previously saluted this flag within one year. If two or more ships are in company only the senior shall salute.

(2) See note under "Ships passing or being passed."

(3) Honors for the Secretary of State, when not a representative of the President, are the same as for other cabinet officers, except the Secretary of the Navy.

Passing in Boat, Close Aboard, with Flag Flying

President of the United States. President of foreign republic. Foreign sovereign. Member of royal family. Secretary of State when en route to foreign country in the capacity of representative of the President.	Full guard and band. Attention by bugle. 4 ruffles and flourishes. National anthem.
Vice-President. Secretary of Navy.	Full guard and band. Attention by bugle. 4 ruffles and flourishes. March. Hand salute from "present arms" until end of flourishes.
Assistant Secretary of Navy.	Full guard and band. Attention by bugle. 4 ruffles and flourishes. March. Hand salute from "present arms" until end of flourishes.
Flag officer.	Guard of day and band. Attention by bugle. Ruffles and flourishes to which entitled. March. Hand salute from "present arms" until end of flourishes.
Commanding officer of or above rank of lieutenant commander with pennant flying.	Attention by bugle. Officers and petty officers on watch, boat keepers, and sentries salute. Others stand at attention.
All officers, passing close aboard, whether in uniform or not.	No general honors. Boat keepers and sentries salute.

NOTE.—By "close aboard" is meant within 600 yards for passing ships, 400 yards for passing officers.
For high personages and foreign ships the term shall be interpreted liberally, and in any case be careful not to render less honor than may be due.

Ships Passing or Being Passed

Foreign, or United States man-of-war flying flag of President of the United States, president of foreign republic, foreign sovereign, or member of royal family. (See Arts. 231 and 236, U. S. N. Regs.)	Man rail unless otherwise ordered. Full guard and band. Attention by bugle. National anthem. Hand salute. Fire national salute.
Foreign, or United States man-of-war flying flag of Secretary of the Navy or Assistant Secretary of the Navy. (See Arts. 239 and 241, U. S. N. Regs.)	Full guard and band. Attention by bugle. National anthem. Hand salute. Gun salute as appropriate.

Foreign, or United States man-of-war, or Coast Guard vessel with or without personal flag flying, whether or not member of fleet, squadron, or division if she has been or is on detached duty.	Guard of day and band. Attention by bugle. National anthem. Hand salute. Gun salute as appropriate.
If United States man-of-war or Coast Guard vessel having neither guard nor band. (See Art. 266, *U. S. N. Regs.*)	"Attention," hand salute.
Vessel of own formation not on detached duty.	"Attention," hand salute. (In tactical evolutions outside of port, none.)

NOTE.—No honors other than "attention" on the bugle or otherwise shall be rendered between vessels while they are engaged in maneuvers or evolutions. When two or more ships are in company, whether at anchor or under way, coming to anchor, or getting under way, they shall be considered as a part of the same formation and as engaged in maneuvers or evolutions, so far as concerns salutes. In case of a ship or ships joining such formation, honors shall not be rendered unless ship or ships have been or are on detached duty. The term "detached duty" in this case does not apply to a ship or ships temporarily out of formation, but only to ships which, by order of competent authority, have been in some port other than the rendezvous of the division, squadron, or fleet to which they may belong or on duty which has kept them away from their immediate division, squadron, or fleet for a period of more than 48 hours. A ship is not considered as on detached duty when she leaves the formation, whether under way or at anchor, for target practice, coaling in the immediate vicinity, or for similar duty. Ships of divisions or squadrons of the fleet getting under way or coming to anchor at about the same time, or in obedience to the same signal, shall be considered as engaged in evolutions, and no honors, other than "attention" on the bugle, shall be rendered as they pass each other. A vessel in full commission, being inspected by the Board of Inspection and Survey, shall be considered as being on detached duty until the inspection is completed.

General Order No. 230

Navy Department
Washington, D.C., November 14, 1932.

PRECEDENCE OF FORCES IN PARADES

1. General Order No. 172 is hereby canceled.

2. In parades of forces which include United States troops the order of precedence will be as follows:

(*a*) Cadets, United States Military Academy.

(*b*) Midshipmen, United States Naval Academy.

(*c*) Cadets, United States Coast Guard.

(*d*) Regular Army.

(*e*) United States Marines.

(*f*) United States Navy.

(*g*) United States Coast Guard.

(*h*) National Guard organizations which have been federally recognized.

(*i*) Marine Corps Reserve.

(*j*) Naval Reserve.

(*k*) Other organizations of the Organized Reserve, National Guard, Naval Militia, Reserve Officers Training Corps, and other training units in the order prescribed by the grand marshal of the parade.

(*l*) Veterans and patriotic organizations in the order prescribed by the grand marshal of the parade.

3. The grand marshal and his staff will in all cases lead the parade. A detachment of police or special forces may be assigned to precede the grand marshal for the purpose of clearing the line of march.

4(*a*). When foreign troops are invited to participate in parades within the territorial jurisdiction of the United States, they will be assigned a position of honor ahead of United States troops, and next after the grand marshal and his staff, except that a small detachment of United States troops will immediately precede the foreign troops as a guard of honor.

(*b*) On occasions when troops of two or more foreign nations participate the order of precedence among them will be determined by the grand marshal in accordance with the one of the following methods which he deems appropriate.

(*c*) When the parade or exercise is in honor of a particular nation, as, for example, in the celebration of a national holiday of that nation, the troops of such nation should be assigned a position in the line ahead of all others.

(*d*) Except as provided in (*c*), the order of precedence among foreign troops will normally be fixed by the relative ranks of the commanders of the forces from which the parade detachments are drawn, but in cases where this method is not applicable, it may be fixed by

(1) The relative ranks of the commanders of the parade detachments; or

(2) The alphabetical order in the English language of the names of the nations concerned.

C. F. ADAMS,
Secretary of the Navy.

CHAPTER V

LEST WE FORGET

Comments on Social Customs of the Naval Officer

"Look about you today! See the confusion and chaos that reign over all questions of doctrine, diet, hygiene, behaviour; the relations of man to man, and above all of sex to sex; and ask yourself whether everything does not already bear the indelible stamp of having been left too long without the discriminating guidance of taste. Where traditional usages are breaking down, what is rising to take their place? Where old institutions are losing their power, where are the substitutes offered by the present age?
—ANTHONY M. LUDOVICI, *A Defence of Aristocracy.*

"Let public apathy starve our material into inaction or degenerate us into an epidemic of scraping and painting, of brightwork and holy stones, if so be it that we remain a personnel determined that the niceties of plain good manners, manners learned at home and polished up with military terms into military courtesy, shall not perish from the sea; if so be it that these manners of Paul Jones, of Lawrence, of Farragut, of Dewey; if these sea manners passed down to us by these sea-gentlemen be preserved through us of today to sea-gentlemen yet unborn; if so be it we remain determined that the heart and soul of the Navy shall not go to hell!"
—CAPTAIN (now Admiral) F. B. UPHAM, U. S. Navy, "Them Haly-Con Days," Naval Institute PROCEEDINGS, XLVI, No. 208.

"Life is not so short, but that there is always time for courtesy."
—EMERSON, *Social Aims.*

THE naval officer will have in an average career relations with the representative citizens and subjects of many countries. It is generally recognized that all the information which he may acquire that pertains to the customs and accepted usage of foreign states will prove useful. This acquisition of knowledge aids the conduct of official business, and conduces to ease in official and social intercourse. But first, it is essential that the naval officer be acquainted with and sensible to the value of our own sea manners, customs, and best usage.

It is believed by many that the tremendous expansion of the commissioned personnel of the Navy in the World War occasioned a laxity in what may be termed the niceties of naval customs and usage. After the United States entered the World War, officers who had had little peace-time training were concerned with strictly professional duties and the acquisition of specialized knowledge to perform efficiently their jobs. Expediency was the rule. Work clothes and the grim business of war rightfully crowded practically everything else from the scene. Finer customs fixed by long usage were relegated to the side. To win the war was the thing. To be sure, the traditional *lex non scripta* of naval etiquette, sea manners, as well as shore manners are best learned in an officer's youth. It is the hope of many that the thread be picked up again and that sea manners receive a rationalized consideration. It is granted that times have changed, but although life itself means change, some social values are as necessary as they are immutable.

Young officers are constantly reminded that they are in all things to set good examples for their men. By the same token, it is logical to assert that as the older officers observe sound and time-honored usages so will the younger officers conform to example and precept. It is admitted that there are different shades of interpretation, for assuredly in "different ships, different long splices." If seniors give scant attention to sea manners, juniors may consider them unworthy of adoption.

The comment upon some of the "small things" that are set forth in this chapter were in the main prompted by experienced officers of the Navy, both on the active and retired lists. The observations range in a general way from ordinary manners and courtesy always expected of the officer aboard ship to a mention of the more common amenities that comprise a part of the *savoir faire* of a man of the world.

In the first class may be placed some of the niceties of naval etiquette that have been observed by outstanding officers that have gone before. In the second class, there is much that is conventional, thereby sanctioned by the cultured, well-bred gentleman in any walk of life.

In reminders that follow, details and manner of execution require the judgment and initiative of the individual officer.

The custom, the principle, and in some cases the sincere *beau geste* are the points to which attention is invited.

On Deck

It was once always customary to send a side boy or messenger to the foot of the accommodation ladder when guests of flag rank came aboard. This insured that the boat would be held snugly alongside, and that parcels or luggage would be expeditiously handled. In short it is a courtesy that may have a practical value and a distinct attention that should not be overlooked.

It was once a custom that the junior officer of the deck, junior officer, or an officer of the deck, if convenient, go to the foot of the accommodation ladder and inform a visiting commanding officer that it was not convenient, if such was the case, for the commanding officer to receive the visitor in person. The captain is often precluded from attending the side because of conferences, courts-martial, inspections, etc. This fine old custom was a courtesy that might save the visiting captain a useless trip up the ladder, for usually he is only making a friendly and informal visit. There was a time when this custom was never neglected.

To give side boys to foreign officers after dark or sunset, when making calls, as well as attending dinners and receptions, was once a gracious courtesy that was often rendered. This is done by various foreign navies today. It is the superlative gesture of giving an extraordinary courtesy to honored guests.

To hold in mind the "sanctity" of the quarter-deck and observe its traditional etiquette—this should be ever foremost in the minds of those who respect their profession and their ship.

Extraordinary Courtesies

Some outstanding examples of extraordinary courtesy follow.

An interesting custom and extraordinary courtesy is that of delaying the "official sunset" in order that regulation day-time honors may be rendered. This was done aboard the U. S. S. *Arizona* at Callao, Peru, in August, 1921, in order that honors and a salute could be rendered the President of Peru, who did not leave the ship until after dark.

Captain Edwin T. Pollock, U. S. Navy (retired) writes:

In Chefoo, China, in 1906, a French ship with a vice admiral arrived and the American rear admiral was required by international courtesy to follow the sunset as set by his senior for evening colors. The French navigator apparently made a mistake in the computation of his "sunset table," for the French flagship made evening colors when the sun was still about fifteen minutes in time above the horizon, and plainly visible. The next day the sun set properly.

When the Prince of Wales passed through the Panama Canal on his cruise to Australia a ship of the Special Service Squadron rendered full honors after dark.

On 4 July, 1923, all ships of the Royal Navy present in Hongkong, by direction of the commander in chief of the British Asiatic Fleet, rendered a 21-gun salute although the only American ship present was the gunboat *Pampanga*, too small to be rated as a saluting ship. It is such sincere and timely gestures that aid in maintaining the cordial relations that should exist between public officers and the inhabitants of friendly states.

One recalls also the aërial salute that was given by Admiral T. P. Magruder, U. S. Navy, to the populace of Wellington, New Zealand, in 1925. Planes were launched in heavy winds and taken aboard in a choppy sea: the gesture was exceptional and timely. Admiral Magruder also executed, as a mark of respect to the Governor of Tasmania, a very difficult naval evolution at high speed, both upon entering and leaving Hobart, Tasmania. It might have been called "cutting a Dido," but the smart effect of the division of cruisers in rendering this exceptional honor was taken as a compliment to the governor and appreciated by the inhabitants. Such things are not soon forgotten.

A most interesting custom still remembered by older officers of the retired list was that of using lanterns after dark to light the way from the gangway to the hatchway leading to the officers' quarters. The anchor watch lined up and held six lanterns for the admiral, four for the captain, and two for a wardroom officer. After the introduction of electric lights, this custom fell into disuse. However, it is reported that, when Admiral W. H. Brownson commanded the armored cruiser squadron, he instituted the practice of using a portable electric lead which carried eight lamps. This is the last record of the old custom.

There is another memory that will always live in the minds of our officers and men, and that is the cheering led by Admiral Beatty when Admiral Rodman's division of United States battleships joined the Grand Fleet as the Sixth Battle Squadron. Admiral Beatty's waving his cap with the cheering blue jackets was a sincere gesture—a momentous occasion, for it was the first time since the days of John Paul Jones that the United States had joined a foreign Navy as a unit.

To digress from mention of dignified courtesy to humorous stupidity, there is a record in our Navy of the officer that in good spirits and purely from a point of view of rendering just due to all men, saluted, with a non-regulation salute in the dead of night, one of his good friends of *our Service*. This exceptional courtesy incurred the government's displeasure, so the story goes, and a court-martial resulted.

THE OFFICERS' MESS

An officers' mess should be comparable to a gentlemen's club in its tone of behavior and conversation. The laxity that has been observed in some ships is attributed to many causes. Some assert that the heavy work incident to fleet schedules and competitions leaves little time for the "fancy stuff." Others state that the "slackening off" is the result of an influx of officers during the World War who did not have proper junior officer training. Another group considers the regulations prohibiting wine in the mess have limited formal entertainment to the extent that the large parties of the "good old days" are no more, and with them have gone the attendant amenities occasioned by the formal dinner. Whatever may be the cause or causes, some of the sea manners and usages that were once long observed and are now in many particulars disregarded deserve a word of attention.

Old Customs That Could Help Modern Wardrooms

(1) Officers were required to be prompt for meals and to seat themselves with the president of the mess. This not only adds distinction and smartness to an officers' mess, but has practical significance in serving food.

(2) It was never considered good form for officers to leave the table while the president of the mess was present without asking him to excuse them. This custom is strictly adhered to in the British, German, French, and Italian Navies.

(3) At strictly formal parties, best usage and custom dictated that cigarettes and cigars should not be lighted until coffee had been served. The informal custom of smoking throughout the meal while at a formal dinner has never been sanctioned by good usage.

(4) One of the oldest and best mess customs was that religion and ladies (politics are included as taboo by some) should not be discussed in a gentlemen's mess.

(5) All officers should feel that the guests of officers in a mess are to a great extent guests of the mess, and anything that may contribute to their comfort and entertainment should be tendered by any member if opportunity presents itself.

(6) It was once customary to have a night each week or month designated as guest night, when the officers dressed; the "Number One" dinner was served; and one was assured in bringing guests aboard that they would receive the most favorable impression of the mess, the ship, and the Service.

(7) No matter what the individual officer thinks, guests will always believe that the "tone" of the mess is a criterion of the breeding of the officers in the mess. Therefore, conversation should not be limited to service trivialities and monotonous talk of shop; neither should a guest in any walk of life be "talked down to." Naval officers have no superiority by "divine right."

(8) The practice on small ships of permitting officers to eat at the mess in dungaree trousers should not be tolerated, except in most exceptional circumstances.

(9) Only extraordinary circumstances are sufficient excuses for officers to wear civilian clothes at mess.

AFTER DINNER IN THE CAPTAIN'S CABIN   (From lithograph in color [1831], *Old Ship Prints,* by E. Keble Chatterton)

scene, on board an East Indiaman, showing the Effects of a heavy Lurch, after dinner.

AT DINNER IN AN EAST INDIAMAN   (From an etching by George Cruikshank [1818], *Old Ship Prints,* by E. Keble Chatterton)

(10) In addition to the formal dinner that should be tendered the captain at a convenient time after assuming command, it is good form to invite the captain to dinner at frequent periods throughout his cruise. It not only enables him to converse with officers in a more informal manner, but also usually it is a change and diversion that a senior officer welcomes. The captain should be given a farewell dinner even though it be an informal one.

(11) The best regulated messes provide themselves with distinctive wardroom visiting cards, but in any event, a wardroom calling committee should call upon all foreign visiting men-of-war as well as coastal foreign army posts. If a small foreign ship enters our ports, the calls are usually made by the wardroom of the flagship, or ships anchoring near the visitor. It is a courtesy that is expected by the foreign ship, and should never be neglected. Custom requires a formal dinner or luncheon in honor of the visitor, but informal dinners may be most enjoyable for host and guests.

(12) The quality of food and manner of service in a mess depend largely upon the interest of the mess. One cannot blame the Navy Department or the Comptroller of the Treasury for a poor mess.

(13) The criterion of a mess is that it shall be one in which officers are proud to bring a distinguished guest at any time, and know that he will receive the same dignified hospitality that he would expect in a gentlemen's club or at gentlemen's dinners. This type of mess is not obtained except by the sincere co-operation of *all members*.

(14) If there is only one officer in the mess when a visiting wardroom officer or a guest of the mess enters, it is that officer's duty to act the host until others entertain the visitor.

A WELL REGULATED WARDROOM AND ITS REGULATIONS

It is the duty and generally a pleasure for the executive officer to regulate the wardroom mess in order to insure that the mess preserve the dignified tone expected of it, and at the same time foster a cordial and friendly atmosphere among messmates.

One of the best conducted and regulated wardrooms in the Battle Fleet based its success on the following rules (they were of course unwritten):

(1) The executive officer saw to it that he was always in the mess "on the bell" for meals. With the exception of breakfast, all officers were expected to be seated with the executive officer.

(2) Furthermore, it was expected that officers leaving the table before the executive officer had finished dinner should carry out the old custom of requesting to be excused.

(3) Officers were encouraged to bring guests aboard for dinner. Sufficient boats for guests were always provided, and officers were enjoined to have guests aboard in time for the scheduled dinners. Care should always be exercised in this respect, for not only do guests feel more at ease if presented to officers of the mess before being seated, but punctuality is a considerable factor in the matter of correct service for a large mess. Moreover, stewards may be held to serving hot and appetizing food in prompt messes.

(4) It was expected that all games played in the mess, such as cards, chess, checkers, etc., would be stopped one-half hour before meal time.

(5) The mess boys of the watch were required to tidy up the mess every two hours. Care in this respect insured that the mess was always neat and presentable.

(6) At frequent intervals special dinner parties were given when all officers were required to wear formal evening dress.

(7) The atmosphere was created that at all times a *guest was the guest of the mess.*

(8) All officers were required when in the messroom to be dressed in complete uniform. A rack for the stowage of caps was installed outside the wardroom.

(9) Attention was given to prompt and correct service of food; strict attention by the head boy to all details of service; menus planned with care; and above all a neat, clean, and well-appointed wardroom was insisted upon. Flowers were arranged in the wardroom when the season and price permitted. In brief, the exercise of discriminating taste was the aim of those charged

with the conduct of mess affairs. A mess as a rule is a composite reflection of its members.

In connection with a mess, it is of great interest to read Colonel Stewart's description of Lord Nelson's routine on the *St. George:*

His hour of rising was 4 or 5 o'clock, and of going to rest about 10; breakfast was never later than 6, and generally nearer to 5 o'clock. A midshipman or two were always of the party, and I have known him send, during the middle watch, to invite the little fellows to breakfast with him, when relieved. At table with them, he would enter into their boyish jokes and be the most youthful of the party. At dinner he invariably had every officer of the ship in their turn, and was both a polite and hospitable host.

In commenting upon Nelson's courtesy to subordinates, and his desire to teach young officers the amenities of polite society, Admiral Mark Kerr, Royal Navy, in *The Sailor's Nelson* writes:

It is impossible to overestimate the value of this [in those days] unusual procedure in forming the discipline, good feeling, and mutual confidence of the generations who have followed him in the naval service; it has been and still is one of the principal priceless legacies that Nelson has bequeathed to the Service, which looks up to him as a model for all time.

Calls Required of the Ensign after He Reports on Board Ship

The young officer should give thought at the outset of his naval career to the fact that there are visits and calls that are required by regulations, by customs, and by courtesy. A personal choice or selection in the matter of visits is not the prerogative of those in official life. Good usage decrees that calls be as scrupulously returned as they are expected to be made.

In delivering verbal communications from senior to junior, it is customary for officers of the Navy to use the form, "Rear Admiral Smith presents his compliments to Captain Brown and says, etc." A junior never presents his compliments to a senior. Upon making a social or official call upon a senior, it is perfectly correct and customary to say "Admiral Smith, I came to pay my respects," or to the orderly before entering the cabin, "Tell the Captain (or Admiral) that Lieutenant Commander Jones should like to pay his respects."

The *Regulations* state that

an officer joining a ship or naval station shall, in addition to report-ing for duty, make a visit of courtesy to his commanding officer or commandant within 48 hours after joining.[1]

Service dress uniform is worn when reporting for duty but the *Uniform Regulations* prescribe that undress (frock coat and sword) be worn when making first call upon commanding offi-cers. This refers to the courtesy visit that is required by the *Regulations*. It is expected that this call be made to the com-manding officer in his cabin on board ship, and to the com-mandant or other senior officer at his office when ashore. This courtesy visit shall be made even though the officer has reported for duty in person to the commanding officer or commandant. There are times when it is not practicable for the young officer to see the commanding officer or commandant when he reports for duty. If such is the case, he will be informed by the execu-tive officer, aide to the commandant, or officer representing the senior officer when it will be convenient to make the courtesy visit. Always ask the executive (if the information is not given you) when it will be convenient to call on the commanding officer.

A courtesy visit should last about ten minutes, unless the caller is requested to stay longer. Learn to make a quick and graceful exit. One should never stand and become involved in long conversation after one has signified by conversation or the act of rising that departure is imminent.

It should also be remembered during calls that seniors will as a rule endeavor at the first meeting to observe the "cut of the junior's jib." Naturalness in demeanor and restraint in conversa-tion are to be recommended for the junior.

The young officer who has been outstanding at Annapolis in scholarship, athletics, or general activities has, it is true, an

[1] *U. S. Navy Regulations* (1920), Sec. 349 (3).

advantage, but it will soon be lost if he attempts "to live on his record." The Service judges and marks the officer on officer-like qualities and results.

Next in order of calls after the courtesy visit to the commanding officer is that to be made upon the commanding officer and wife at their quarters ashore. Ascertain whether or not there is a regular "at home"; if not, call and leave cards as soon as possible. This call should be followed by a courtesy visit ashore to the executive officer and wife (if married); if not married, respects are paid to the executive officer in his stateroom aboard ship. These two important calls should be followed by calls upon the heads of departments (your own first), and the next senior officer in your department. Every effort should be made to pay short courtesy visits upon all the married officers of the wardroom before detachment. It is also expected that the ensign will make social calls upon all the married commissioned officers of his mess. The Service has always made a particular point of paying prompt calls upon all newly married couples. The commanding officer and his wife, as well as other seniors, pay this call upon the most junior ensign and his bride.

In the social world, party calls are not in all cases made as unfailingly as they once were. Nevertheless, the Service in general observes the old custom. As a rule those of about "the same time and grade" do not always pay "bread and butter" calls, but a junior should make a short courtesy visit within a few days after a dinner given by a senior, at which the junior was an invited guest. Senior officers and their wives as a rule pay party calls to young hosts and hostesses who have given dinners in their express honor.

In conclusion, a thoughtful officer will, at the outset of his social and professional career, give more than a thought to the fact that his professional reports of fitness will commence the day he reports aboard his first ship and continue until he leaves the active list. Consequently, it follows that where reports of fitness become the high responsibility of the senior in relation to the junior, the senior will observe the manners of the junior both afloat and ashore; that his officer-like qualities will be carefully noted. It is a foregone conclusion that the young offi-cer's attitude toward the Service will be reflected as a rule by his attention to duty, and his observance or non-observance of the customs and best usage of the Navy.

"Uniform Regulations"

The *Uniform Regulations* enjoin officers and men to provide themselves with the correct uniform and therein prescribe all details of dress. The following excerpts from *Uniform Regulations* comprise the principles upon which proper authority en-forces the provisions of the *Uniform Regulations*.

The uniform, with its various insignia and devices, is designed primarily to indicate on sight those belonging to the naval service; to show at a glance their rank, corps, or rating, and hence the au-thority and responsibility imposed by law upon those wearing it.

It should be a matter of pride with officers and men in the naval service to be habitually neatly and smartly dressed, to see that their uniforms are scrupulously clean, that their lace, devices, and in-signia are bright and free from tarnish and corrosion, and that they are promptly renewed when necessary. They should see that their clothes and equipment are made of the best material, and that they are conspicuous for these characteristics rather than for contrary ones. There is no question but that those who are properly and smartly dressed at once create a far better impression than those who fail in this respect, who wear ill-fitting or stained clothes, or who may be careless or negligent in permitting their stripes or insignia to become tarnished or corroded.[1]

Club Etiquette

Naval officers are often given cards to clubs for the short stays of the ship or the fleet in ports both at home and abroad. It is a privilege that the Navy has always enjoyed, and under no condition should it be abused. For the benefit of young officers who have never been honorary members of the larger or more exclusive clubs, a few "navigational aids" are not amiss.

The visitor has no special rights in the club, but is expected to conform to the club rules, the same as any member. In fact,

[1] *Uniform Regulations, U. S. Navy*, Chap. 1.

dignified courtesy should be rendered to all members, remembering always that the uniform and rank of the officer permit him to enjoy the facilities of clubs, while often some men wait many years to become members. Club members gauge the social and intellectual caliber of the Navy by the officers they meet in their short stay in port. Although there are all kinds of clubs, the better clubs are not "back-slapping, political-rally" organizations, and are therefore not fit places for large class reunions and the gayer parties that should be held elsewhere. There is an air of dignity about the best clubs, both at home and abroad, such as is found in the best homes. Men of affairs, men of letters, and "those who spin not" use a club for meeting other members, both in a business and social sense, as well as to take advantage of facilities such as the library, the reading- and writing-rooms, and the dining-room. To many it is their home. Ofttimes men of great wealth and affluence, after a family has been dispersed, prefer permanent residence at clubs and, of course, expect the same atmosphere to prevail that once obtained in their homes. In no sense is a club a hotel, and the better ones are not fraternal organizations. A well-known club man once remarked:

In a very smart London club, you keep your hat on and glare about. In Paris you take your hat off and behave with such courtesy and politeness as seems to you an affectation. In New York you take your hat off and behave as though the rooms were empty; but as though you were being observed through loopholes in the walls.

Possibly these remarks are ultra-sophisticated but they adequately express the "tone" of the smart and more exclusive clubs.

Officers who have been given cards as guests of a club for a stated period of time should sign the club register, that is, if the courtesy that has been extended is accepted. This formality has a practical reason. The servants know who you are, and members are able to know what officers have visited the club. Leaving cards or signing the register permits club members to look for old friends, as well as know the names of those for whom special courtesies may be extended. One should also observe whether or not there is a card board and, if so, leave a visiting card on the board. This is always customary in British clubs. Leaving a card signifies that you have appreciated the invitation and have paid your respects to the members. Senior officers leave their cards when convenient in person or send them by a member of the staff.

An officer should be prompt in meeting all financial obligations incurred at a club where he is tendered the privilege of signing checks. It is embarrassing for a senior officer to receive an official letter after sailing, to the effect that an officer under his command sailed without paying his club debts. There is a certain stigma attached to the non-payment of club debts. "Tailors sometimes have to wait a short time, but club bills are paid promptly," so saith the old clubman.

It is customary for the senior officer of a division or squadron and commanding officers of ships acting singly to address a letter to the club before sailing, in which he expresses thanks for the kindnesses and courtesies that have been tendered the officers of his command during the stay of the ship or ships in port. This letter is usually addressed to the secretary of the club. In some cases, the letters are addressed to the president of the club.

In clubs where an officer has been a member or guest for a long period of time, such as is the usual practice for "China coast sailors" and the gunboat officers, and the officer is about to leave for other duty or home, it is customary to leave on the card board before his departure a *"p.p.c."* card (*pour prendre congé*). This is an ordinary visiting card with *p.p.c.* written in the corner. By this card, a rule of etiquette is utilized to bid good-bye to all members. One, of course, calls upon one's personal friends and bids them good-bye.

It would be difficult to improve on Emily Post's remarks on good manners in clubs:

A perfect clubman is another word for the perfect gentleman. . . . Good manners in clubs are the same as good manners elsewhere— only a little more so. A club is for the pleasure and convenience of many; it is never intended as a stage setting for a "star" or "clown" or "monologist." There is no place where a person has greater need of constraint and consideration for the reserves of others than in a club. In every club there is a reading-room or library where conversation is not allowed; there are books and easy chairs and good light for reading both by day and night; and it is one of the unbreakable rules not to speak to anybody who is reading or writing.

When two people are sitting by themselves and talking, another should on no account join them unless he is an intimate friend of both. To be a mere acquaintance, or, still less, to have been introduced to one of them, gives no privilege whatever.[1]

It is also well to remember that the more exclusive clubs have customs which one calls in the Navy "special rates"—R.H.I.P. That is, the oldest members have certain corners or small rooms in which they lounge, certain tables they habitually use in the dining-rooms, certain desirable chairs that for years they have occupied near the windows on the street. Observation on the part of the young officer will usually disclose this distinct deference that is paid to age and rank.

In conclusion, an excellent rule for a young man to obey in a meeting of gentlemen, whether in clubs or out, is George Washington's 66th "Rule of Civility," "Be not forward but friendly and courteous; the first to salute, hear, and answer, and be not pensive when it's a time to converse."

General Courtesy

It is an unwritten law that warrant officers and junior officers remove their caps when in the wardroom country; also that all officers uncover when passing through the captain's or admiral's country. This is not done when in full dress or with sword.

Those who are versed in the niceties of old custom and usage always remove their caps when passing through the crew's quarters at meal times.

When officers enter the sick bay on inspection trips and otherwise, it has been customary for them to remove their caps. This custom is probably derived from the old mark of respect paid

[1] Emily Post, *Etiquette*. (By permission Funk & Wagnalls Co.)

the sick and suffering. Men were about ready for "slipping the cable" when they were admitted to "sick bays" in the days of sail.

Strictly speaking, officers are not supposed to uncover in the open except for divine worship, funerals, and other religious ceremonies. Since standing at attention and rendering the hand salute is the highest respect that one pays the colors or the commander in chief of the Navy afloat or ashore, it should suffice for the meeting with gentlemen or ladies in the open. The doffing of the headdress passed when it was decreed that the salute to flag and superiors would be the hand salute. This, of course, does not apply to receptions and social occasions on deck.

The very old courtesy of passing a senior going in the same direction with a "By your leave, Sir," is not supposed to be forgotten when the midshipman leaves the Naval Academy.

In walking with a senior ashore, or acting as an aide, the position of honor is to the right. An aide should be to the left and one or two paces in the rear when approaching presentations or meetings between seniors, whether it be military, naval, or civil officers. If the aide is to make the introductions, he should step to the side, facing both officers who are presented. The custom of the "right hand rule" is very old. It is quaintly expressed in Washington's 30th "Rule of Civility:"

In walking, the highest place in most countries seems to be on the right hand, therefore place yourself on the left of him whom you desire to honor; but if three walk together the middle place is the most honorable. The wall is usually given to the most worthy if two walk together.

The above rule applies to riding in carriages or automobiles with seniors. It has become an Army regulation and a Naval Academy regulation not to salute an officer driving an automobile.

A proper "gangway" for seniors should be scrupulously observed. Again, one reads in Washington's 29th "Rule of Civility":

When you meet with one of greater quality than yourself, stop and retire, especially if it be at a door or any straight place to give way for him to pass.

Toasts Afloat and Ashore

The custom of welcoming guests at a repast by special libations in honor of the head of the state of the visitor, or the country from which the guest hails, or the organization to which he belongs, is very ancient. In olden days it was also customary for the host first to take a sip of the cup to show that the beverage was not poisoned. This custom is still followed in parts of Scotland. A survival of the custom lingers in the usage that is observed when a sip is poured in the glass of the host before filling the glasses of the guests. This should be done by waiters.

Although "official drinking" antedates the Caesars, it is of interest that the term toast is of Anglo-Saxon derivation. A piece of toast was at one time placed in the glass with certain wines and beverages. The following quotations indicate the custom of the day:

It happened that on a publick day a celebrated beauty of those times [of Charles II] was in the Cross Bath [at Bath] when one of the crowd of her admirers took a glass of water in which the fair one stood, and drank her health to the company. There was in the place a gay fellow, half-fuddled, who offered to jump in, and swore, tho' he liked not the liquor, he would have the *toast* [making an allusion to the usage of the times of drinking with a toast at the bottom of the glass]. Tho' he was opposed in his resolution, this whim gave foundation to the present honour which is done to the lady we mention in our liquors, who has ever since been called a *toast*.

—*Tatler,* No. 24 (4 June, 1709).

> Let the toast pass
> Drink to the lass
> I'll warrant she'll prove excuse for the glass.
> —SHERIDAN, *School for Scandal,* iii, 3.

> Go fetch me a quart of sack; put a toast in 't.
> —SHAKESPEARE, *Merry Wives of Windsor,* III, v, 3.

It is universally acknowledged that at official dinners given in honor of visiting foreign officials, toasts are to be drunk first to the head of the state, or to the country, or to the organization of the guests. For example, at a dinner given by an Italian admiral to an American admiral, the Italian would propose a toast to the President of the United States, and shortly afterwards the senior honored guest, the American admiral, would propose a toast to the King of Italy. There are occasions where some confusion might arise in those messes where a toast is always drunk at dinner to the sovereign. For example, it was once observed in a British mess at a dinner that was not official, that the president of the mess toasted the King, then shortly afterwards he proposed a toast to the United States Navy. The proper reply by the American officer should have been a toast to the British Navy. At an official dinner the Britisher would toast "the President of the United States" and the senior American reply "to the King."*

Because of General Order No. 99 and the Eighteenth Amendment, toasts nearly died in the Service afloat. They may be revived in the future and they may not, but it is part of the social education of a naval officer to know how they are given in all foreign navies, and to know what to do if the occasion arises.

Ceremonies differ somewhat as to the time when the first and ceremonial toasts are drunk. At an official dinner given, for example, by a British admiral to an American admiral, the routine may be as follows: The British admiral at a point before completion of the dinner, usually at or after dessert, rises and toasts the President of the United States, the orchestra playing "The Star Spangled Banner," upon the completion of the toast. After the officers are seated and a minute or so afterwards, the American admiral should rise and toast "The King"; immediately thereupon the orchestra will play "God Save the King." After these toasts, short speeches are sometimes made, followed with a toast to the respective Services. It is understood that there are British military messes wherein no one but the King may be toasted. This was especially waived at one time for Admiral Farragut, an extraordinary courtesy.

Officers of the Royal Navy have the privilege of remaining

* See Appendix D for British Admiralty order.

seated when they toast the sovereign. Some authorities write that this honor was accorded the Royal Navy by William IV, while the popular service opinion is that it was Charles II who established the custom. The story goes that Charles II, when returning to England in 1660 in the *Royal Charles,* bumped his head because of the low overhead of the wardroom when replying to a toast that had been drunk to him. He made the statement forthwith that royal naval officers would never again rise to toast the British sovereign. The late Marquis of Milford Haven, then Admiral of the Fleet and at that time the Prince of Battenburg, established the custom of rising in the British Navy only when the toast to the King was followed by "God Save the King." Officers in the royal yacht rise to toast the king. This is in all probability a custom that arose from the desire of the officers of the royal yacht to be distinctive in this respect.

Commander Beckett, R.N., writes that he was given the following quaint toasts by an old officer as the customary secondary toasts in the days of Nelson:

Monday night, "Our ships at sea"
Tuesday night, "Our men"
Wednesday night, "Ourselves" (As no one is likely to concern themselves with our welfare)
Thursday night, "A bloody war or a sickly season"
Friday night, "A willing foe and sea-room"
Saturday night, "Sweethearts and wives"
Sunday night, "Absent friends"

In the British Service at the present time the youngest member of the mess is called upon to reply on Saturday night to the toast on behalf of "The Ladies."

Although the manner of toasting in military and naval messes is not in all respects uniform, some general principles may be outlined:

(1) Do not drink a toast that is proposed to you or your Service. All drink to the President, King, or a dignitary.

(2) The highest officials as a rule propose toasts to the heads of the state. The host honors the guest first.

(3) At smaller dinners and semi-formal ones, the toast may be drunk to the Navy of the visiting country, the country of the visitors, and in some cases to the senior officer and officers of the squadron or ship. These toasts may also follow the toasts to the heads of the respective states.

(4) Replies to toasts should be of similar nature and of corresponding subjects.

(5) Toasts to sovereigns and heads of states should be short and not prefaced by irrelevant remarks.

The French, with the politeness characteristic of their race, usually say "I have the honor, etc." At a dinner for a French admiral or senior French officer, the American officer would say, "I have the honor to propose a toast to the President of the French Republic." The French officer would reply, "It is my great honor to propose a toast to the President of the United States" or simply "To the President of the United States." At regular mess dinners in the British Navy, the senior member of the mess proposes the toast "The King," and all members in a low tone repeat "The King" and drink a sip of the toast.

The German Admiralty has published recently a book called *Handbook for Relations with Foreign Navies* wherein various toasts are set forth for all occasions. Among these toasts are:

Messieurs,

C'est un grand honneur et un vif plaisir pour nous autres Allemands d'avoir l'occasion aujourd'hui (ces jours-ci) de voir parmi nous des représentants de la Marine Française. C'est pourquoi je prends la liberté de prier mes compatriotes (camarades, collègues) de s'associer avec moi pour souhaiter à ces Messieurs bien cordialement la bienvenue en Allemagne (à bord), et je vous demande de vous joindre à moi pour porter un toast à la santé des Officiers Français ici présents.

Messieurs,

J'ai l'honneur de proposer un toast pour (à la santé de) le Président de la République Française.

Messieurs,

J'ai l'honneur de vous proposer de lever vos verres et de boire (de les vider) à la santé des Officiers de la Marine . . . (à la santé et à la prospérité de la Marine . . .).

It also contains such cordial expressions as,

I request my fellow countrymen to raise their glasses and join me in the toast of . . .

I ask the officers of the . . . to rise and to drink the health of . . . wishing them success always and everywhere.

And in now drinking the health of . . . we testify our keen appreciation of what they have done for us and wish them happy days and good luck.

The Royal Italian Naval Academy, by its textbook on *Most Prevalent Usage in Social and International Relations,* teaches in regard to toasts:

As a rule toasts should be few and short.

At dinners aboard that are not strictly private, it is advisable to adopt the English usage of a single toast to the King (the simple words, long live the King). If there are foreign guests, however, it will be well to drink a toast of the occasion, by saying a few cordial words of welcome and concluding with homage to the nation of the guest. It is best to speak in one's own tongue, if the others are not known well. It is to be remembered in such case that utmost brevity is indispensable.

Much care should be taken in the choice of the subject, all political allusions being avoided, unless specially authorized or directed. Good subjects may be drawn from naval history by recalling glorious feats of arms, possibly common to the two navies, and finding in them reasons for predicting glory and prosperity for the future.

To a toast of this nature reply is made by the ranking member of the visiting body, who follows a similar course. If the first toast is made in honor of the Navy and its representatives, reply is made in the name of the whole Navy, expressing the deepest appreciation for the complimentary words, etc., etc., and giving assurance of ineffaceable memory of the days past in such pleasant company, everlasting gratitude for the cordial hospitality received, etc., etc.

At official dinners attended by high authorities it is necessary that all toasts be previously agreed upon at least as to the spirit and the subject to be treated.

This is particularly necessary at dinners attended by sovereigns or princes of royal blood, in which case, if there has been no means of previous understanding with someone in the suite, it is preferable to abstain from any manifestation whatever.

In some foreign countries (northern) it is customary not to make any toasts, but to drink successively to the health of each individual guest, expressing one's own wishes with a look or gesture. It is proper to reply by at least one sip and a nod of the head, and then to return the compliment a few minutes later.

In those countries, it may happen that while at table in a public place, a polite acquaintance may send a waiter to inform you that he wishes to drink to your health. In such case it is proper for everyone to remain seated, make a gesture of thanks and, turning to the gracious person, take at least one sip, and then return the courtesy.

In countries of non-European civilization, other customs prevail, all of which it would be impossible to recall. In every case and wherever it may be it will be well to show the greatest cordiality without, however, considering oneself obliged to drink or eat the food and drink to which one is not accustomed.

Short dignified exchanges of toasts are more agreeable than the interminable speeches that have become a part of so many banquets and official dinners.

For this reason, it is well never to go to an official dinner without some thought of a few concise remarks that will be apropos of the occasion. Even though the word has been passed beforehand that there will be no speeches, it does not always hold; possibly the "few words" that are expected are not classified as speeches. At any rate, it is safe to be prepared. A well-told joke or anecdote; short, sincere remarks addressed to the host or hosts, in the spirit of the occasion—this is the real secret of effective after-dinner speaking. One may also be drafted as a toastmaster at some period in one's career.

A very successful toastmaster told the writer that he always learned all that he could about those who were to respond to toasts, with particular emphasis upon any exceptional services or duties that they had performed or honors they had received. He disclosed this information in short, concise, but pleasing introductions. Moreover, he never failed to make a short comment on the toasts proposed, and tempered the spirit of his com-

The Midshipman's Birth (Original spelling) (Courtesy Naval Records and Library, Navy Department)

mentaries to the mood of the toasts. He always interspersed his introductions with short anecdotes and jokes. The great secret, he said, was to relate short "yarns" in which various guests present had participated, but under no circumstances to indulge in stories that were unpleasant or sarcastic, and never make a diner the butt of too strong a joke. But after all is said, the true toastmaster, like the actor, is born and not made.

Even though grape juice is used, the time-honored custom of toasting at a formal dinner in honor of foreign officers should be carried out. At informal dinners, a short word of welcome is in good form, and may or may not be followed by a toast to guests.

OFFICER AND GENTLEMAN

Attention is invited to the two terms that are supposed to be synonymous—"officer and gentleman." The officer corps attains its highest distinction when the two words are inseparable. It is not the duty of the officer to break needlessly those niceties in custom and usage that have been thoroughly tested in the past; for, as Cardinal Newman said in his classical definition of a gentleman, "He even supports institutions as venerable, beautiful, or useful, to which he does not assent."

The Service will never go astray by a thoughtful adherence to standards of conduct that were tested many years before the present active list entered the Navy. The Service has certain olden usages that are worthy of respect and, no matter how pressing duties become, there is time for their observance. It is not tradition and custom alone that compel these observances; instinct also lends its voice. Some say that times have changed. Yes, they have changed in many ways, but good manners, punctilious courtesy without sycophancy, attention to those niceties not in the regulation book, all based on loyalty and consideration for others, remain the hall mark of the officer and the gentleman.

CHAPTER VI

SOCIAL USAGE—PRESCRIBED AND PROSCRIBED

"As you from this day start the world as a man, I trust that your future conduct in life will prove you both an officer and a gentleman. Recollect that you must be a seaman to be an officer; and also that you cannot be a good officer without being a gentleman."
—ADMIRAL LORD NELSON
To a young man just appointed a midshipman.

"The favorites of society and what it calls whole souls are able men, and of more spirit than wit, who have no uncomfortable egoism, but who exactly fill the hour and the company, contented and contenting, at a marriage or a funeral, a ball or a iury, a water party or a shooting match."
—RALPH WALDO EMERSON

"Manners maketh man."
—WILLIAM OF WYKEMAN

Nor stand so much on your gentility,
Which is an airy, and mere borrowed thing,
From dead men's dust, and bones: and none of yours
Except you make, or hold it.
—BEN JONSON

MONTAIGNE, whose *Essays* have been one of the best sellers for ten generations, and whose work has gone into seventy-five European editions with translations in all civilized tongues. wrote:

I have often seene men proove unmanerely by too much maners, and importunate by over-much curtesie. The knowledge of entertainment is otherwise a profitable knowledge.[1]

By all means, it is the "profitable knowledge" that should be gained. No point that adds to the order, ease, and decorum of official and social intercourse should be taken lightly by those of the Service. As Joseph Hergesheimer implies, true elegance is more than that supposed to obtain by giving orchids, drinking champagne, and wearing dinner coats. In fact the worthy goal is

[1] John Florio, *Translations of the Essayes of Michael Lord of Montaigne*, XIII, 1st Book.

that ease that marks the well bred who are unconscious of "manners"; by some it is called the "cultus of the imperturbable."[1]

The heritage of the Navy is one of superior behavior and unquestioned honesty. Superior behavior comprises self-restraint, consideration for others, as well as gracious conformance with the best social usage of the time. The steadfastness of honor has become a tradition—a fashioner of character.

It is certainly not the privilege of all to have the excellent advantages in childhood of environment and training that some enjoy. However, in the humblest of homes a foundation is laid that is beyond price when children are taught the simple yet basic amenities—to pay proper respect to age and office; to treat ladies with chivalrous regard; to aid the unfortunate and helpless; and above all to meet life with a sense of decency and fair play. Such training leaves an indelible stamp.

Without this foundation, manners and so-called "polish" are superficial. Gentility is more than skin deep and the outward show without the inner spirit is to cultured and thoughtful people comparable to the impression of a gangster in a "tail coat" at a night club; a burlesque queen attempting to play Lady Vere de Vere at a ball; or a Tammany "heeler" attending a lecture on honest governments. Gold braid never made an officer; and a uniform, a *man*.

Early training is required but, after the fundamentals are gained in childhood and early youth, it will take careful observation of good manners in others, a searching self-criticism and vigilant attention to deportment and bearing in order that one may eventually feel at ease in any company, no matter how formal, official, or dignified the assembly. An officer should ever reveal possessions that make him worth meeting.

No attempt will be made to define "gentleman." It is one of the most abused terms in the English language. We all have a conception of the ideal, well knowing that it lies between the "gent" of certain circles and the contemptible, conceited, ar-

---

[1] NOTE.—A term that has become classic since Austin Dobson in the *New Chesterfield* explains Chesterfield's scheme of conduct for his son in *Eighteenth Century Vignettes*.

rogant cad found in higher circles. The exact term fits neither those who are afraid they will not be taken as "gentlemen" nor those who tell the world they are "gentlemen." It is rather a matter of character. Human behavior is somewhat a relative term after all.

A proper appreciation of social values and the exercise of superior manners require no justification. Neither are good manners incompatible with the rôle of seaman, notwithstanding the extreme "he-man" and "hairy-chested-sailorman" school of thought. Suffren, Jervis, Howe, Nelson, Perry, Lawrence, Decatur, Porter, Farragut, and Dewey were gentlemen. They knew the importance of dignified ceremony, the effect of gracious demeanor in diplomatic dealings, and the respect that should be accorded their seniors in age and office.

Again, the Service sometimes forgets that the foreign officials' impression of the culture of the United States is formed to a large extent by their contact with the officers of the diplomatic corps and the Navy. Do we not as a rule judge the people of a country by their official representatives? By *Naval Regulations,* it is the duty of the naval officer to respect the customs of foreign lands, while to learn some of the outstanding customs, modes of living, and social amenities comprises an important phase of the liberal education of any man. We do not roam the world as free-lance writers, critics of manners, and sociologists; rather it is our duty to keep in mind that we are usually official guests and as such to criticize the hosts is to commit a breach of etiquette that is inexcusable. We as Americans have no monopoly on customs or manners. It may be profitable to spend more time in mending our own fences, correcting our own shortcomings, and less in criticism of the other races of the world.

It was told of the British bluejacket, but could be equally indicative of the egoism of some of our own tourists, that in a South American country, Jack ashore said to his shipmate, "Why, these bloomin' fools are so ignorant that they call a hat a sombrero." Only a story; nevertheless, it makes an emphatic point.

Good manners require in their international aspect a reasonable conformance to the best usage of the foreign states. We revert again to consideration for others and self-restraint. Of course, the American finds in foreign lands a certain amount of antiquated, narrow ceremonial, as well as forms of stilted etiquette that border in our opinion on servility. Some of it is mummery to puppets, but do not lean over backwards to evade "while in Rome do as the Romans do"; that is, if one wishes to attend an interesting "show."

In a study of our Foreign Service, Mowrer writes that,

Regardless of whether we, in our wisdom might be able to improve upon these rules, our agents should follow punctiliously the prevailing rules of diplomatic or court etiquette. To do otherwise is to be needlessly boorish. We may properly expect foreign agents in Washington to accede, on public occasions to our home customs; our own agents abroad should be equally scrupulous not to offend the sensibilities of the people with whom they have to work and to whom they aspire to be able, perhaps, to influence.[1]

This brings us to an important rule in official social relations, that is, to ascertain in advance what will be expected—the ceremonies and customs that shall obtain on certain occasions. This policy if pursued has two practical advantages. First, all ceremonies, such as presentations, levees, and audiences go more smoothly when all know the "drill." Second, although senior officers are at times required by virtue of rank to attend official ceremonials, juniors may by advance information forego the "pleasure," if not in sympathy with the ceremonial or participants (for example, some Protestants would not desire a Papal audience, and some Catholics would forego presentation to the Archbishop of Canterbury). In fact, in recent years quite a fright was given a naval surgeon when, after a Papal audience, he was told by a brother officer, as a "wise crack," that the Papal Secretary of State would like to see all Masons in the next chamber. The surgeon glanced in and saw only the Swiss guard standing erect with sharp halberds. For a short time the doctor's expression was a cross between the portrait of a "primitive" saint and a victim of the Inquisition.

[1] Paul Scott Mowrer, *Our Foreign Service* (1924), p. 328.

With inquiry, all details may generally be ascertained in advance of official functions. Then too, where the occasion is that of a luncheon or dinner, the senior officer will often be called upon to say a "few words," whether he knows or does not know the significance of the memorial, celebration, anniversary, or feast day. So preparedness should be the rule. Formal or informal inquiry through the United States consular or diplomatic channels will secure the desired advance information. This is part of the business of the Foreign Service. A vice-consul once made haste to inform a naval officer not under any circumstances to inquire how his friend, a Mexican general, lost the use of an eye. The eye was lost by impact with a champagne cork in a celebration by the Mexicans for what they considered the expulsion of Pershing from Mexico, at the time the American Army pursued the bandit Villa.

George Washington, in his 39th "Rule of Civility," wrote: "In writing or speaking, give to every person his due title according to his degree and custom of the place." This excellent rule is universal in its application. It happens that in the thousands of extant letters written by Washington few mistakes are found in titles and points of address. Again, it is well to be forehanded enough to find out who will be at the ceremonial, celebration, or dinner. How are they addressed? What is their official title? What is the correct etiquette of the occasion? A young American naval officer, in England, knowing well the correct form of address, addressed the wife of an Earl as "Mrs." ——. For a second her embarrassment was apparent, for it was probably the first time in her life that she had been so addressed. It should be remembered that she had the same right to a title that the naval officer had to his rank—it was fixed by law. The title was not even a custom, upon which many United States titles (excepting the military and naval) depend. The individual should be given the benefit of the doubt, but where titles are established by law, be they civilian, military, or naval, one should be precise in giving "every person his due."

Besides, scrupulous attention to official amenities is a factor that is conducive to good morale. Particularly on foreign duty how many times one has heard, in substance, "Our captain knows what to do at the right time and the right place." It goes without saying that this engenders pride in ship and Service, it imbues junior officers with the desire to emulate at all times the action of the superior, and to learn from example what to do and when to do it when the time comes. This spirit of emulation is strikingly noticeable in other phases of the naval profession, but we are here concerned with social usage, ceremonies, and customs. The true spirit of the gentleman aids considerably in a competent exercise of the art of command.

Captain Basil Hall, Royal Navy, who wrote a most detailed and descriptive journal of his career on the sea, said in this connection over a hundred years ago:

And certainly as far as my own observation and inquiries have gone, I have found reason to believe, that those officers who are the best informed and the best bred, and who possess most of the true spirit of gentlemen, are not only the safest to trust in command of others, but are always the readiest to yield that prompt and cheerful obedience to their superiors, which is the mainspring of good order. Such men respect themselves so justly and value their own true dignity of character so much, and are at all times so sensitively alive to the humiliation of incurring reproach, that they are extremely cautious how they expose themselves to merited censure. From the early and constant exercise of genuine politeness, they become habitually considerate of the feelings of others; and thus, by the combined action of these great principles of manners, officers of this stamp contrive to get through far more work, and generally do it much better, than persons of less refinement. Moreover, they consider nothing beneath their closest attention which falls within the limits of their duty; and, as a leading part of this principle, they are the most patient as well as vigilant superintendents of the labours of those placed under their authority, of any men I have ever seen.

The worth of these observations has not changed through the years.

So-called grand manners, "rococo etiquette"—the entrance of the grand seignoir, for example—do not in all cases indicate consistently good manners. There is a differentiation. Someone recently wrote that as a rule when anyone takes ill in the night at a French pension, it is the American who goes for the doctor. This statement implied that the count and the baron would probably lie abed.

There are rules of civility that have been vested with the authority of good usage. Experience has proved their worth. Our generation did not make them, nor did our fathers; they will exist when our last cruise is over. There is a marked universality to some of them. The Chinese sage Confucius "saw the courtesies as coming from the heart" and wrote that "when they are practiced with all the heart, a moral elevation issues."

After the fall of Rome, "a revolution," writes Gibbon, "which will ever be remembered, and is still felt by the nations of the earth," manners and social codes of the various classes became vague and in some instances non-existent. The Norman, William the Conqueror, introduced the beginnings of the medieval institution of chivalry with the conquest of England. This was a civilizing force that instituted certain rules for peace and war in contrast to the savage fight-to-the-death, and influenced those who bore arms to observe codes of courtesy and self-control that had scarcely existed since the fall of Roman civilization. The organization of the Church by William also aided to ameliorate the general condition of savagery.

It was much later that we find the first collection of rules for the deportment and manners of gentlemen, although an unwritten code existed for gentlemen-at-arms. From this first book of etiquette came the "Rules of Civility" that George Washington certainly emulated, if his career be inspected from this angle.

The original rules styled *Bienséance de la Conversation entre les Hommes* were composed and collated by the *pensionnaires* of the French Jesuit College of La Fleche in 1595. They were sent to their brothers at Pont à Mousson where Father Perin translated them into Latin, adding a chapter of his own on behavior at the table. Father Perin's edition appeared in 1617. Editions were published in Spanish, German, and Bohemian. A French edition appeared in 1640, and at the same time Francis Hawkins published an English edition in London.

This book in its various translations was used as a rule book in many of the great institutions of learning that were charged with the education of the young gentlemen of the day. There was some plagiarization in England. A copy stating that it was "Newly revised and much enlarged" of date 1698 is to be found in the British Museum.

Obadiah Walker, Master of University College, Oxford, called his book, *Youth Behaviour*. From this source possibly came the English versions as transcribed by George Washington in his youth.

Rules of Civility and Decent Behaviour in Company and Conversation as reflected throughout the life of Washington were most probably learned from his brothers, Augustine and Lawrence, and not from the Reverend James Mayre as explained by Maurice Conway, for research "fails to establish the fact"[1] that "Washington ever attended a regular school."[2] These rules, though old fashioned and quaint, carry in essence that fundamental precept of any social code—polite deference and respect to others.

It would be preposterous to state that the memorization of a set of rules will create in any sense a gentleman. In the last analysis, it is a reflection of the inner man. The rules only give a directive to the spirit. For as James I said to his óld nurse, "I'll mak' your son a baronet gin ye like, Luckie, but the de'il himself couldna mak' him a gentleman."

SOME NAVAL SOCIAL CUSTOMS

Cards and Visits

In civilian life, formal visits are not so much in vogue as they once were. In military and naval life they fulfill a more useful purpose than in civilian life and are still made as they always were and probably always will be. Good usage has long decreed in the Navy that juniors and seniors should meet in each other's homes, with emphasis that the first call should be made by the

[1] NOTE.—The new edition of Charles Moore (Houghton Mifflin, 1926) clears up disputed points.

[2] John C. Fitzpatrick, *George Washington Himself* (1933), pp. 19 and 517.

junior on the senior, but in the case of a late comer or a newly married couple, calls are made first by those longer on the ship or station. Of course, the commanding officer is always called upon first by his juniors, irrespective of his time in the ship or at the station.

Calls in reality merely serve the purpose of permitting naval officers and their families to become acquainted; furthermore, they permit juniors and seniors to meet at other times than in the official discharge of their duties. Such meetings permit the senior to get the "cut of the jib" of the junior. But it works both ways, for in informal conversation a junior may learn at times semi-official and private views of a senior on subjects that will tend to aid the junior in his duties. There will always be a certain amount of formality connected with the career of an officer, and by means of calls and social visits upon seniors the young officer develops a *savoir-faire* in these matters within his own Service, before extensive contact on his part with officials of another country, where foreign languages are often employed and in general a more formal atmosphere will exist. The young officer and wife will also have the opportunity of acting as host and hostess to all ranks when their visits are returned. Dignified cordiality, graciousness, and good conversation mark those who excel as hosts and hostesses. The "jazz age" has placed perhaps too much accent on "matters liquid" as the mark of the most popular host and hostesses. Or must "prohibition" be blamed? The "New Deal" will tell.

A dinner invitation should not be tendered without sending a card or in some cases writing a note asking that the formality of a visit be waived, if the host and hostess have not called upon the invited one. It is mandatory that first calls be returned. There are situations in the Navy where it is practically physically impossible for senior officers and their wives to return all calls. The question is definitely settled, if on the advice of the senior officer a reception at his home signifies that all calls are returned.

A bachelor's call is returned by leaving a card at the officer's club; but if he is more than a mere acquaintance it is correct to call informally at his rooms or home. It is, of course, understood that unless invited in the company of her husband, a lady does not return the call of a bachelor.

Card Etiquette

Cards should be left when making all formal calls or attending certain afternoon receptions, teas, and garden parties. An old socialite once said, "Always carry your cards. Have them convenient. Look out for the tray."

When the call is upon a lady living in a hotel or apartment house, cards are left at the desk. It is good form to write her name across the top of the card to insure that she receives it. This prevents the embarrassment of some and surprise of others should the card be placed in the wrong box.

If not received when calling upon the sick, it is proper that a card be left with the words "to inquire" written on it. Cards should also be left for friends who have suffered great grief or bereavement. Notes are, of course, sent to close friends.

Captain Niblack wrote in "Letters from a Retired Rear Admiral to His Son,"[1]

It is curious how important small matters may, on occasions, become, as for instance who should leave his visiting card on whom. On the continent of Europe, and in the diplomatic corps the world over, in general terms the last-comer makes the first call. This is also agreed to in all navies, and followed in all armies. While Great Britain and the United States officially subscribe to this, in everyday life and among women folks the opposite custom obtains, and everyone is expected to call upon the newcomer. In the Navy officially among officers, a commanding officer of a ship, division, or squadron makes the first call on his superior in command of a ship, division, squadron, or naval station. Among those not in command and among the wives, there is no real rule respected, and it leads to uncertainties, misunderstandings, and heartburnings. In all cases, the first call should be made and returned in person, and the expectation is that it will be. In the diplomatic corps it is, in fact, often bluffed through, and careless diplomats have been known to rely on the office boy or the stationer from whom visiting cards

[1] U. S. Naval Institute PROCEEDINGS, XLI, No. 157.

are ordered, to make the first round of card-leaving visits. In all navies, calls are made in person and returned in person within twenty-four hours.

Aside from any mere formality or formalism, the exchange of visits and of visiting cards implies a "recognition" which forms the entire basis of social or official relations, and any one who belittles it is a nonentity, except in the narrow local orbit of his greatness.

In many localities a *"p.p.c."* (*pour prendre congé*) card is used by either ladies or gentlemen to denote that they are leaving the vicinity for some time, or for good. *"P.p.c."* is merely written on the card. Such a card is either left at the door or mailed. It will under no circumstance relieve one of the courtesy of saying goodbye to one's best friends, or thanking in person or by note those who have been most kind.

It is not good form to leave more than three cards for the ladies of the house, regardless of the number of daughters or visitors. The old rule holds that a lady never leaves cards on a gentleman, and that a gentleman always leaves cards for the gentlemen of the house and the ladies.

The custom of turning up the corners of cards is not standard in the United States. In some localities, it means a call upon all the ladies of the house where the number is unknown; in other places it signifies a call made upon all the household. In still other sections it is supposed to denote that the call was made in person. There are some who invariably do this and assert it signifies nothing in particular. It will suffice to say that one should be guided by local customs, when determined by the best usage. Nevertheless the custom of turning up the corner of calling cards has not entered the standard usage of card etiquette in this country.

When a maid or butler says that "Madam is not at home," it means usually that she is not receiving. This is perfectly correct and is not as some people imagine a rebuff. It is well that juniors in the Navy receive when practicable—unless they have regular "at homes," a custom that is more often followed by seniors.

In some cities of the Orient, it is customary, when calling on English, American, and frequently French nationals, to leave cards in a little box provided for the purpose. The "not at home" sign is usually up. In a few days after cards are left, one is usually invited to the home called upon for tea or possibly dinner.

In England, one usually "signs the book" when making official calls at the homes of senior officials, military and naval. This register is at the doorway of the house. One signs and departs. Visiting officers who have so registered are generally invited later to tea.

All officers on duty in Washington are expected to leave cards upon the President of the United States. Officers are, of course, not received when calls are made. Of late those who call have been invited to White House musicales. It is also customary that cards be left on the chief of Naval Operations and his wife. An invitation from the White House requires a reply by hand, and should never be mailed. A White House invitation takes precedence over all other invitations. It is for us in the United States comparable to what "a royal command" is to the foreigner.

If there is any doubt as to who should make the first call, do not stand on the doubt *but make the call.* Cards serve a useful purpose when left on those who do not know you personally, permitting them to have at hand the names of those who called—a valuable reference in the preparation of lists for future social events.

Carry sufficient cards at all times so that when needed they are readily accessible. On some occasions visiting cards are used for announcements by butlers and thereby save some very humorous mispronunciations of names.

Card etiquette in the Navy is to all practical purposes uniform, although determined by custom alone. There are no regulations on the subject. The rules of civilians vary in detail, depending upon the locality. It is well in all matters social to inquire as to the local customs and to conform to local practices.

Invitations at Home and Abroad

Formal invitations must always be replied to "by hand" in the formal third person style and in the prescribed form. The writing must be spaced with the proper indentations conforming to the formal invitation.

Dinner invitations must be declined or accepted as soon as possible after receipt. A reply should be made within twenty-four hours. Informal dinner invitations require the same prompt answer as formal invitations.

The hour and date of the dinner must be placed in the note of acceptance, although it is not required in notes of regret. This holds for all replies to invitations of a formal nature.

"*R.s.v.p.*" (*répondez s'il vous plaît*) invitations of all descriptions must be replied to. The custom is growing in the United States of putting "Please reply to——," instead of "*r.s.v.p.*"

The words "levee dress" on British invitations mean the dress that one should wear at a royal levee, which, of course, is "full dress"; whether or not sword is worn and other details are matters of inquiry.

"Afternoon dress" on an invitation signifies morning coats and top hats. At such functions, foreign military and naval officers never wear uniform but, instead, the correct civilian dress.

Where "smoking" is placed in the lower left corner it signifies dinner coats and is usually employed for stag parties and certain sporting events held at night. This term is often used by the French.

Informal written invitations should always be replied to by hand. It is a moot point whether or not mention of a previous engagement should be made in a note of regret.

In foreign services, replies are usually made to flag lieutenants and aides-de-camp. Replies to invitations of royalty are made to the Lord Chamberlain, or to equerries. To whom the reply is to be sent is usually found in the lower left corner of the invitation.

Inasmuch as French is a diplomatic language and the tongue of *politesse* throughout most of the world, it is well to reply to a French invitation in French. Some of our United States embassies and chancelleries use the French language for social invitations. In all other cases reply to the invitation in English.

When several formal invitations are replied to from the same ship, it is good practice to send the individual replies ashore by officer messenger to the embassy or consulate, where they will usually be dispatched by messenger to the proper address.

When invitations are issued for ships' receptions, large balls on board, and formal dinner parties, it is good form and a great convenience to have the pier from which boats leave placed in the lower corner of the invitation. In large affairs a card should be issued that will give admittance to boats at the pier or landing designated thereon. This is a great convenience to civilians who naturally know little about the water fronts and piers of their cities.

Formal Dinners

Flag Lieutenants' and Aides' Duties Abroad

The flag lieutenant or officer charged with the details, after determining the number of guests, should make out a neat seating diagram and submit it to the admiral or senior officer for his approval. Precedence must be carefully considered and if in doubt when on a foreign station, by all means make inquiries to the senior United States official ashore or a member of his staff. These matters possibly bear more weight with foreigners than with us. Nevertheless, the records show there have been cases of dispute among United States officials.

Check the menu with the steward, see that flowers are ordered and then arranged. Do not forget the place cards. Give a written memorandum to the officer of the deck as to the time when boat will be sent for the guests. It is good practice to ascertain personally that the coxswain knows for whom he is going. If there is a large party and only one boat trip, instructions should be given for the coxswain to await a certain length of time. It is good practice to give the coxswain a list of the guests.

Inform the admiral or senior officer when his guests are approaching the ship. An officer should go to the lower ladder to aid the ladies of the party as well as the elderly gentlemen. Escort the ladies to the room reserved as a cloakroom for them. Insure that as many introductions as possible are made before dinner. See that the steward announces dinner promptly and properly. Assist guests with the seating diagram. If a large dinner, small cards with the dinner partners of the gentlemen will aid in prompt seating. Observe all service and, if necessary, in a low tone speak to the "head boy" if there is any irregularity.

The flag lieutenant is supposed to assist the admiral at all times in seeing that guests are comfortable and their wishes gratified. The musical program is usually left to the flag lieutenant. He should check the bandmaster's program in advance; and if toasts are required and the national airs of foreign states are to be rendered, make a written memorandum as to details for the information of the bandmaster. Finally, check and ascertain that the bandmaster thoroughly understands the signals of execution for national airs.

At formal dinner parties one should always divide the time in conversation with the ladies on either side. Even if not introduced before being seated, custom has decreed that the presence of those seated next to each other at a formal dinner will suffice for an introduction.

SEATING FOR FORMAL LUNCHEONS AND DINNERS*

At small dinners and luncheons, it is customary for the flag officer or host to sit at the head of the table, and the flag lieutenant opposite and at the other end. Seating then takes place in order of seniority from the admiral's (or host's) right. It is customary to give this place of honor to the senior lady guest (other than the host's wife), unless the meal is in honor of a high ranking guest. He should then be given the seat of honor.

It is customary in the U. S. Navy, when the admiral is guest of

* In the Army, all retired officers rank after active officers of the same grade. In the Navy, retired officers rank with their grade and are given precedence as determined by date of commission in the grade. Exception is the Chief of Naval Operations who, by law, ranks next after an Admiral-of-the-Navy.

honor at a dinner given by a junior admiral or a captain, to seat the admiral to the right of the host who does not yield his seat. In this respect, strict continental custom is not followed.

In the wardroom, if the longitudinal seating is used, it is customary to place the senior guest from the cabin in the center of the table. If the captain and admiral are both invited to a wardroom dinner, it would be correct to place each at the center and opposite to each other, or the admiral and captain may be seated to the right and left of the president of the mess.

The following instructions, as paraphrased from the instructions for Italian naval officers, and followed generally by the French, British, German, and Japanese, give the general usage for the seating and arrangements at formal repasts. They are submitted as a guide.

(1) For a large number of guests a seating diagram should be made and placed in a convenient place for the observation of the guests. Names may be placed on individual menus, or place cards used. For smaller dinners an aide should quietly inform gentlemen of the location of their seats, and also the names of the ladies they are requested to escort to the table.

(2) All instructions emphasize the care that should be taken in the assignment of places. Strict attention must be paid to the rank of the guests and their relative precedence.

(3) Before going to the table, all effort should be made to have the guests meet each other: this adds to congeniality.

(4) At large formal luncheons and dinners, the one who invites (the host) sits at the center of one of the longitudinal sides of the table, generally opposite the entrance door. At the center opposite him is the highest ranking guest belonging to the ship. However, if there are among the guests, a person, military or civilian, whose rank is senior to the highest ranking guest from the ship [for example, an admiral is the host; chief of staff, a rear admiral, the second senior on board; and the senior guest a Senator, Congressman, or visiting vice-admiral or rear admiral], then such person sits opposite the one extending the invitation, unless it be a person of exceptionally high office and

precedence, in which case he takes the host's place while the latter sits opposite.

The commander of a ship yields his place likewise to the commander of his division, squadron, or fleet.

Presidents, sovereigns, and princes of royal blood always preside over the repast in which they participate. Likewise it is well that the seating arrangement be approved by someone in their suite.

(5) With the exception of such special cases, seats will be distributed as follows: At the right of the host sits the highest ranking guest not belonging to the ship; at the left of the host, the one immediately following the highest ranking guest. The third and fourth in precedence are seated respectively to the right and left of the one having the central seat on the other side of the table, and so on down the list.

EXAMPLES

Guest of honor opposite the host

Seniority

(1) American vice-admiral, *host*
(2) British vice-admiral, *guest of honor*
(3) U. S. rear admiral
(4) U. S. rear admiral, chief of staff
(5) Captain, R.N.
(6) Captain, U.S.N.
(7) Captain, R.N.
(8) Captain, U.S.N.
(9) Commander, R.N.
(10) Commander, U.S.N.
(11) Flag lieutenant, R.N.
(12) Flag lieutenant, U.S.N.

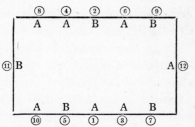

A senior in the same organization takes the seat of the host

Seniority

(1) C. in C., U. S. Fleet, admiral
(2) Vice-admiral, R.N., *guest of honor*
(3) Vice-admiral, U.S.N., *host*

(4) Rear admiral, U.S.N.
(5) Rear admiral, U.S.N., chief of staff
(6) Captain, U.S.N.
(7) Captain, R.N.
(8) Captain, U.S.N.
(9) Colonel, U.S.A.
(10) Captain, R.N.
(11) Commander, R.N.
(12) Commander, U.S.N.
(13) Flag lieutenant, R.N.
(14) Flag lieutenant, U.S.N.

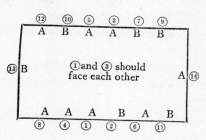

However, persons belonging to the ship are seated between guests from the outside. Those belonging to the ship are likewise seated by rank and longevity, but not always strictly so. As the Italians put it,

Attention must be paid to foreign languages spoken by each, professional congeniality with the guests from outside, and, in a word, all the elements contributing towards maintaining the most animated and interesting conversation. . . .

(6) If there are matrons, elderly ladies, and young ladies, the two former classes occupy the first seats in the order of precedence of their respective husbands or fathers (but all ladies before very young ladies). In seating gentlemen among ladies, care should be taken not to seat near relatives (husband and wife, father and daughter, etc.) together.

(7) At luncheon and dinner aboard ship, all the ladies, even the wife of the host, are considered as guests. If only one lady is invited, she is requested to sit opposite the host.

On the other hand, at luncheons ashore, the wife of the host presides over the occasion. In case she is absent, a lady of the family or the wife of the highest ranking officer among the host's brother officers is requested to take this place.

(8) At formal repasts very young boys and girls must not take part even if they belong to the family of the host. (The continental custom prescribes eighteen years as the minimum age for attendance at formal dinners.)

(9) The Italian rules with true Latin gallantry suggest "that

it is rather a polite custom to put bouquets of flowers at the ladies' places on the table, or to distribute them before sitting down at the table."

Keep conversation on the best possible plane and avoid if possible the talk of shop, unless questioned. Also refrain from a discussion of women, death, religion, politics, and surgical operations. The rule should never be deviated from for, even though one speak well of one who has died in high office, someone may be present who is not in sympathy with the name discussed. In other words, make all guests comfortable and at ease. This is only done by avoiding embarrassing and doleful topics of conversation. Be a pleasant fellow but for goodness' sake do not be a Pollyanna.

Presentations and Audiences

Wear the prescribed uniform and arrive at the prescribed time. Yes, a few minutes ahead of time.

Remember that the old word "Sir" is always correct in replying to royalty, nobility, or those of high officialdom. It is preferable and customary to use "Sire" in replying to sovereigns.

At any presentation learn in advance the ceremonial, if this be possible. Maintain a military bearing but endeavor to feel at ease.

In either formal or informal conversation, it is considered very bad form to question royalty or nobility. It is never correct to turn directly away after formal presentation to commoner or king, but rather to back away a few steps and if necessary to the side.

Some of the ancient ceremonies observed by courts, clergy, and foreign naval and military organizations are most interesting, and should afford pleasing memories for after years.

At some official receptions on the Continent, guests of honor are announced individually and are expected to step forward and bow to the assembly. Consequently, it is well to be prepared to be announced and presented *tout seul*. This requires all the poise and dignity that the average person is able to muster, but as an experienced foreign-service official said, "The best rule is to take it easy with a smile."

COMMODORE MATTHEW C. PERRY, U. S. NAVY—The Japanese characters describe the picture: "North America, a country with republican government. Copy of direct portrait of the Chief Admiral Matthew C. Perry, Special Envoy and Plenipotentiary of the Sovereign, as he appeared in conference on landing at Yokohama Province off Sagami." (By an unknown Japanese artist)

The matter of curtsies for ladies will not be discussed. The opinion is ventured that unless the lady learned to curtsy as a child or in her youth it is seldom made with grace. Nevertheless, the rule stands without comment that all ladies of all races curtsy when presented to sovereigns and to those of the blood royal. Ladies whose husbands are heads of republican states would, of course, not curtsy to sovereigns or the blood royal.

Under no condition is it expected that young women or matrons curtsy to our own officials. The late White House usher wrote in his memoranda:

Mrs. Levi Leiter, a wealthy Chicago and Washington social leader and mother of Lady Curzon, insisted upon addressing the President and Mrs. Taft as "Excellency," much to their amusement, but Taft didn't think it funny when Mrs. Wickersham and Mrs. Meyer would curtsy to him. It annoyed him until he spluttered.[1]

One kneels during a papal audience and is supposed to touch lips to the papal ring when His Holiness blesses visitors in the Vatican. The "toe kissing" may be dismissed as a camp meeting myth.

Letters of Appreciation and Thanks

The naval officer, before or just after leaving port, must never neglect the amenity of writing notes of thanks, of appreciation, and of farewell to those clubs, societies, officials, and individuals who rendered courtesies and favors to him and his command. In fact, it is all the thanks that many receive for their courtesies and their kindness to officers of the Fleet.

Some of the expressions of thanks in this day of fast communications may take the form of dispatches. Although dispatches lack the personal touch of the letter, they are in better form for promulgation by rapid communications to others who are concerned.

The Fighting Man in Gentle Company

Brusqueness, "hard boiled" exterior, the accentuated "he-man" effect, with indifference and disdain for the more refined

[1] Irvin H. Hoover, "White House Notebook," *Saturday Evening Post*, 31 March, 1934, by courteous permission of the copyright owners, Houghton Mifflin Co.

arts, are not the attributes of gentility. Such traits usually lead the individual to become an exemplar of the antithesis of good manners. A superficial examination will show that aggressive and unpleasant strains in social intercourse are conspicuously absent in a Nelson, a Wellington, a Washington, a Farragut, and a Lee.

A chivalric character is expected to be the hallmark of the officer corps. This in essence means a consideration of others in differentiation to the aggressiveness and "chip-on-the-shoulder" attitude of certain classes and individuals. Strength of character may be displayed without bombast; dignity, without frigidity; friendliness, without garrulousness; while an appreciation of art, music, and the *belles-lettres* should not lessen the essential professional qualifications of the officer.

It is important that the officer corps acquire the tastes of refined society and enlightened men. It is well that thought be given to the civilian attitude, and that discussions pertaining to "shop" and war should not monopolize the conversation with those not of the profession of arms. Your gauge as a warrior and qualifications as an officer are not exemplified by whetting swords in the presence of refined society, or by displaying indifference to the manners and tastes that mark the finer types of the social order. Castiglione wrote in 1528 in his *Book of the Courtier,*

Because to such men as this, one might justly say that which a brave lady jestingly said in gentle company to one whom I will not name at present [supposed to have been a brave soldier of fortune, one Captain Fracassa] who, being invited by her out of compliment to dance, refused not only that but to listen to the music, and many other entertainments proposed to him, saying always that such silly trifles were not his business; so at last the lady said, "What is your business then?" He replied with a sour look, "to fight." Then the lady at once said, "Now, that you are in no war and out of fighting time, I should think it were a good thing to have yourself well oiled, and to stow yourself with all your battle harness in a closet until you be needed, lest you grow more rusty than you are." And so, amid much laughter from the bystanders, she left the discomfited fellow to his silly presumption.

In conclusion, it may be safely said that the code of a gentleman may not be compassed within a few written rules, or in a volume as far as that goes. To some extent, it is a progressive education throughout life. There are many commendable, terse private codes of conduct. And from those examined, one has been selected, the code of a once active naval officer, a gentleman who loved the sea and who was the beloved sovereign of a vast empire—the late George V.

The code, which is said to have been framed and hung in his bed chamber, is:

Teach me to be obedient to the rules of the game.

Teach me to distinguish between sentiment and sentimentality, admiring the one and despising the other.

Teach me neither to proffer nor to receive cheap praise.

If I am called upon to suffer, let me be like a well-bred beast that goes away to suffer in silence.

Teach me to win if I may; if I may not, teach me to be a good loser.

Teach me neither to cry for the moon nor to cry over spilt milk.

It would be logical to end these notes with the "Code of a King." But for purposes of contrast, a final point is presented —an observation that not only will mark the catholicity of good manners, but also will exemplify the impressions created by the possessor of good manners.

Mr. R. D. Blumenfeld, onetime American newspaper reporter, now the doyen of Fleet Street editors and an outstanding personage in the British newspaper world, was recalling a short time ago the high spots of his successful career. He spoke of the celebrities he knew intimately, of the rulers and political leaders who had trusted him with many confidences. When asked who was the greatest, he dismissed them all. Blumenfeld named Jimmy Aylett, a plain, smiling, cheerful, silent, poor man of Essex, "a natural poet, a philosopher, a true gentleman." Blumenfeld said,

Jimmy Aylett was my week-end cottage gardner thirty years ago. He was eighty. He was born next door, as his father and grandfather and great-grandfather before him. He knew the earth which gave to his spade and his hoe, and what it could stand and could produce. He knew all about clouds and rain and sun.

Jimmy Aylett lived his simple, honest, beautiful life without violence, without temper, without malice. He went to church o' Sundays with a little bunch of flowers in his cleanly brushed Sunday coat. He had the courtesy and the gallantry of the courtier. He knew naught of London or the world. His philosophy lay in Mother Earth and what she would provide. He was kind to dogs and hated traps for rabbits. Always in his pocket there was an apple or a pear or a few dusty sweets for children.

Blumenfeld considers Jimmy Aylett the greatest man he has ever known,

for he taught me above all things that the important things in life are not to be achieved in the making of money or in the chasing of social rainbows.

The life of a Jimmy Aylett should not be dismissed as irrelevant in any study of social relations. After all, meetings of humanity "are the stuff that outward existence is made of"— and manners constitute one fine art that may be cultivated by all.

PART III

SYMBOLS OF GREAT TRADITION

CHAPTER VII

THE FLAG OF THE UNITED STATES

"A thoughtful mind when it sees a nation's flag, sees not the flag only, but the nation itself, and whatever may be its symbol, its insignia, he reads chiefly in the flag, the governments, the principles, the truths, the history, which belongs to the nation."

HENRY WARD BEECHER

"The Stars and Stripes have, therefore, served as an invitation to all the races of the world and our liberal naturalization laws make it a simple matter for an alien to become a citizen."

ADMIRAL GEORGE H. PREBLE, U. S. NAVY.

"Life on a man-of-war is well calculated to inspire love for our national flag . . . the ceremony with which the colors are hoisted in the morning and lowered at night when the sunset gun is fired . . . the salutes in its honor at home and abroad, the never ceasing watch for its appearance at sea or in foreign ports, the constant reference to it in nautical conversation, the carrying it in all small boats, are only a few of the ways in which it deepens its hold upon heart and memory."

ELIZABETH DOUGLAS VAN DENBURG[1]

" . . . And yet though silent it speaks to us—speaks to us of the past of the men and women who went before us and of the records they wrote upon it."

WOODROW WILSON

FROM TIME immemorial, flags, standards, and banners have been flown by kings, noblemen, military and civil organizations, as well as by religious bodies and faiths, in order to denote by visual symbol the distinctive character of those who claimed the colors or insignia. In the earliest recorded history, it was by such devices that the presence of the supreme commander was made known; that the camps of military units and tribes were differentiated; that enemies were marked from friends. Banners as distinctive tribal devices were used by the Tribes of Israel. David in the Psalms wrote, "We will rejoice in thy salvation, and in the name of our God we will set up our banners." Indeed, it is recorded that the wise Solomon said, "Terrible as an army with banners." The units of the army of ancient Egypt had dis-

---

[1] *My Voyage in the U. S. Frigate "Congress."*

tinctive standards. The chariot of Darius, the Persian, carried
its distinctive badge. Later, the eagle standards of the Caesars
were known by the barbaric tribes at the outposts of the known
world.

Likewise have flags and symbols played a conspicuous part in
the history of religion. The fanatical fervor of the Crusades,
which was inspired by the Cross as well as the Crescent, has
been unsurpassed in its intensity in all history. It is recorded
that in the sixth century Saint Augustine and his followers carried to Canterbury banners of the Cross of Christianity. Richard
the Lion Hearted bore the "Cross of Saint George" to the Crusades. In fact, the history of the Crusades, as well as the bitter
feelings and cruel wars of Moor and Christian in Western Europe, were symbolized by allusion to the conflict of the banners
of the Cross and of the Crescent.

In the Middle Ages when chivalry was at its height, the noble-
man, knight, and squire each had his distinctive device. Many
of these banners were carried to the Crusades and were accorded
a devotion by their followers that was in reality an act of worship.
The banners that were brought back were sacredly preserved,
and counterparts of the insignia were in time placed on the
seals, symbols, and flags of the respective countries. It was in
this romantic and religious age that heraldry came into being,
and it is from this point that the expert is able to trace the evolution and changes, as well as the fixed symbols that comprise the
history of flags and standards. Even in the formulation of the
Flag Code of the United States certain ancient but established
principles of heraldry govern.

The effect of the Crusades upon European art, architecture,
and letters is incalculable. The Cross previously surmounted
many crowns, but after the "Holy Wars," in practically all distinctive Christian devices the motif of the Cross was predomi-
nant; it was the symbol of countries, kings, and leaders. The
triple cross flag of Great Britain, as well as the flags of Norway,
Sweden, Denmark, Germany, and Italy carry to this day the tradition of the devotion that the early symbolism inspired. Robert
Phillips, in his study of the American flag, wrote:

"I HAVEN'T BEGUN TO FIGHT"—John Paul Jones. (From painting by Henry Mosler. Copyright The Knapp Co., Inc., by courtesy American Lithograph Co., Inc.)

Out of the chaos and romance of this golden epoch there emerged a universal addiction to the display of personal and family coats of arms, and of the colors of knightly and religious orders. The records of the time teem with allusions to standards, banners, banderolls, guidons, gonfalons, pennons, pennoncels.

In this connection and for those who are curious as to the earliest arms and banners arising from the spirit of the Crusades, one is referred to a quaint and interesting book, *Knowledge of All the Kingdoms, Lands, and Lordships That Are in the World.* This book was written by a Spanish Franciscan in the middle of the fourteenth century, and sets forth a detailed and faithful description of the arms and devices of each land as well as those of the ruling kings and lords.

It is only of comparatively recent date that a nationalistic significance has been given to the flags of certain states, that is, recent in comparison to the long period that flags were distinctive of the leaders, whether king or baron. In fact, the now outmoded theory of the divine right of kings, and a slow dissipation of monarchial myth caused what was originally the "King's Colors" to become the colors of the state or kingdom. The "King's Colors" of the dominant sovereign became in time the banner of united countries and states. Before the establishment of a state or national flag, we have record of the *fleur-de-lis* of the Bourbons, the black eagle of the Hohenzollerns, the double eagle of the Hapsburgs and the Romanoffs. They were originally the flags of a royal or princely house. The double-headed eagles of imperial Austria and Russia symbolized their claim in a vague, traditional way to the rule of both the former Eastern and Western Roman Empires. Napoleon carried on the Roman tradition by the adoption of the eagles of the Caesars. For an army standard he took bees as an imperial device. In our day certain royal arms have been removed from the flags of once powerful empires. At this writing (1933) Germany has reverted to the flag of Imperial Germany.

It is claimed that the flag, called the Dannebrog, of Denmark, is the oldest national flag of a present day state. It is tradition that the flag was adopted in 1219 after the Danish King Waldemar beheld at a critical point in battle a shining cross in the sky. The red swallow-tailed flag with the white cross was then adopted and has remained the flag of the country until the present time. The second oldest flag is that of Switzerland, a white Greek cross on a red field, adopted in the seventeenth century. It is interesting to note that the flag of the Red Cross is that of Switzerland with the colors reversed. The X-like cross that has been placed on many flags, both public and private, is the Cross of Saint Andrew, the patron saint of Russia.

Scotland also has a prior claim to Saint Andrew. Peter the Great in 1698 established the order of Saint Andrew, and the distinctive cross was carried on flags, medals, and insignia.

Most national flags in their present form are of a recent date. The royal standard of Spain was adopted originally in 1785. The tri-color of France was born of the French Revolution and supplanted the *fleur-de-lis* of the Bourbons in 1794. The standard of Great Britain was adopted in 1801. The British flag perpetuates the union of England, Scotland, and Ireland, and is a combination of three crosses: Saint George, Saint Andrew, and Saint Patrick.

The oriental flags have not been considered as to precedence of age, although what is known of their traditionary origin presents an absorbing story. As far back as A.D. 1169, the Emperor of Japan used the red disc of the sun as the royal emblem. It was only after contact with the Occident that Japan, in 1859, adopted the red sun with diverging rays on a white field. China officially promulgated the design of its flag in 1826, a blue dragon with a green head biting at a red ball. It is curious that this flag was triangular and of deep yellow material. In reality the emblems of the flags of Japan and Imperial China antedate all flags of the world.

The flag of the United States is among the oldest of the national standards of the world. This remark should be qualified with the fact that the forty-eighth star was added to the original design in 1912 on the admission of the last state, Arizona, to the Union.

The American flag in its development to that of one with

forty-eight stars carries with it the high lights of United States military and naval tradition from the struggles of the weak Colonies under Washington to the present day. Although there is dispute as to where the flag was first flown in battle, and question as to minor details in the first design and place of manufacture, the following chronological sequence will give in general the history of the flag.

For about seventy years before the Revolutionary War, the American Colonists used the red ensign of Great Britain with distinctive devices for the various Colonies, such as British Colonies and dependencies use today.

The banner of Saint George was the ancient flag of England (a white field with a red cross). As early as the fourteenth century the badge of Saint George was universally worn by the soldiery of England. In the late war, Admiral Sir Roger Keyes gave the signal "Saint George for England" as the dispatch of execution in the daring Zeebruge attack. The Cross of St. George formed the national colors of England until 1606, when by royal proclamation the Cross of St. Andrew (a white cross on a blue field), carried by the Scots in the Crusades, was added to it.

We are well assured that the flag of St. George was in use in Massachusetts at an early date, for in 1635 a complaint was entered, "that the ensign at Salem was defaced"; viz., one part of the red cross was taken out. It was not done in disrespect to England, but "upon the opinion that the red cross was given to the King of England by the Pope, as an ensign of victory, so a superstitious thing, and a relic of anti-Christ." The court gave no verdict, and after referring the matter to the next higher court, a new flag was proposed and the matter referred to the crown for the purpose of obtaining "the judgment of the most wise and godly there."

Cabot and the early English explorers flew as the national flag of England—the Cross of Saint George; but as stated before, James I after the unification of England and Scotland, superimposed upon the English cross the Scottish Cross of Saint Andrew, thereby giving to Britain the first union flag. It was 102 years later that this flag was named the Union Jack by Queen Anne.

The first union flag (although not then so called) was decreed by a proclamation of James I on 12 April, 1606. Although the realms of England and Scotland had not been united, the King thought that a common flag would effect a closer union. No differentiation was prescribed for men-of-war and merchantmen, but in reality a distinction was made in that royal ships flew a jack on the bowsprit, and a pennant aloft. It seems reasonable to assume that this flag was carried by the Jamestown Colonists when they landed in Virginia and by the Mayflower Colonists at Plymouth Rock at a later date in 1620.

The Union flag became distinctive of the Royal Navy in 1634. The land forces and the merchant ships flew either the Cross of Saint George or that of Saint Andrew. After the execution of Charles I, in 1649, the English ships reverted to the old flag of Saint George. From all accounts the American Colonists preferred the Union flag during this period. It was in 1707 that Queen Anne decreed that a flag of a red field with a "Union Jack" in the canton, should now be flown by all who had previously carried the flags of either Saint Andrew or Saint George. This flag in general design is the present well-known "red ensign" of the British Merchant Service.

The British Colonies in America at an early date placed a distinctive Colonial design on the Union flag. Up to 1776 four main changes had been made in the basic design. In 1737, the United Colonies of New England were authorized to use a blue flag, with the red cross of Saint George in a white canton, and in the upper corner of the canton next to the staff, a globe representing the world.

One of the popular designs of pre-Revolutionary days was that of a red field with a tree instead of a globe in the canton.

Unions of countries and states have to a large degree always been characterized by the union of distinctive insignia on the flag. In 1649 a new union flag was designed for the British Navy, and in design symbolized the union of England and Ireland. In 1658 the old Union Jack was reintroduced with the "harpe" imposed thereon for Ireland. It is of record that in 1660 the "harpe" was removed, "it being offensive to the King." It was only in 1801 that the British flag became the flag that we know today.

Although the "Union" of Washington's "Great Union Flag" of 1776 was supposed to stand for the union of the United Colonies, it is certain that the traditional ties to the mother country were not forgotten, for in the canton were the crosses of Saint Andrew and Saint George.

SOME EARLY FLAGS BORNE BY UNITS OF THE CONTINENTAL ARMY

Date	Description	Remarks
1775 Bedford Flag	Designed originally in England for Three County Troop in King Philip's War. A maroon ground with mailed arm holding a short sword, on a scroll the motto *Vince aut morire* (conquer or die).	Carried by Cornet Nathaniel Page at Concord.
1775	No illustration has been preserved. A red ground with the Connecticut motto *qui transtulit sustinet* (He who transplanted still sustains); on the reverse side a pine tree with the early motto of Massachusetts, "an appeal to heaven." It is almost identical with the Connecticut State flag of today.	Said to have been a present from John Hancock to General Putnam for the gallant fight of his troops at Bunker Hill. First unfurled at Prospect Hill, Boston.
1775 Philadelphia Light Horse Troop Flag	Of yellow silk 40″ by 30″ with a shield and elaborate rosette design of blue and silver. L.H. was also intertwined on the flag, and underneath the motto, "For these we strive." In the upper left-hand corner were 13 blue and silver stripes, the first flag that symbolized the thirteen Colonies by stripes.	This flag was first carried by the Philadelphia Troop of Light Horse when it escorted Washington from Philadelphia to New York to take command of the Continental Army at Cambridge. Probably carried at battle of Trenton; the Light Horse Troop was there.

Date	Description	Remarks
1 Jan. 1776	Had 7 red and 6 white stripes with the cross of Saint Andrew and St. George on the blue field of the canton.	This flag was hoisted over the troops of George Washington about 1 or 2 January, 1776, on Prospect Hill; at Charlestown on 3d; at Cambridge on 4th. It was designed primarily for naval use. Washington wrote 4 August, 1776, "We hoisted the Union flag in compliment to the United Colonies and saluted it with 13 guns." Tradition relates that Commodore Esek Hopkins sailed in February, 1776, from Philadelphia "amidst the acclamation of thousands assembled on the joyful occasion, with the display of a Union Flag with 13 stripes emblematical of the thirteen Colonies."

One observes from the above outline that Revolutionary flags of all descriptions were carried. Some of them were intended to be fierce Revolutionary banners, while others expressed the fervor and seriousness of the patriotic Colonists. The Great Union or Cambridge flag was never authorized by Congress and was in reality "half British." It was on 4 July, 1776, that the Declaration of Independence terminated forever the "King's Colors" and the Great Union flag in the United Colonies.

EARLY FLAGS USED AT SEA

The Great Union flag was designed primarily for use at sea, but various other flags were worn by Continental ships, state ships, and privateers.

"Don't Tread on Me" Flag

Thirteen stripes without a union, with a rattlesnake undulating across the flag, and underneath the motto, "Don't tread on me." It is reported that it was hoisted by Hopkins, 5 December, 1775, at the mainmast of the *Alfred* at the time Lieutenant John Paul Jones raised the Grand Union flag. A portrait of Commodore Hopkins was printed in London in August, 1776, and it clearly shows on his right the "Don't Tread on Me" flag, while on his left may be observed the "Liberty Tree" flag (Pine tree on white field with inscription "Liberty Tree" at top and "Appeal to God" underneath).

Washington's Navy Ensign or *Pine Tree Flag*

Green pine tree on white field bearing inscription, "An Appeal to Heaven." It was adopted in 1775 and carried by some of the first naval vessels of the United States. It is noted that the pine tree was used on various New England flags, because it had previous to the Revolution been a symbol on banners and flags of some of the New England Colonies.

Merchant and Privateer Ensign

A plain flag of seven red stripes and six white ones without a union, used at sea from 1775 until 1795.

OTHER FLAGS OF THE WAR FOR AMERICAN INDEPENDENCE

Gadsden's Standard, February, 1776

A bright yellow flag with a coiled rattlesnake in the center and underneath the motto, "Don't Tread on Me." This flag has a peculiar interest in that Gadsden, a member of the Naval Committee, presented it to Congress with the request that it be designated as the personal command flag of Commodore Hopkins, the commander in chief of the Navy. So far as can be learned, nothing was ever done about it, and the flag hung for some time in Congress. Nevertheless, a chart of early flags published by the Washington Bi-Centennial Congressional Committee states underneath a cut of this flag that it was hoisted by Hopkins on the *Alfred*. It is regretted that no proof is to be found to this effect.

Pine Tree Flag, 1775-1776-1777

The outstanding device on the majority of these flags was a pine tree with the motto, "An Appeal to Heaven" underneath. This type of flag was used by the floating batteries of the Delaware. It was borne by the Massachusetts and New Hampshire regiments. John Fiske writes that this flag was carried by many naval vessels until the adoption of the new flag in 1776.

There were many unique flags carried by troops in the War of the Revolution. The Culpepper Minute Men, commanded by Patrick Henry, had the snake with the two mottoes: "Liberty or Death" and "Don't Tread on Me." Morgan's Rifles had "1776" on their flag, with the words "XI Virginia Regiment" and "Morgan's Rifle Corps" devised thereon. Count Pulaski, who so gallantly cast his lot with the American Colonists and lost his life for the cause, carried into his last battle at Savannah, Georgia, a crimson silk banner covered with many devices.

There is still preserved the flag used by the Washington Light Infantry. The fiancée of Colonel William Washington hastily made this flag of a red curtain. This flag saw victory at Cowpens, on 17 January, 1781, and was carried at the battle of Eutaw Springs which was conceded a British victory.

JOHN PAUL JONES'S CONNECTION WITH THE EARLY AMERICAN FLAG

John Paul Jones was so closely connected with the first American flags afloat, that it is relevant to flag history to mention his association with the tradition of the first "breaking" of the flag, and the first salute to the Stars and Stripes.

Paul Jones's commission as a first lieutenant in the first organization of the American Navy was dated 22 December, 1775, and was presented to him in Independence Hall, by John Hancock in person. It is recorded that immediately upon receipt of his commission, in the company of John Hancock, Thomas Jefferson, and others, he repaired on board the *Alfred*, the flagship of Commodore Hopkins. Captain Saltonstall, the flag captain, was not aboard, and for that reason it has been related that Hancock directed that Lieutenant Jones take charge. He immediately hoisted to the masthead a new ensign, probably the first "flag of America" ever displayed at the mast of an American man-of-war. Admiral Preble in his exhaustive and authoritative study of flags was of the opinion that the flag hoisted by Jones was in all probability the "Union Flag" which was hoisted two weeks later over Washington's Army at Boston. But later writers seem to agree that it was a combination of the "rattlesnake" flag and the "pine tree" flag. This flag had the rattlesnake coiled around the pine tree and the motto, "Don't Tread on Me" underneath. We are certain that the snake was on the flag, for Jones wrote later in his journal:

For my own part, I could never see how or why a venomous serpent could be the combatant emblem of a brave and honest folk, fighting to be free. Of course I had no choice, but to break the pennant as it was given to me. But I always abhorred the device and was glad when it was discarded for one much more symmetrical as well as appropriate a year or so later.

The Union flag was flown when this little force that marked the beginning of the American Navy sailed from Philadelphia. The order of the day that prescribed the sailing of the fleet down the Delaware on 17 February, 1776, specifically said that all vessels should fly "Saint George's ensign with stripes at the mizzen-peak." In all probability this was the Grand Union flag at the hoist of honor, with "the standard at the main top." The standard referred to must have been the "rattlesnake" flag (i.e., seven red stripes, six white stripes, a rattlesnake placed diagonally on the flag, with the motto, "Don't Tread on Me" underneath).

The first operation of the infant Navy was against New Providence in the Bahamas. A writer for the London *Ladies Magazine* wrote at the time that the American ships there had colors "striped under the Union with thirteen stripes and their standard a rattlesnake." This checks closely with the order of the day.

The First Star Spangled Banner

It is to be regretted that we shall never know who stood up in the Continental Congress on Saturday, 14 June, 1777, and motioned for the adoption of the resolution which read that

the flag of the thirteen United States be thirteen stripes, alternate red and white; that the union be thirteen stars, white in a blue field representing a new constellation.

This marks the birth of the flag in practically all respects as we know it today. Colonel Nicholas Smith in his book on the flag wrote:

A flag was wanted to harmonize with the growing spirit of Americanism, one that would beautifully symbolize the aspirations of the thirteen states.

One of the most curious coincidences in American naval history is the fact that at the same hour that the new flag was adopted the daring Jones was ordered to command the *Ranger.* His orders and the flag adoption were not in the same bill, but passed in the same hour. Jones was surely cognizant of this event, for afterwards he wrote in his ever ardent style,

That flag and I were twins; born in the same hour from the same womb of destiny. We cannot be parted in life or death. So long as we can float, we shall float together. If we must sink, we shall go down as one.

After honors, glory, bitterness, and vicissitudes, all that is mortal of John Paul Jones rests at Annapolis under the flag he so gallantly defended.

The Official United States Flag's Baptism of Fire

It has long been a point of discussion and dispute as to where the first official United States flag went into battle. There are three claimants for the honor. Fort Stanwix (Schuyler), now Rome, New York, is the oldest contender for the honor. Colonel Peter Gansevoort then in command defended the fort on 3 August, 1777, against a force composed of British and Indians. Massachusetts re-enforcements brought the news of the adoption by Congress of an official flag. It is recorded that the soldiers cut up their shirts to make the white stripes; scarlet material to form the red, so tradition states, was secured from red flannel petticoats of officers' wives; while material for the blue union was secured from Captain Abraham Swartwout's blue cloth coat. A voucher is extant stating that the captain was paid by Congress for the loss of his coat. But whether this flag was the Grand Union or the Stars and Stripes is still questioned by historians. Of all claims, it has the most popular belief.

After the engagement at Fort Schuyler came the battle of Bennington. The two American flags carried in that battle are still in existence. They are curious flags in design. A good part of one of them is well preserved. The flag has a blue canton with thirteen stars painted thereon. A part of the green field is still attached to the canton.

The other flag is now in the possession of the Bennington Battle Monument and Historical Association. It is certainly a "Stars and Stripes" of a peculiar size and design. The flag is 10 feet long and 5.5 feet wide, with seven white stripes and six red stripes. The striping makes both the bottom and top stripe white. In this connection, it is of interest that when the original certificate of the Society of the Cincinnati was designed in Paris, the engraver used this arrangement of stripes, because it was in accordance with the rules of heraldry. The canton of the flag spanned nine stripes instead of the present seven; it was blue with thirteen white stars. Eleven stars were arranged in an arch, with one in each upper corner. All the stars are seven pointed, with the point directed upwards. Large Arabic numerals "76" are under the arch. It is the oldest Stars and Stripes in existence.

Although there are no records to the effect, it is quite possible that General Gates in command of American troops flew some description of "Stars and Stripes" at the surrender of General Burgoyne in the decisive battle of Saratoga.

There is a third claim that the new official flag was first flown in action at Cooch's Bridge, near Newark, Delaware, on 3 September, 1777. Here Maxwell's advance corps met the British under Howe, and Washington wrote "pretty smart skirmishing" occurred. No reference can be found in official records that the flag was flown there. This corps had been through Philadelphia on its southern march to check the advance of the British, and there is every reason to believe that an official flag was secured in Philadelphia, inasmuch as it had been adopted by Congress on 14 June, but was not officially promulgated until 3 September.

Under date of 12 September, 1932, Mr. C. W. Heathcote, of West Chester, Pennsylvania, in a letter to the New York *Times,* brings additional evidence as to the presence of the first official flag at the Battle of Brandywine. He writes:

However, for the first critical battle of the Revolution, the battle of the Brandywine, the official flag floated. In carrying on research for a considerable period of time, I found a copy of a sermon preached by the Rev. Joab Trout, a chaplain near Washington's headquarters on the eve of the battle, September 10, 1777. He said, "It is a solemn moment, Brethren, does not the solemn voice of nature seem to echo the sympathies of the hour? The flag of our country droops heavily from yonder staff; the breeze has died away along the green plains of Chadd's Ford, the plain that lies before us, glittering in the sunlight, the heights of the Brandywine arising gloomy and grand beyond the waters of yonder stream. All Nature holds a pause of solemn silence on the eve of the uproar, of the bloodshed and strife of tomorrow."

We believe we are correct in assuming that the flag the chaplain refers to is the official flag. It is not likely that Washington would fly any other from his headquarters, and, inasmuch as he was ever correct in matters of etiquette, would not fly the Stars and Stripes until he received its official promulgation. We, therefore, believe that the new United States flag received its baptism in the battle of the Brandywine. The above information is presented as an interesting side light of flag history, although the question of "first flying in battle" has not been definitely settled by historians

THE FIRST UNITED STATES FLAG IN EUROPEAN WATERS

Tradition records that Captain John Paul Jones was presented a flag for the *Ranger* that had been made from the best silk gowns of the ladies of Portsmouth, New Hampshire. Jones furnished the specifications, and it is recorded that the work was done at a quilting party. It is of interest that the white stars were cut from the bridal dress of one Helen Seary. It is most probable that this is the flag that was first saluted at Quiberon Bay, France. Jones describes this most important salute in American history as follows:

I also demanded and obtained a salute from the Flag of France both at Quiberon and at Brest, before the treaty of alliance was announced.

This official report was made to the American Board of Admiralty in March, 1781, as a reply to certain questions that they had propounded. History records the fact that Jones saluted the French Admiral La Motte Picquet with thirteen guns, while the return salute to Jones was nine guns. In the thirteen-gun salute, it was intended that there should be one gun for each state. It is also a matter of record that Jones ascertained in advance that his salute to the white flag of the Bourbons would be returned, although he was disappointed that it would not be returned gun for gun. A kingdom at that time gave a republic (Holland, for example) only nine guns. This is the first record of a salute of honor to the Stars and Stripes at sea.

That Jones's flag received the first salute on 14 February, 1778, is generally accepted; but in this connection it is of historic importance to know that John Adams wrote in a letter to Josiah Quincy that the first American vessel to receive a salute from a foreign power was the *Andrea Doria* in November, 1776, at St. Eustatius in the Dutch West Indies. The flag carried by the *Doria* was probably the Grand Union flag. It was certainly not the Stars and Stripes. Cooper wrote: "For this indiscretion the Dutch Governor was subsequently displaced."

It is of great interest that the salute to the flag in France was rendered before the Treaty of Alliance with France, the first and only treaty of alliance that the United States government has ever made. Had it not been for French aid, it is very doubtful whether the United States would have won the War of Independence.

The first five vessels commissioned by the Congress in December, 1775, carried the first flag of the new Navy. John Adams, a member of the Marine Committee, wrote,

The first was named *Alfred,* in honor of the greatest Navy that ever existed; the second, *Columbus,* after the discoverer of this quarter of the globe; the third, *Cortez,* after the discoverer of the northern part of the continent; the fourth, *Andrea Doria,* in honor of the great Genoese admiral; and the fifth, *Providence,* the name of the town where she was purchased and the residence of Governor Hopkins and his brother Esek, whom we appointed the first captain.

It is true that a salute to the American flag was rendered by the Dutch on 16 November, 1776, after the *Doria* had saluted the Dutch flag, as set forth in John Adams' letter. Nevertheless, it was not a salute to the authorized Stars and Stripes. It is highly probable that the *Andrea Doria,* commanded by Isaiah Robinson, wore the "Union Flag" that Washington hoisted over his army at Cambridge, a flag that was never legalized. The St. Eustatius salute was given by the Dutch about eight months before the legal birth of the Stars and Stripes.

THE FLAG IN EUROPEAN WATERS

Jones had the supreme honor of carrying this first flag into an action on the seas. As Buell in exuberance writes,

This was the first edition of the Stars and Stripes that Europe ever saw; the first to be saluted by the guns of a European naval power, but far beyond, and beyond anything, it was the first and last flag that ever went down or ever will go down flying on the ship that conquered and captured the ship that sunk her.

Be that as it may, it is a glorious tradition for a sea service to start with. Jones in his report eloquently describes the sinking of his vessel, the *Bon Homme Richard,* after those of his crew that were alive had been transferred to the ship of his foe, H.M.S. *Serapis.* Jones writes,

The ensign-gaff shot away in action had been fished and put in place soon after firing ceased, and ours torn and tattered was left flying when we abandoned her. As she plunged down by the head at last her taffrail momentarily rose in the air so the very last vestige mortal eye ever saw of the *Bon Homme Richard* was the defiant waving of her unconquered and unstrucken flag as she went down. And as I had given them the good old ship as their sepulcher, I now bequeathed to my immortal dead the flag they had so desperately defended, for their winding sheet.

Tradition records that this was the flag carried out of Portsmouth in the *Ranger*. But Jones's report contradicts the tradition. The Stars and Stripes that Jones flew on the *Serapis* after taking her as prize is preserved. It has twelve stars in the canton. It is a tradition that one star was cut off and given to President Lincoln as a gift.

The New Flag 1795

After Vermont and Kentucky had been admitted to the Union, they strongly requested to be included in the symbolism of the United States flag. After considerable involved debate in the House of Representatives, a bill was passed that provided that from first day of May, 1795, the flag of the United States be fifteen stripes of alternate red and white; that the union be fifteen white stars in a blue field. This bill was approved by President Washington 13 January, 1794. It was passed by a vote of fifty yeas to forty-two nays.

The Last Alteration to the Flag

For twenty-two years the flag of 1795 was hoisted ashore and afloat, over civilian, military, and naval activities. It was the conquering flag in thirteen out of eighteen naval battles of the War of 1812. It was truly the flag of our golden age on the sea. It had inspired in 1814 at Fort McHenry the words of the stirring song "The Star Spangled Banner," that in 1931 became our official and legal national anthem. The epic of America was taking shape, and from the frontiers five new states were admitted to the Union. There was again considerable debate on the change in the flag. Representative Wendover in a speech on the floor said:

And even on those who predicted that in nine months the striped bunting would be swept from the seas, it possessed the wonderful charm, that before the nine months had elapsed, "fir buildt frigates" and "Yankee Cock Boats" were magnified in ships of the line; and his Majesty's faithful officers, careful for the preservation of British oak, sought protection for their frigates under the convoy of 74-gun ships.

It is interesting to note that in that time there was no uniformity in the number of stripes of the flag. Wendover said,

That, on the hall of Congress, whence laws emanate, has but thirteen, and those of the navy yard and marine barracks have each eighteen. Nor can I omit to mention the flag under which the last Congress sat during its first session, which from some cause or other unknown had but nine stripes.

In reality it was a ragtime period of flag manufacture; there was little uniformity.

A bill was finally passed that provided from the Fourth day of July, 1818:

The flag of the United States be thirteen horizontal stripes of alternate red and white; that the union have twenty white stars in a blue field; that one star be added on the admission of every new state in the Union; and that the admission shall take place on the 4th of July next succeeding such admission.

The bill passed on 31 March, 1818, and was signed by President Monroe on 4 April, 1818.

The signing of this bill marked the settlement of the troublesome national flag question. By the admission of states in the years that followed, the flag of forty-eight stars as we know it today became fixed in appearance and design. It is safe to assume that none will be added and none taken away. An Act of Congress on 26 October, 1912, decreed that there should be from henceforth forty-eight stars arranged in six horizontal rows of eight each, with five-pointed stars, one point on each star directed upwards.

"THE STAR SPANGLED BANNER"

After years of inactivity, bickering, attempts by cliques and individuals to secure recognition of other words and music, on 21 April, 1930, the House adopted the words and music of "The Star Spangled Banner" as the national anthem. It became a law after being adopted by the Senate on 3 March, 1931. Although Congress three times rejected the bill of the late Congressman Linthicum of Maryland, he finally presented a petition which was reported to bear 5,000,000 signatures that were obtained through the co-operation of various patriotic societies. Without commenting on the musical merits of "The Star Spangled Banner," it is interesting to note that when the argument was advanced that the song was pitched too high for popular singing, Mr. Linthicum was instrumental in bringing about a hearing before the House Judiciary Committee at which two sopranos sang and the Navy Band played the strains. The passage of the bill indicates approval (See note, p. 187).

In brief, the history of "The Star Spangled Banner" is here given. Francis Scott Key was inspired to write the words of "The Star Spangled Banner" during the bombardment of Fort McHenry, by a British fleet in 1812. Dr. William Beanes, a prominent and old resident of Upper Marlborough, Maryland, was made prisoner by General Ross of the British Army and confined on Vice-Admiral Sir George Cockrane's flagship, H.M.S. *Surprise*. Francis Scott Key, a very close friend of Dr. Beanes, determined to request the doctor's release and for that reason repaired on the flagship. Admiral Cockrane received Key most cordially; he consented to release Dr. Beanes but informed him that, in view of important operations, it would be necessary for them to remain aboard for a few days.

On the night of 13 September, 1814, the heavy shelling took place. Key, with Beanes and John Skinner, of Baltimore, who accompanied Key, were transferred to the British tender *Minden* just before the attack. After a night of bombardment, Francis Scott Key looked out at dawn towards the fort of his homeland for signs of life. His vision was greeted by "The Star Spangled Banner," although torn and shell-rent, it still floated over the gallant defenders of the old fort. It was then that he wrote the first draft of the song, inscribing the words on the back of an old envelope.[1] His reference to the "foe's haughty host" al-

[1] The original draft of "The Star Spangled Banner" was purchased by the city of Baltimore in 1934 and is now exhibited in the Walters Art Gallery of that city.

luded to the British soldiers of General Ross at North Point.

The motives that gave birth to our national anthem need no commentary. The tradition for our reflection is that noble sentiment, pride in country and flag inspired the legal national anthem of our country. Maryland now observes 14 September as Defenders' Day. The flag that flew through the night may now be seen in the National Museum, Washington. It is pierced with eleven shot holes.

The Star Spangled Banner

Oh, say, can you see by the dawn's early light,
What so proudly we hailed at the twilight's last gleaming;
Whose broad stripes and bright stars, through the perilous fight
O'er the ramparts we watched, were so gallantly streaming?
And the rockets' red glare, the bombs bursting in air,
Gave proof through the night that our flag was still there.

First Chorus

Oh, say, does the star-spangled banner yet wave
O'er the land of the free and the home of the brave?

On the shore, dimly seen thro' the mists of the deep,
Where the foe's haughty host in dread silence reposes,
What is that which the breeze, o'er the towering steep,
As it fitfully blows, half conceals, half discloses?
Now it catches the gleam of the morning's first beam,
In full glory reflected now shines on the stream.

Second Chorus

'Tis the star-spangled banner, oh! long may it wave
O'er the land of the free and the home of the brave.

And where is that band who so vauntingly swore,
That the havoc of war and the battle's confusion
A home and a Country should leave us no more?
Their blood has wash'd out their foul footsteps' pollution;
No refuge could save the hireling or slave
From the terror of flight or the gloom of the grave.

Third Chorus

And the star-spangled banner in triumph doth wave
O'er the land of the free and the home of the brave.

Oh! thus be it ever when free men shall stand
Between their loved home and the war's desolation.
Blest with vict'ry and peace, may the heav'n rescued land
Praise the Pow'r that has made and preserved us a Nation.
Then conquer we must, when our cause it is just,
And this be our motto, "In God is our trust."

Fourth Chorus

And the star-spangled banner in triumph shall wave
O'er the land of the free and the home of the brave.

The fourteenth of June is now observed in practically all
states as Flag Day. There is no law that decrees that this day
shall be observed. "Its observance is based rather on custom
and conventionality, which are often of greater authority than
are decrees and statutes."

FEDERAL LAW AGAINST DESECRATION

There is but one federal statute which protects the flag
throughout the country from desecration. This law provides
that a trade mark cannot be registered which consists of or comprises among other things, "The flag, coat of arms, or other
insignia of the United States or any simulation thereof" (33
Stat. L., p. 725, Feb. 20, 1905). Also penalties have been enacted by Congress for desecration, mutilation, or improper use
of the flag in the District of Columbia (Feb. 8, 1917, 39 Stat.
L., p. 900).

Fringed flags are permitted the infantry and cavalry, but are
not to fly from flag poles. The banners of infantry are called
"colors"; of cavalry, "standards"; of the Navy, "ensigns."

SYMBOLISM OF THE FLAG

The National Flag Conference of 1924, in an appeal to the
honor and loyalty that should be accorded our colors and to
the significance of its history, concluded:

It embodies the essence of patriotism. Its spirit is the spirit of the American nation. Its history is the history of the American people. Emblazoned upon its folds in letters of living light are the names and fame of our heroic dead, the Fathers of the Republic, who devoted upon its altars their lives, their fortunes, and their sacred honor. Twice-told tales of national honor and glory cluster thickly about it. Ever victorious, it has emerged triumphant from eight great national conflicts. It flew at Saratoga, at Yorktown, at Palo Alto, at Gettysburg, at Manila Bay, at Chateau-Thierry. It bears witness to the immense expansion of our national boundaries, the development of our national resources, and the splendid structure of our civilization. It prophesies the triumph of popular government, of civic and religious liberty, and of national righteousness throughout the world.

The symbolism of the flag as understood by the Service is not quite so sweeping, but probably more intensive in its restricted compass. It is difficult to interpret this attitude, but it is assuredly neither the "eagle screaming," Fourth-of-July platitudes, nor the Ku Klux Klan, "100 per cent" credo. Nor is it the approval of a demagogic appeal to "Old Glory" that often smacks of a thin veneer of patriotism subtly concealing motives of self-aggrandizement to organizations and the selfish interests of the individual. Most enlightened men believe that much strife, graft, and needless bloodshed have been perpetrated in the name of patriotism and religion. It is sufficient to say that the Service has been educated and trained "under the flag"; that individuals are sworn to defend the Constitution, and as in the past, so in the future, the Service will consider it the highest and most solemn duty to defend the flag against all enemies. Such training and duty conduce to a symbolism that falls in the category of those sacred things of the spirit, which are seldom paraded in public.

THE FLAG SALUTE AT COLORS ON BOARD SHIP

The salute to the quarter-deck with its venerable history has been explained, but the date when the flag salute at colors became a regulation is not so generally known.

The first order that can be found on the subject is that of Admiral James E. Jouett. The squadron order was dated 22 November, 1884, and read:

The attention of the squadron is called to the fact that at colors no custom has hitherto prevailed of giving appropriate recognition, by salute or otherwise, to the flag, the emblem, not only of the national authority at home, but of liberty and progress throughout the world. Under the conviction that such a recognition is fitting and desirable, and that the custom, if adopted by all, should be the spontaneous expression of a general sentiment, the commander in chief deems it only necessary to express the wish that on board the ships of the North Atlantic Squadron all officers and men who may be on deck at colors will uncover, as far as practicable without serious interruption to the occupation of the moment.

It is interesting to note that in 1884 all salutes were rendered by removing the headdress. And although there was a ceremony for the guard and others who were on duty at colors, the above order clearly indicates that others in the vicinity paid no attention to the ceremony. The custom of standing at attention and saluting became in time a naval regulation. Thus the "wish" of an admiral became the order of our day.

THE FLAG CODE

In order that the officers of the Service may have the best opinion and collected usage pertaining to flag etiquette, there is set forth the Flag Code adopted at the National Flag Conference, Washington, D.C., June 14-15, 1923, and as revised and endorsed at the Second National Flag Conference, Washington, May 15, 1924. The original Flag Conference was convened at the call of the American Legion in Memorial Continental Hall of the National Society Daughters of the American Revolution.

The attention of officers is invited to the fact that the following Flag Code is to be used as a guide—the best obtainable. The code is in the nature of a formulation of customs and conventions gained from best usage and expert authority. They are not statutes and are therefore not enforceable.

DESCRIPTION OF THE FLAG[1]

The Flag of the United States of America has 13 horizontal stripes —seven red, and six white—the red and white stripes alternating, and a union which consists of white stars of five points on a blue field placed in the upper quarter next the staff and extending to the lower edge of the fourth red stripe from the top. The number of stars is the same as the number of States in the Union. The canton or union now contains 48 stars arranged in six horizontal and eight vertical rows, each star with one point upward. On the admission of a State into the Union a star will be added to the Union of the Flag, and such addition will take effect on the 4th day of July next succeeding such admission. The proportions of the Flag, as described by Executive Order of President Taft, October 29, 1912, are as follows:

Hoist (width) of flag	1.
Fly (length) of flag	1.9
Hoist (width) of union	7/13
Fly (length) of union	0.76
Width of each stripe	1/13
Diameter of star	0.0616

THE SHIELD OF THE UNITED STATES OF AMERICA

The shield of the United States of America has 13 vertical stripes, 7 white and 6 red, with a blue chief without stars.

PROPER MANNER OF DISPLAYING THE FLAG

There are certain fundamental rules of heraldry which, if understood generally, would indicate the proper method of displaying the Flag. The matter becomes a very simple one if it is kept in mind that the National Flag represents the living country and is itself considered as a living thing. The union of the Flag is the honor point; the right arm is the sword arm, and therefore the point of danger and hence the place of honor.

[1] Professor Allen Westcott writes: "Chief credit for the present design of the flag is generally accorded to Captain Samuel Chester Reid, famous privateer's man of the War of 1812 and hero of the battle at Fayal between the privateer *General Armstrong* and three British men-of-war. Reid, who was then harbor-master at New York, suggested in 1818 to Representative Wendover that the flag have thirteen stripes and a star for each state, with the stars in parallel rows for military use but arranged in one great star for other purposes. This design, without specification as to the arrangement of the stars, was adopted by Act of Congress 4 April, 1818, and a new flag of twenty stars, made by Mrs. Reid, was hoisted on the Capitol on 13 April following. (See Preble, *History of the Flag of the United States*, pp. 339-50.)"

1. The Flag should be displayed only from sunrise to sunset, or between such hours as may be designated by proper authority. It should be displayed on National and State holidays, and historic and special occasions. The Flag should always be hoisted briskly and lowered slowly and ceremoniously.

2. When carried in a procession with another flag or flags, the Flag of the United States of America should be either on the marching right, i.e., the Flag's own right, or when there is a line of other flags, the Flag of the United States of America may be in front of the center of that line.

3. When displayed with another flag against a wall from cross staffs, the Flag of the United States of America should be on the right, the Flag's own right, and its staff should be in front of the staff of the other flag.

4. When a number of flags of States or cities or pennants of societies are grouped and displayed from staffs with the Flag of the United States of America, the latter should be at the center of the highest point of the group.

5. When flags of States or cities or pennants of societies are flown on the same halyard with the Flag of the United States of America, the latter should always be at the peak. When flown from adjacent staffs the Flag of the United States of America should be hoisted first and lowered last. No such flag or pennant flown in the former position should be placed above, or in the latter position to the right of the Flag of the United States of America, i.e., to the observer's left.

6. When flags of two or more nations are displayed they should be flown from separate staffs of the same height and the flags should be of approximately equal size. (International usage forbids the display of the flag of one nation above that of another nation in time of peace.)

7. When the Flag is displayed from a staff projecting horizontally or at an angle from the window sill, balcony, or front of building, the union of the Flag should go clear to the peak of the staff unless the Flag is at half-staff. (When the Flag is suspended over a sidewalk from a rope, extending from a house to a pole at the edge of the sidewalk, the Flag should be hoisted out from the building towards the pole, union first.)

8. When the Flag is displayed in a manner other than by being flown from a staff it should be displayed flat, whether indoors or out.

When displayed either horizontally or vertically against a wall, the union should be uppermost and to the Flag's own right, i.e., to the observer's left. When displayed in a window it should be displayed the same way, that is, with the union or blue field to the left of the observer in the street. When festoons, rosettes, or drapings of blue, white and red are desired, bunting should be used, but never the Flag.

9. When the Flag is displayed over the middle of the street, as between buildings, the Flag should be suspended vertically with the union to the north in an east and west street or to the east in a north and south street.

10. When used on a speaker's platform, the Flag, if displayed flat, should be displayed above and behind the speaker. If flown from a staff it should be in the position of honor, at the speaker's right. It should never be used to cover the speaker's desk, or to drape over the front of the platform.

11. When used in connection with the unveiling of a statue or monument, the Flag should form a distinctive feature during the ceremony, but the Flag itself should never be used as the covering for the statue.

12. When flown at half-staff, the Flag should be hoisted to the peak for an instant, then lowered to the half-staff position; but before lowering the Flag for the day, it is raised again to the peak. By half-staff is meant hauling down the Flag to one-half the distance between the top and the bottom of the staff. If local conditions require, divergence from this position is permissible. On Memorial Day, May thirtieth, the Flag is displayed at half-staff from sunrise until noon and at full staff from noon until sunset; for the Nation lives and the Flag is the symbol of the living Nation.

13. Flags flown from fixed staffs are placed at half-staff to indicate mourning. When the Flag is displayed on a small staff, as when carried in parade, mourning is indicated by attaching two streamers of black crêpe to the spear head, allowing the streamers to fall naturally. Crêpe is used on the flag-staff only by order of the President.

14. When used to cover a casket, the Flag should be placed so that the union is at the head and over the left shoulder. The Flag should not be lowered into the grave nor allowed to touch the ground. The casket should be carried foot first.

15. When the Flag is displayed in the body of the church, it should be from a staff placed in the position of honor at the congregation's right as they face the clergyman. The service flag, the state flag, or

PROPER MANNER OF DISPLAYING THE FLAG—Note in the upper right corner the proper method of flying a flag or pennant on the same staff with the national ensign. *No flag* is ever hoisted above the national ensign; but during church services aboard ship the church pennant is hoisted above the flag of the United States. (From "The Flag Code" adopted at the National Flag Conference)

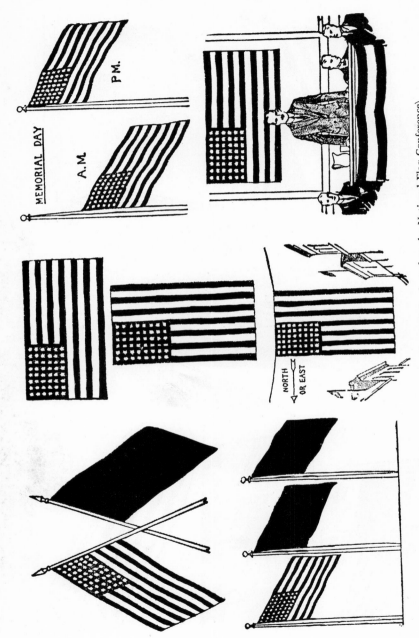

PROPER MANNER OF DISPLAYING THE FLAG (From "The Flag Code" adopted at the National Flag Conference)

other flag should be at the left of the congregation. If in the chancel or on the platform, the Flag of the United States of America should be placed on the clergyman's right as he faces the congregation and the other flags at his left.

16. When the Flag is in such condition that it is no longer a fitting emblem for display, it should not be cast aside or used in any way that might be viewed as disrespectful to the national colors, but should be destroyed as a whole, privately, preferably by burning or by some other method in harmony with the reverence and respect we owe to the emblem representing our country.

CAUTIONS

1. Do not permit disrespect to be shown to the Flag of the United States of America.

2. Do not dip the Flag of the United States of America to any person or any thing. The regimental color, state flag, organization, or institutional flag will render this honor.

3. Do not display the Flag with the union down except as a signal of distress.

4. Do not place any other flag or pennant above or, if on the same level, to the right of the Flag of the United States of America.

5. Do not let the Flag touch the ground or the floor, or trail in the water.

6. Do not place any object or emblem of any kind on or above the Flag of the United States of America.

7. Do not use the Flag as drapery in any form whatever. Use bunting of blue, white, and red.

8. Do not fasten the Flag in such manner as will permit it to be easily torn.

9. Do not drape the Flag over the hood, top, sides, or back of a vehicle, or of a railroad train or boat. When the Flag is displayed on a motor car the staff should be affixed firmly to the chassis, or clamped to the radiator cap.

10. Do not display the Flag on a float in a parade except from a staff.

11. Do not use the Flag as a covering for a ceiling.

12. Do not carry the Flag flat or horizontally but always aloft and free.

13. Do not use the Flag as a portion of a costume or of an athletic uniform. Do not embroider it upon cushions or handkerchiefs nor print it on paper napkins or boxes.

14. Do not put lettering of any kind upon the Flag.

15. Do not use the Flag in any form of advertising nor fasten an advertising sign to a pole from which the Flag is flying.

16. Do not display, use, or store the Flag in such a manner as will permit it to be easily soiled or damaged.

PROPER USE OF BUNTING

Bunting of blue, white, and red should be used for covering a speaker's desk, draping over the front of a platform, and for decoration in general. Bunting should be arranged with the blue above, the white in the middle, and the red below.

SALUTE TO THE FLAG

During the ceremony of hoisting or lowering the Flag, or when the Flag is passing in parade or in a review, all persons present should face the Flag, stand at attention, and salute. Those present in uniform should render the right-hand salute. When not in uniform, men should remove the headdress with the right hand and hold it at the left shoulder, the hand being over the heart. Women should salute by placing the right hand over the heart. The salute to the Flag in the moving column is rendered at the moment the Flag passes.

SALUTE WHEN GIVING THE PLEDGE TO THE FLAG

In pledging allegiance to the Flag of the United States of America the approved practice in schools, which is suitable also for civilian adults, is as follows:

Standing with the right hand over the heart, all repeat together the following pledge:

"I pledge allegiance to the Flag of the United States of America and to the Republic for which it stands.

"One Nation indivisible, with liberty and justice for all."

At the words "to the Flag," the right hand is extended, palm upward, toward the Flag and this position is held until the end, when the hand, after the words "justice for all," drops to the side.

However, civilian adults will always show full respect to the Flag when the pledge is being given, by merely standing at attention, men removing their headdress. Persons in uniform should render the right-hand salute.

SALUTE TO THE NATIONAL ANTHEM

When the National Anthem is played and no Flag is displayed, all present should stand and face toward the music. Those in uniform should salute at the first note of the Anthem, retaining this position until the last note of the Anthem. All others should stand at attention, men removing their headdress. When the Flag is displayed, the regular "Salute to the Flag" should be given.

NOTES ON THE FLAG[1]

When displayed either horizontally or vertically against a wall, in a show window, or elsewhere.

The blue field is uppermost and to the flag's own right, that is, to the observer's left.

In a window, the flag is displayed the same way, that is, with the blue field to the left of the observer in the street.

NOTE.—The reason for displaying the flag with the blue field uppermost and to the flag's own *right* (the observer's *left*) is this: The blue field, according to the rules of heraldry, is the honor point and should, therefore, occupy the position of danger. But the position of danger is the position of the arm which holds the sword, that is, the right arm. Therefore, the blue field of the flag, which faces the observer, should be to its right.

A simple "rule-of-thumb" that tells how to display the flag correctly in either a horizontal or vertical position is this: We always speak of the flag as the Stars and Stripes, never as the stripes and stars. Therefore, when we look at the flag it should read "stars and stripes," that is, the stars (in the blue field) should come first.

When carried in a horizontal position by a number of people, as is sometimes done in parades.

The blue field is at the right (flag's own right) and front.

NOTE.—However, it is a violation of the Flag Code to carry the flag in this manner and it is to be regretted that it is ever done. Everything possible should be done to discourage the practice, which, however good the intentions of those concerned may be, is considered by

[1] *Reserve Officers' Manual, U. S. Navy* (1932).

most people as an unnatural, unusual, and undignified display of the
flag. When carried this way, the flag is often allowed to sag in an
ungainly manner, frequently touching the ground, which sometimes
leads to the abuse of using the sagging flag as a receptacle for hats
and other articles. Hence, it is most desirable that the practice be
discontinued.

When used to cover a casket.

The flag should be placed so that the union is at the head of
the casket and over the left shoulder of the deceased.

NOTE.—The casket should be carried foot first.

The flag must not be lowered into the grave, nor allowed to
touch the ground.

The position of the blue field is reversed on a casket to indicate mourning. With the blue field on the right as the flag
faces the coffin it may be said that the flag is embracing the deceased who in life had served the flag.

*To indicate mourning when the flag is not on a staff but is
displayed flat.*

A black crêpe bowknot, either with or without streamers, is
placed at the fastening points.

NOTE.—Since the flag symbolizes the nation, it should be half-
masted or dressed with crêpe only in cases where it is appropriate to
indicate that the nation mourns. If it is desired to show that a state,
a city, a club, or a society mourns, then the state, city, club, or society
flag should be half-masted or dressed in crêpe. The flag should not
be both half-masted and dressed with crêpe, nor should it ever be
tied in the middle with crêpe to indicate mourning.

INTERESTING FLAG HISTORY AND EXTRAORDINARY SALUTES

The Turkish Flag Flies over Bainbridge in Command of a United States Frigate

In September, 1800, the 26-year-old Captain William Bainbridge in the United States ship *George Washington*, first American man-of-war to enter the Mediterranean, delivered tribute
from the United States government to the Dey of Algiers. The

Dey, after much protest on Bainbridge's part, commandeered the *George Washington* for use in sending a special ambassador to the Sultan of Turkey with money and rich gifts.

The American Consul, General Richard O'Brien, in a report to Bainbridge setting forth in official form the history of the negotiations and formal protest, wrote:[1]

We went on board; the Turkish flag was hoisted at the main of the United States ship, and was saluted with seven guns, as customary.

Painful is the detail, but it contains a narrative of facts. To the truth thereof, witness my hand and seal of office, at Algiers, this 9th day of October, 1800.

Captain Bainbridge[2] wrote at the time to a friend:

The Dey of Algiers, soon after my arrival, made a demand that the United States' ship, *George Washington,* should carry an ambassador to Constantinople with presents to the amount of five or six hundred thousand dollars, and upwards of two hundred Turkish passengers. Every effort was made by me to evade this demand but it availed nothing. The light in which the chief of this regency looks upon the people of the United States may be inferred from his style of expression. He remarked to me, "You pay me tribute, by which you become my slaves; I have therefore a right to order you as I may think proper." The unpleasant situation in which I am placed must convince you that I have no alternative left but compliance, or a renewal of hostilities against our commerce. The loss of the frigate and the fear of slavery for myself and crew were the least circumstances to be apprehended, but I knew our valuable commerce in these seas would fall a sacrifice to the corsairs of this power, as we have here no cruisers to protect it. . . . I hope I may never again be sent to Algiers with tribute unless I am authorized to deliver it from the mouth of our cannon. . . .

Tunis on Request Salutes First

The first national salute by the Regency of Tunis to the U. S. flag was fired to the flagship *North Carolina*, Commodore John Rodgers, in February, 1827. This salute was fired at the request

[1] "American State Papers," II, *Foreign Affairs*, p. 353.
[2] *Life and Service of Commander Wm. Bainbridge, U.S.N.*, 1897, pp. 44-45.

of Dr. S. D. Heap, U. S. Consul General to Tunis. The salute was immediately returned by the *North Carolina*.[1]

Washington's Birthday under Confederate and United States Flags

The Pensacola Navy Yard, fort, barracks, and hospital had been seized by the troops of Alabama and Florida. A secession flag had been hoisted in place of the United States flag. This new flag antedated the Confederate flag and had thirteen stars and stripes, with a blue field and white star in the center. The U.S. frigate *Sabine* and the sloops *Brooklyn* and *St. Louis* were in the offing. Such was the situation when on 22 February, 1861, the hostile forces each saluted in memory of the Father of his Country. The following description was given by a correspondent of *Harper's Weekly:*

At noon on the twenty-second some secession guns in the navy yard, to the right of the hospital, most unexpectedly to us opened a salute; soon after a puff of smoke rolled up from Fort Barrancas, and hid their flag of one star and many stripes, and they were hardly fairly at it before Berryman's port showed a lightning flash, and column of smoke shooting out, paused an instant, rose, and then the breeze striking it in the center, bore it to leeward in an N-like shape over the vessel, while a beautiful ring hung for a moment over the flag at the main then melted softly away, while one could hear exclamations of delight from our men on the ramparts. It was a grand, pleasing but withal melancholy sight; these white puffs of smoke shrouding different flags, and yet honoring one man.

Flag's First Salute by a Foreign Power

Jones fired thirteen guns to the French Admiral La Motte Piquet, on 14 February, 1778, in Quiberon Bay off the coast of France. The salute was returned by nine guns from the French flagship.

Flag Carried around the World

Captain Robert Gray, sailing from Boston on 30 September, 1787, in command of the sloop *Washington,* took command of

[1] Letter from Dr. Heap to his father, Dr. John Heap, Carlisle, Pennsylvania, dated 15 February, 1827.

the *Columbia* in the northwest country. The *Columbia* sailed from Boston at the same time. Gray sailed with a cargo of guns to China and returned to Boston on 10 August, 1790, "having carried the thirteen stars and thirteen stripes for the first time around the world."

Flag Hoisted over the Louisiana Purchase

The Stars and Stripes were first hoisted in Louisiana, 20 December, 1803. It was not until 10 March, 1804, that the formal transfer of upper Louisiana took place. St. Louis, Missouri, has the unique distinction of having been under three flags in twenty-four hours. On 9 March, 1804, the Spanish flag was hauled down and that of France was hoisted. On 10 March, 1804, the flag of the United States was raised for the first time over the vast territory of upper Louisiana.

First Waves from an Old World Fort

By the grace of God, a few Marines, and thirty-odd Greeks, Lieutenant Presley N. O'Bannon, U. S. Marine Corps, a Kentuckian, took the battery that defended the city of Derne, Tripoli. O'Bannon routed the enemy, turned the guns on the fleeing Tripolitans, and planted the flag on the fort.

Hoisted over the Castle of Chapultepec, Mexico

After General Santa Anna had been forced out of Mexico City by Pillow's and Quitman's Divisions, Captain Benjamin S. Roberts, of Vermont, on orders planted a stand of colors on the ancient palace of the Montezumas.

Lowering and Raising the Flag at Fort Sumter

On Sunday, 14 April, 1861, the United States flag of Fort Sumter was lowered and saluted with fifty guns during the lowering, by order of Major Robert Anderson, U. S. Army, in command. A premature discharge of a gun during the salute resulted in the death of a United States soldier, the first fatality of the Civil War. The fort had made a game defense but could not withstand the heavy Confederate bombardment. The lowering of this flag marks the beginning of the bloody, long drawn-out Civil War.

The Confederates were not forced from Fort Sumter until 17 February, 1865. To celebrate and mark the restoration, it was ordered that on Washington's birthday, 1865, West Point and all forts, arsenals, and garrisons in the United States fire a national salute. "General Order No. 50," Adjutant General's Office, Washington, of date 27 March, 1865, ordered:

That at the hour of noon on the fourteenth day of April, 1865, Brevet Major General Anderson will raise and plant upon the ruins of Fort Sumter, in Charleston Harbor, the same U.S. flag which floated over the battlements of that fort during the rebel assault, and which was lowered and saluted by him and the small force of his command when the works were evacuated on the fourteenth day of April, 1861.

That the flag, when raised, be saluted by 100 guns from Fort Sumter, and by a national salute from every fort and rebel battery that fired upon Fort Sumter.

The American Flag Replaces That of Spain at Santiago

Admiral Sampson and Commander Schley defeated the Spanish fleet of the gallant Spanish Admiral Pasçual Cervera after it emerged on 3 July, 1898, from the harbor of Santiago, Cuba. The harbor had been unsuccessfully sealed by the daring deed of Lieutenant Richmond Pearson Hobson in the *Merrimac*. The naval action and the success of the United States Army in the battle of San Juan Hill and El Caney forced the surrender of Santiago on 17 July, 1898. General Castellanos formally surrendered the government to General John Brooke, U. S. Army, on 1 January, 1899, and the Spanish flag with the arms of Ferdinand and Isabella, the sovereigns for whom Columbus discovered the new world, was lowered on Morro, Havana. By this act the last vestige of Spanish sovereignty was lost in this hemisphere.

The Spanish Lieutenant Müller y Tejerio wrote 17 July, 1898 in regard to the surrender of Santiago:

In conformity with the terms of the capitulation, the surrender of the city to the American Army took place today. At 9 P.M., the Spanish flag was hoisted on Punta Blanca Fort and saluted by twenty-one

SPAR DECK OF THE U.S.S. *Hartford*—Note the short jackets, cap and straw hat worn by the two officers in the foreground. (From a photograph entered in the clerk's office for Eastern District of Louisiana, 10 November, 1864)

guns; shortly after it was lowered. At 9:30 Generals Toral and Shafter, commander in chief of the Spanish and American forces, respectively, the latter accompanied by his staff and many of the commanders and officers of the American fleet, witnessed the marching by, under arms, of a company of the former, representing all the Spanish forces, as it was difficult to assemble them. The American forces presented arms and beat a march.

The heights of Conosa were the theater of this sad scene. . . .

The troops having evacuated the city, 1,000 men of the United States Army entered it, hoisting the flag of that nation at the Palace and Morro Castle.[1]

Flag Flies over Manila in the Philippines

Commodore Dewey and the American Asiatic Fleet destroyed and captured the Spanish fleet of Admiral Montojo at Manila on 1 May, 1898. It was not until 12 August, 1898, that the protocol of agreement was signed between Spain and the United States. On 13 August, Dewey sent the following dispatch to Washington:

Manila, August 13. Secretary Navy, Washington: Manila surrendered today to the American land and naval forces, after a combined attack. A division of the squadron shelled the forts and entrenchments at Malate on the south side of the city, driving back the enemy, our Army advancing from that side at the same time. City surrendered about five o'clock, the American flag being hoisted by Lieutenant Thomas M. Brumby. About 7,000 prisoners were taken. The squadron had no casualties; none of the vessels were injured.

On August 7, General Wesley Merritt and I demanded the surrender of the city, which the Spanish general refused.

DEWEY

The Discovery of the North Pole by a Naval Officer

The world was excited on receipt of the following message: "Indian Head Harbor, via Cape Roy, N.F., September 6, 1909. To Associated Press, New York: 'Stars and Stripes' nailed to North Pole. PEARY."

[1] The American ensign hoisted over the Morro at the harbor entrance was a yacht ensign. This flag was sent by Captain E. T. Pollock (retired) in 1933, to the Naval Academy.

It was after twenty years of polar exploration that Robert E. Peary, civil engineer officer, United States Navy, on 6 April, 1909, reached the top of the earth. The fragment of the flag he deposited there in a glass bottle was a part of the silken flag presented to him by his wife fifteen years before. Small fragments had been left by Peary at all his "farthest norths" in the years that preceded his discovery.

'Stars and Stripes" Fly over British Parliament

The flag of the United States flew over the highest spire of the British parliament building on 20 April, 1917, the first foreign flag ever to fly there. This was in celebration of the entry of the United States in the World War. War was declared on 6 April, 1917.

Byrd Makes First Flight in Airplane over North and South Poles

On 9 May, 1926, Lieutenant Commander Richard Evelyn Byrd, U. S. Navy (Retired),[1] made the first airplane flight over the North Pole. A weighted American flag was dropped by him on the calculated "top of the earth." On 29 November, 1929, Commander Byrd flew over the South Pole in an airplane, and from a trap door in the plane dropped an American flag weighted with a stone brought from the grave of his comrade, dear friend, and pilot on the North Pole flight, Floyd Bennet, former Chief Aviation Pilot, U. S. Navy. At a later date, Byrd made another flight over the Pole and in memory of Scott and Amundsen dropped the flags of their respective countries, on the "bottom of the earth."

The Origin of the Term "Old Glory"

The story that the writer has found in various books and papers states that Captain William Driver, of Salem, Massachusetts, gave the name "Old Glory" to a flag that was presented to him by a committee of ladies, in 1831, in recognition of some special kindness rendered by him. The original "Old Glory" was hoisted on his brig, the *Charles Daggett.*

[1] Afterward commissioned by Congress Rear Admiral (Retired).

At the time of the occupation of Nashville, Tennessee, by the Federal troops, on 25 February, 1862, a United States flag was first hoisted by the Sixth Ohio Volunteers, but was hauled down a few minutes later and Driver's original "Old Glory" hoisted in its place.

In an article titled "Adventures of Old Glory," William E. Beard,[1] the author, relates how

Captain Driver, at the time of the occupation of Nashville, retired from the sea and residing in the Tennessee city, had sacredly preserved his flag during the exciting times of secession and had the distinction of raising it with his own hands over the state house. Nashville thus became the only city over which the original "Old Glory" ever floated as an emblem of war.

[1] William E. Beard, "Adventures of Old Glory," Naval Institute PROCEEDINGS, LIII, No. 289. The author acknowledges an indebtedness to Mr. Beard for the use of dispatches quoted and valuable information relating to the flag.

NOTE.—To secure the petitions in support of the measure that ultimately made the "Star Spangled Banner" the legal national anthem, great credit must go to a Spanish-American War veteran, "Daddy" Joyce, who worked zealously for nine years on this measure. Mrs. Harvey L. Miller, Chairman of the National Legislation Committee of the Veterans of Foreign Wars Ladies' Auxiliaries, gained mainly by her own efforts the final legislative support required to pass the Linthicum Bill.

CHAPTER VIII

THE GOLDEN AGE
NAVAL WAR 1812-1815

"This war should be studied with increasing diligence; the pride of two peoples to whom naval affairs are so generally familiar has cleared all the details and laid bare all the episodes, and at every step can be seen that great truth, that there is only success for those who know how to prepare for it."

—ADMIRAL JURIEN DE LA GRAVIÉRE[1]

"The material results were not very good, at least in their effect on Great Britain, whose enormous Navy did not feel in the slightest degree the loss of a few frigates and sloops. But morally the result was of inestimable benefit to the United States. The victories kept up the spirits of the people, cast down by the defeats on land; practically decided in favor of the Americans the chief question in dispute—Great Britain's right of search and imprisonment—and gave the Navy, and thereby the country, a worldwide reputation."

—ROOSEVELT[2]

Men, if still we dare to argue that we're just as good as they,
We can seek the God of Battle on our knees, and humbly pray
That the work we leave behind us, when our earthly race is run,
May be half as well completed as our Father's work was done.
—CAPTAIN RONALD HOPWOOD, R.N.[3]

"What you from your fathers have inherited,
Earn it, in order to possess it."

—GOETHE

GOLDEN age is a general term applied to the most brilliant portion of a phase of history or department of activity. Such ages in a particular field of human endeavor tower above other periods, as mankind looks back along the bridge that links the present with the past. To students of these divisions of history, generally accepted as epochal, there may be found a wealth of material and a source of inspiration and thought that should lead to a better knowledge of mankind's stumbling advance.

Liberally educated minds are in general agreement as to the

[1] *Guerres Maritimes.*　　[2] *Naval War of 1812.*　　[3] *Our Fathers.*

superlative place of these ages in history. For example, the greatness of the Roman Empire and the ancient glory of Greece are beyond controversy. Few qualified men will dispute the profound impress that Homer, Sophocles, Socrates, Plato, and Vergil gave to letters and philosophy. The genius that stamped the golden ages of sculpture and art gives today to artists and connoisseurs their highest inspiration and appreciation. It cannot be gainsaid that thoughtful men will ever cease to marvel at noble artistry and superb skill, well knowing that there are few Pericleses, Michael Angelos, Raphaels, Dantes, Miltons, Shakespeares, and Goethes in a score of centuries—giants, who gave to successive ages definitive criteria that serve to mark progression or retrogression in their respective spheres of intellectual and artistic activity.

In the profession of arms ashore and afloat, there have been golden ages when leaders of unquestioned superiority were followed by men so inspired by ardent loyalty and devotion to cause, that for long periods all made for victory. One recalls the campaigns of Caesar, Gustavus Adolphus, Frederick the Great, and Napoleon, the success of the mariners of Elizabethan England as well as the superb genius that was exemplified in all that Lord Nelson directed.

Recorded history contains a plethora of golden ages of all descriptions of achievement and glory in the categories of letters, science, art, and the military-naval profession. We are here concerned with achievement on the sea, and more specifically of the United States at war at sea. Indeed in the naval profession there must be standards—measuring rods. It is doubtful that any United States naval campaign ever exceeded the brilliant exploits, the fine leadership, the high morale of crew, and the superb seamanship of the Naval War of 1812.

It is not merely a heroic saga for lovers of high adventure. The impetus that the Navy of 1812 gave to a new service is incalculable; the wealth of tradition that was bequeathed as a heritage is priceless. The unselfish devotion to duty that characterized the leaders and the majority of the men is a refreshing chapter of our nation's history.

In such a study, for what should one search? It is not necessary that one look for lessons in seamanship, for to wear, box-haul, or reef sail on a frigate, are arts that are dead. But rather to mark the intrepid spirit of the sea officers of 1812, their unqualified honor, their bravery and their gallantry, with their mastery of profession, is to review even with a discount of the frailty of human nature, the fundamental qualities of great leadership at apogee.

Past deeds tend to inspire the accomplishment of future action. The Navy is supposed to be and is bred to arms. Therefore, when an appreciation of tradition and the weight of inspiration waxes cold within us; when routine duties become dull; when years of attention to the details have dulled the imagination, let us turn back to the refreshing study of the exploits of our own officers and the men who went before us and with tremendous odds against them won the respect of their powerful adversary and the praise of the great powers of the world. For what? For what we all aspire to when the call comes—*preparedness, action,* and *victory*.

There will come an hour in every officer's career when he experiences the need of precedent, inspiration, memory of another's greatness. Personalities of golden ages give the profession of arms these precedents. But they will not be acquired except by thoughtful study, meditation, and an effort to retain in vision their distinct images.

That the United States Naval War 1812-1815 is our naval golden age is a thesis that is strongly supported and to that end certain pertinent proof will be introduced.

The War of 1812 was fought primarily over opposite views of the United States and Great Britain as to the rights of belligerents and neutrals on the sea. It was the result of long conflict of the British doctrine, "once a subject always a subject," with the American law of citizenship requiring five years of residence and the execution of certain forms. Moreover, there was the British system of impressing crews for men-of-war which had been a customary practice in the British Navy, and which had caused much bitterness when the British extended the policy to the search of American ships for British seamen. Also, Great Britain held that she had the right to search any neutral ship for property and the nationals of her enemies. Of course, due to impressment in the British Navy, many British seamen deserted and sailed under the American flag. Roosevelt, in his *Naval War of 1812,* said: "Equally probable is it that the American blockade runners were guilty of a great deal of fraud or less thinly veiled perjury."

Many incidents over a period of years led up to this "second war of the Revolution." The Navy had never forgotten the *Chesapeake-Leopard* affair when, without declaration of war, H.M.S. *Leopard* (54 guns) made a surprise attack on U.S.S. *Chesapeake* (38 guns); killed or wounded twenty-two of the crew; and took off four alleged deserters. One alleged deserter was hanged by the British. Captain James Barron was suspended from duty for five years on charges that his ship was not ready for action. The British captain received a letter of commendation from his admiral which stated:

You have conducted yourself most properly. I hope you mind the published accounts as little as I do. We must make allowances for the state of the populace in a country where law and every tie, both civil and religious, is treated so lightly.

The small, weak service knew that events were moving on to conflict.

What was the caliber and character of the officers and men of the Navy? What type of training and discipline had this "substantially similar" branch of the English race afloat? The officers and men had had for the most part very active service. Traditions had been made. Some of the older officers and men had served in the War of the Revolution and recounted tales of Barney, Jones, and the roving privateering of the preceding century. It had been a hard, rough school, but it had developed skilled seamen.

The officers were all practical seamen. In the small United States Navy their promotion had been won mainly by their skill in ship handling and their attention to the drill of their crews, both in seamanship and gunnery. Their metal had been tried against the French, and at Tripoli their prowess against the Moors had become history. Theodore Roosevelt refers particularly to the officers' devotion to duty and flag.

Beyond almost any of his countrymen, he [the American naval officer] worshipped the Gridiron Flag and, having been brought up in the Navy, regarded its honor as its own. It was, perhaps, the Navy alone that thought itself a match, ship against ship, for Great Britain. The remainder of the nation pinned its faith to the Army, or rather to that weakest of weak reeds, the Militia. The officers of the Navy, with their strong *ésprit de corps,* their jealousy of their own name and record, and the knowledge, by actual experience, that the British ships sailed no faster and were no better handled than their own, had no desire to shirk a conflict with any foe, and having tried their bravery in actual service, they made it doubly formidable by cool, wary skill.

General apathy on the part of the legislative branch of the government caused the little service to band together more closely, to maintain the highest discipline and morale. For in 1808 the Navy had in commission one frigate and two smaller vessels. Jefferson did not desire to build a Navy but considered that 257 small defense gunboats could protect the coasts. He wrote to a friend:

Believing that gunboats are the only water defense which can be useful to us and protect us from the ruinous folly of a Navy, I am pleased with everything which promises to improve them.

The administration of the Navy Department was grossly inefficient for a period of years prior to 1812. When it was proposed to lay up the small Navy in port during the war, it was extremely fortunate for the Navy and the country that Charles Stewart and William Bainbridge were in Washington. Their ardent protests helped to prevent the execution of this policy.

The seamen of this period were as efficient and competent in their spheres as the officers. They were shrewd, bold, and daring. For the most part, their training had been acquired in the Merchant Service, with the exception of a scattering of the man-of-war's men who were in the War of the Revolution, in the two victories of the *Constellation,* and possibly some who were with

Sail Plan of the U. S. Frigate *Constitution*, "Old Ironsides" (See footnote, opposite page)—"Her deck once red with heroes' blood, Where knelt the vanquished foe,"—Oliver Wendell Holmes. (From pen and ink drawing, Courtesy Naval Records and Library, Navy Department)

Decatur when he cut out the *Philadelphia* at Tripoli with a handful of men. These seamen of 1812 already had traditions to live up to. Training and the "sea habit" were theirs. Before entering the Service, they had followed their calling in the East India trade; or run the blockade to France with the Baltimore clippers; or sailed in the whalers of New Bedford to the border of the Antarctic; and most of the New Englanders had in their youth been to the Grand Banks after cod and halibut. Sailor-men all.

This sturdy stock of the New World may have overemphasized the abstract word "liberty," but they knew it did not lie in impressment on British ships. They detested the British Navy, the British flag, in other words, the system; but they had no particular grudge against those of their own blood, the English seamen.

In general, there was very little difference between the Yankee and British sailor. At that time, they looked much alike and had the same speech. Both English and American seamen were then the boldest, coolest, and most intelligent seamen in the world. Roosevelt comments:

What choice there was, was in favor of the American. In point of courage there was no difference whatever. The *Essex* and the *Lawrence,* as well as the *Frolic* and the *Reindeer,* were defended with the same stubborn, desperate, cool bravery that marks the English race on both sides of the Atlantic. But the American was a free citizen, anyone's equal, a voter with a personal interest in his country's welfare, and, above all, without the degrading fear of the press gang perpetually before his eyes.

So much for the seamen—what kind of ships did they fight?

The frigates of 1812 did credit to their builders. They were for the most part fast sailers, and, in the hands of trained seamen, they were handled with consummate skill. It is true that the

FOOTNOTE.—Note the aftermost fore-and-aft sail, the ringtail (sail) abaft spanker. The triangular sail on the mizzenmast and above the spanker is a gaff topsail. The sails on the yards of the foremast from the deck aloft are: foresail, fore topsail, and to the right fore-top-studding sail; fore-topgallant sail, and to the right the fore-topgallant-studding sail; fore royal, and to the right fore-royal-studding sail; fore skysail. Note the staysails spread fore and aft between the fore and main and between the main and mizzen.

American 44-gun frigate was a more formidable ship than the British 38's, but the statement has often been made by British historians, particularly by James, that they were "disguised line of battle ships." This is not true. The smallest line of battle ships of that day, the 74, threw a broadside of 1,032 pounds, while the real broadside of the United States frigate *United States* threw a normal 846 pounds and a real 786 pounds. In fact, the British ship of the line compared to the United States frigate in broadside threw three to two, or two to one. Credit must be given where due, and although it is to the credit of the Service and the builders of its ships that the American frigates surpassed the British frigates in armament, it was in the use of the guns that the superiority was marked. Roosevelt goes into detail to compare the weight of broadside, and in their well-known actions he itemizes the guns and carronades and gives the following totals:

Constitution		*Guerrière*
Broadside, Nominal ...736		Broadside ....556 lb.
Real 684		
United States		*Macedonian*
Broadside, Nominal ...846		Broadside ....547 lb.
Real 786		
Constitution		*Java*
Broadside, Nominal ...704		Broadside ....576 lb.
Real 654		

The *Constitution* found the 42-pound carronades too heavy, and in the *Java* action carried 10 less than in the *Guerrière* action. Long 18's were the largest British guns employed in the above actions against United States' long 24's, but the defeat may be ascribed to superior seamanship and gunnery on the part of the Americans. The gunnery superiority has been conceded by various British writers.

In a most comprehensive study and authoritative text on the customs and history of the British seamen, *The British Tar in Fact and Fiction,* by Commander Robinson, Royal Navy, and John Leyland, one marks a British opinion:

After Trafalgar, the Navy stood at the height of its splendour, and its officers felt the fullest confidence in their prowess. They had despised their foes, and when they encountered the young American Navy they despised their new foes also. They had begun to pay less attention to gunnery, and the failure in this matter, resting partly upon too much pride and self-confidence, prepared the way for many discomfitures. . . . The lesson of the war is so clear that it should be unnecessary to point it out. Two races had met in conflict, each of them high in intelligence, and each of them possessing the true fighting edge, and the victory often went in the single-ship actions to that side which had earned it by thoroughness of preparation. Here we notice also that when equality of fighting power is reached, and ships and squadrons are handled equally well by their officers generally, it is the quality of the gunnery officers and seamen gunners that tells most in the deadly effect of the gunfire, and thus it was that the seamen of the United States, in the War of 1812-15, often with some advantage in the weight of their broadsides, exercised in many of these minor actions the deciding influence for success.

War had been declared. Yet what went by the name of a Navy Department had done little to meet the approaching crisis. It is unthinkable that a weak Navy such as ours, with war imminent, should have been so widely scattered. With the exception of Commodore John Rodgers' squadron, it would be difficult to conceive of greater naval unpreparedness. The *Constellation, Chesapeake, Adams*, and *John Adams* were out of commission. The *Constitution* was at Annapolis shipping a new crew. But by the twenty-first of June, all of Commodore John Rodgers' squadron was ready with the exception of the *Essex*. The doughty, competent old Commodore's broad command pennant flew on the 44-gun frigate *President*. With him were the *United States* (44), *Congress* (38), *Hornet* (18), and *Argus* (16). We must not forget that Captain Stephen Decatur commanded the *United States;* and Lieutenant James Lawrence, the *Hornet*. Rodgers started the cruise and the war by calling all hands to quarters and in sailor style said:

Now lads, we have got something to do that will shake the rust from our jackets. War is declared! We shall have another dash at our old enemies. It is the very thing you have long wanted. The rascals have been bullying over us these ten years, and I am glad the time has come when we can have satisfaction.

Rodgers sailed within an hour after war was declared. He had been watching the situation; knew that a British convoy from Jamaica had sailed on 20 May and should be off our coast; and decided that a bold, powerful stroke should be made at once. By prompt sailing, after concentration on 21 June, he missed the orders from the Navy Department to the effect that he establish a patrol on the coast. Some time after this move he wrote:

My calculations were even if I did not succeed in destroying the convoy, that leaving the coast as we did would distract the enemy, oblige him to concentrate a considerable portion of his active navy, and at the same time prevent his single cruisers lying before any of our principal ports, from their not knowing to which and at what moment, we might return.

Frost, in *We Build a Navy*, says: "This idea was an inspiration of genius and stamps Rodgers as the leading strategist of our early Navy."

It is regretted that due to the scope of this work only the salient features of various actions may be examined, the headlines of the actions, the deeds that live on in the traditions of our Service.

After the *Constitution* sailed from Annapolis with new gun crews, she fell in with Broke's squadron off the coast. Here the brilliant seamanship of Hull and his first lieutenant, Morris, was displayed in escaping by kedge hauling. Although it looked as if escape was impossible, Captain Hull calmly told Lieutenant Morris: "Let's lay broadside to them, Mr. Morris, and fight the whole. If they sink us, we'll go down like men!"

The *Essex* was not ready for sea and so Captain David Porter did not sail with Rodgers. But his later ventures and long thrilling cruise in the Pacific fill pages of naval history.

The *Essex* was not properly armed, for instead of the usual 18- or 24-pound long guns, she was given but six long 12's and the rest of the broadside were carronades, a very useful short-range, point-blank gun, but of no use for long-range work. Porter protested, but the Navy Department of the day refused to change the armament.

But here we gain a useful lesson, a fine tradition. After protest and recommendation to improve the commands, the sea officers of this day redoubled their efforts to make the most of what they had. This Porter did. He knew that with his carronades he would have to fight close action and attempt whenever possible to carry the day by boarding. Farragut, who afterwards became a distinguished admiral of the Navy, was a midshipman on board and wrote:

Every day the crew was exercised at the great guns, small arms, and single stick. And I may mention here the fact that I have never been on board a ship where the crew of the old *Essex* was represented but that I found them to be the best swordsmen on board. They had been so thoroughly trained as boarders that every man was prepared for such an emergency, with his cutlass as sharp as a razor, a dirk made by the ship's armorer out of a file, and a pistol.

Porter's officers and crew always reflected this training and drill. This is the David Porter who, after the shortcomings of Jeffersonian naval policy were apparent, said:

The vital error, if not criminal neglect of the government, is in not introducing the naval element into the Navy Department. Experienced officers would have avoided the terrible mistakes which have been committed within my recollection, and we would have had now such a respectable force of frigates that Great Britain would not have dared to go to war with us, for fear of having her commerce destroyed. Thirty frigates on our side would make her respect us.

Did we learn a lesson? Did the last three administrations by their naval policy really lead to disarmament or did they weaken the power of the Navy to support their policy in the Pacific? What is the result of ponderous moral pretensions without power? Upon whom will the blame rest when a Navy has to fight that has been made purposely inadequate? To reflect upon such questions is certainly the duty of the Service. At this writing (1934) laws have been passed and measures taken to bring the Navy to treaty strength.

But back to the golden age. One of the most decisive and

intense frigate duels in our history occurred during the twenty-five minutes that it took Hull in the *Constitution* to dismast and defeat the *Guerrière,* commanded by the gallant Dacres. This victory was the sea-Saratoga of the War of 1812; it bolstered up the administration; raised the morale of the people; and gave the Navy a high mark at which to shoot.

Much inspiration for the officer of today may be derived from an examination of the action of Hull. Smith, a gun sponger, who wrote the most vivid narrative extant of the action, said,

Hull was now all animation. He saw the decisive moment had come. With great energy, yet calmness of manner, he passed around among the officers and men, addressing to them words of confidence and encouragement. "Men," said he, "now do your duty. Your officers cannot have entire command over you now. Each man must do all in his power for his country." The Stars and Stripes never floated more proudly than they did at that moment. All was silent beneath them, save the occasional order from an officer, or the low sound of the movement of our implements of war! *Every man stood firm to his post.*

There's a tradition never to forget. It was reported by the three survivors of the U.S.S. *Akron* that, when the great dirigible crashed in the Atlantic, *every man stood firm to his post.*

News was widespread of the *Constitution-Guerrière* action. The London *Times* wrote: "Never before in the history of the world did an English frigate strike to an American." John Paul Jones's victory should not have been forgotten so soon, for not only did the *Serapis* strike but Jones sailed away in her after seeing his command, the *Bon Homme Richard,* sink with colors flying.

For high adventure, one should read of that grand old sailor Barney, of Baltimore, who started a privateering cruise in the Baltimore schooner *Rossie.* Barney's capture of the *General Monk* in the War of the Revolution and a review of his sea career of forty years cause one to conclude that he was a master seaman and an officer who knew no fear. Barney had the distinction of serving in two wars, as well as in the Navy of France. He was perhaps at his best as a privateersman, for once in eleven days he captured twelve ships.

Next came Decatur in the *United States* and captured the *Macedonian*. It was a long-range gunnery duel in contrast to Hull's close action in the *Guerrière* fight. The *United States* and the *Macedonian* compared in size and armament with the *Constitution* and *Guerrière*. By the system of British tonnage measurements, the *Constitution* was 1,426 to 1,338 for the *Guerrière*. The Yankees carried 24 pounders while the British considered 18 pounders more effective. The United States frigates were about one inch thicker. The British considered that the increased weight would make clumsy sailers. But a seaman's heart must have thrilled at Decatur's seamanship and maneuvers in the *Macedonian* duel. British gunnery was very poor and in ninety minutes Decatur had inflicted 104 casualties. With 11 casualties in the *United States,* Decatur achieved a complete victory.

Bainbridge gained a victory in the *Constitution*. He fought the *Java* in probably the fiercest frigate action of the "second war for American Independence." Bainbridge was badly wounded but kept his station on deck. Lieutenant Aylwin fell with wounds that caused his death—Aylwin who saw also the battle ensign of the *Guerrière* lowered. Another Yankee victory! Bainbridge was fêted in Boston. "Old Ironsides" was laid up for overhaul. The British Admiralty issued orders that British frigates were not to engage American 44's in single action.

Then James Lawrence's immortal tradition—the battle cry of the Golden Age! The criticism of Lawrence's judgment in fighting the *Shannon* under the able Broke will not be discussed. There is a variance of opinion. Suffice it to say that Lawrence was a chivalrous soul, as ambitious as a Nelson, as brave as John Paul Jones. He landed with Porter in Tripoli; he made that hazardous climb over the *Philadelphia's* side with Stephen Decatur; he thirsted for fame and the superiority of American arms. Broke was a brilliant and competent captain. After devastating and superior gunfire, Broke boarded the *Chesapeake*. His men were seasoned and experienced; Lawrence had taken over a new ship, and there had been little drill together.

Lawrence fell mortally wounded. After being carried below to the cockpit, he would cry out:

Go on deck, and order them to fire faster and to fight the ship till she sinks; never strike, let the colors wave while I live.

When he knew that the defeat was decisive, he said over and over again: "Don't give up the ship, blow her up."

The fighting had been fierce, and 146 Yankees had been killed or wounded; Lawrence lived four days after the action and, in the intense suffering of mind and body, kept saying "Don't give up the ship." What indomitable courage, what devotion to duty! Nelsonian in every attribute. Before his death he talked to his officers of why he failed. Washington Irving wrote:

It was thus he devoted the last of his moments to usefulness and instruction, teaching his friends how to improve upon his precedent, showing the survivors the way out of the wreck to rise.

Lawrence left us a double tradition, to fight a ship of equal strength with chances of victory and to realize that an officer's greatness lies in his willingness to admit mistakes, so that others may profit by the lessons of experience.

Next, we lost the *Argus* to the British *Pelican*. Allen, the American captain, had poor gunners; he had not devoted enough time to drills. In the first few minutes, a shot tore Allen's leg off. He fell but, by raising up from the deck, he continued to give orders. He fainted; his life blood ebbed; he died at his post. His ship was taken by boarding; his crew left their posts. It is a dark spot, this leaving their posts by the crew—the Captain died at his.

The American *Enterprise* met the *Boxer*. Both ships were evenly matched. Captain Blyth of the *Boxer* was killed in the first few minutes of action. Burrows was mortally wounded, and he too lay on the quarter-deck voicing the tradition of Lawrence, repeating that the colors must not be struck. Just before his death, Burrows received the sword of the enemy and said, "I am satisfied, I die contented."

Each captain did his duty, each died as a promising naval career seemed to show ahead. Burrows, the American, and Blyth, the Englishman, were buried side by side at Portland, Maine.

Finally, there was brave Macdonough on Lake Champlain.

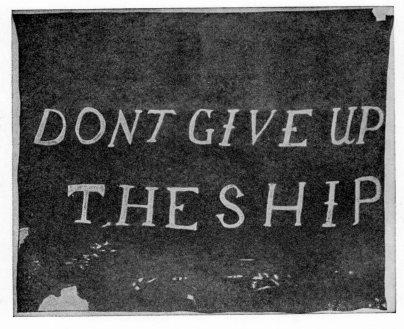

PERRY'S BATTLE FLAG (From *Makers of Naval Tradition,* by Alden and Earle)

We have met the enemy and they are ours: Two Ships, two Brigs one Schooner & one Sloop.

Yours, with great respect and esteem

O H Perry.

FACSIMILE OF PERRY'S DESPATCH

After the action, Sir George Prevost made great haste to return to Canada, and the northern frontier was never again seriously menaced. There is little doubt that Macdonough's splendid victory had a decided effect on the peace negotiations.

After a detailed and comprehensive study of Macdonough in the *Naval War of 1812*, Roosevelt said:

But Macdonough in this battle won a higher fame than any other commander of the war, British or American. He had a decidedly superior force to contend against, the officers and men of the two sides being about on a par in every respect; and it was solely owing to his foresight and resource that he won the victory. He forced the British to engage at a disadvantage by his excellent choice of position; and he prepared beforehand for every possible contingency. His personal prowess had already been shown at the cost of the rovers of Tripoli. . . . His skill, seamanship, quick eye, readiness of resource, and indomitable pluck are beyond all praise. Down to the time of the Civil War, he is the greatest figure in our naval history. A thoroughly religious man, he was as generous and humane as he was skillful and brave; one of the greatest of our sea captains, he has left a stainless name behind him.

We had some defeats, losing the *Essex* and the *President*. Chauncey made history on Lake Ontario. Perry prepared his squadron on Lake Erie. But there could be no more fit conclusion to this sketch of the golden age than to carry always in our memory Perry's action after the conference with his captains on the *Lawrence*. He brought back a flag that hangs today in a place of great honor at Annapolis. It was of blue, with rough white muslin letters, the words thereon being those of the chivalrous Lawrence, "DON'T GIVE UP THE SHIP." He told his captains that it would be the battle signal. Frost appropriately says in his detailed study of the War of 1812,

Ah! what a battle flag to fight under! Every vessel of our Navy should today carry an exact copy of this famous flag to be hoisted before going into action.

Some of the outstanding actions of this heroic age of the Navy have been presented. Purposely, details have been omitted. The tactics of the single-ship action and the general strategy such as that on the Lakes will only be learned by a study of the naval history. Mistakes were certainly made, some of them glaring ones. Commander Frost writes,

A blanket approval of all the events of our early history does not distinguish between the excellent, the good, and the mediocre. It lowers our standard of measuring ability.[1]

It is for critical analysis of historical data to disclose those mistakes in methods. We are concerned here with the motives that inspired the Service and their total effect on the outcome of the war. The greater tradition is not the advisability of action on Lawrence's part but rather how he fought and how he died.

The spirit of the offensive, a cardinal principle of war, was not new to the officers of 1812. It was to a great extent a heritage from the War of the Revolution. For example, when Captain Pearson testified at his court-martial for losing the *Serapis* to John Paul Jones, he stated,

Long before the close of the action, it became clearly apparent that the American ship was dominated by a command will of the most unalterable resolution, and there could be no doubt that the intention of her commander was, if he could not conquer to sink alongside. And this desperate resolve of the American captain was fully shared and fiercely seconded by every one of his ship's company.

Such a great tradition in a service lives. More than three decades afterwards, Stephen Decatur in his report to the Secretary of the Navy relative to the capture of the *Macedonian* declares:

The enthusiasm of every officer, seaman, and marine on board this ship on discovering the enemy—their steady conduct in battle, the precision of their fire could not be surpassed. Where all met my fullest expectations, it would be unjust in me to discriminate.[2]

Could any sea captain expect more?

In summary, the United States Navy won at sea because it demonstrated that a well-drilled Navy, although poor and small,

[1] H. H. Frost, preface to *We Build a Navy*.
[2] Report of Stephen Decatur to the Hon. Paul Hamilton, written at sea 30 October, 1812.

may win single-ship actions with a larger sea power; that American frigates were as well constructed as any in the world became a settled question. The theory was proved that accuracy in gunnery is largely dependent upon drill and practice at sea. In the training of officers and men it must be noted that the majority of the sailors were trained in the hard school of merchantmen, while many of the officers learned their seamanship and gunnery in privateers; took part in the short war at sea with France; and fought the corsairs of the Barbary Coast. Sailors are made on oceans and there is no substitute for "the sea habit!"

The things that men fight for must never be underestimated. Although this age is slightly cynical towards idealism, it has been a general rule that golden ages are marked by ideals, and in the great military-naval ages by a fervent belief in cause. This was true in the War of 1812. In short, it was a readiness to risk all in defense of the political principles upon which the new republic had been founded, that generated the inestimable driving force, an imponderable, that spurred a small infant Navy to face fearlessly the world's largest and most seasoned sea power. In an estimate of the traditions that are ours as a result of this war on the sea, it seems that enthusiasm, loyalty, and the will to win led to impressive "practical" results.

PART IV
THE SEA

CHAPTER IX
NAUTICAL WORDS AND NAVAL EXPRESSIONS

"Out of monuments, names, wordes, proverbs, private recordes and evidences, fragments of stories, passages of books, and the like, we doe save and recover somewhat from the deluge of time."

—BACON

"It should be of greatest interest to all who wear the naval uniform to know as much as possible of the customs and traditions of their service. One should be entirely conversant, one should be proud to be conversant, with the odd expressions and strange terms with which the naval vocabulary is so plentifully flavored."

—Reserve Officers' Manual, U. S. Navy (1932)

"It's very odd that sailor-men should talk so very queer."

—Ingoldsby Legends

IN A study of the derivation of nautical terms and expressions, one is impressed with their polyglot mixture. The English sea terms were derived from Greek, Latin, Italian, Spanish, French, and Dutch sources. Although many of the words have an English sound, men of the sea are responsible for giving them the English shape after borrowing the sea terms from foreign sources.

Logan Pearsall Smith writes:

Our oldest sea terms divide themselves into two main classes, and are derived from the two far-distant corners of Europe, where, in prehistoric times, men of European races first built themselves ships and ventured on the sea. These places were in the South among the islands and peninsulas of Greece, and in the North along the shores and shallows of the North Sea and the Baltic. From Greece the arts of navigation spread with their appropriate terms over the Mediterranean, while the sailors of the North carried their Teutonic speech along the coasts of the Atlantic. Gradually, these two vocabularies met and mingled, and the sea vocabularies of England and the other European countries are largely made up of a mixture of these North Sea and these Mediterranean terms. The most English and anciently established ones in our language are, of course, of Northern origin, and consist of those words which the Angles and Saxons brought with them to England, and which safely survived the Norman Conquest. But among these old inherited terms are a few which, though they belong also to the South, have not been borrowed from thence, but descend to us from a time, thousands of years ago, when the Northern and Southern races dwelt together, and shared in a common language. Indeed, in sorting our words, we must put a few of them aside as belonging to the Aryan speech, from which not only most of the languages of Europe, but those of the Hindoos and Persians, descend.[1]

In the glossary of the language of the sea that follows, it must be kept in mind that the great thalassocracies contributed directly and indirectly to the language of the English-speaking mariner. Apart from the customary meaning of the terms for those afloat, the philologist finds in them much of interest. Usage has shaped pronunciation in many cases. The lexicographer may not agree in pronunciation with the sailor when he says "starburd" for starboard; "focsul" for forecastle; "boy" for buoy; "tāckle" for tackle; and even "starn" for stern; but why should not sailors "in ships" differ in speech from those who occasionally go "on ships"?

Admiral. The title may be traced to the Arabic *Amir-al-Bahr* or admiral (commander) of the seas. *Bahr* was dropped and the Romans called the admiral *Bahrs,* "Sarraccenorum Admirati" introducing the "d" into the Latin form. It was a title of great dignity. The term was introduced into Europe during the Crusades. There is record of its use first by the Sicilians and then by the Genoese.

The first English admiral appointed was a William de Leyburn with title of "Admiral of the Sea of the King of England." This appointment was made by Edward I in 1297. The wide powers of this office gradually merged into the title of Lord High Admiral of England. We find in the time of Edward II that the Latinized term *Admiralius* had been Anglicized as *Admyrall.*

There is record of the first extant Royal Commission to a British Naval Officer. It was dated 1302 when Gervase Aland

---

[1] Logan Pearsall Smith, *Words and Idioms* (4th Ed.) (1933), pp. 2-3.

was appointed "Captain and Admiral." Authorities are of the opinion that the title of "Captain" delegated executive command, while that of "Admiral" delegated legal powers.

Queen Anne at one time acted as Lord High Admiral of England upon the death of her consort who had the title. It is said that the Earl of Berkeley is the only officer not of royal blood to win the flag of Lord High Admiral. At the age of twenty he had his second command, the *Litchfield*. At twenty-three he commanded the *Boyne* (80). At twenty-seven he was made Vice-Admiral of the Blue, and the next year Vice-Admiral of the Red. On 29 March, 1719, at the age of thirty-eight, he hoisted his flag on the *Dorsetshire*, as Lord High Admiral, with the title Vice-Admiral of England and First Lord of the Admiralty.

The Sicilians and Genoese at the beginning of the Crusades conferred the honor of admiral on the commander of a squadron of ships.

Louis IX, "St. Louis," introduced the title of admiral into France. At that time, the rank of admiral was equivalent to a Marshal of France; but their prerogatives became so great that Richelieu took the title and suppressed it in others. In 1669, Louis XIV revived the title but he made no appointments. Nevertheless the power was enormous in later appointments. When the Duke de Penthierre gave up the title, in 1759, he received an annual grant equivalent to $30,000 a year until the French Revolution. In France, fifty-nine persons in all have held the high title. Napoleon, in 1805, made Murat a "grand admiral"; but the post was purely honorary. The title of "grand admiral" was never revived after the 1830 Revolution.

We have had three admirals of the U. S. Navy: Farragut, Porter, and Dewey.

From the beginning of our Navy, the need of higher naval commissions was urged. John Paul Jones wrote to Robert Morris in 1776,

I am convinced that the parity in rank between sea and land or marine officers is of more consequence to the harmony of the service than has generally been imagined.

He sets forth the British system and then adds:

Were that regulation to take place in our Navy, it would prevent numberless disputes and duellings that otherwise would be unavoidable.

The relative ranks with the Army were fixed on 15 November, 1776. The four highest naval grades were not established, moreover, for nearly a hundred years; captain was the highest grade.

Secretary Upshur wrote in his annual report for 1841,

The rank of Admiral is known in all the navies of the world except our own; it has existed through a long course of past ages; and has been fully tested in the experience of all nations. It still exists and is still approved. . . . Our naval officers are often subjected to serious difficulties and embarrassments in the interchange of civilities with those of other countries or foreign stations. . . .

Repeated attempts were made by the Secretaries of the Navy and by the press, but the opinion prevailed that the title of admiral had a royal and authoritative flavor, and Congress did not create the grade until 16 July, 1862.

The Secretary of the Navy repeatedly recommended the establishment of the grades vice-admiral, rear admiral, and commodore. The 16 July, 1862, Act provided for nine grades of commissioned officers and carried the authority to appoint nine rear admirals.

Résumé of Flag-Officer Legislation

1864—Authorization to appoint a vice-admiral from the rear admirals of 1862. Farragut was appointed first vice-admiral.

1865—A bill made Farragut admiral and permitted one vice-admiral (David Dixon Porter) and ten rear admirals.

1870—Admiral Farragut died, and Vice Admiral David Dixon Porter became admiral and Rear Admiral Rowan became vice-admiral.

1875—Congress provided that grades of admiral and vice-admiral should not be filled by promotion. In other words, the grades were abolished upon the death of Rowan and Porter.

15 August, 1882—The number of rear admirals on the active list was reduced to six. "Rules and Regulations for the govern-

ment of the Navy of the United States" made the following provision:

Sea officers of the Navy of the United States shall take rank in the following order: admiral, vice-admiral, rear admiral, captain, commander (hereafter called master commander), lieutenant.

2 March, 1899—The President was authorized to appoint "An Admiral of the Navy." Dewey was appointed and held the title until his death on 16 January, 1917.

3 March, 1899—The Navy Personnel Act made provision for eighteen rear admirals. For purpose of pay, the grade was divided in halves. The upper nine received the same pay and allowances as major generals; the lower half, the pay and allowances of brigadier generals.

13 May, 1908—Navy Personnel Act of 1899 was changed with different pay rates for "rear admirals, first nine"—"rear admirals, second nine."

3 March, 1915—The Naval Appropriation Act authorized that the commanders in chief of the Atlantic, Pacific, and Asiatic Fleets should have the ranks of admiral while on that duty and the seconds in command, the ranks of vice-admiral while on that duty.

20 August, 1916—The number of officers in the different grades was increased, and provision was made for pay and allowance of staff officers of flag rank as well as the line.

29 August, 1916—The Chief of Naval Operations was given the rank and pay of admiral and took the rank after the admiral of the Navy. There is no Admiral of the Navy at the present time and no one was appointed to this grade in the World War.

22 May, 1917—The Act of 3 March, 1915, was repeated, and the President was and is now authorized to make a selection of six officers for the commands of the fleets (usually considered Atlantic, Pacific, and Asiatic), three of which shall while assigned to the duty have the rank and pay of admiral and three, the rank and pay of vice-admiral.

Admiral, Vice. This office in the British Service may be traced to the vice-admiral of the United Kingdom which was the evolution of the ancient title lieutenant admiral or lieutenant of the Admiralty. It later became vice-admiral of England, in 1672; then became vice-admiral of Great Britain in 1707; and finally, vice-admiral of the United Kingdom, in 1801. In 1876 the office was not held and remained vacant until 1901 when King Edward VII revived it.

On 21 December, 1864, the grade of vice-admiral was introduced into the American Navy. David Glasgow Farragut was the first vice-admiral. When Farragut was promoted to admiral in July, 1886, Rear Admiral David D. Porter was then made a vice-admiral. When Farragut died in August, 1870, Porter was made Admiral of the Navy, and Stephen C. Rowan was made a vice-admiral. After the deaths of Admiral Porter and Vice-Admiral Rowan, the grades became extinct until the Act of 3 March, 1915.

Admiral, Rear. In order that the natural son of Charles II, Henry Duke of Grafton, could at tender years hold the title vice-admiral of England, Admiral Arthur Herbert was made the first "rear admiral of England." This office was not held until 1895 when it was revived as was that of vice-admiral of the United Kingdom by Edward VII. Both offices are now held but carry no emoluments.

These high honorary titles brought the terms into English nautical phraseology, and for that reason are mentioned for their historical value.

The Act of 16 July, 1862, to a marked degree reorganized the Navy, authorized the commissioning of not more than nine rear admirals on the active list and nine on the reserve or retired list. The first rear admirals were selected for distinguished service. Afterwards vacancies were filled by regular promotion.

Ahoy. This was once the dreaded war cry of the Vikings—a distinct nautical hail.

Aiguillette. There are various theories and traditions as to the origin of this term. The best known is that of the aide-de-camp, or henchman, of the superior who carried the rope and pegs for tethering the knight's horse, and thereby became the "ear mark" of the one near the leader. Another tradition relates that it was the rope of the provost marshal used in hanging the condemned. It was a badge of office of a personal aide. It is a custom that aides to the President of the United States, royalty, and viceroys wear aiguillettes on the right side, and that aides to all other senior officers and dignitaries wear them on the left side. Naval aiguillettes are blue and gold, while those of the Marine Corps and the Army are red and gold.

Anchor. This term is derived from a Greek word for hook or crook. Sailors say today "drop the hook," or refer to the anchor as "the old mud hook." The original Greek meaning has been lost, and the word has today only one connotation—the *terminus technicus* for a means of holding a ship when she is not under way.

Dr. Giles, the eminent scholar of things Chinese, writes that ships with anchors, rudders, and oars were used as early as 2000 B.C. It is recorded that Emperor Yü even invented the anchor; but emperors in those days took much credit that belonged to their subjects. The Chinese have a word for anchor, spoken "ting" and written with the character "stone." The present Chinese word is spoken "mao" and written with the character "metal." Emperor Yü was said to be the first to use chains fore and aft. The peculiar noise of chain running out gave rise to the Chinese mariners expression "cat" or "iron cat" which in Chinese signifies "mao."

Bags of sand or stone were used as anchors by the early navigators. In time, stone anchors were used by the Greeks and Romans. Expert stone cutters began to make stone anchors. In the book of Stephanus Byzantius, titled *De Urbibis,* there is the statement that the town of Ancyra in Egypt derived its name from the manufacture of anchors in its quarries.

Large lead trunks which are exhibited as Greek anchors may be found in the archeological collections of the Museum Boreli at Marseilles, the British Museum in London, the Old Museum in Berlin, and in many smaller museums of Southern Europe.

The Romans used the anchor as a symbol for wealth and

commerce, while the Greeks gave to it the significance of hope and steadiness, a meaning that persists in religion and heraldry today. The symbolism of the Greeks was carried on by the early Christians with a meaning of steadfastness, hope, and salvation. Pictures of anchors comparable in shape to those used today may be seen in the Catacombs. The drawing was sometimes accompanied by such an inscription as *spes in Christo.* The foul anchor with the line wound around the shank may be found on the world renowned sculptures of the Temple of Neptune at Rome.

"Articles for the Government of the Navy." (Discussed in Chapter III.) Some provisions of the Code of Oléron, from which in a historic sense the English and American articles of war were derived, are:

Any one who committed a murder at sea was to be bound to the corpse and buried alive with it.

Theft on board was treated with boiling tar and feathers.

Sleeping on watch was punished with dipping in the sea.

When the captain wished to discharge the crew or certain members of the crew, he was to give notice of his intention by taking away the mess cloth for three meals in succession; hence the expression and act of "giving notice."

In certain circumstances the captain was always to consult the crew and act according to the wishes of the majority as to whether the weather was suitable for sailing.

Aye Aye. Aye is old English for "yes."

Back. The wind backs when it changes counter-clockwise, but veers when it changes clockwise. Square sails are backed or aback when the wind blows on their forward side thrusting them against the mast. Should this occur through a shift of wind, the effect of a heavy sea, or a careless helmsman, a ship is said to be taken aback. To back water with oars is the opposite from a regular stroke, *i.e.,* to push instead of to pull. To back a piece of gear means to rig or set up a preventer. To back an anchor means the practice of sending an extra anchor to the bottom or holding ground with its shank made fast on the chain of the first anchor in order to back it or assist it. It also means to shackle or otherwise secure the extra anchor to the chain near the lower anchor before letting go. "To back chain" is sometimes confused with "to veer chain" but it generally refers to easing out a few fathoms before letting go the anchor.

Beach Comber. Originally one who searched beaches and foreshores for material washed up from wrecked or stranded ships. Beach combing in winter after a blow was quite a profitable business for the longshoremen of British ports and watering places in the old days. It has been stated that "in the happy pre-war era of gold, such a beach as that of Brighton, Hastings, or Ramsgate yielded up many a golden guinea after it had been bared by a winter gale." The expression today connotes tramps of the sea, unreliable drifters. It is also applied in some cases to impoverished and stranded landsmen in foreign sea ports.

This is a term rather in vogue among sailors in the Pacific. It is applied to certain roving characters, who, without attaching themselves permanently to any vessel, ship now and then for a short cruise in a whaler; but upon the condition only of being honorably discharged the very next time the anchor takes hold of the bottom; no matter where. They are mostly a reckless, rollicking set, wedded to the Pacific, and never dreaming of ever doubling Cape Horn again on a homeward-bound passage. Hence their reputation is a bad one.
        —HERMAN MELVILLE, *Omoo*

The old beach comber: gaunt, grim-visaged, eager-eyed, tar-smelling and tatooed: a ship deserter, runaway: the jetsam and the flotsam of the waters of the world in human guise.
        —FRANK COWAN, *Australia*, "A Charcoal Sketch"

Binnacle. Originally spelled "bittacle." About the size of a large corn bin or cupboard in which was stowed a compass, log board, lighted candle or lamp at night, and other navigation gear.

Bitter End.
A bitter end is but the turn of a cable about the bits, and veare it

out little and little, and the bitter's end is that part of the cable doth stay within board.

—*Seaman's Grammer* (1653) vii

Bleeding a Buoy. To let the water out.

Bluejacket. The first uniform that was ever officially sanctioned for sailors in the Royal Navy was a short blue jacket open in the front.

Blue Peter. A flag, "blue pierced with white," was used in the British Navy from 1777 as a general recall flag. In a quarter of a century the term "blue peter" was used by all to designate this flag. Civilians knew its significance for merchant ships and convoys in the French wars and would not sail until the escorting man-of-war hoisted the blue peter for passengers to come aboard.

There is on record a piece of doggerel, autographed "Emma," written when Nelson sailed in 1801:

> Silent grief and sad forebodings
> (Lest I ne'er should see him more)
> Fill my heart when gallant Nelson
> Hoists blue peter at the fore.

Boarders. Even in 1885 one reads:

They are men detailed to attack the enemy by boarding. They are armed with pistols and cutlasses and led by the executive officer. They are summoned by verbal order and by the springing of the rattle, and assembled in the part of the ship designated, keeping under cover as much as possible.

—*U. S. Marine Encyclopedia*

Boats. Derived from Anglo-Saxon "bat" that stood for boat, small ship, vessel.

Barge—"Served for state and ease (as for carrying the generall, admiralls, and prynce captains)." It was the admiral's boat and was rigged for ten or twelve oars.

Gig—The 1815 edition of Flaconer's *Dictionary of the Marine* calls it "A long narrow boat . . . generally rowing six to eight oars, and is mostly the private property of the captain or commander."

Dinghy or Dinghey—An Indian word and taken from the East India Company's service.

Boatswain. The Saxon word "swein" meant a boy or servant, therefore, boatswain. The "boat" refers to the ships and not to her boats. "Cockswain" has a similar derivation. "Cock" is an old word for a type of small boat.

He is to be very particular in having ready at all times a sufficient number of mats, plats, knippers, points, and gaskets so that no delay may be experienced when they are wanted.

—*Naval Regulations* (1824)

The ships were usually commanded by "batsuen" (boatswain) in the eleventh century.

Boatswain's Pipe. Discussed in detail in the chapter on "Ceremonies and Honors."

The parts of the pipe are the buoy, gun, keel, shackle.

The first reference to "call" on the whistle was about 1671; but the use of the whistle at sea antedates Carthaginian sea power.

Bomber. It is curious how the term bomber came to be adopted in the British Army. After the first battle of Ypres, when hand grenades were generally used, designated men in each company were given the official name of "grenadiers." The Grenadier Guards raised serious objection to this order and based their protest on the exclusive right to the name. The colonel in command of the First Battalion, Grenadier Guards, protested to the War Office and drew attention to the fact that after Waterloo the name had been given to his historic organization in order to commemorate the English Guards' part in overthrowing Napoleon's Grenadiers of the Guard. The bitter controversy was finally referred to the King. In May, 1916, it was officially promulgated that "at His Majesty's 'expressed wish' the word 'bomber' should be universally substituted for 'grenadier.'"

Bottomry Bond. A lien placed on a vessel by a master in order to obtain money to get the vessel home. The funds secured are only used for repairs. This is resorted to only when the master is out of communication with the ship's owners. Such a lien takes priority for first payment over all mortgages. A lien on cargo is a respondentia bond.

Brig. As a name for a sailing vessel this term did not come into use until latter part of eighteenth century. Mentioned by Johnson in his dictionary of 1760. It is a contraction of the older word "brigantine" or "brigandine" from robber or brigand. This was originally a general term for the fast sailing vessel used by pirates of the Mediterranean.

Buccaneers. The term was first given to early Frenchmen in Haiti, who were the original cowboys of that island. The word "boucan" was of Caribbean origin, meaning a dealer in smoked-dried meats.

In the Caribbean area, the hunters placed meat to dry on wooden lattice work, known as "boucans." "The boucanners" eventually took to privateering and general lawlessness. After the Treaty of Ryswick, buccaneer became the common word for pirate.

Bugle. Bugle is derived from the French, and originally meant "wild ox." Therefore, bugle horn, meaning wild ox horn, became the first expression. It was and remains in some parts of the world the true horn of the chase. Joseph Haydn, the celebrated musician, wrote the first bugle calls in about 1793, and they were at a much later date introduced into Navies.

Bumboat. A boat selling supplies, provisions, and articles to ships. The most popular derivation is from "boomboat," signifying boats permitted to lie at booms. A British source accounts for the term as derived from "bomboat," a vessel in which beer is carried to soldiers on duty.

Buoys. Floating beacons which by shape and color give the mariner valuable navigational information. The types in use in the United States comprise can, nun, spar, cask, bell, whistle, and lighted buoys. In coming from seaward, red buoys mark the starboard, or right, side of the channel and black buoys, the port, or left, side. A convenient way of remembering this is "red, right, returning." Red buoys are on the right when returning from sea. Dangers and obstructions which may be passed on either side are marked by buoys with black and red horizontal stripes and may be left on either hand. Buoys indicating the fairway are marked with black and white vertical stripes and should be passed close to. Sunken wrecks are marked by red and white obstruction buoys. In foreign countries, green buoys are frequently used to mark sunken wrecks. Quarantine buoys are yellow. White buoys are used for special purposes not connected with navigation such as race courses, special anchorages, etc. The starboard and port buoys are numbered from the seaward end of the channel, black buoys bearing odd numbers and red buoys, even numbers. Perches with balls, cages, etc., will, when placed on buoys, be at the turning points, the color and number indicating the side on which they shall be passed. A spar buoy moored close by a bell or lighted buoy is called a marker buoy. A buoy that floats visibly is said to be watching.

Buttons (On cuffs of British midshipmen). As in other matters of uniform, the origin of certain insignia and distinctions of dress is not definitely recorded but it is generally agreed in the case of midshipmen that buttons were placed on the cuffs for a purpose. One must remember that the British midshipman enters the Navy today at the age of thirteen, and in former years he entered at a younger age.

A British commentator wrote:

In the earlier days of the last century, small mites of boys eight or nine years old and even younger, were sent to sea. When these small boys were first at sea, they were one and all so woefully homesick that they had continuous cases of sniffles, and for the first part of their term of service they were forever rubbing their poor little homesick and dripping eyes and noses on the cuffs of their coats. This was so detrimental to the appearance of their uniforms, that it led to the sewing on of buttons.

Commander W. N. T. Beckett, R.N., writes:

Snotty is a slang term for a midshipman and is derived from the allegation that these officers used to make their sleeves do duty as handkerchiefs, and that to obviate this practice buttons were placed on the cuffs. The term "wart" is used to demonstrate the fact that a midshipman is an excrescence on the face of nature.

Captain. From "caput," the head or chief, and "thane," a Saxon title of honor first conferred by King Athelstan. The evolution of the commanding officer of ships comes from the batsuen (boatswain) or the rector in the eleventh century, when the boatswain usually steered if the rector was aboard, to the rank of captain in 1370. The master, although he sailed the ship, was of lower rank than the captain. In a British order in council in 1748, the relative rank was settled with the Army by dividing Navy captains into three grades. It was deemed at that time that any officer in command was entitled to the title of captain while in command, regardless of rank. All captains not eligible on the list for promotion to rear admiral were originally called "masters and commanders" and had "C" after their names. The rank was shortened to commander in 1794. The term "cdr." in the British Navy was used after the names of commanders in 1826.

"Post captain," a term used in the Royal Navy and once known in the American Navy, distinguished captains commanding frigates from master commanders or commanders next in rank. There never was a commission of "post captain." In 1747, the rank of captain was first clearly defined in the British Navy. Captains who commanded post ships took rank, if of three years standing, with colonels in the Army. Until the year 1824 the Royal Navy list classed such captains as post captains.

Until 1862, captain was the highest commissioned officer in the United States Navy, and according to his duty ranked with lieutenant colonel, colonel, or brigadier general.

Cargo. Comes directly from Latin *cargo* or *carga,* a load, freight. Old commercial document Anglo-Saxon "cark," meaning a load.

Cathead. Projections in bows for rigging tackles for purpose of hoisting anchor aboard—"To cat and fish." The term appears in English as early as 1626. Cat carved on wooden timber for good luck; hence the term cathead.

Caulk, To Take a. To take a sleep or nap; came from the days when it was taken on the deck, and one's back became marked by the pitch of the seams.

Chains. Where shrouds were secured to platforms on the ship's side, "chains" were used to brace the platform. This platform was used for leadsmen to stand upon when heaving the lead, and today means that platform or position from which the lead is hove.

Chantey.[1] Gershom Bradford gives an excellent description of chantey. He writes that it was

a song formerly always and now rarely sung aboard ship to lighten and unify labor at the capstan, sheets, and halyards. The soloist is known as the chanty-man and is usually a man of leadership in the forecastle. He is something of an improviser, for those especially successful made their verses applicable to the existing conditions in the ship, indulging in slight hits at the peculiarities of the different officers, the vociferousness of the chorus indicating the relative delight with which these squibs are received by the men. This was the only privilege allowed to pass in the old days of iron-fisted discipline. They were composed for various kinds of work such as capstan chanties, which were timed to be rhythmic with the steady tread around the capstan. They usually dwell upon the joys of being homeward-bound and farewells to the port (and ladies) when heaving up the anchor to leave. The topsail halyard chanties are the most stirring as they, at their best, are sung in a gale when the reefed topsail is being mastheaded. There are also long pull and short pull shanties.[2]

As Arnold Bennett once remarked about limericks, the best chanties are not for general publication. They were for the most part tuneful and melodious, and smack of the romantic age of sail. Pronounce as if spelled *shanty.*

[1] See page 279 for more information on chanteys.
[2] Gershom Bradford, *A Glossary of Sea Terms,* New York: Yachting, Inc., 1927.

Chaplain. Chaplains have been carried aboard warships from the earliest days. Charles I appointed a chaplain to each ship of the fleet of England. Chaplains and doctors were once paid by the seamen. The chaplain received from each seaman four pence per month. The chaplains did not live in the wardroom until the end of the eighteenth century. The chaplain, purser, and doctor on almost all ships messed in their respective cabins. There is record of chaplains messing regularly with the captains. In the old days, the chaplain had the authority to give a midshipman six pence for learning a psalm. Tradition gives the origin of the title as follows: St. Martin divided his coat with a poor beggar on a cold wintry day outside of Amiens. It is related that the coat was "miraculously preserved" and thereby became a sacred banner for the Kings of France. This cloak or cape (French *chape*) was preserved in an oratory that took the name of *chapelle,* while the gentleman charged with its keeping was called the *chapelain.*

We read that in 1678 Henry Teonge, Chaplain of the *Bristol* (48), had "piggs," "ghoose," and that "strange liquor punch." He records that he first tasted punch on board. Nevertheless, from the events of his diary, he was certainly a pious and orthodox chaplain. There is record of Eli Vallette, a chaplain of the United States Navy, 26 February, 1800.

Charlie Noble. Sailor's nautical name for the galley smoke-pipe. Derived from the British merchant service Captain Charlie Noble, who required a high polish on the galley funnel. The funnel of his galley was of copper and its brightness became known in all ports visited.

Chart. From Latin *charta,* Greek *charte,* a kind of papyrus. In middle English, the chart or maps were known as "scacards" or seacards. There are many references in the early day to "the cards" for the charts.

Chit. (Hindu word *chitti.*) Letter, note, voucher, or receipt. It came from the old East India Company. The word has wide use in the Far East and is used throughout the British Army

BATTLE MANEUVERS   (Drawing by Commander G. D. Hull, U. S. Navy)

and Navy. The United States Navy has used the word for many years. It was probably gained by the Navy on the Asiatic Station many years ago from the "pidgin" English.

Clerks. The institution of "captain's clerk" as the United States Navy knew it came from the British Navy. There was no commission or warrant for the duties but although the Captain appointed the clerk and dismissed him if necessary, he was considered an officer of the Navy.

The acme of position of official clerical work was in time the "commodore's secretary" or "commodore's clerk." This billet grew into the flag secretary of today. Both the "commodore's secretary" and "captain's clerk" wore a uniform much like that of the midshipmen of their day. They lived with the midshipmen in the "after cockpit." In fact, a few became midshipmen.

In the early days should no civilian be employed by the captain, a midshipman was appointed to the office. In 1779, Commodore John Paul Jones appointed Midshipman Nathaniel Fanning as "commodore's secretary."

In 1835, one finds secretaries to "commander of squadron commanding in chief" and to "commander of squadron." There were also the titles "clerk to commander of squadron" and "clerk to commander of ship," as well as "clerk to paymaster" at a later time. The top secretaries in time were ranked with lieutenants in the matter of certain privileges, such as messing in the wardroom.

A derivative of the old "purser's steward" was the clerk to paymaster or paymaster's clerk. In time the work of the "clerk to commander of ship" was done by a midshipman, while later the chief yeoman ordered to perform the clerical duties of the captain became styled the "captain's writer." The "ship's writer" was the title given to the chief yeoman who assisted the executive officer. At the present time, an ensign of the line is designated as the "ship's secretary" and is responsible for the paperwork in the captain's office. The executive officer is assisted in clerical work by an ensign of the line called the "aide to the executive officer." The supply officer due to the increase of reports and paper-work has as assistants pay clerks and yeomen.

Clipper. Properly taken from old English "clip," meaning to run, fly swiftly.

Commander. As explained under "captain," the lower grades of captains were originally styled "master and commander" and commanded small ships of war. The title was introduced in England by William III and was originally "commandeur." The British first appointed commanders as second in command on large ships, in 1827. It is recorded that the Navy was much in opposition to this innovation.

It was introduced in the United States Navy in 1838 when the law read that "master commandants" should be known as "commanders."

The pay bill approved 3 March, 1835, recognized the title. A commander was originally supposed

to command vessels of the third and fourth classes; may be employed as chief of staff to a commodore, or duty under a bureau; or as aid to a flag officer of either grade or shore stations.[1]

Commission Pennant. "The distinctive mark of a ship of the Navy in commission, other than the national ensign, is a flag or pennant, at a masthead." *U. S. Navy Regulations,* 321 (1).

In the days of chivalry, knights rated a small pointed flag or pennon. The mark of a squire was a long pennant very similar to the "coachwhip pennant" of modern men-of-war. Bannerets ranked the knight and took precedence below a baron. They carried a knight's pennon with a slit in the end. It was customary to create barons on the battlefield by the king or general cutting off part of the fly of the pennon. This square flag was then a symbol of increased rank. Edward, the Black Prince, after battle tore the tail off the pennon of Lord John Chandos saying, "Sir John, behold, here is your banner; God send you much joy and honor with it." One may trace directly from these customs, the commission pennant, "coachwhip," broad command pennant, and broad flags worn by commanding officers

[1] *Marine Encyclopedia* (1881).

of ships, and by commodores, as well as the square flags of the admirals of our own and other navies.

When Maarten Harpertszoon Tromp, the Dutch admiral, hoisted a broom at his masthead, to indicate his intention to sweep the English from the sea, the English admiral hoisted a *horsewhip*, indicating his intention to chastise the insolent Dutchman. Ever since that time, the narrow, or coachwhip pennant, symbolizing the original horsewhip, has been the distinctive mark of a vessel of war, adopted by all nations.[1]

Commodore. This title came from Holland. In the Dutch Wars of 1652, there were not sufficient admirals and the Dutch desired to create others without calling them admirals. The title was brought to England by William III. The broad command pennant or burgee was used by the Dutch at the same time. The rank was officially recognized by the British in 1806. The American Navy used the rank as an honorary title in the Revolution—"Commodore" John Paul Jones; "Commodore" Esek Hopkins, appointed as "commander in chief."

Until 1861 all captains in the United States Navy, commanding or having commanded squadrons, were recognized as commodore, though never commissioned as such. They wore a broad pennant distinctive of that rank. In 1862 it was established as a fixed rank, as in July of that year eighteen were commissioned on the active list and seventeen on the retired list.

A captain in the United States Navy, who commands a flotilla or squadron of destroyers is called a "commodore" by courtesy. The British Admiralty continues to make appointments of a small number of commodores. The broad stripe of rank is worn by those appointed and the "burgee" of a commodore is flown.

Commodore's Privilege. An open fly.

Compass. Some writers hold that the Chinese made use of the compass long before European navigators. This rather interesting statement has never been verified by conclusive proof. The early Chinese records disclose that the Chinese knew of the extraordinary properties of the magnet, but in all the docu-

[1] Admiral George H. Preble, U.S.N., *History and Origin of the American Flag.*

ments relating to voyages at that earliest date no mention is made of the magnet as an aid to direction and navigation.

The Arabians were acquainted with the magnet ashore as well as the Greeks who used it for purposes of instruction in their academies. Plato wrote of the magnet in a humorous vein when he spoke of its use by jealous husbands to detect wifely virtue; but there is no record of its use at sea.

The following interesting description of what may have been a compass was recently found in a Latin volume dealing with the art of ship handling.[1]

Take a number of small iron bars (needles) and paint them with a mixture of cinabro and oprimento well powdered and mixed with the blood of the crest of a rooster. Heat them well and, after the Astrologer has carried them next to his skin for a period of a full lunation, lay them on straws floating on the water and they will point south.

In 1248, about 1,000 years later, Brunetto Latini, a Florentine, made reference in his poem "Tresor" to the instrument used on the Norman ships:

In a tub of water placed in the center of the ship there floats the Mariniere, which is a round piece of cork with a thin hollow shaft filled with lodestone inserted through its center so that it lies parallel to the plane of the water, and the quill of a goose sealed at both ends, also inserted through the cork at right angles to the one filled with lodestone; over this there lays a bird's skin with the *fleur-de-lis* upon it, and even as our august King is our constant guide on the land, so does the *fleur-de-lis* upon the Mariniere guide the mariner by constantly pointing to Boreas (north) no matter how the ship may go.

The *fleur-de-lis* has remained to this day on the north point of practically all compass cards.

About 1295, Messere Flavio Gioja, an Amalfitan, gave to the world the first practical compass. He used a large copper bowl instead of the wooden tub of the Mariniere in order that,

---

[1] Captain John M. L. Gorett, M.S.R., C.C.A., in his comprehensive compass research brought to light the Latin book, title and author unknown, with the title page missing. He places its writing in the third century A.D.

when the ship's head swung in azimuth, the current of the electro-magnetic induction was such as to dampen the oscillations of the compass and thereby bring the needle to rest sooner than the old method in the wooden tub. He balanced the compass card on a vertical shaft in the bowl and placed on the card all the cardinal points of the compass. The *fleur-de-lis* was left for the north point and, although Gioja was not the first to use the symbol, it was indeed a graceful compliment to Charles d'Anjou, whose armorial device it was, and who at the time was the reigning King of Sicily.

Prince Henry, the Navigator, Don Enrico, the Fifteenth Infante, did much to perfect the compass by his establishment of a school for navigation in Portugal in 1480. When Vasco da Gama sailed on July 18, 1497, it may be correctly said that his compass cards were the result of Norman invention, Italian adaptation, and Portuguese improvement.

Con, Conn. A very old word and the exact derivation is not known. It was used in 1520 in the present sense of directing the steering. One writer says that it "undoubtedly had an affinity to cunning."

Cook. Michael Scott in *Tom Cringle's Log* writes:

The cook of a man-of-war is no small beer; he is his Majesty's warrant-officer, a much bigger wig than a poor little mid, with whom it is condescension on his part to jest.

It seems to be a sort of rule, that no old sailor who has not lost a limb or an eye, at least, shall be eligible to the office, but as the kind of maiming is so far circumscribed that all cooks must have two arms, a laughable proportion of them have but one leg. Besides the honour, the perquisites are good; accordingly, all old quartermasters, captains of top, etc., look forward to the cook down, as cardinals to the pope down.

In the seventeenth century the cook was, in most cases, an unscrupulous individual. For many years, it was the custom that the cook received his meat from the steward, and was by order to cook it and give it to "such persons as are chosen by every mess (mess cooks) for the fetching of it away from him." We learn in many cases that cooks were bribed to furnish double rations to a mess. In the time of Charles II, men who had been maimed in the Dutch Wars were given appointments as cooks in the Royal Navy. We have record of John Gamble who, although minus both arms "in fight the 11th of August 1673," was recommended for cook of the navy ship *Sweepstakes* while James Davis, "who lost all the lower part of his face in the engagement 28 May, 1692," was made cook of the *Revenge*. The record reads, "that forasmuch as he is not able to eat sea biscuit or meat that he would be permitted to perform cook's duty by deputy."

Coxswain or *Cockswain*. From "cock," a small boat, and "swain," a servant. It originally meant one who had charge of a boat and a crew in the absence of an officer.

It was once the custom that in single-banked boats the coxswain pulled the stroke oar; the boat was generally steered by an officer; in double-banked boats the coxswains usually steered.

Crew. Probably from old Norman word "acrue," meaning to increase; to accrue, closely allied to recruit.

Cruiser. Derived from "crusal" or fast, light vessel used by pirates in the Mediterranean. They were not essentially fighting vessels, but were used for raiding and pillaging.

Cut of His Jib. In the days of sailing ships, nationality and rigs could often be distinguished by their jibs. A Spanish ship, for example, had a small jib or none at all; the large French ships often had two jibs; English ships seldom but one.

From ships, the phrase was extended to apply to men; approximately enough, for the nose, like the jib, is the first part of its wearer to arrive.

Cutting a Dido. A rather recent expression and one used considerably in some sections by shorefolk. H. M. S. *Dido,* a very smart and clean ship in commission about thirty years ago in the British fleet. The *Dido* cruised around the fleet often as a "show off" before anchoring, hence "to cut a dido."

Dago. From James, the Spanish patron saint, called Iago, Santiago, San Diego, Diego. Yankee sailors first called Spanish sailors "Diego men" or "Dagos." Extended to the Latin race, then restricted by usage to Italians.

Dead Marine. An empty bottle, "a marine," "a dead marine." In the old days of hard drinking at sea, this expression was generally accepted as synonymous with an empty bottle. The story is told that William IV, when Duke of Clarence and Lord High Admiral, at an official dinner said, pointing at some empty bottles, "Take away those marines." A dignified and elderly major of Marines present rose from the table and said: "May I respectfully ask why your Royal Highness applies the name of the corps to which I have the honor to belong to an empty bottle?" The Duke, with that tact and characteristic grace that was his, retorted promptly, "I call them marines because they are good fellows who have done their duty and are ready to do it again."

In Grose's *Dictionary of the Vulgar Tongue,* one finds under the word "marine officer" the libelous explanation, "an empty bottle."

Dead Reckoning. A reckoning kept so as to give the theoretical position of a ship without the aid of objects on land, of sights, etc. It consists of plotting on a chart (map) the distance believed to have been covered along each course which has been steered. On a long voyage the navigator runs it from noon to noon.

In the seventeenth and early eighteenth centuries, this was always referred to as "deduced reckoning" or "deduced position." The old log books had a column for entering the "deduced position" but because of lack of space at the top of the column, it became a general custom to write "ded reckoning." Mariners referred to this position by its shorter and abbreviated top-of-column term, which by another strange change in spelling but with the same pronunciation became "dead reckoning."

Derrick. From the name of Thomas Derrick, a well-known hangman of the time of Queen Elizabeth. Derrick, an ingenious fellow, devised a spar with a topping lift and purchase for his gruesome work, instead of using the old-fashioned rope method. Derrick was the executioner of the Earl of Essex in 1601.

Devil to Pay. "The devil to pay and only half a bucket of pitch" was the original expression. This is understood when it is known that the "devil" was the longest and most difficult seam to pay and was found near the garboard strake; hence, "between the devil and the deep blue sea." "Pay" is from the French word *poix,* meaning pitch, "to pay the seams" or "to pitch the seams."

Ditty Box. The small box carried by sailors in which is kept letters, small souvenirs, and needles and thread. These articles were kept formerly in a bag of "Dittis" or "Manchester stuff"; hence a "ditty box." Possibly derived from the Saxon word "dite," meaning tidy.

Doctrine of the Last Fair Chance. A doctrine which provides and asserts that a person in authority shall, when a collision is imminent, do all that is possible to avert or lessen the damage of the disaster.

Dog Watch. Several possible origins are given. It may have come from "docked" or short watch. Admiral Cradock, in his *Whispers from the Fleet,* called it a watch "curtailed."

Dutch Courage. This term, used by the English-speaking world, is of nautical origin and may be traced to the Dutch in their days of sea power. It is related that when Cornelius Van Tromp and de Ruyter were in command, Dutch sailors were given, before going into battle, suitable libations of the well-known "square-faced gin." The English, who were their enemies at the time, called the effects of this practice "Dutch courage."

Dutchman's Breeches. Mariners look for that small patch of blue sky that denotes the breaking up of a gale. No matter how small the patch, it has been said to be "enough to make a pair of breeches for a Dutchman."

East. Old Norse *Austr;* Anglo-Saxon *easte.* All from the Latin *Aurora,* meaning the dawn.

Embargo. From Spanish *embarger,* to arrest.

Engineer Corps. At the present time this is not a distinct corps in the United States Navy, although there are officers assigned for engineering duties only. The first appointment of an engineer in the United States Navy was in 1836; the first in the British Navy in 1837. The corps was not incorporated in the United States Navy *Register* nor regularly organized until 1843.

Ensign (flag). Direct from old Norman *enseigne.* Anglo-Saxon *segne* meant flag. *Signum* in Latin meant sign. Signal comes from the same root word.

The British Navy borrowed the word from land service in the sixteenth century when the large flag was hoisted on the poop of sea vessels. One may read in *The Theorike and Practike of Moderne Warres,* in 1598, that

we Englishmen do call them [ensigns] of late "colours" by reason of the variety of colours they may be made of, whereby they may be the better noted and known to the companie.

Ensign bearer, shortened to ensign, was the rank of a young officer in the French Army at an early date, and was introduced into the French Navy as a naval rank. After the British in 1861 adopted the rank of sub-lieutenant to supplant the rank of mate, the American Navy in 1862 adopted ensign to denote passed midshipman.

Epaulettes. They were common in the French service long before they were introduced in the British Army. The British Navy first used them as an optional part of the dress, although no uniforms were standardized. In time, British officers in France were not recognized as commissioned officers without them. Nelson met Captains Ball and Shephard in France and wrote in regard to these officers, "They wore fine epaulettes, for which I think them coxcombs. They have not visited me, and I shall not count their acquaintance." Epaulettes were originally dubbed "swabs" and are so known today. This ornament of uniform consisted originally of bunches of ribbon.

Executive Officer. The second in command of ships of the United States Navy. Captain W. T. Truxtun, writing in 1881, said:

The title of executive officer is of quite recent date and has been the cause of much discussion, bad temper, and bitter opposition. It has grown from the ashes of the old first lieutenant and finds its parallel in the Army adjutant, and in all corporations or factories employing large bodies of men, in the name of superintendent or manager. The executive officer holds by far the most onerous, most difficult, and most thankless office on board ship. . . . He is held responsible for the cleanliness of the ship, her good order, neat and man-of-war-like appearance, and above all, he is to do as he is told by his captain, to promulgate and execute his orders; and, last of all his duties, never to go ashore except on the sheet anchor.

Eyes of the Ship. Most of the early ships had in the bow carved heads of mythological monsters or patrons; hence the terms "figurehead," "forecastle head," "the heads," and the term "eyes of the ship" followed from the eyes of the figures placed there.

Fathom. From Anglo-Saxon *faehom;* Dutch *vadem;* Latin *patene,* act of stretching two arms wide as rough measurement of six feet.

Figureheads. Research does not disclose when the custom of placing figures and images over the prow, cutwater, and between the "eyes of the ship" began. We do know that the ancient Phoenicians, Egyptians, Greeks, Carthaginians, and Romans, as well as the Norsemen, placed images of animals, great leaders, and the deities over the prows of their war vessels. It was originally a superstitious custom intended to propitiate the gods of storms. The early Greeks named their vessels of war after goddesses and had an image of the goddess aboard. Spanish galleons in the sixteenth century carried aboard images of patron saints of the ships.

The *Constitution,* "Old Ironsides," had originally a figurehead of Hercules. Later Andrew Jackson's figure in wood was placed there but the head was sawed off in a mysterious way by a navy yard clique of opposite politics. The *Constitution* later carried a carved scroll. One of the most famous figureheads in America is that of the one-time Chief of the Delaware Indians, Tamanend. This stern Indian chief once adorned that proud old ship of the line, the U.S.S. *Delaware*. In order to preserve this fine old relic of sail and reminder of tradition, the Naval Academy Class of 1891 donated the amount necessary to cast a duplicate in bronze and with suitable ceremony left it as the "patron saint" of the "wooden" midshipmen, "the god of 2.5" (lowest passing mark). The old figurehead of Tamanend is called Tecumseh, a name and a memory that no Naval Academy man shall ever forget.

Figureheads, in some cases, and shields on the majority of ships were worn as late as 1909. They were both removed prior to the new instructions for painting ships effective late in 1908. White hulls were then changed to the slate or man-of-war color we know today.

Figureheads went off merchant ships with the passing of the clippers. The clippers were truly aristocrats of the sea, and figureheads crowned their harmony of design. One notes at the present a revival of figureheads and scrolls on some of the larger and newest yachts.

Flag Officer. A designation of those who have attained the rank of rear admiral and the grades senior thereto. It comprises in the United States Navy rear admiral, vice-admiral, and admiral. The President of the United States appoints vice-admirals and admirals by letter. Officers revert to rear admiral upon the completion of the duties requiring the two senior grades of flag rank.

The United States Navy had "flag officers" before the square flag was flown and before the grade of admiral was created by Congress. On 16 January, 1857, an Act of Congress directed that "captains in command of squadrons" should be denominated *flag officers*. The square flag was not prescribed at the time.

The following order is of interest in that it is a *forerunner of the rank of admiral and prescribed the flag* (See "Admiral") :

NAVY DEPARTMENT,
May 18, 1858.

It is hereby ordered that in lieu of the broad pennant now worn by "flag officers" in command of squadrons, they shall wear a plain blue flag of dimensions proportionate to the different classes of vessels prescribed for the jack in the table of allowances approved July 20, 1854.

Flag officers whose date of commission as captain is over twenty years shall wear it at the fore; all others at the mizzen.

ISAAC TOUCEY,
Secretary of the Navy

Admiral George H. Preble observed that
This order introduced the flags of vice and rear admirals into our Navy, although the title was considered too aristocratic sounding for republican ears at the time.

Fleet. From Anglo-Saxon *floet, floetan;* old Spanish *flota;* hence, flotilla.

Flogging.

May 10 (1834). At 6:30 p.m. punished at the gangway with one dozen of "the cats." Thomas Frazier and Thomas Webb, also Peter Hudson six, with "the cats."[1]

In 1799, Congress passed a law that restricted a commander of a naval vessel to no more than twelve lashes on the bare back of a sailor or marine, unless more were ordered by decision of a court-martial. This law was abused in many instances. In 1850, Senator John P. Hale (New Hampshire) a liberal and champion of the "under dog," added an anti-flogging clause to the Naval Appropriation Bill. Commodore Uriah P. Levy had been instrumental in interesting Senator Hale in the measure.

In 1851-53, Commodore R. F. Stockton, Senator from California, further restricted flogging by legislation. On 17 July, 1862, Congress finally abolished flogging entirely.

The Navy Department reported that "it would be utterly impracticable to have an efficient Navy without this form of punishment." The Department reported that the "colt" (a single whip) was in most instances used instead of the "cat-o'-nine-tails." Senator Hale showed where a seaman had been

---

[1] A flogging entry from the log of the U.S.S. *Constitution.*

THE NAVY AND FLOGGING—Captain Uriah P. Levy exhibiting the cat-o'-nine-tails and describing its use to a group of statesmen in Washington. The abolition of corporal punishment in the United States Navy was largely due to Captain Levy's efforts. (From *Puck's Pictorial History*)

On 28 March, 1939, British government disclosed that Admiralty had asked it to abolish the centuries-old punishment of flogging in the British Navy. Until 1881 the cat-o'-nine-tails was used frequently for various breaches of discipline. Corporal punishment is now authorized, however, only for mutiny and "closely allied officers" in peace time, the maximum sentence being 25 lashes.

sentenced by court-martial "to receive 500 lashes, and actually received 400." This was given in twelve-lash installments.

Many sailors as well as writers had long advocated reform in punishment. But strange as it may seem, groups of sailors presented memorials to Congress requesting no change in the system, stating that without drastic punishment the good men would have to do the work of the shirkers. After the act was passed, Secretary of the Navy Gideon Welles reported on 4 December, 1862, that it was impossible to re-enlist the better class of seamen. The sober, hard-working men considered that they had been performing duties of the shirkers and the indolent. This led to a change in the enlistment system and the training of the Navy.

Forecastle. In the twelfth century, castles to fight from, similar to those towers of wood used ashore, were placed forward and aft on the Norman ships. The word forecastle survived. The only trace of aftercastle is found in the *ax* cut on the wash deck gear of the quarter-deck divisions of the British Service.

Foul Anchor. An anchor that is foul of the cable or chain. The symbol is found in various Admiralty and Navy crests. This device is also on the cap badge of the American naval officer, the collar of the midshipman, and the buttons and cap badges of the British officer. It is regarded by many true sailors as an emblem of careless and poor seamanship, although artistic to the landsmen, and is sometimes called the "sailor's disgrace." It was the badge of Lord Howard of Effingham in 1601, when he was Lord High Admiral, and was used first in this connection as a naval seal. As a badge, it was used previous to this time.

Frigate. A name originally designating a class of Mediterranean vessels which used both oars and sails. "The English were the first to use frigates on the ocean for war or commerce."

Furl. Probably from the old English "furdle," corruption of "fardle," meaning to make up in a bundle.

Futtock Shrouds. Futtock is a contracted term for "foot

hooks," for the toes have to be hooked or bent around the rat-lines to go over them.

Gale. From old Norse *galem,* Danish *gal,* mad or furious. But-ler in the seventeenth century, wrote:

When the wind blows not too hard, so that the ship may bear out her topsail a-trip (that is, fully hoisted, no reefs) it is called a loon gale; when it blows much wind it is called a swift and strong gale, or at least a fresh gale.

He describes the conditions when no sail could be carried as a tempest and this was considered a degree higher than a storm. The force of wind in nautical miles per hour, with equivalent designations such as "calm," "light airs," "fresh breeze," "gale," and "full gale" are employed today for logging weather. They were originally devised by Admiral Beaufort, R.N., and are known as the Beaufort scale or table.

Galley Yarn. A scuttle-butt rumor, a rumor. In the early days the cook was usually the originator of all startling news passed on to the crew.

Gangway. From Anglo-Saxon *gang,* to go; make a passage in, or cut out, or through.

Gig. The captain's boat. It is usually a light boat of whaler build with a gilded arrow on each bow. Much pride is taken in the gig; the general appearance of the crew and the cleanli-ness and neatness of the boat are usually excellent indications of the condition of the ship. In a gig under oars, it is customary for the captain to steer the boat and make the landing, after which the coxswain who is stroke oarsman takes charge.

Gig Stroke. A stroke used by the single-banked crew of gigs, requiring a distinct pause after each stroke of the oars. This stroke has fallen into disuse in the United States Navy and will soon be only a memory.

Gig and Galley.
The clinker-built "gig," as a substitute for the pinnace as the cap-tain's boat, came in with the nineteenth century. The 1815 edition of Falconer calls it "A long, narrow boat used for expedition, gen-

erally rowed with six or eight oars, and is mostly the *private property* of the captain or commander." The one-horse, two-wheeled vehicle called by the same name was introduced only a few years earlier, and the two land and sea terms may have the same etymology. Elisha Coles (1692 A.D.) and Bailey (1724-90) in their dictionaries give, as the *only* meaning of word "gig," a "wanton woman!" but "gigmanity" in a man-of-war has always been as much a guarantee of "respectability" afloat as Carlyle assures us it was ashore. The term "galley," now so universal for the long six-oared "gig" of the captain of a man-of-war, is not older on board ship than the middle of the nineteenth century, and at the date of the Crimean War was exclusively applied to the boat of the captain of a line-of-battle ship; but it has never been officially recognized by the Admiralty. In Crimean days it was an unpardonable offense for an officer of the watch, when the captain of a line-of-battle ship ordered his boat, to call away the "1st gig" instead of the "galley."[1]

Give Quarter. Came from a practice that originated in the wars between the Dutch and the Spaniards, when a captured officer was given life and liberty for a ransom fee estimated at one-quarter of his yearly pay.

Glass. Employed nautically to refer to such articles of the mariner's craft as barometers, telescopes, and time glasses. "How's the glass?" means, "What is the barometer doing?" "To flog" or "to sweat the glass" was a sharp practice of olden days, whereby the "glass" was agitated; the sand flowed faster; and the watch was more quickly terminated. "Clear glass" was used in reference to the heaving of the chip log and signified to clear all sand out of one end of the glass before heaving the log. "To cook a glass" meant to heat either a time glass or a telescope in order to remove moisture.

Grape. Small iron balls an inch or so in diameter bound together in clusters. This type of ammunition played an effective part in our early frigate actions.

Grog. A sailor's expression for watered rum. Admiral Vernon, R.N., in 1740 ordered that the rum be watered. It was Vernon's

[1] Rear Admiral Sir R. Massie Blomfield, R.N., "Man-of-War Boats, II," *Mariner's Mirror,* Vol. II, No. 1, p. 7, Jan., 1912.

custom to wear a cloak of a coarse material, called "grogram" (kind of taffeta). His nickname was "Old Grog"; hence the name applied to the beverage. Sailors of long ago sang:

> For grog is our starboard, our larboard,
> Our mainmast, our mizen, our log—
> At sea, or ashore, or when harbour'd,
> The mariner's compass is grog.

The legislation that led to the abolishment of grog in the Navy is of some historic interest. The spirit ration when abolished consisted of "two dips" a day and in lieu thereof a commutation of five cents per day.

Gustavus V. Fox, Assistant Secretary of the Navy, wrote Senator J. W. Grimes, "I beg of you for the enduring good of the Service . . . to add a proviso abolishing the spirit ration. . . ."[1] Senator Grimes championed the bill that abolished a spirit or rum ration aboard United States men-of-war.[2]

On 23 May, 1872, Congress made provision for a liberal issue of coffee and prescribed its use—"an additional ration of coffee and sugar to be served at his [the seaman's] first turning out. . . ."

"General Order 99," of 1 June, 1914, signed by Secretary of the Navy Josephus Daniels, prohibited "the use or introduction for drinking purposes of alcoholic liquors on board any naval vessel, or within any navy yard or station. . . ."

"General Order 244," of 21 March, 1934, signed by Secretary of the Navy Claude A. Swanson, permitted intoxicating liquors on naval shore establishments and confined such use to "officers' quarters, officers' messes, and officers' clubs. . . ."

Guard and Band for Colors. Although originally a ceremony at sunrise, Lord Saint Vincent established a new regulation after the mutinies in order to make it a most impressive ceremony. The British Navy in 1844 for the sake of uniformity set a fixed time for this ceremony.

---

[1] Letter from Hon. G. V. Fox to Hon. J. W. Grimes, 28 May, 1862.
[2] "On September 1, 1862, the spirit ration shall forever cease and thereafter no distilled spirituous liquor shall be admitted on board vessels of war, except as medicine and upon the order and under the control of the medical officer of such vessel and to be used only for medical purposes." *U. S. Stat.,* Vol. 12, p. 565.

Guess or *Guest Warp Ropes*.

A rope carried to a distant object in order to warp a vessel towards it, or to make fast a boat. "Haul out" also meant to haul out in its original sense. A ship's boat would come alongside, the crew would be ordered aboard, and the boat would be made fast while alongside to a guess warp and "hauled out."[3]

Gun, Son of a. In the early days, sailors were permitted to keep their "wives" on board. The term was actually used to refer to children born alongside the guns of the broadsides. In fact, the expression questioned the legitimacy of anyone. The old definition of a man-o'-war's man was,

Begotten in the galley and born under a gun. Every hair a rope yarn, every tooth a marline spike; every finger a fish hook and in his blood right good Stockholm tar.

A British officer commanding a brig off the Spanish coast in 1835 wrote in his diary,

This day the surgeon informed me that a woman on board had been laboring in child for twelve hours, and if I could see my way to permit the firing of a broadside to leeward, nature would be assisted by the shock. I complied with the request and she was delivered of a fine male child.

The Gunnery Department surely made a perfect score.

Gunnel (Gunwale). Whale comes from Anglo-Saxon *wala*, a "weal," a strip, a ridge. First in English in 1330. Derived from the custom of firing the top row of guns over planking which had been re-enforced by "wales"; hence "gunwales."

Gunnery. Although China had powder long before its invention in Europe, 1330 is given as the date of the invention of gunpowder. The Spaniards were armed with cannon in a sea fight against the English and the people of Poitou, off Rochelle in 1392. This is the first battle wherein mention is made of artillery in Navies. In 1824, Blunt, in his *Theory and Practice of Seamanship*, stated on the fly sheet that "the whole formed a

[3] Smythe, *Sailor's Word Book*.

useful compendium to the officer, to instruct him when young, and to remind him when old."

He writes in regard to gunnery:

The machines, which owe their rise to the invention of gunpowder, have now totally supplanted the others; so that there is scarcely any but the sword remaining of all the weapons used by the ancients. Our naval battles are therefore almost always decided by fire arms, of which there are several kinds, known by the general name of artillery. In a ship of war, fire arms are distinguished in the cannon mounted upon carriages, swivel cannon, grenades, and musketry. Besides these machines, there are several others used in merchant ships and privateers, as cohorns, cardbines, fire arrows, organs, stinkpots, etc.

In the British *Naval Regulations* (1790) the following may be found under "The Gunner":

Also every gunner ought to know that it is a wholesome thing for him to eat and drink a little meat before he doth discharge any piece of artillery, because the fume of saltpetre and brimstone will otherwise be hurtful to his brain, so it is very unwholesome to him to shoot in any piece of ordnance while his stomach is full.

Melville writing of the quarter gunners and gunners' mates refers to them as,

a class full of unaccountable whimsies. They were continually grumbling and growling about the batteries; running in and out among the guns; driving the sailors away from them, and cursing and swearing as if all their consciences had been powder singed and made callous by their calling.

Hammocks. Christopher Columbus in 1498 in the Bahamas found that the natives used woven cotton nets as beds, called by them "hammacs." The Spanish changed the word to *hamaco*. The Spanish spelling was used when the word entered the English nautical vocabulary in the Elizabethan reign.

In 1596, they are officially mentioned as hanging "cabbons" or "beddes." After an action, as many sails as possible were expended to provide new hammocks and white trousers for the crew. "Up hammocks" and "down hammocks" are expressions derived from the days when hammocks were stowed in topside,

Top: Reefing Topsails. Center: Lowering a Lifeboat on the Quarter. Bottom: Heaving the Chip Log—Note young seaman with hourglass, also spare chip log and reel on the deck. (From *Heck's Iconographic Encyclopedia*)

upper-deck nettings; hence comes the meaning "up all hammocks."

Hand, Lend a Hand or *Bear a.* Long usage has decreed that "lend a hand" is a request for assistance, while "bear a hand" implies an order.

Handsomely. An order meaning slowly and carefully.

Harter Act. By this act and law, a ship owner is protected against claims for damage incurred through the acts of the ship's officers or crew, provided the ship was seaworthy and was fully equipped and manned on leaving port.

Harvest Moon.

The phenomenon, in high latitudes, of several moonlight nights at the full moon nearest the autumnal equinox in which that body rises nearly at the same time. The moon ordinarily rises later each night by an average of 51 minutes, but at this time she is coming northward very rapidlly in declination, causing an earlier rising which almost overcomes the natural retardation due to her eastward movement of revolution.[1]

Haul. It means literally to pull or to drag. The wind "hauls" when it changes in direction with the sun. When a ship's course is so changed that her head lies nearer the wind, she is "hauled up." "To haul off" is to remove to a greater distance.

Hawse Pipes. Hawse is an old name for throat; and, since the head was forward as well as the "eyes," the term throat pipe or hawse pipe came into being.

Hawser. In some of the older English books of the sea, the term "haulter" is found, possibly referring to holding a ship, as an animal is held, by a halter.

Holystones. So named because fragments of broken monuments from Saint Nicholas church, Great Yarmouth, England, were used at one time to scrub the decks of ships of the British Navy. Holystones were also called in the British service, "ecclesiatical bricks." The name is now used for bricks, sand stones, or medium-soft sand rock utilized for the scrubbing of

[1] Gershom Bradford, *A Glossary of Sea Terms*, New York: Yachting, Inc., 1927.

wooden decks. They were moved fore and aft on the wet decks by means of a wooden handle placed in a depression of the stone. Holystones were of sufficient importance to become the subject of a general order issued by the Secretary of the Navy.

General Order 215 of March 5, 1931, states:

1. The use of holystones for cleaning the wooden decks of naval vessels wears down the decks so rapidly that their repair or replacement has become an item of expense to the Navy Department which cannot be met under limited appropriations.

2. . . . .

3. It is therefore directed that the use of holystones or similar material for cleaning wooden decks be restricted to the removal of stains.

Idlers. Falconer's *Marine Dictionary* (Revised 1815) defines "idlers" as all those on board a ship of war, who from being liable to constant day duty are not subjected to keep night watch, but nevertheless must go up on deck if all hands are called during the night. The term today includes sick bay attendants, cooks, yeomen, etc.

Jamaica Discipline. A name for the "Articles for the Government of Pirate Ships," in the eighteenth century. The articles stipulated that the captain took two shares of all stolen booty, the officers one and one-half and one and one-quarter, depending upon rank, while all the crew shared alike. In order to prevent quarrels and brawls aboard ship, gambling and the bringing of women aboard ship was prohibited. Indulgence in strong drink could only take place on deck after 8:00 P.M.

Java or "Jamoke." Used by bluejackets of the United States Navy to designate coffee. For twenty years before "grog" was legislated out of the Navy, the rum ration had been diminished, while tea and coffee were "experimentally supplied as a substitute." In the Congressional Bill of 23 May, 1872, further provision was made for "an additional ration of coffee and sugar to be served at his [the bluejacket's] first turning out." The United States Navy uses more coffee per man than any other military or naval organization in the world.

Keelhauling. A call down or reprimand; "getting on the carpet" is its general meaning as used by older seamen. In the early days this term signified one of the most drastic and cruel forms of punishment. The victim was hoisted by a whip or light tackle to a fore yardarm, and thence dropped into the sea. A weight was attached to the unfortunate to insure that he would sink deep enough for a whip to drag him under the keel and up again to the opposite yardarm on the other side.

There is record that this was originally a punishment in vogue among the pirates of the Mediterranean in the sixteenth century, and that it was afterwards introduced into the English and the Dutch Navies.

Boteler describes this punishment in a book, called *Dialogical Discourse on Marine Affairs,* written probably about 1630, but published in 1685, and dedicated to Samuel Pepys, as follows:

The duckinge at the marine yarde arme is when a malefactor by haveing a rope fastened under his arms and about his middle and under his breech is thus hoysted up to the end of the yarde from whence he is againe violently let fall into the sea, sometimes twice, sometimes three, severall tymes, one after the other, and if the offense be very fowle, he is also drawn under the very keele of the shippe, the which is called keele-rakinge, and whilst he is thus under water a great gunne is given fyre unto, right over his head, ye which is done as well to astonish him the more with thunder thereof, which much troubles him, as to give wareinge unto all others to looke out and beware of his harms.

Knots and Fathoms. Leslie, in *Old Sea Wings, Ways, and Words,* states:

To appreciate the term "knot," a slight acquaintance with the rule of three is desirable. Thus, if the ship goes one mile in one hour, how far does she go in a half minute. Having found the distance, which is about eight fathoms, measure off on the log line as many such spaces as may seem necessary, marking them in the knots. Then when the log is hove, the number of knots that will pass off the reel while the half minute sand glass is running will correspond to the number of miles that the ship will go in an hour. This is why "she goes ten knots" is right and "she goes ten knots an hour" is wrong.

Many junior officers make this mistake and confuse knots with miles per hour.

Captain Gershom Bradford describes in detail the old method of computing speed:

Chip log is a device now restricted to a few sailing vessels. It consists of a wooden quadrant about 5 inches in radius, with lead placed in the circular edge, which causes it to float upright. It is made fast to a log line by a three-part bridle. The part fitted to the upper corner has a socket and a pin which pulls out when a strain is placed upon it with the desire to haul it aboard. The chip is cast over (streamed) with the pin in position. The first 15 or 30 fathoms of line is called the stray line which is marked by a piece of red bunting. The line from this point is divided into parts of 47 feet 3 inches, each called a knot. They are marked by pieces of cord tucked through the strands with knots in their ends corresponding to the number of knots out. Each knot is subdivided into fifths and marked with a white rag. The log line is allowed to run out while a 28-second glass is emptying itself. The result is the rate of speed of the vessel. The length of the knot was derived from the proportion that one hour (3,600 sec.) is to 28 seconds as one mile (6,080 ft.) is to the length of a knot (47 ft. 3 in.) . The clipper ship *Flying Cloud*[1] off Cape Horn once ran out 18 knots and there was still a little sand in the glass."

Langridge. Knife blades, old nails, copper slugs, iron bolts, and scraps of metal in cans. Used in cannon at the time of the War of American Independence and War of 1812. Bayonet blades bound with rope yarn were shot from cannon for the purpose of cutting rigging in order to effect the fall of masts. There were shells of that time known as starshots, chain shots, "sausages," double headers, "porcupines," and "hedge hogs."

---

[1] The American clipper *Flying Cloud,* one of the fastest and most famous clippers ever built. Designed by Donald McKay, launched in 1851, length 225 ft., beam 40 ft. 8 in., depth 21 ft. 6 in., tonnage 1,782. On first voyage, sailed from New York to San Francisco in 80 days 21 hours, the fastest passage up to that time. The British *Cutty Sark* was constructed of teak and built to beat the *Thermopylæ,* which on one occasion did the run between London and Melbourne from land to land by the Cape of God Hope in 59 days. The *Cutty Sark* did the run from Shanghai to London in 98 days. It was said figuratively of the captains of these famous ships, that they "padlocked" their topgallant sheets in rounding the Horn. Ships of graceful lines, fleecy white sails, lofty tapering spars—all gone, as well as the sturdy souls who manned them.

Larboard. The "load board" was the left side of the ship, in distinction to the right side of a ship where the steering gear was carried, known as "steer board." Larboard was confused with starboard and hence the term "port" or loading entrance was adopted.

The expression "steer bord" may be traced to the Vikings. Viking ships have been found in a remarkable state of preservation, wherein the remains of chieftains were buried. From these ships the arrangement for steering on the right or starboard quarter may be observed in detail. The Gokstadt ship discovered in 1880 was built of oak, was 72 feet long and 15 feet 6 inches beam, and had a displacement of about 30 tons. The quarter rudder was used by the Vikings in the ninth century, but about the twelfth century a second rudder was placed on the larboard side. Eventually the stern rudder replaced the two quarter rudders.

Lashing Broom to Fore Topmast. Maarten Harpertszoon Tromp, a Dutch admiral, ordered that brooms be lashed to the masts when the great sailor sailed to meet the fleet of Cromwell. This gesture signified that he would sweep the English Channel of the English Navy. Tradition tells us that the English wore horsewhips at the masthead, and that the coachwhip pennants were derived therefrom.

The American Navy has for many years hoisted brooms at the mastheads of the ships that won the battle efficiency pennants. Even before the present form of competition, brooms were hoisted by ships standing one in gunnery, also in engineering competition. Christmas trees are hoisted at both the foremast and mainmast trucks of United States ships during the Yuletide. The tips of yards are also decorated with evergreens.

Launch Cannonade. This short piece of ordnance was in reality the forerunner of the anti-aircraft gun. It was the most effective gun of its time for shooting at sharpshooters in the tops. It is recorded that by a launch cannonade the mizzentop of the *Chesapeake* was cleaned of sharpshooters before the daring Broke boarded her from the British *Shannon*.

Lieutenant. A word derived from the French, meaning "holding in lieu of" or "one who replaces."

The introduction of this rank into the British Navy in 1580 was for the purpose of providing the captain with an assistant and qualified relief if necessary. The first lieutenant was for years, both in the British and American Services, the executive officer of the ship. In smaller British ships, the title First Lieutenant still obtains, and he is referred to unofficially as No. 1.

In the latter part of the Elizabethan reign, the following rule is on record:

The lieutenant must have a care that he carry not himself proudly or presumptiously, nor that his captain give him power or authority to intermeddle with the master's office; for where there is heart burning between the lieutenant and master, it will make it burst out into open discontent and then will follow mischief and factions among the company.

Lieutenant Commander. This title was introduced in the United States Navy in 1862 with the reorganization of the Service. Previous to this time, all lieutenants in command of smaller men-of-war were called "lieutenant commanding." For example, in the roster of the North Atlantic Blockading Squadron in 1862 one reads:

(U.S.S.) *Valley City,* Lieut. Commanding S. C. Chaplin, bearing the flag of Flag Officer Goldsborough; also (U.S.S.) *Commander Perry,* Lieutenant Commanding C. W. Flusser.

The title lieutenant commander was derived from the term "lieut. commanding."

"Limey." A friendly name that through the years has been used by American bluejackets in referring to British bluejackets and merchant sailors in particular, and when pluralized, to Britishers in general. It was derived from the old practice in the British Navy of giving lime juice as an anti-scorbutic. In order to combat the evil of scurvy, lime or lemon juice was issued from the time of the early French wars until this century. Until 1860, this anti-scorbute was obtained from Malta and

Sicily; in fact, it was the juice of the lemon, then called a lime. Medical authorities then considered the acid quality of citron fruit an excellent means to combat scurvy. Due to the expense and difficulty of getting lime juice from the Mediterranean area, the British authorities commenced after 1860 to secure lime juice from St. Kitts in the West Indies. Scurvy cropped up again in the British Navy during the World War, and a committee of experts were delegated to study the question. It was found that certain vitamins played a most important part. Investigation disclosed that lime juice contains a negligible percentage of those vitamins, while lemon juice had a large percentage. The acid quality had little or nothing to do with the prevention of scurvy. Scurvy, that dread disease of sailors, has been practically eliminated by short voyages and modern refrigeration, but the old word "limey" lives on.

Loggerhead. The word was derived from "logger-heat," a piece of iron on a long handle used for melting pitch. The iron after heating was placed in the cold pitch. It was a deadly weapon when men came to "loggerheads."

Long Ship. An expression once used in our Service and still used in the British Service to signify a ship in which it was a long time between drinks or a long way from the fount of hospitality. There are ships of a naval service today that hoist a green pennant in port at noon to signify that the time for the cup that cheers has arrived and friends are welcomed aboard.

Lucky Bag. Now a small compartment or large locker where masters-at-arms stow articles of clothing, bedding, etc., picked up on the decks. Originally, these articles were placed in a bag called the "lucky bag" which was in the custody of the master-at-arms. In a narrative of a cruise in the U.S.S. *Columbia* in 1838, the writer relates that the bag was brought to the mainmast once a month, and the owners of the articles "if their names are on them, get them again, with a few lashes for their carelessness in leaving them about the deck." The term "lucky" in this case is sailor's humor for "unfortunate."

Marines. At least five centuries before the Christian Era, the Phoenicians and the Greeks used marines. The marines were the fighting men, while the seamen were the rowers. There is mention of marines in the time of Darius, King of Persia, about 497 B.C. In the battle of Lade between the Greeks and the Persians, one hundred Greek ships had forty armed citizens on board, and those were picked men. The Greeks called these sea soldiers *epibatoe*. The Scandinavians called them *bat-karler* or sea soldiers. They have been called *supra-salientes,* a word still retained in the Spanish *sobiesaliente,* and as a military term meaning "over-leapers." In 1740, three regiments of marines were raised in the American Colonies and were assembled at New York.

The United States Marine Corps antedates the organization of the regular Navy, and even the Declaration of Independence. On 10 November, 1775, the Continental Congress to promote a "publick defense"

Resolved, That two battalions of Marines be raised consisting of one colonel, two lieutenant colonels, two majors. . . . That particular care be taken that no person be appointed to offices, or enlisted into said battalions, but such as are good seamen or so acquainted with maritime affairs as to be able to serve to advantage by sea when required; that they be enlisted and commissioned to serve for and during the present war between Great Britain and the Colonies. . . . That they be distinguished by the names of the First and Second Battalions of American Marines.

Lieutenant Wallingford of the Marines lost his life under Jones in the *Ranger-Drake* action. Lieutenant O'Bannon of the Marines "planted the American Flag for the first time on a fortress in the Old World." That was at Tripoli. The first officer killed in the *Constitution-Guerrière* fight was Lieutenant Bush of the Marines.

Admiral Luce wrote:

The United States Marine Corps has well sustained the high reputation for steadfast courage and loyalty which has been handed down to it from the days of Themistocles.

THE UNITED STATES MARINE CORPS WAS AUTHORIZED BY THE CONTINENTAL CONGRESS OF THE UNITED COLONIES NOV 10 1775. DISBANDED AT THE CLOSE OF THE REVOLUTIONARY WAR 1782. REORGANIZED AND PERMANENTLY ESTABLISHED UNDER THE CONSTITUTION OF THE UNITED STATES JULY 11 1798.

BIRTH OF THE UNITED STATES MARINE CORPS, 10 November, 1775—"Per Mare et Terram." (From a painting by J. Joseph Capolino. Courtesy Marine Corps Recruiting Bureau, Philadelphia)

It would require a long essay to trace the history of the Marine Corps from the British Navy in 1664 to our present organization. The first corps was known as the Admiral's Maritime Regiment and was commanded by the Duke of York (later James II). Its history is long and interesting. In 1802, they were styled Royal Marines by order of the King as a mark of the King's pleasure for their conduct during the War of the French Revolution and their action during the great mutiny.

In 1827, new colors were presented to the Chatham Division of the Royal Marines, and at the presentation a device or badge was given them. The Duke of Clarence said:

From the difficulty of selecting any particular places to inscribe on these standards, your Sovereign has been pleased to adopt "The Great Globe itself," as the most proper and distinct badge . . . the anchor which is your distinctive bearing was also adopted.

The cap device of the American marine was formerly a bugle; but in 1869 a metal hemisphere on an anchor and surmounted by an eagle was adopted.

Martinet. A stickler for discipline, "a sundowner." The name comes from a French army officer, the Marquis de Martinet. A "cat-of-nine-tails" is still called in French nautical slang a "martinet."

Master. Six things required of a master in the Elizabethan age were "the cards (charts), the compass, the tides, the time, the wind, and the ship's way." The detailed duties of a master in the United States Navy are outlined elsewhere.

Master-at-Arms. Master-at-arms evolved from the sea corporal and was introduced into the Royal Navy during the reign of Charles I. "His department included all the muskets, carbines, pistols, swords; and he exercised the ship's company, seeing that their bandoliers before going into action were filled with good powder." In the early days of the U.S.S. *Constitution* and other ships, there is record of drill under arms for the seamen under the direction of the master-at-arms. He not only had police duties and was "chief of police," but was supposed to be qualified in close order fighting under arms. Records of more than a hundred years ago indicate that these drills were received by the crew with no more enthusiastic welcome than today.

Mate. An old rank in the Navy. The mate, although an officer, was not in the line of promotion and held his position by appointment. He usually messed in the steerage or with the warrant officers and was ordered to duty in charge of boats, mate of the deck, or any special duty prescribed by the commanding officer. This term must not be confused with boatswain's mate, gunner's mate, etc.

Mess. Mess comes from the Latin word *mensa,* meaning table; Spanish word *mesa,* table; also, a Gothic word *mes,* meaning a dish; hence, a mess of pottage. The word in English originally denoted four, and at large dinners the diners were seated in fours. Shakespeare wrote of Henry's four sons as his "mess of sons" (*II Henry VI,* Act I). The word mess, meaning confusion, is from the German *mischen,* meaning to mix.

Messmates. Those eating together, comrades.

"Messmate before shipmate, shipmate before stranger, stranger before a dog."[1]

Midshipman. Men or boys originally stationed amidship to carry messages, to carry up ammunition, and to relay messages from aft to the gundecks. It was a ship's rating in the British Navy until the end of the Napoleonic wars. A midshipman could be disrated at any time by the captain. In 1740, admirals and captains were permitted a certain number of followers; and in some cases a flag officer was permitted fifty. They were rated midshipmen, tailors, barbers, fiddlers, footmen, and stewards. It was in 1815 that midshipmen became a naval rank in the British Service. The midshipman's time on the books counted towards promotion as a lieutenant, for two years of the six years' service required at sea had to be served as a midshipman or mate. Often midshipmen were entered on the books a year or so before actual service. It was a British personnel problem in 1755 how

[1] Smythe, *Sailors' Word Book.*

to breed up officers and gentlemen who should be able seamen, skilled to manage a ship and maintain a sea fight judiciously, of discretion and courage and able to speak to the seamen in their own language.

"Middy" is the term used most frequently by elderly ladies, land-going writers of sea stories, and in the "movies."

Until the advent of steam the life of the midshipman was often most disagreeable. The food was bad; the quarters cramped and located below the water line; and the duties were onerous and manifold. Without the full status of an officer and still not a member of the crew, his position aboard ship was quite indefinite until regulations became more specific. The *United States Naval Regulations* (1818) state: "The commanding officers will consider the midshipmen as a class of officers, meriting in an especial degree their fostering care." From all accounts this "fostering care" was capable of wide interpretation.

This apprenticeship for a commission is set forth in a realistic manner by Rear Admiral Baron Jeffrey de Raigersfeld in *The Life of a Sea Officer*. As to midshipmen, it is recorded:

In the latter part of the eighteenth century it was not uncommon for midshipmen to be flogged, mastheaded, and disrated, if not turned before the mast.

Admiral de Raigersfeld writes of his midshipman days under Captain, afterwards Admiral Lord, Collingwood:

On board the *Mediator* all these punishments were inflected at various times; and one morning after breakfast, while at anchor in St. John's Road, Antigua, all the midshipmen were sent for into the captain's cabin, and four of us were tied up one after the other to the breech of one of the guns, and flogged upon our bare bottoms with a cat-o'-nine-tails, by the boatswain of the ship; some received six lashes, some seven, and myself three. No doubt we all deserved it, and were thankful that we were punished in the cabin instead of upon deck, which was not uncommon in other ships of the fleet.

The practice of carrying babies as midshipmen on the books in order to gain seniority was not limited to the British Service. Samuel Barron of the United States Navy was appointed, when only a little more than two years of age, a midshipman from Virginia. Samuel Barron was born 28 November, 1809, and appointed a midshipman 1 January, 1812. He commenced his sea service in his eleventh year, and in 1825 was a midshipman in the frigate *Brandywine* when that ship took Lafayette to France after his visit to the United States. It was suggested in the United States Naval Institute PROCEEDINGS (LIX, No. 365) that after the death of Barron's father, a commodore of the same name, this appointment was secured not only to provide for the son's future but also "to afford some additional government compensation for the mother and family."

As to the many duties of the "young gentlemen" (midshipmen were so referred to before Nelson's time), Rear Admiral J. K. Taussig, U. S. Navy, told the writer that he was ordered with another midshipman to heave the lead from the chains of the *Newark* upon her departure from New York City in 1899, notwithstanding the fact that both of the young gentlemen were in dress uniform. Rear Admiral Taussig also relates that due to a mix-up in a salute from a British captain to an American rear admiral, his senior officer ordered him as a midshipman "to go aboard that British ship and make the British captain feel sorry for his mistake." It took courage, quick wits, and above all the spirit of youth to perform creditably the duties of a midshipman at sea. After all, the most amusing and thrilling events in a sea officer's career take place in his midshipman and junior officer days.

As a contrast of the education of the old Navy and the new, the *United States Naval Regulations* (1818) state under the duties of the chaplain, "He is likewise to teach the other youths of the ship (outside of instruction of midshipmen) according to such orders as he shall receive from the captain." On 1 June, 1933, President Franklin D. Roosevelt delivered diplomas to 432 members of the class of 1933. Graduates for the first time in our naval history received the degree of Bachelor of Science. Of the graduates, 216 were commissioned ensigns of the line.

To classify a midshipman as an officer has always been subject to qualification. The present *United States Navy Regulations* (1920) state that, "Midshipmen are by law officers in a qualified sense. They are classed as being of the line." In other days, their relative rank, as established in the reorganization of the Navy by the Act of 1815, was as follows:

The order in which officers shall take precedence and command in the ship to which they belong is as follows:

Captain or commander
Lieutenants, agreeably to date or number of their commissions
Master
Master's mate
Boatswain
Gunner
Carpenter
Midshipman

In days of sail midshipmen in our Navy often called each other "reefers" in familiar conversation.

The old title "passed midshipman" in the United States Navy meant originally a midshipman who had passed his examination, entitling him to promotion to a lieutenant. When the title of ensign was introduced into the United States Navy, those awaiting promotion were called midshipmen while under-graduates were called cadet midshipmen. In 1819 a board, of which Commander Bainbridge was senior member, met in New York to give the first examinations that had ever been given midshipmen in our Navy for promotion. This, incidentally, was the first examination of any kind instituted for officers in the American Navy.

Moor. From Dutch word *marren,* to tie, to fasten.

Not Room to Swing a Cat. A very old naval expression, meaning not room to swing a cat-of-nine-tails—low over head.

Oakum. Derived from the old Anglo-Saxon word *oecumbe;* in the eighteenth century it was spelled *ockam.*

Oar. Utilized by mankind at the dawn of history but our word comes from the *ayr* of the Middle Ages.

Officer—Officials. The following interesting history was taken from a foreign service examination pamphlet issued by the Department of State:

Historically, the employment of the word "officer" to denote a person holding a military or naval command as representative of the State, and not as deriving his authority from his own powers or privileges, marks an entire change in the character of the armed forces of civilized nations. Originally signifying an official, one who performs an assigned duty (Latin, *officium*), an agent, and in the fifteenth century actually meaning the subordinate of such an official (even today a constable is so called), the word seems to have acquired a military significance late in the sixteenth century.

It was at this time that armies, though not yet "standing," came to be constituted almost exclusively of professional soldiers in the king's pay. Mercenaries, and great numbers of mercenaries, had always existed, and their captains were not feudal magnates. But the bond between mercenaries and their captains was entirely personal, and the bond between the captain and the sovereign was of the nature of a contract. The non-mercenary portion of the older armies was feudal in character. It was the lord and not a king's officer who commanded it, and he commanded in virtue of his rights, not of a warrant or commission.[1]

Open Muster. The general muster in the American Navy was derived from the British open muster. The British "mustering by the open list" was forced upon the British Service to counteract the sharp practices of pursers in underpaying men. The original idea was that each member of the crew would report who he was and for what he was paid. General muster was abolished in the American Navy in 1914. Division quarters each morning was introduced by Admiral Kempenfeldt, R.N., in 1780.

Passing to Windward. Vessels were supposed to pass to leeward of their superiors. This was strictly observed if the inferior happened to be a merchantman. For it was then written:

If the opposite procedure took place, it is as accounted as unmannerly a trick as if the constable of a parish should jostle for the wall with a justice of the peace dwelling in the same county.

---

[1] At sea the relatively clear partition of actual duties amongst the authorities of a ship brought the adoption of the term "officer" somewhat earlier.

Whether in men-of-war or merchantmen the weather side was the traditional side at sea for the admiral and captain, the starboard side is the "sacred ground" when the ship is at anchor, and in the days of sail with the wind aft, it is explained as the side where

he [the captain] can feel the wind and weather upon his cheek, can sniff the land, or sight the coming squall. It was once always customary for all weather gangways to be used by superiors.

Paying Your Footing. The following anecdote gives the meaning of this old expression. Captain's Clerk Mr. E. G. Wines, U. S. Navy, who served on the U.S.S. *Constellation* 1829-31 wrote:

On the twenty-first of August [1829] I went for the first time to the main top-gallant masthead—to me a dizzy height. . . . The old tars laughed heartily at my timidity. I asked them if they were never afraid. "Afraid!" they replied, "what good would it do to be afraid? Mr. Wines, have you never been in a top before?" "No." "Then you must pay for your footing" was the next thing. Paying for your footing is treating all hands to a glass of grog on your first visit to a top. This they never fail to demand, always promising in return, to teach you all they know themselves about the rigging of the ship. At first I offered them money. "Oh," said they, "give us the grog, what good will money do us here?" I then told them I would pay my footing in their own way, if they would get permission from the first lieutenant. I thought this would stagger them, but was mistaken. "Poh! Poh!" they replied, "never mind the first lieutenant, send it up by a boy and call it water." More than two years afterwards, I asked the captain of the top if I didn't owe him a glass of grog. "Yes, Sir, I believe you do, Sir. Why, Sir, I believe it's to pay your footing in the main top, Sir."

Paymaster (Purser). Records of the fourteenth century show "clerks" or "bursers" in English ships. In the early days their pay came from profit in the sale of supplies, which sometimes led to the purchase of assignment, to lucrative positions. In 1842, the British Navy created the title paymaster and purser.

Melville, writing of life on the U.S.S. *United States* in 1843, says:

Of all the non-combatants of a man-of-war, the purser perhaps stands foremost in importance; though he is but a member of the gunroom mess, yet usage seems to assign him a conventional station somewhat above that of the equals in Navy rank—the chaplain, surgeon, and professor.

The purser's steward in those days acted as postmaster.

The title purser was derived from bursar. This was the old name for keeper of the cash, and hence the word disburser or one who pays out money. The term "burse magister" may be found in the English Merchant Marine in the time of Henry VI. The title purser was used in the United States Navy from its birth until 1860. The pursers were civilian appointments made only for a vessel's cruise. Their compensation was based upon a commission on expenditures. By a general order, legalized by Act of Congress in 1854, pursers of more than twelve years' service were to rank with commanders and those of less than twelve years, with Lieutenants, and to take rank with surgeons according to date of commission. In 1860, it was enacted that pursers in the Navy of the United States should thereafter be styled "paymasters." They were designated supply officers in 1917 and were authorized to be addressed by the military titles, ensign, lieutenant, lieutenant commander, commander, captain, and rear admiral. This order gave military titles to all officers of the Staff Corps.

Pea-Coat. The exact derivation of the name is not known. For two hundred years, it has been the name for the heavier top coat worn by seafaring men in cold weather. The coat was originally made of a material called pilot cloth.

Port. Larboard signified the left side on board ship in the United States Navy until about 1846. It is recorded that in that year the following word was passed on board an American man-of-war cruising off the coast of Africa:

Do you hear there fore and aft? The word "larboard" is to be forever dropped in the United States Navy, and the word "port" is substituted. Any man using the word "larboard" will be punished.

The British Navy made the change some years before. Admiral Penrose Fitzgerald states in his memoirs that the word

QUARTERMASTERS WHO STEERED U.S.S. *Hartford* IN THE BATTLE OF MOBILE BAY, 5 AUGUST, 1864.—Left to right: Joseph Tessier, John McFarland, Van Ness, and James Ford. Note the size of the wheel, the "spit-kid" for the helmsman, the large binnacles, and the lee helmsman in the background. (From a photograph entered in the clerk's office for Eastern District of Louisiana, to November, 1864)

"port" was adopted in the British Navy from the orders of the Portuguese Tagus River pilots (See "Starboard").

Porthole. James Baker, a shipbuilder, ordered by King Henry VI (1485) who desired heavier guns on his ships, pierced the sides of *The Great Harry.* Baker resorted to the French method of a water-tight door to close the opening when the battery was not in use. This door was called a port; hence the term porthole which was originally a hole for a gun.

Professors of Mathematics. The first appointments were made in 1831 for the purpose of instructing midshipmen aboard ship. Eventually, this practice was found impracticable, but after the establishment of the Naval Academy the professors then on the list were detailed to duty at the Academy. Professors of mathematics were at an early date detailed to the Naval Observatory. The first appointment of a professor of mathematics was given to Professor Elisha Fitch, 25 September, 1831. Professor Fitch served until his death, 15 October, 1839.

Promotion. From the London *Times,* Thursday, 10 January, 1828:

Quick Promotion—Colonel Arbuthnot, who commands the 73d Highland Regiment, quartered at the Tower, is only 21 years of age.

Slow Promotion—There are three middys on board the *Victory* at Portsmouth—one is 40, another is 42, and another 45 years of age.

Captain Hopwood, R.N., writes:

> Count not upon certain promotion,
> But rather to gain it aspire;
> Though the sight-line end on the target,
> There cometh, perchance, a miss-fire.

Quarter-Deck. From the *Marine Encyclopedia* (1881) prepared by officers of the Navy:

The upper deck abaft the mainmast. Naval etiquette requires all persons to salute coming on the quarter-deck, and to conduct themselves in decorous manner while thereon.

The starboard side in port and the weather side at sea are reserved for the use of the commanding and executive officers, and officer of the deck

Irrespective of design or type of ship, there will always be a part of the deck set aside for ceremonies and honors.

Quartermaster. A quartermaster had originally nothing to do with steering a ship, but was assigned to specific duties of looking after troop quarters. In later years these men were retained aboard after troops debarked and were assigned to other duties. The military use the word in its original connotation.

Rogue's March. An old tune played when drumming bad characters out of a ship or a regiment.

Rogue's Yarn. The yarn in rope which is twisted either the opposite way from the other yarns, or is colored. This is a means to detect the theft of government cordage.

Rope.* Ropes are called lines by sailors. Old sailors assert there are seven ropes on a ship, although some are called lanyards—the manrope, headrope, handrope, footrope, bellrope, buoyrope, and diprope.

That master mariner of sail, Captain Felix Riesenberg, in his review of the first edition of this book, writes:

I can think of a few more, such as wheel rope or tiller rope, back-ropes (the head stays, from the martingale up, aft, to the cat heads), mast rope (used in sending up and down masts), yard rope (same for yards, boltrope (on sails), and ridgerope (on ship's awnings).

Round Robin.

This morning we all signed a round robin, setting forth our "willingness to return to duty on the liberation of the three men." Our names are written in radiating lines, like the spokes of a wheel, so that there are no leading names on the list.

Query—"Is it from this custom of signing dangerous papers that the term 'ring leader' was derived?"—William M. Davis.

Round Turn. To take a turn around a bitt or bollard, to check a strain or weight.

"To bring up with a round turn" is nautical phraseology for a "call-down" or reprimand.

---

* Admiral Hugh Rodman, U. S. Navy (Retired), with 32 years' sea service and all early days under sail, adds to "ropes": Anchor rope (small boats), boltrope, yokerope, wheel or tiller rope, yardrope, mastrope, backrope, and bullrope.

Rudder. Originally placed on "steer board" or starboard side of Viking ships. Derived from the old Anglo-Saxon *rother,* that which guides. The sternpost rudder came into use in the twelfth century. In 1262, there is record of ships paying certain dues if they had "helm-rothers," and smaller dues for "hand-rothers." This is considered as a distinction between the quarter rudder and the sternpost rudder.

Running. Originally to impose upon the credulity of a "green horn" at sea, whether it be a man or a midshipman. In a description of a cruise in the *Constellation,* a hundred years ago: "The men were fond as the 'reefers' of 'running' each other, and imposing upon the credulity of landsmen." Confined now generally to midshipman slang and connotes mild hazing: as junior officers signify "kidding" or "leg pulling."

Sailing Master. This was the title for a warrant (warranted) officer as early as 1798. In the *Regulations of the United States Navy,* issued by command of the President, 25 January, 1802, certain duties required of the sailing master were:

To inspect the provisions and stores. . . . To take care of the ballast. . . . To give directions for stowing the hold and spirit-room. Trimming the ship, and preservation of the provisions; to take special care of the rigging; to navigate the ship and see that the log and log book are duly kept.

These duties are now assigned to executive, navigator, and first lieutenant. In 1813, there were 162 sailing masters on the list of the Navy. George Farragut, father of the Admiral, was on this list. The title was changed to master in 1839. In 1846, the term "masters in the line of promotion" was used to signify certain of the grade of passed midshipmen to fill the vacancies by death of the old-time masters. In 1861, there were 36 of the grade on the active list. In 1862, on reorganization of the Navy, they were all merged into the grades. Then master became a commissioned grade between lieutenant and ensign, with the duties of a watch officer. In 1881, there were 4 old-time warranted masters on the retired list.

Sailor. From Middle English *saylor,* root unknown.

On shipboard, one who has made a long sea voyage other than his first, and who is qualified to go aloft and tend the sails. A sailor is not necessarily a seaman.[1]

Mariner is usually restricted to legal documents. Technically speaking, sailor means one before the mast; nevertheless, that Farragut was a great sailor will not be denied.

Salt Junk and Hard-Tack. At one time the principal diet of seafaring men, and stood for salted meat and sea biscuits. This expression is seldom heard today. One who has eaten of the old hard-tack fully agrees with Charles XII when he said "It is not good but it can be eaten." In old sea narratives mention is made of "lobscowse," a delicacy in its day, although easy to prepare—potatoes and salt beef hashed together.

Junk was originally a vegetable fiber from which rope was made. In time the word junk was used in referring to old rope. The meat, in sailing ship days, was carried in the "harness cask." Probably as a result of its resemblance to old rope, both in texture and stringiness, it was called salt horse or salt junk.

Schooner. The schooner is an American rig, and the type was originally built in Gloucester, Massachusetts, in 1713. Andrew Robinson, shipbuilder, had not decided on a name for the new rig, and tradition relates that as she left the ways a bystander sung out, "See how she scoons." Robinson heard this remark and said, "A schooner she shall be."

Scuttle. This meant "hold" in Anglo-Saxon. In reality, to scuttle a ship means literally to hole her.

Scuttle Butt. The sailors' well or source of fresh drinking water.

Melville, in *White Jacket,* describes the scuttle butt in the U.S.S. *United States,* 1843:

The scuttle butt is a goodly, round, painted cask, standing on end, and with its upper head removed showing a narrow circular shelf within where rest a number of tin cups for the accommodation of

[1] *Brande and Cox.*

drinkers. Central within the scuttle butt itself stands an iron pump, which, connecting with the immense water tanks in the hold, furnished an unfailing supply of the much admired Pale Ale. . . .

A long road to the present day Frigidaire drinking fountains aboard ship.

Sea.

The sea was called *saivs* from a root *si* or *siv*, the Greek *seiō*, to shake; it meant the tossed-about water in contradistinction to stagnant or running water.[1]

Sea Time. There is record in the earliest days of navigation of a division of the sea day into watches.

Pigafetta, in his detailed account of Magellan's ill-fated voyage, refers to the captain-general when he

ordered that three watches should be set at night. The first was at the beginning of the night, the second at midnight, and the third towards break of day, which is commonly called *la diane,* otherwise the star of the break of day.

Sir Henry Mainwaring explains the early watches in his *Seaman's Dictionary,*

at the sea the ship's company is divided into two parts, the one called the starboard watch, the other the larboard watch. The master is the chief of the starboard and his right-hand mate, of the larboard. These are in their turns to watch, trim sails, pump, and do all duties for four hours; and then the other watch is to relieve them. Four hours they call a whole watch.

It is believed that "dog watches" came at a later date than the time of the *Seaman's Dictionary.*

Sandglasses were in use ashore before the clock era. Due to the rolling and pitching of a ship, sandglasses remained for many years as ships' timepieces after the pendulum clock was invented. Mainwaring in his description of heaving the log, says:

One stands by with a minute glass, whilst another out of the gallery lets fall the log; just as the log falls into the water the other turns the glass, and just when the glass is even out he cries "stop"; then he

[1] Max Müller.

stops and reckons how many fathoms are run out; so gives his judgment.

It appears that before ship's bells the sandglass was turned each half hour for the "trick at the wheel." This original watch probably lasted only one-half hour, due to its strenuous nature. Lyde writes in his *Friends Adventure* that one sailor

sat down on a low stool by the helm, to look after the sandglass and to call to pump, which they had to do every half hour because the ship leaked so much.

Ships' bells came in later. The first clue that can be found is from the author of an anonymous book of travel and adventure. He wrote in the middle of the seventeenth century and describes a Dutch ship which he boarded in Leghorn, Italy. Among other things this unknown writer said:

Every half hour the steersman . . . at the ringing of a bell is changed. The bell is rung also every time they change the watch and for prayers, breakfast, and dinner.

The eight strokes on the bell is derived from the turns of the hour glass during the watch. The hour glass went, the ship's bell remains.

An old custom, once strictly observed, was that of having the oldest man in the ship, be he admiral or jack-of-the-dust, strike eight bells at midnight, on December thirty-first. This was immediately followed by eight bells for the New Year and always struck by the youngest boy on board. It was, of course, the only time of the year when sixteen bells were struck.

An old ship bell from H.M.S. *Conqueror* has this inscription, *Tempus Omnia Vincit.*

Shackle. This word is traced to the Anglo-Saxon *sceacul,* or link of a chain.

Shakedown Cruise. A cruise made in a new vessel for the purpose of testing machinery, adjusting instruments, and getting officers and men familiar with administration and drill aboard.

Shipmate. "A term once dearer than brother, but the habit of short cruises is weakening it."[1]

[1] Smythe, *Sailors' Word Book.*

Shipping Over. Since men first followed the sea, imagination has pictured the end of the cruise, the getting "paid off," the decommissioning, the shore leave, and shore duty. Often the sailor exclaims, "Never again!" and that he will quit the sea; but the idle boasts usually come to naught, and the old-timer is back aboard, after a little hectic life ashore. In 1843, the following conversation took place after a long cruise on an American man-of-war. It is heard in substance today, but without the nautical verbiage of deep-water men of other days. "Sink the sea!" cried a forecastle man. "Once more ashore, and you'll never catch old Boom bolt afloat. I mean to settle down in a sail loft. Shipmates, take me by the arms and swab up the lee scuppers with me, but mean to steer a clam cart before I go again to a ship's wheel. Let the Navy go by the board, to sea agin, I won't."

"Start my soul-bolts, maties, if any more blue peters and sailing signals fly at my fore!" cried the captain of the head. "My wages will buy a wheelbarrow if nothing more."

"I have taken my last dose of salts," cried the captain of the waist . . . "Blast the sea shipmates!" says I.

Needless to say, after spending their accumulated wages, nine out of the ten shipped over.

In commentary, Melville said:

But do men ever hate the thing they love? Do men forswear the hearth and the homestead? What then must the Navy be?

Thus it was and ever shall be.

Show a Leg. An expression used generally by boatswains' mates and masters-at-arms to rouse and turn out sleeping men. "Rouse and shine" has been corrupted to "rise and shine" in the American Navy.

The call "show a leg" is derived from the days when women were carried at sea, "the wives of seamen," the women who put out a purser's stockinged leg for identification were not required to turn out at first call.

The old original call, says Commander Beckett, R.N., was,

Out or down there, out or down there, all hands, rouse out, rouse out, rouse out. Lash and carry, lash and carry, show a leg or else a purser's stocking. Rouse and shine, rouse and shine. Lash up and stow, lash up and stow, lash up and stow, it's tomorrow morning and the sun's a-scorching your (bloody) eyes out.

Shrouds. When cordage was of inferior grade, so many stays of rope were used to support a mast athwartships that the mast was practically obscured in the manner that a shroud covers a corpse.

Sick Bay. Originally called "sick berth." The term probably was introduced by Lord St. Vincent in 1798. After round bows were introduced about 1811, the contour of the bulkhead effected the change of name to "sick bay."

Silence in a Man-of-War. The American Navy has always insisted, as the British Navy did at an earlier date, that silence be observed at all drills and evolutions. When Napoleon was aboard the *Bellerophon* in July, 1815, he remarked as the ship was getting under way:

Your method of performing this evolution is quite different to the French. What I admire most in your ship is the extreme silence and orderly conduct of your men. On board a French ship everyone calls and gives orders and they gabble like so many geese.

Skin of a Ship. The outer planking or plating of a ship is called the "skin." It is believed that there is a direct connection with our ancestral sailors of many centuries ago, who first sailed the seas in wicker-work coracles covered with the skins of animals. The skins were sewed together at "seams." Both "skin" and "seam" have lived in the language of seamen.

Skipper. Derived from the Scandinavian word *schiffe,* meaning ship; or the Dutch word *Schipper,* which means captain.

Sky Pilot. The chaplain aboard ship is called the *padre* or "sky pilot" by sailormen. The older sailormen had a religious vein that was mingled with superstition. The bluejackets of sail seldom showed any fear for a hereafter. Their philosophy as expressed by an old sky pilot was, that since they lived hard, worked

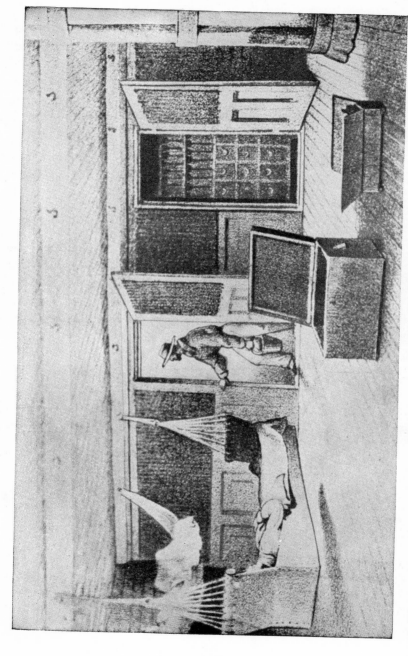

SICK BAY OF AN AMERICAN NAVAL VESSEL ABOUT 1845—Note the canvas hospital cot and type of hammock in use at that time. The "loblolly boy" is wearing a straw hat as uniform of that period. Medicine chest and instrument case stand open on the deck. (After Horner)

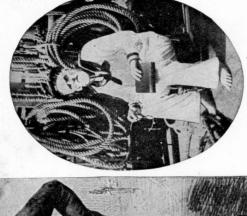

An Old-timer (Courtesy J. M. Colasanti, from *Our Navy and Defenders*)

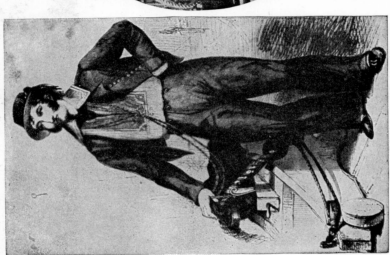

Boatswain's Mate George Brown (From *Stewart's
Naval Magazine* [1836])

SAILORMEN ALL

Chief Gunner's Mate Andrew Newman
(1876)

hard, and died hard, they thought it would be hard indeed to have to go to hell.

Slops. A general term for ready-made clothes and outfits furnished seamen. The name was first used in this sense by Maydman, in 1691. The word is an old one, for in Chaucer's time *sloppe* designated a kind of breeches.

In an original manuscript account of Queen Elizabeth, one finds an order to John Fortescue to deliver some Naples fustian for "sloppe for Jack Green, our Foole."

Snow. A two-masted, square-rigged vessel with a boom mainsail set on a trysail mast, and often with a spritsail rigged beneath the bowsprit. The rig was most common at sea in the War of American Independence. It is said to be pronounced as rhyming with "cow." A model may be seen in the Smithsonian Institution, Washington, D.C.

Speaking Trumpet or Megaphone. History records that Alexander the Great used one in 335 B.C. It is used by the officer of the watch for hailings, and is of particular use in wind and fresh breezes.

Splicing the Main Brace. Tradition relates that, in the days of sail, those who performed this rather important and difficult task of marlinespike seamanship received upon completion of the job an extra ration of rum.

A copy of the following historic message may be seen today in the United States Navy Department. The dispatch was sent or "signal made," as the British say, by Admiral Sir David Beatty, R.N., to the Allied Fleet at Rosyth on 11 November, 1918.

The Armistice commenced at 11:00 today, Monday, and the customary method in the H. M. Service of celebrating an occasion is to be carried out by the ships' companies splicing the main brace at 19:00 today. Hands are to make and mend clothes.

It is interesting to observe that in the address one may read, "Negative 6.B.S." The Sixth Battle Squadron was composed of American ships under the command of Rear Admiral Hugh Rodman, U. S. Navy, and was operating under the orders of

Beatty. Spirits were forbidden in the United States Navy, but there is pleasant recollection of cases where some American officers and men visited the ships of their British allies on that memorable day.

Sprit. From old Saxon with very ancient meaning "to sprout." We have the bowsprit which sprouts out from the bow. The spritsail in older ships was set under the bowsprit.

Steerage. A term that is rapidly becoming supplanted by junior officers' mess. In the *Marine Encyclopedia* (1881), a steerage officer was

an officer living or messing in the steerage. Steerage officers in the U. S. Navy are clerks, midshipmen, cadet midshipmen, mates, cadet engineers, ensigns when not in charge of a watch or division, and all officers ranking with ensign.

Sundowner. Derived from the strict captains who once required that all officers and men be aboard by sunset; now used for a martinet or strict disciplinarian.

Sun Over the Yardarm or Fore Yard. In other days the well known expression meaning, about time for the first drink, "a nooner."

Supercargo. Much of the early success of the British and American China and Indian trade was due to these business diplomats who handle the sale and collection of cargo. E. Keble Chatterton writes:

He has to combine the ability of a banker and merchant, the tact of an ambassador and the loyalty and incorruptibility of an honest man. . . . His job was to sell the vessel's cargo, buy a new one, and establish relations with the highest Indian natives or with the loftiest Chinese officials.

In 1690, French priests were given free passage out to the Orient in English ships, in order that their knowledge of languages and conditions might be utilized in the capacity of supercargoes. An idea of the tremendous amount of business with the huge profits of those days may be seen in the investment of £430,000 by England's East India Company in 1674, whose ships brought home £860,000 worth of commodities. In New England's early maritime development and China trade, the supercargoes were oft-times the scions of families of shipowners, and their trade reports were some of the earliest submitted to our government.

*Superstitions, Sailors'.** Literature abounds in superstitions and explanations that the early mariners gave to phenomena actually observed at sea. Some of the great superstitions of the sea arose from the love of travelers to exaggerate in relating great adventures after long voyages to distant, strange lands.

Many volumes have been written of the superstitions of men of the sea, from the journey of the Argonauts and legend of floating rocks on through *Flying Dutchman* days to the pig tattooed on a modern sailor's foot as a charm against drowning.

The phenomena of the sea, waterspouts, phosphorescence, St. Elmo's light, winds and storms, enchanted islands and rocks, mermaids, and sea monsters, all have in the seagoing races numerous legends, superstitions, and customs of propitiation with charms against dangerous effects.

Phantom ships and apparitions were often reported by mariners. Sailors to a great degree still believe in omens and prognostics. The "Friday superstition" still obtains among landsmen as well as among seamen. There is an old proverb, "Friday's noon come when it will it comes too soon."

Shakespeare alludes to luck days in *King John*, III, 1; in *Macbeth*, IV, 1; and in *A Winter's Tale*, III, 3—" 'Tis a lucky day, boy, and will do good deeds on't."

The "Fore-Topman," who recorded in an entertaining and vivid style life in "Old Ironsides," in 1839-41 wrote:

Many clever writers have affirmed that sailors are generally the most superstitious beings in existence, and I believe with some reason, for since my sojourn on the boundless ocean, I have never seen an accident occur on shipboard but what someone would step up with prophetic countenance, and engross the attention of every bystander with a relation of some little circumstance that he had taken notice

* Lieut. Comdr. A. W. Meyerson, former Imperial Russian Navy, reports old Russian Navy superstitions: Bad luck to whistle aboard ship; to kill sea gulls or albatross; to have priest and woman aboard ship together; to come on deck without a hat. Never write the port of destination in a log book until reached. Always scratch a mast to get a wind.

of prior to the occurrence, which he considered as a forewarning.
. . . Sailors put great faith in the predictions of fortune tellers or
persons supposed to be skilled in magic charms.

Surgeons (Medical Corps). The title surgeon cannot be found
in any record of the British Navy before 1557. However, there is
little doubt that some went to sea before that date. Doctors of
medicine commanded regiments of cavalry and infantry in the
civil wars of Charles I's time.

The title is a contraction of the French word *chirurgien,* or is
from the Latin *chirurgus* and from the Greek originally, and
means "operating with the hand." Gallant old Sir William
Monson says:

The surgeon is to be placed in the hold where he should be in no
danger of shot; for there cannot be a greater disheartening of the
company than in his miscarrying, whereby, they will be deprived of
all help for hurt and wounded men.

Taking a Sight. This term is well known by all who follow
the sea as the act of taking with sextant or octant the altitude
of the sun, moon, or stars; but it has another meaning. Captain
Marryat refers to it as the act of spreading the fingers out and
placing the right thumb to the nose. Rabelais gives it the same
meaning in his *Pantagruel* (Book II).

Tar. General name for a sailor and derived from the old custom of a sailor tarring his trousers, as well as other wearing
apparal, in order to make them water proof.

Tarpaulin Muster. In practice, the term is applied to a collection of money by a group of sailors. For example, if a popular
shipmate was discharged from the service without funds, his
messmates would spread a blanket and his friends would drop
money thereon. Also at times used to collect money for the
family of a deceased shipmate.

Tattooing. The *Century Dictionary* defines tattoo:

To mark, as the surface of the body, with indelible patterns produced by pricking the skin and inserting different pigments in the
punctures. *Sailors and others mark the skin with legends, love em-*

*blems, etc.; and some uncivilized peoples, especially the New Zea-
landers and the Dyaks of Borneo, cover large surfaces of the body
with ornamental patterns in this way.* . . .

"They [the Tahitians] have a custom . . . which they call
Tattowing. They prick the skin so as just not to cause blood."[1]

Although savage races have from early times decorated the
body with designs, which were supposed to give beauty to the
individual, one must examine other reasons for the origin with
the military and seagoing. It is thought that seafaring men imi-
tated at an early date the custom as practiced by the military.

Tattooing was the original identification tag of the soldier.
Various researches that have been made arrived at the conclusion
that the art of tattooing with Europeans originated as a mark of
identification for the dead and wounded on the field of battle.
It was by such an identification that Edith, the Swan Neck, found
the body of Harold on the field of Hastings. Tattooing was
also once used to mark permanently a thief or a deserter. Charles
Kingsley wrote in *Hereward the Wake,*

May not our soldiers' and sailors' fashion of tattooing the arms and
chests with strange devices be a remnant of the very fashion kept
up, if not originated, by the desire that the corpse be recognized
after death?

In this connection, due to the custom of refusing burial to
Protestants in wholly Catholic communities and islands, as in
the islands of Madeira when at one period a Protestant stranger
was not permitted to be buried upon the island, the sailormen,
irrespective of creed, found a way to insure a shore burial. The
Reverend Fitch W. Taylor, a chaplain of the United States Navy,
wrote in 1838:

And so prevalent was this refusal of the rites of burial to Protestants,
by Catholic communities, that there is even a custom among sailors
to have a cross tattooed upon their arms, that if by chance they should
die in a Roman Catholic country, their bodies might be respected,
and be allowed a quiet interment on the shore.

[1] Cook, *First Voyage*, I, xvii.

From a means of identification, tattooing in time became the fashion of sailormen of all nations. It was as much a part of the sailor as was nautical phraseology; it marked him as a mariner. Even now elaborate tattooing is considered by many sailors to give an added degree of "saltiness" to the one tattooed.

The practice of tattooing in the United States Navy is on the wane, though most of the older men and a considerable number of the older officers are tattooed. Commenting on the new type of man, an old chief boatswain's mate, remarked:

Yes, sir, we had bracelets tattooed on our arms, but the "rookies" now wear wrist watches, and what hurts me is where we tattooed our girl's name and the ports we made is today just a place where these landsmen wear garters. No, sir! She ain't what she used to be.

Since the practice is dying out, it may be well to comment briefly on some of the conventional designs of tattooing that will soon be no more as the old school passes on—"old sailors never die, they just sail away." The design varied from a small crest, anchor, star, or shield to a large design of Christ on the Cross, flanked by the two thieves. The latter design, pricked on the sailor's back, was the *chef d'œuvre* of the tattoo "professor"; but due to its size and the time required for execution, it was one of the most painful pieces of work. Nudes were once quite popular, but it was required on re-enlistment that the girls be dressed. This was done by tattooing a dress of color over the nude. "Miss Liberty" in red and blue was one of the favorite costumes.

In order to express profound sentiment for the girls ashore, initials of the fair ones would be tattooed on the arms or legs. Sometimes the sailor's initials as well as those of the girl would be intertwined in a heart. One of the most competent and artistic of the "professors" of tattooing told the writer that sometimes the girl would have the identical design tattooed on her body after the sailor had submitted to the pricking. It was a token of true love. A sailor once told the writer that "the initials help you to remember their names." Some of the more robust fellows would have a dagger that appeared to pierce the skin with a motto, "death before dishonor." The cross is sometimes used alone as a design, but more frequently it takes the form of a tombstone placed under a willow tree. A sailor stands by the stone, and underneath or on the cross is placed "In memoriam" to "father" or "mother" or both. The word "hold" was sometimes tattooed on the fingers of one hand, and "fast" on the fingers of the other. It was considered by the more superstitious that a pig tattooed on the foot was an effective means of preventing death by drowning. As the designs pass out, some of the younger men have a log of the ports and the years in which they were visited, tattooed on the forearm. This is a convenient means of refreshing the memory.

Tattoo work may be partially removed by means of acid; it is most painful and a blur always remains under the skin.

To Break a Flag. "To stop" when used with reference to flags means to make up in order "to break" from masthead in order to insure flag or pennant will fly free and not foul the rigging, or for a quick signal—breakdown or guide flags. "Hoist" is used in regulations and old general orders in reference to personal flags of flag officers. Whether a personal flag is "to be broken" or "to be hoisted" depends upon type of ship, and whether or not there is danger of fouling in making the hoist. The method governs the term. They should not be interchanged. Precedent does not decree that the term "break" is correct in all cases.

In reference to battle flags Admiral Dewey at Manila Bay wrote: "We broke our flags from the mastheads with the conviction that we were to see the end of the story. . . ."

"Upon the completion of the reading of his orders, he will direct the commanding officer to break his flag."[1]

Extracts from chronology of Lord Nelson:[2]

1797, February 13th. Hoisted Broad Pendant on board *Captain.*
April 1st, Hoisted his flag. (After promotion Rear Admiral).
1798, March 29th, Broke his flag on board the *Vanguard.*

[1] Commander Battle Force, letter 1 August, 1932. (See change in Command Ceremony Letter, Chap. IV.)
[2] Admiral Mark Kerr, R.N., *The Sailor's Nelson.*

1801, January 17. Hoisted his flag on board the *San Josef*. [After promotion Vice Admiral of the Blue.]

To Box the Compass. It is derived from the Spanish *boxar*, to sail around.

To Saw Away the Bulwarks. The first record of this practice in the American Navy is found in the chase of the American cruisers *Lexington, Dolphin,* and *Reprisal* by an English ship of the line. The *Dolphin* and *Lexington* by separating escaped with little difficulty but it is recorded by Cooper in his *Naval History* that the

Reprisal, commanded by Lambert Wickes, was so hard pressed as to be obliged to saw her bulwarks, and even to cut away some of her timbers; expedients that were then much in favor among the seamen of the day, although of questionable utility.

This questionable practice was supposed to limber a ship and make her sail faster.

The *Reprisal* took Dr. Franklin to France. The sheltering of American men-of-war and French prizes was so vigorously protested by the English that France ordered the *Reprisal* and *Lexington* seized until word was given that they would leave France. The *Lexington*, the first vessel of the American Navy to have borne the American flag (not the later official one) in a victory on the seas, shortly after sailing from France was captured by the *Alert* in a prolonged gun duel, and thus ended her career of great usefulness. The *Reprisal* met a sad fate. On her voyage to the American shores, the ship foundered and all the officers and crew were lost, with the exception of the cook. Thus ended the career of Captain Lambert Wickes, one of our most outstanding and brilliant officers, to whom small space is given in the average naval history. It must be remembered that not only did these two cruisers make many captures of prizes in European waters, but also were the first two of our national cruisers to dispute British commerce in those seas.

To Skylark. An expression that is distinctly nautical. Lark, meaning a spree, is a corruption of the old Anglo-Saxon word

A Scene between Decks (W. J. Huggins, 1833) (From *The British Tar in Fact and Fiction*, by Commander Charles N. Robinson, R.N.)

lac, to play or have fun. The word skylark was derived from the practice of young sailors laying aloft to royal yards and sliding down the backstays. A skyraker or skyscraper is any sail above the fore, main, or mizzen royal.

To Whistle for a Wind. A very old expression of sailing-ship days. It is derived from the expression "you can whistle for it if you want it," and came from the custom of supplying a certain number of drinkers in English taverns and ale houses with whistles in order to summon the drawer for refills of tankards.

Tom Sawyer's Traverse. An old term that at the present time is not used in the Navy. It meant the course and movements of a "soldiering" (no reflection on the Army) sailor to kill time, such as frequent trips and long stays at the scuttle butt and in the head.

Transom. In sailing ships a transom was a horizontal timber that was a part of the stern frame and sternpost. This beam or timber was used as a seat; hence, any seat that is built in officers' country and is a permanent fixture is by usage called a transom.

Typhoon. A corruption of the Chinese *t'ai-fun,* or great wind. In connection with wind, it is of interest that the word "windfall" came about as the result of the old custom that some of the British nobility held lands on condition that no timber would be cut except for the Royal Navy; but those trees blown down by wind were exempt. It was usually considered a godsend when gales effected windfalls.

Up the Pole. Means "on the water wagon" or not drinking at the time. It was originally a term for "a sheet in the wind" or "a little high," hence "up the pole."

Wardroom. In the early part of the eighteenth century, there was a compartment aboard British ships and below the "great cabin," called the "wardrobe." It was utilized for storage of valuable articles taken from prizes. The officers' staterooms were near by. When the wardrobe was empty and, particularly on cruises out, the lieutenants met there for lounging and for meals. In time the compartment was used entirely as an officers' messroom and the name was changed to wardroom. Such was the designation of the lieutenants' messroom when the United States Navy came into being.

Watch Marks. Now a term for the red tape on the upper part of the left sleeve of a fireman in the Navy and the white tape at the same place on the right sleeve of the seaman. This tape takes the name "watch mark" from the old custom of the days of sail when men wore a thin red braid on the upper part of the right or left sleeve to denote whether the wearer belonged to the starboard watch or port watch. The latter custom was discontinued in the British Navy in the 1870's.

Watches. Herman Melville, in *White Jacket,* describes life on the U.S.S. *United States* in 1843. Speaking of watches and details, he writes:

Now the fore, main, and mizen topmen of each watch, starboard and larboard, are at sea, respectively, subdivided into quarter watches. . . . Besides these topmen who are always made up of active sailors, there are sheet-anchor men, old veterans, all whose place is on the forecastle; the fore yards and anchors, and all the sails on the bowsprit being under their care. . . . These are the fellows, that it does your soul good to look at; hearty members of the old guard; grim sea grenadiers. . . . Then there is the after guard stationed on the quarter-deck, who under the quartermaster and the quarter gunners attend to the mainsail and spanker, and help haul the main brace, and other ropes. . . . (The quartermasters and after guard.) They acquire the name of "sea dandies" and silk socks gentry. . . . Then there are the waisters, always stationed on the gundeck. These haul aft the fore and main sheets, besides being subject to ignoble duties, attending to the draining and sewerage below hatches. . . . They are the tag-rag and bobtail of the crew and he who is good for nothing else is good enough for a waister.

Weigh. Anglo-Saxon *woeg.*

To lift the anchor from the ground. This term must not be confounded with "way" as is often the case. A vessel is *under weigh* from the moment her anchor is *weighed,* or off the ground (or as soon as she has slipped her moorings) , even though she may have no *way* on her.[1]

Wherry. Said to be another form of the word "ferry," because wherries in early days were often ferry boats on rivers.

Women at Sea. Women were carried on many British men-of-war until after the beginning of the nineteenth century. There is record of Mary Ann Talbot, who received a pension of £20 a year "for wounds received in action when she was before the mast in the Navy." Rebecca Anne Johnson served on a Whitby collier for seven years when in 1808 her sex was discovered. It is related that her mother served at sea and fell at the battle of Copenhagen as a member of a gun's crew.

The marriage of two sailors as reported in a London journal is of interest.

At St. Dunstane's in the East, in May, 1802, David Jones was married to Anne Robinson. They had been old shipmates on board *Le Seine,* frigate on the West Indian Station, during most part of the war, where the lady bore a most conspicuous part in the different actions in which the frigate was engaged. She was always an attendant in the surgeon's department and waited upon Jones in his wounded state. An attachment took place which ended in their union.

Wreck. From old English *wrack* or seaweed; cast ashore; drifted or driven ashore.

In the statute of Westminster the first [3, Edw. I, C.4], the time of limitation of claims given by the charter of Henry II is extended to a year and a day, . . . and it enacts that, if a man, a dog, or a cat escape alive, the vessel shall not be adjudged as a wreck.[2]

SOME PROVERBS AND PHRASES OF THE SEA

"The genius, wit, and spirit of a nation are discovered in its proverbs."

Davy Jones's Locker.

A familiar name among sailors for Death, formerly for the evil

[1] Ansted, *A Dictionary of Sea Terms* (1933).
[2] Blackstone, *Com.,* I, viii.

spirit who was supposed to preside over the demons of the sea. He was thought to be in all storms, and was sometimes seen of gigantic height, showing three rows of sharp teeth in his enormous mouth, opening great frightful eyes, and nostrils which emitted blue flames. The ocean is still termed by sailors Davy Jones's locker.

—WILLIAM A. WHEELER

As ships go to Old Davy, Lord knows how, Sirs,
While heaven is blue enough for Dutchman's trowsers

—THOMAS HOOD, "Love and Lunacy"

He dies, by not a single sigh deplor'd.
To Davy Jones' locker, let him go,
And with old Neptune booze below.

—JOHN WOLCOTT, "Ode to the K——

He That Would Bring Home the Wealth of the Indies Must Carry the Wealth of the Indies with Him.

As the Spanish proverb says, "He who would bring home the wealth of the Indies must carry the wealth of the Indies with him." So it is in traveling; a man must carry knowledge with him, if he would bring home knowledge. Boswell. "The proverb, I suppose, sir, means, he must carry a large stock with him to trade with." Johnson. "Yes, Sir."

—JAMES BOSWELL, *The Life of Samuel Johnson.*

It Is an Ill Wind That Blows No Man Good. This very old expression came directly from the sea and is derived from the fact that every wind is a fair wind for some ship under sail.

It is found in Heywood (1546); Richard Edwards, *Damon and Pythias* (1571); Shakespeare, *II Henry IV*, v. 3, and *III Henry VI*, ii. 5; Scott, *Rob Roy* (1817), xxvii; Dickens, *Pickwick Papers* (1837), xxxi, etc.

Like a Fish Out of Water.

Ne that a monk, whan he is rekkeles,
Is like to a fish that is waterles.

—CHAUCER, *Prologue to Canterbury Tales.*

Shipshape and Bristol Fashion. Neat, clean, all rigging coiled and flemished down.

There was no foolish gilding and ginger-bread work, to take the

HIGH SEAS IN THE WAR ZONE.—A remarkable picture of the U.S.S. *O'Brien*, Commander Charles A. Blakely, taken from another destroyer, December, 1917, while on escort duty in waters south of Ireland. This terrific gale will be remembered by many officers and men of the Queenstown destroyers.

eye of landsmen and passengers but everything was "shipshape and Bristol fashion!"

Sail, quoth the King;
Hold, quoth the Wind.

This is a proper admonition to kings that however great their power may be over their subjects, the wind, seas, and weather will not obey them, let them bluster and threaten as much as they please.
—*The Gentlemen's Magazine* (1738), viii, 474.

The Fish That Is Bred in the Sea Swims Best.

"My lord mayor," he said, "there is a proverb in my country which says, 'Fish swim best that's bred in the sea,' which means, I take it, that men do best what they are trained for."
—Sir E. Bulwer Lytton, *The Last of the Barons.*

To Be Above Board. To have nothing concealed, nothing below deck, frank, honest, open minded.

Now, for my part, d'ye see, I'm for carrying things above board, I'm not for keeping anything under hatches, so that if you b'ent as willing as I, say so a'God's name, there's no harm done."
William Congreve, *Love for Love,* iii, 7.

To Be at Sea. To be doubtful; to "mull" around; to be hesitant.

"To say the old man was at sea would be too feeble an expression."—G. W. Cable.

To Be Three Sheets in the Wind. An old definition in Webster's *International Dictionary* reads, "a sheet in the wind," *drunk;* "three sheets in the wind," *very drunk.*

To Catch a Crab. To fail to keep in stroke in rowing and ofttimes thereby to jam and foul other oars. The Venetians call a green hand or novice at rowing a "crab."

"It was a scene of much confusion—the half-drunken boat's crew catching crabs, and falling forward upon the others."
—F. Marryat, *Peter Simple,* xxviii.

To Know One by the Cut of His Jib. To size up; to make a personal estimate of; to judge character and capabilities by appearance.

"A vessel is known by the cut of her jibsail; hence the popular phrase, to know a man by the cut of his jib."—HOTTEN.

"We shall be very good friends, sir, I'll answer for it, if I may judge from the cut of his jib."

—F. MARRYAT, *Jacob Faithful*, vi.

To Rejoice the Cockles of One's Heart. To gladden and to cheer. Derived probably from the old English term "cockling seas," or short and quick ones; hence, applicable to that which brings short, quick heart beats. The cockles of the heart are of course unknown to doctors and surgeons.

To Shoot Charlie Noble. To clean the galley smokepipe of soot and dirt by firing a pistol therein.

Between Wind and Water. That part just below the water line when sailing in smooth water that becomes exposed when the ship rolls. It refers to the vulnerable part of anything.

> And just e'en as he meant, sir,
> To loggerheads they went, sir,
> And then he let fly at her
> A shot 'twixt wind and water,
> That won this fair maid's heart.
> —WILLIAM CONGREVE, *Love for Love*, iii, 15.

To Write in Water.

> Men's evil manners live in brass; their virtues
> We write in water.
> —SHAKESPEARE, *Henry VIII*, iv, 2

On John Keats's tombstone in Rome, one may read:
This grave contains all that was mortal of a young English poet, who on his deathbed, in the bitterness of his heart at the malicious power of his enemies, desired these words to be engraved on his tombstone: "Here lies one whose name was writ in water."

Life of Reilly (spelled by men-o'-war's men, "Riley"). This term filtered into the American Navy from Broadway. It means a sailorman's good time and all that goes with it; or sometimes used by sailors to refer to an easy ship, where reveille is a little later, and early liberty and good chow are the rule.

It is related that a Broadway actor by the name of Reilly was in the habit of "painting the town" after he had accumulated enough money. In off-stage periods it became a common expression for any actor who had enough to live well on, to reply when asked what he was doing, "I am leading the life of Reilly."

> Beneath this sod an iceman sleeps,
> They brought him here today;
> He lived the life of Reilly
> While Reilly was away.

Wet Your Whistle. To take a drink of liquor.

> As any jay she light was and jolyf,
> So was hir joly whistle wel ywet.
> —CHAUCER, *Reeve's Tale*, I, 235.

Slipped His Cable (Slipped His Wind). Means he died.

"You gave him the right stuff, Doctor," said Hawes jocosely, "and he wont slip his wind this time." The surgeon acquiesced.
> —C. READE, *Never Too Late.*

Chantey (continued). Because the well-known American chanteys have passed from the sea, there is printed hereunder some authoritative, first-hand information on the subject, from a letter "To The Editor of The New York *Times:*"

> Whiskey is the life of man
> O, whiskey Johnny!
> I'll drink whiskey while I can
> Oh, whiskey Johnny.

. . . Your correspondent is correct in saying that "Whiskey Johnny" starts with a "Ho," but in the twelve years that I served on square-rigged vessels I never heard the line "Whiskey killed my sister Sue." The first line was, invariably, "Ho, whiskey is the life of man," and, as I remember, the following stanzas rather contradicted this assertion by detailing the dire effects of drinking whiskey.

There are, or used to be, three kinds of chanteys—single-pull, double-pull, and capstan, or marching. The first, as its name implies, was used where tremendous effort was required and single pulls, with a breathing spell in between, were all that could reasonably be asked of men—hauling aft the main-sheet is an example. "Haul on the bowline" is a single-pull chantey, and the pull comes on the last word "haul"; in some ships the pull was made immediately after the word and, in my experience, it gave the best results. "Haul on the bowline" was not nearly as popular as "Haul Away, Jo" or "Oh, Do, My Johnny Bowker," both single-pulls; "Paddy Doyle's Boots" was invariably used for bunting the sail on top of the yard, when furling any of the courses or lower square-sails.

The double-pulls were used for fairly long pulls, such as mast-heading the topsails, or even to' gallant sails in vessels with single to' gallant yards. The chanteyman sang a line and the hands pulled twice on each bit of chorus; for instance, in "Blow, Boys, Blow," the chanteyman sang "A Yankee ship came down the river" (chorus) "BLOW, boys, BLOW." "And all her sails they shone like silver" (chorus), "BLOW, my bully boys, BLOW," the pulls coming only on what your correspondent calls upper-case.

There are dozens of double-pulls; probably the most popular was "Blow the Man Down," with "Whiskey for My Johnny" and "Reuben Ranzo" close seconds. A good chanteyman made up his lines as he went along, after the first line or two, but naturally the choruses remained the same.

Capstan chanteys could be, and were, almost any song with a good rhythm and chorus; "Away for Rio" (pronounced rye-o) being perhaps the most popular; also "A-Roving"; but I've hove up the anchor many times to "Marching through Georgia." . . .

Incidentally, the only chantey I know of that is written in a minor key is "On the Plains of Mexico" and is of American origin.

WILLIAM APPLEBYE-ROBINSON.

Cornwall, N.Y., Jan. 20, 1939.

IRON MEN IN WOODEN SHIPS

The following excerpts are taken from a scurrilous but entertaining work, called *The Wooden World*, first published in 1707, by Edward Ward, one-time British seaman. Plain Ned Ward ran an inn after retiring from the sea. He wrote various compositions, coarse but always descriptive, and with engaging frankness and wit. Some of the bawdier extracts would not be appropriate in a work of this description. Acknowledgment to

JACK ON A CRUISE (Published by **R.** Sayer and **J.** Bennett, 1780)—"Avast, there!
Back your mainsail." Note the sailor's shore togs. This picture when found on
mugs and jugs is much prized by collectors of nautical pottery. (From *The
British Tar in Fact and Fiction*, by Commander Charles N. Robinson, R.N.)

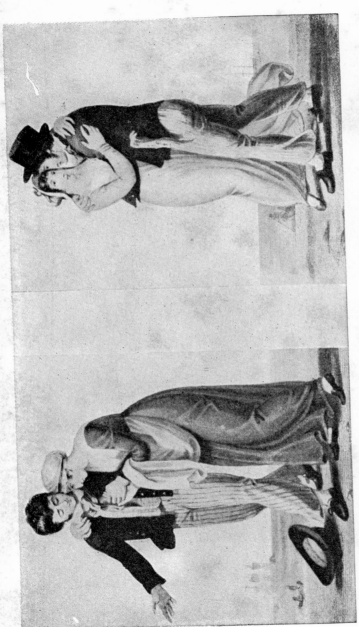

THE SAILOR'S FAREWELL.
Dear Nancy, dispel all thy bosom's alarms,
I fear not the storms on the main;
Not long on the ocean I part from thy charms
Till I meet thy embraces again.

THE SAILOR'S RETURN
Adieu to the danger of tempest and war
No more from my Nancy I part,
No more from her presence I wander afar
To give a deep sigh to her heart.
R. COOPER.—H. COURBOLD, 1814.

(From *The British Tar in Fact and Fiction*, by Commander Charles N. Robinson, R.N.)

Geoffrey Callender for the extracts from a new edition of *The Wooden World*.

Sea Captain. Upon his first popping up, the lieutenants sheer off to the other side, as if he was a ghost indeed; for 'tis impudence for any to approach him within the length of a boat hook.

A Sea Lieutenant is a gentleman, he'll tell you, by his commission, and hence it is he always carries it about with him to give you demonstration proof, in case you call it in question: He lays it out as often as he does his watch, and believes both together convincing proofs of his gentility.

A Sea Chaplain is one that in his junior days was brought up in the fear of the Lord; but the university reasoned him out of it at last, and he has ofttimes thanked his good stars for it.

The Master of a Ship of War. His language is all heathen Greek to a cobbler; and he cannot have so much as a tooth drawn ashore without carrying his interpreter. It is the aftmost grinders aloft, on the starboard quarter, will he cry to the all-wondering operator.

The Purser is a kind of Pythagorean philosopher, not because of his pocket holes, for his breeches are commonly well lined, but for his many transmigrations, having lived in various regions, and rubbed through many callings, before he came to be a purser in the Navy.

The Surgeon. He adjusts his prescriptions, as a country shoemaker does his lasts; he makes one and the same recipe serve to a hundred various tempers and circumstances. For there's no standing upon niceties, he cries, with fellows that have the constitution of a horse.

The Gunner. As heavy as his guns are, they are certainly more active than he is, and do the King fifty times more service, for his grand amusement is eating and drinking; his sleeps are moderate enough, just to suffice nature, and make him ready for a fresh attack: Were it not for these, he would be a list man, for his mates do all his other business for him.

The Carpenter. Tho' he is generally but a rough-hewn fellow, yet he values himself upon a well-built hull; and as for his intellects, they are much about the same model with the master's, for he has little more of the mathematicks than the boatswain.

The Boatswain. It is not so much his fine silver-coil, as the illustrious chain that it hangs by, that is the distinguishing badge of his post, and which he's as proud of as my Lord Mayor is of his and prouder.

He has a thousand pretty phrases and expressions pickt up at Billingsgate and elsewhere, which he never sends abroad without bedecking them with all the embroider'd oaths and curses that can be had for love or money.

He has wit in his liquor, that's certain, for though he's often tipsy, it's at other men's cost.

A Sea Cook. The captain's cook and he are opposites as well in their practice as in their habitations, and seldom or never make incursions into each other's provinces. . . . He cooks by the hour glass as the parsons preach sermons. . . .

A Midship-man. He's elevated as high as Flamsteed, in his own conceit, and is often times shewing you a sample of his ingenuity. He can prove the purser a rogue by Gunter's scale, and compose a bowl of punch by the rules of trigonometry. . . . He's one that sometimes passes under the discipline of the cane or fist; that is when he is guilty of that great sin of omission of not giving timely notice of the captain's going from or coming into the ship.

The Captain's Steward. But he's too staunch a knave to trust to vain hopes and fair promises; so he takes care to make hay while the sun shines; and shuffles and cuts with everyone that has to do with him.

A Sailor. He's one that is the greatest prisoner, and the greatest rambler in Christendom; there is not a corner of the world but he visits . . . but when he does get ashore he pays it off with a vengeance; for knowing his time to be but short, he crowds much in a little room and lives as fast as possible.

APPENDIX A

A LUCKY BAG OF FACTS AND TRADITION

THE United States Navy has had but four fleet actions, but in each one it captured and destroyed every enemy ship.

No United States man-of-war has ever mutinied or been in the hands of mutineers, while in other navies whole squadrons and fleets have mutinied.

The Marine Corps has never experienced a mutiny of any description, and through the years has been conspicuous for adherence to its motto, *Semper Fidelis.*

The United States Navy is the only Navy in the world that has in its possession a British royal standard taken by capture. This standard, now at the United States Naval Academy, was captured by Commodore Chauncey at York, Canada.

The United States Navy possesses in "Old Ironsides" the most successful and historic frigate that ever sailed the seas. She battered down enough of the stone forts of Tripoli to contribute directly to the treaty with that Barbary State. She escaped from Broke's squadron of six ships after a four-day chase. It was by the unparalleled seamanship and masterly stratagem of Captain Hull that the *Constitution* made her escape without losing a man, a gun, a boat, or an anchor. Hull's first lieutenant called it, "the advantages to be expected from perseverance under the most discouraging circumstances as long as any chance of escape may remain." She defeated the *Guerrière,* a crack British frigate, dismasting her twenty-five minutes after firing the first broadside, and she shot every spar out of the British frigate *Java.* It is a tradition that the *Constitution* did not take in her royals for this fight. She captured the British *Cyane* and *Levant* at the same time. They were smaller than "Old Ironsides," with a combined armament of 55 guns to the *Constitution's* 52, but the more effective long 24's of the American frigate and Captain Stewart's excellent maneuvers carried the day.

THE BURNING OF THE "PHILADELPHIA"

The burning and boarding of the *Philadelphia* was commented upon by Lord Nelson as the most bold and daring act of the age. The U.S.S. *Philadelphia* had been captured and was moored near the combination palace and fort of the Bashaw of Tripoli. The Tripolitans had a brig, two schooners, and a galley moored near by. A battery of 110 guns from the shore bore on the *Philadelphia*. The audacious Decatur in a 60-ton ketch manned by 74 officers and men not only boarded the *Philadelphia* at night, but also fired and destroyed her after forcing overboard the Barbary pirate crew. Decatur made good his escape with only one man wounded. The American lieutenant was later promoted at the age of twenty-four to captain.

OFFICERS AND MEN OF THE NAVY IN THE WAR OF REVOLUTION

The list of officers of the Continental Navy comprised about 330 names. This roster includes the officers commissioned in France. There are no complete lists extant of the medical officers, pursers, midshipmen, and warrant officers. It is estimated that the number of petty officers and seamen of the Continental Navy reached a total of approximately 3,000 men.

PRIVATEERS AND LETTERS OF MARQUE

The majority of naval historians have under-emphasized the work of the United States privateers. The Library of Congress has compiled a list of about 1,700 "letters of marque" which were issued to the privateers of the Continental Navy. It has been estimated that the total number of private vessels carrying arms totaled 2,000 ships, with 18,000 guns, and 70,000 men.

FIRST COMMISSION FOR OFFICER AFLOAT

The first commission issued by President Washington to an officer afloat was issued to Captain Hopley Yeaton, master of a revenue cutter. The Continental Navy had been disbanded and the sole maritime defense was revenue cutters (now Coast Guard). This historic document, dated 21 March, 1791, bears the signatures of both Washington and Jefferson. The Coast Guard had searched for years for this first commission and by a coincidence secured it at the time of this writing from Miss Mary Yeaton, great granddaughter of Captain Yeaton.

EARLY SALUTE OF 17 GUNS

The Naval Regulations (1818) state:

The anniversary of the independence of the United States; and of the birth of General George Washington are to be celebrated by salutes of 17 guns, from every vessel in port, of the rate of a sloop of war and upwards.

It is most probable that a salute of 17 guns was decided as proper, in view of Washington's rank as the senior general of the Army.

RECRUITING FOR THE NEW NAVY

The last section of the *Naval Regulations* (1818) gives some idea of "Jack ashore" of the day and also of the system of recruiting men. The last article states:

That seamen should be rescued, as far as practicable, from the fangs of rapacious landlords and others who frequently taking advantage of their habits of intoxication, and generally unsuspicious characters swindle them of the whole amount advanced to them by the recruiting officer, and to the prejudice of the seamen and of the Service generally, leave them in a naked and destitute condition at the time of their appearance on board.

The section ends with advice to the recruiting officer to prevent the swindling of the men, by inducing them "to repair on board the receiving ship." The final words of the section are touched with a shade of irony, "and to take every means in his power to render [to the recruit] the Service as pleasing as possible."

"REGULATIONS" OF OTHER DAYS

Article XX.

When any man returns on board of the ship in a state of intoxication, all officers are directed to keep away from him and not to exchange a sentence with him. His mess mates are to be called; they will take charge of him, lead him forward, and lash him up in his hammock, if in the opinion of the officer of the deck it is necessary.

Article VII [Conduct expected of midshipmen].

The first lieutenant will report all improprieties, which will be properly noticed; only the gentlemanly and well behaved will be indulged.[1]

AN ATTEMPT AT MUTINY

For attempting to incite a mutiny, Midshipman Philip Spencer and two seamen were hanged at the yardarm of the United States brig *Somers*. The hangings took place in late November, 1842, while the *Somers* was en route from Liberia to New York. Spencer, who was the son of the Honorable John C. Spencer, then Secretary of War under President Tyler, conspired with seamen Cromwell and Small to kill the officers, seize the ship, and go on a pirating expedition. Cromwell protested his innocence; Small confessed. There was overwhelming proof of Cromwell's guilt, and both seamen were hanged at the same yardarm with Spencer.

Commander Alexander Slidell Mackenzie, U. S. Navy, in command, was a stern, pious officer. He considered that his actions were warranted as, "Safety, our lives, and the honor of the flag entrusted to our charge, require the prisoners be put to death."

The national flag was hoisted at sea; drums rolled; a gun fired; and the crew walked away at the whips, hoisting the three in the air. Captain Mackenzie then talked to his crew, asked them for three cheers, and wrote:

Three heartier cheers never went up from the deck of an American ship. In that electric moment I verily believe the purest and loftiest patriotism burst forth from the breasts of even the worst conspirators.

The captain then had the ensign half-masted, and read the service for the dead. He concluded:

Preserve us from the dangers of the seas, and the violence of enemies; bless the United States, watch over all that are upon the deep, and protect the inhabitants of the land in peace and quiet, through Jesus Christ, our Lord.

---

[1] Commodore U. P. Levy, U. S. Navy, *Manual of Internal Rules and Regulations for Men of War* (1862).

In a rough sea and by lantern light the bodies of Spencer, Cromwell, and Small were committed to the deep. The church pennant was hoisted above the ensign, and the crew dismissed after singing the Hundredth Psalm.

Commander Mackenzie was tried by a court-martial on the charge of murder. The general court-martial was convened at the Brooklyn Navy Yard on 2 February, 1843, and lasted for six weeks. Mackenzie was honorably acquitted and the verdict was approved by President Tyler.

THE LEGEND OF SANTA BARBARA, THE PATRON SAINT OF CANNONEERS AND ORDNANCE MEN

"Santa Barbara Virgin and Martyr" is said to have lived at the close of the third and beginning of the fourth century of the Christian Era. In the Roman, the Greek, and the Russian calendars, her feast day is celebrated on 4 December, the presumed anniversary of her martyrdom.[1]

Her rich father Dioscorus denounced his lovely and erudite daughter for becoming a Christian and beheaded her himself after she had been condemned by the Governor. Dioscorus was struck by lightning and killed. Santa Barbara has from that time been considered the protectress against lightning, thunder, and flame and, of course, when gunpowder was used by Europeans, she became the "patron saint of cannoneers and ordnance men."

The first official recognition was by the cannoneers of Lille, France, who were commissioned in 1417 by letters patent as the "Confreres de Sainte Barbe." Other countries of Europe followed. A picture of Santa Barbara hangs in the office of the Chief of the Bureau of Ordnance.

"OLD IRONSIDES"

Our most famous and historic ship, the U.S.S. *Constitution*, under Captain Isaac Hull, captured H.M.S. *Guerrière* on 19 August, 1812. In that brilliant action, Moses Smith, sponger of No. 1 gun, records,

[1] *Organization and Administration of the Bureau of Ordnance, U. S. Navy* (1923).

Several shots now entered our hull. One of the largest the enemy could command struck us, but the plank was so hard it fell out and sank in the waters. This was afterwards noticed and the cry arose: "Huzza! Her sides are made of iron! See where the shots fell out!" From that circumstance, the name of the *Constitution* was garnished with the familiar title, "Old Ironsides."

One Bell in the Last Dog Watch

This is a British naval custom. Lieutenant Commander R. C. Lowry, R.N., writes,

There is an old story that one bell has been struck at 6:30 P.M., instead of five bells, since the mutinies of 1797. In one port, the signal to mutiny was to be the striking of five bells in the dog watches; the officers got wind of this and, instead of striking five bells, ordered one to be struck, and the mutiny was averted. How true this may be is not known, but it is quite a common yarn.

Interesting First Events of the History of the Navy

Thus we may dispose of the question of priority in this fashion: John Manley, under a Massachusetts commission and under the Pine Tree Banner, was the first to make a British naval vessel strike her flag. John Paul Jones was the first to raise the Grand Union or American flag on a ship of war. Esek Hopkins was the first commander under a commission of Congress to carry the Grand Union flag in naval operations and to make a capture under it. John Barry was the first under a commission of the Congress and under the Grand Union flag to fight a battle with a British warship and make it strike its colors. These may be regarded as fundamental data in considering the much and often acrimoniously debated question: who was the Father of the American Navy.[1]

Naval Academy established at Annapolis 10 August, 1845; transferred to Newport, Rhode Island, on 5 May, 1861; and again established at Annapolis in September, 1865. Naval War College established at Newport, Rhode Island, 6 October, 1884. The Postgraduate School was established at Annapolis, 1 October, 1909.

Naval Bureau of Medicine and Surgery of the Navy was or-

[1] Willis Fletcher Johnson.

ganized in 1842, by Dr. W. P. C. Barton. He was the first chief and the senior surgeon of the Navy at the time of his death.[1]

The first separate office to administer personnel was the Bureau of Navigation created in July, 1862. At the same time were created the Bureau of Equipment and Recruiting and the Bureau of Steam Engineering.

The first Naval Militia was established by the State of Massachusetts 29 March, 1890.

The first naval officer to become an admiral was David Glasgow Farragut, so appointed on 25 July, 1866.

The first naval officer to become a commodore was John Barry, senior officer in the Navy, appointed in 1794 after the Navy was reorganized.

The first naval officer to become an engineer in the U. S. Navy was Charles Haynes Haswell. He was commissioned 19 February, 1836, by Secretary of the Navy Dickerson to design steam power equipment. Bureau of Steam Engineering created in 1862.

The first navy yard that was acquired after the establishment of the Navy Department 30 April, 1798, was the Portsmouth Navy Yard, Portsmouth, New Hampshire. The property embraced 58.18 acres and had been in use as a shipbuilding yard. The price was $5,500.

The first American warship of iron using steam was the *Michigan*, built at Erie, Pennsylvania, under Act of Congress 9 September, 1842. She was fabricated in Pittsburgh and transported in parts to Erie where she was completed and launched in 1844. On 17 June, 1905, she was renamed the *Wolverine* and officially stricken from the naval list 12 March, 1927.

First warship with propelling machinery below the water line was the screw warship *Princeton*, designed by John Ericsson in 1841.

The first paddle-wheeled steam warships were the U.S.S. *Mississippi* and U.S.S. *Missouri*, finished in 1841. *The Fulton the First* of 2,745 tons was built by Robert Fulton in 1814-15 for the Navy at a cost of $320,000.

[1] *Military Surgeon*, XLVI.

First United States warship to be docked in a Government dry dock was the *Delaware* at the Norfolk dry dock, Portsmouth, Virginia, on the anniversary of the battle of Bunker Hill, 17 June, 1833.

First United States warship to circumnavigate the world was the U.S.S. *Vincennes,* commanded by Commander William Bolton Finch. The *Vincennes* left New York 3 September, 1826, and returned via Cape of Good Hope on 8 June, 1830.

The first hospital ship definitely assigned for the purpose was the U.S.S. *Solace,* fitted out in 1898. The idea and general supervision of fitting out is credited to Admiral William Knickerbocker Van Reypen. *Navy Register* (1864) lists *Red Rover* as "Hospital Steamer."

The first battleship and forerunner of the dreadnought was the U.S.S. *Maine.* The keel was laid 17 October, 1888, and the vessel was launched in 1890. The *Maine* was destroyed by a mysterious explosion in the harbor of Havana, Cuba, 15 February, 1898. This hastened the declaration of war with Spain. Of a crew of 354, only 16 escaped injury or death. The *Maine* had 12-inch side armor and two 10-inch guns in each of the two turrets.

The first electrically propelled vessel of the Navy was the *Langley* (former collier *Jupiter*). The *Langley* was commissioned 7 April, 1913, and converted to an aircraft carrier 21 April, 1920.

The first large floating dry dock of the Navy was the *Dewey,* now at Olongapo, Philippine Islands. This dock was towed there from the Chesapeake Bay, a distance of 13,000 miles. The passage took 150 days.

The first Protestant services in California were conducted near the end of June, 1846, by Commander J. B. Montgomery, U. S. Navy, at Yerba Buena plaza, San Francisco. He requested permission to hold services after finding no Protestant church ashore. Montgomery, who commanded the U.S.S. *Portsmouth,* also hoisted the Stars and Stripes ashore at San Francisco on 9 July, 1846, when official news of the war with Mexico reached him.

The first commander in chief of the Army and Navy to hold

divine service for Navy personnel was President Franklin D. Roosevelt. On Easter Sunday, 1 April, 1934, the President in the absence of a chaplain, stood on the quarter-deck of the *Nourmahal* and read the service from the *Episcopal Book of Common Prayer*. The officers and men of the U.S.S. *Ellis* were present. The flag of the President flew from the yacht.

The first chief of Bureau of Construction, Equipment, and Repair was a captain (line officer) of the Navy, although the law required the chief "to be a skilled naval constructor." By the Act of 3 March, 1853, John Lenthall, a naval constructor, was appointed Chief of Bureau. The present Bureau of Construction and Repair dates from 5 July, 1862. Lenthal remained Chief of Bureau until 1871. He was not a naval officer until 1866 when Congress provided that naval constructors should have the rank and pay of officers of the Navy.

Before the passing of this Act of 1866,

the naval constructors employed at the several navy yards and stations were not regularly commissioned naval officers, as they are at the present time, but their standing was somewhat similar to that of a foreman in a navy yard, as they were employed or laid off as the exigencies of the work in hand required.[1]

The first surgeon and surgeon's mate were authorized by the Act of 6 January, 1776. The surgeon was commissioned while the mate was a warrant officer. In 1777, an examination was provided for both surgeons and surgeon's mates. The pay of the first surgeons was increased in 1789 to $50.00 per month from $21.33 to $25.00 per month.

The first civil engineers of the staff corps were appointed in 1867. Their status had been that of civil employees before this date. In 1871, a law provided that they have such rank as the President might fix. For many years ten officers comprised this corps.

The first dental corps was established in 1912. The original act provided for a corps that could be expanded to one dentist for 1,500 of enlisted personnel.

[1] From paper read before Postgraduate Department on 22 May, 1913, by Naval Constructor [now Admiral in Construction Corps] W. G. Du Bose, U. S. Navy.

The nurse corps (female) was authorized by an Act of Congress in 1908.

The first general board of the Navy was established by Navy Department order of 13 March, 1900. Confidential instructions were originally issued for its guidance. The general board has no executive functions and therefore acts in an advisory capacity.

BRIEF HISTORY OF ORIGIN OF NAVY DEPARTMENT

The first agency to handle naval matters was the Marine Committee of three members, established by Congress in legislation of 1775.

In November, 1776, a "Continental Navy Board" was established to consist of three competent persons and to be subordinate to the Marine Committee.

In October, 1779, a Board of Admiralty succeeded the Marine Committee, and its subordinate Continental Navy Board was given direct control of all naval and marine affairs. The Board of Admiralty consisted of five commissioners: two of the Board to be members of Congress and three to be appointed.

In February, 1781, the Board of Admiralty was succeeded by a Secretary of Marine who had all powers of the preceding board.

In August, 1781, an Agent of Marine was appointed, who took over all duties of agents, boards, and committees previously established.

In August, 1789, a law placed the Navy under the Secretary of War and there it remained for nine years.

In April, 1798, a Navy Department was established "at the Seat of Government" under the control of a "Secretary of the Navy." This marked the beginning of the present organization, the Navy Department. Government navy yards were established in 1800 and 1801. The Secretary of the Navy was directed by the President to purchase and establish navy yards at Portsmouth, New Hampshire, Boston, Massachusetts, New York, New York, Philadelphia, Pennsylvania, and Gosport, near Norfolk, Virginia. These yards are today on the original sites with the exception of the yard at Philadelphia, which was moved to League Island in 1868.

In February, 1815, a "Board of Commissioners" was created to supplement the Navy Department and serve under the Secretary. The board was comprised of captains of the Navy who received appointments from the President subject to confirmation by the Senate. This board was in existence for twenty-seven years.

Origin and Development of the Bureaus of the Department

In August, 1842, the "Board of Commissioners" was abolished and five bureaus were established under the Secretary of the Navy.

(1) A Bureau of Yards and Docks.
(2) A Bureau of Construction, Equipment, and Repair.
(3) A Bureau of Provisions and Clothing.
(4) A Bureau of Ordnance and Hydrography.
(5) A Bureau of Medicine and Surgery.[1]

In July, 1862, the Navy Department was reorganized and eight bureaus provided by law.

(1) A Bureau of Yards and Docks.
(2) A Bureau of Equipment and Recruiting.
(3) A Bureau of Navigation.
(4) A Bureau of Ordnance.
(5) A Bureau of Construction and Repair.
(6) A Bureau of Steam Engineering.
(7) A Bureau of Provisions and Clothing.
(8) A Bureau of Medicine and Surgery.

The present organization of the Navy Department is not given, but at this writing a decided change in organization is proposed and may be effected within the next year.

[1] Matthew F. Maury, a junior line officer of the Navy, did much to effect the bureau system by his "broadsides" on the failings of the "Navy Board"; he wrote under the *nom de plume* of "Harry Bluff."

NOTES ON NAVAL UNIFORMS

The navies of the world have conformed in no small degree to the British in uniform regulations; all navies have differences in details. The French Navy influenced the British Navy somewhat, as in the matter of wearing epaulets, while other navies had official uniforms before the British. It is of interest to note how we gained the "navy blue."

British naval officers meeting at their favorite rendezvous at Will's Coffee House, Scotland Yard, decided in 1745 that they would petition the Admiralty for an official uniform in order to standardize as in other navies of the day. This was done, and the Admiralty asked certain officers to appear in what they considered a good design. Some liked grey with red facings; Captain Philip Saumerez is reported by tradition to have worn a blue uniform with white facings.

Blue and white was chosen by the Admiralty. The story goes that since George II must make the final decision, he selected the colors from the riding habit of the First Lord's wife, the Duchess of Bedford, who was riding in the park. But it is told that to gain his Majesty's consent, the Duchess wore the colors already selected by her husband. Women have always had something to do with the Navy.

The cocked hat is an evolution from the early soft, wide-brimmed hat. The brim was first turned up on one side and then the other. Cocked hats were originally worn athwartships by naval officers. They were worn fore and aft in the British Navy by captains and below in 1795. This was required of all officers in 1825. Three "turn ups" were made to make the three-cornered hats of Colonial times. Nelson's cocked hat was triangular with the back turned up. Enlisted men wore low cocked hats until about 1780.

The epaulet is a glorified, decorative amplification of the shoulder strap. The original shoulder strap had its practical use as a device to prevent the bandolier from slipping off the shoulder. In the early days of the United States Navy, lieutenants of the line wore one epaulet on the left shoulder, except "when in command"; then the piece of decorative accouterment could be shifted to the starboard side.

Oak leaves have been used as insignia by various corps and ranks of the United States Navy since the earliest days. This decorative device was probably adopted originally as a symbol of the excellent oaken ships of the United States. In those days the government had great concern of its live oak for shipbuilding. At Boston and in other navy yards, huge oak logs were preserved under water for years.

Sailors' bell-bottomed trousers are worn large at the bottom in order to roll up easily above the knees for scrubbing decks. This type of trousers was of great practical value when seamen went overboard in shallow water to land pulling boats.

The black silk neckerchief was originally a "sweat rag." Black hid the dirt. It was worn both around the forehead and the neck. Some men used the neckerchief in "pigtail" days to protect their jackets. Black neckerchiefs were used long before Nelson's death. They were probably worn at Nelson's funeral in the manner of the ship's company of the *Berwick*, who in mourning for their captain in 1794 cut the neckerchief in two and wore half around the arm and half around the hat.

The three rows of tape on the collar of the British bluejacket's jumper was authorized in 1857. Lieutenant Commander Lowry, R.N., writes:

One of the members of the committee which drew up the 1890 uniform regulations has since said that they then suggested two rows of tape, but that the Admiralty for no stated reason decided on three, the question of commemorating Nelson's three victories never being mentioned.

It is likely that the three lines of braid on the collar of a bluejacket's blouse were selected for decorative effect and have no special significance, tradition to the contrary notwithstanding.

The Origin of "Checkered Painting" of Wooden Ships

The U.S.S. *Constitution* ("Old Ironsides") carries today the traditional outboard design of paintwork, i.e., the white stripe with the black gunports. It is well established that this method of painting originated with Lord Nelson. Before Nelson attained high command, ships of the British Navy were painted buff, black, or buff and black. Black and white was used for side painting, but before Nelson's order the lines of the wales (strakes of thick outside planking) were painted white, and this gave a very narrow white band. It was ordered by Nelson that the white stripes follow the lines of the deck. Black strakes between were made wider and gun lids were painted black. This gave the well-known checkered broadside. After Trafalgar and probably in memory of Nelson, this method of painting became universal in the British Navy. It was soon adopted by other navies and, from that day until sails of war left the sea, it became the general design. The inboard work was in time painted white. Red was used for many years. Tradition tells us that this color had a most practical value in that it did not show so glaringly the traces of blood incident to battle.

In Memory of Vasco da Gama

The port side is designated the "honor side" in the Portuguese Navy in memory of the great navigator, da Gama, first to double Cape of Good Hope holding Africa on the port hand.

An Official Letter of Commodore "Joe" Fyffe, U. S. Navy

U.S.S. *Monocacy*, 3rd rate.
Wusung, China. [1875]

Honl. Geo. M. Robeson,
　Secretary of the Navy.
Sir:

I am given to understand that my fair country women in these seas, consider that I am wanting in the graces and accomplishments, necessary to a perfect character; that I am rough and bearish; and in fact "little better than the wicked."

I have too much respect for these ladies to doubt the justice of their sentence. I humble myself before them and promise by God's blessing and a little assistance from the gentle sex to become, in time, everything that they can wish.

In order to enable me to fulfill this vow, I request, in accordance with the admirable custom growing so much in fashion in the Navy, that my family may be permitted to live with me on board this ship.

Also my grand mother

Not that I have the honor to possess such a venerable relative, but my wife has one she will lend me with pleasure; who will bring among us the stately and ceremonious manners of that indefinite period called "Old Times"; and who will prove a chastening corrective to all hands of us, for she has, for about a hundred years, cultivated that natural flow of eloquence so charming in her sex; and a soft answer never turns away *her* wrath, for she is as deaf as a post.

Very respectfully,

Your obedient servant,

JOSEPH FYFFE,

Commander, Comdg.

Essex, FIRST AMERICAN MAN-OF-WAR TO DOUBLE CAPE OF GOOD HOPE AND CAPE HORN AND TO FIGHT IN THE PACIFIC

The *Essex*, built in 1799 by the patriotism of the people of Salem, Mass., cost $154,686.77; fastest sailer in Navy for several years; and took the largest number of prizes of any vessel in the War of 1812.

Captain David Porter, in command of *Essex*, rounded Cape Horn in 1813 and stood in Valparaiso for supplies. His object was to break up British navigation. He succeeded so well that it was only a short time until his major problem was to dispose of the merchant ship prizes and prisoners. Midshipman David G. Farragut was one of the youthful prize masters.

The final and fateful engagement came when the *Essex* was defeated by the British ship of war *Phoebe*. In that fight, some of the deeds of Porter's heroic crew are truly blood stirring. "Dying men who had hardly ever attracted notice among the ship's company uttered sentiments worthy of Washington."

A young Scotchman by birth, named Bissley, on losing a leg, said: "I hope I have this day proved myself worthy of the country of my adoption. I am of no longer use to you or her, so good-bye," and with that he plunged through a port. John Ripley, who had been wounded in like fashion, also jumped overboard.

THE UNITED STATES COAST GUARD

Semper Paratus

The Coast Guard is unique in that no other nation has a comparable organization. This difference may be marked by reading the act wherein it is provided that the Coast Guard shall constitute a part of the military forces of the United States and shall operate under the Treasury Department in time of peace, and operate as a part of the Navy, subject to the orders of the Secretary of the Navy, in time of war or when the President shall so direct.

Men who follow the sea should be informed of some of the historic high lights and the general duties of this active sea-going service. The Coast Guard was known originally as the Revenue Marine, but by an act of the First Congress, approved by President Washington on 4 August, 1790, the Revenue Cutter Service was created. This act placed the service under the Treasury Department. No Navy Department existed at the time. It was provided in the later act of 2 March, 1799, that the cutters "shall, whenever the President of the United States shall so direct, co-operate with the Navy of the United States."

The Revenue Cutter Service, later the U. S. Coast Guard, has fought side by side with the Navy in every war at sea in which the United States has been engaged. In the war without declaration with France in 1798-99, vessels of this service cruised against French privateers in the Caribbean Sea. The cutter *Pickering* made two cruises and captured ten prizes.

At the outbreak of the War of 1812, the Revenue Cutter Service was prepared with its sixteen cutters "to defend the coast and commerce of the country as far as the calibre of their guns and size of their vessels would admit." Those 125-ton cutters had many stubborn engagements with landing parties and boarders, but let the enemy of the day comment on the fight with the Revenue Cutter *Surveyor* at Gloster Point, Virginia, on 10 June, 1813.

His Majesty's Ship *Narcissus*

SIR: Your gallant and desperate attempt to defend your vessel against more than double your number, on the night of the 12th inst., excited such admiration on the part of your opponents, as I have seldom witnessed, and induced me to return you the sword you had so nobly used, in testimony of mine. Our poor fellows have severely suffered occasioned chiefly, if not solely, by the precautions you had taken to prevent surprise; in short, I am at a loss which to admire most, the previous engagement on board the *Surveyor*, or the determined manner by which her deck was disputed, inch by inch.

You have my most sincere wishes for the immediate parole and speedy exchange of yourself and brave crew; and I cannot but regret, that I myself have no influence that way, otherwise it should be forthcoming.

I am, sir, with much respect,

Your most obedient,

JOHN CRERIE.[1]

Of such stuff is the tradition of gallantry born.

Down the years, in the Mexican War, the Civil War, the Spanish-American War, and the World War, high standards of duty and a seaman's job well done have crowned the efforts of the Coast Guard.

The late Rear Admiral F. C. Billard, U. S. Coast Guard, defined the community of interest with the Navy and the high professional standards of his Service when he wrote:

Having fought as a part of the Navy in all our wars, and taking an especial pride in being fully prepared to perform creditable service in the Navy whenever called upon, the officers and men of the Coast Guard are inspired not only by the high tradition and fine history of their own service, but also by the splendid traditions, history, and indoctrination of the United States Navy. They have thus two rich heritages to be proud of and two standards of the same lofty character to live up to.

DUTIES AND FUNCTIONS OF THE U. S. COAST GUARD[2]

The Coast Guard is charged with the enforcement of the maritime laws of the United States, the saving of life and property and render-

[1] Captain H. D. Smith, *Early History of U. S. Revenue Marine* (1932), p. 27.
[2] *Tide Rips* (Coast Guard Academy Year Book), 1934.

ing of assistance to vessels in distress, and the performance of miscellaneous duties for other government departments.

The duties under law enforcement include:

Prevention of smuggling, and enforcement of customs laws.

Enforcement of navigation and other laws governing merchant vessels and motor boats.

Enforcement of rules and regulations governing the anchorage of vessels, with Coast Guard officers assigned as captains of the port.

Enforcement of law to provide for safety of life on navigable waters during regattas or marine parades.

Examining merchant seamen for certificates as lifeboatmen.

Enforcement of the law relative to oil pollution.

Enforcement of laws relating to immigration, quarantine, and neutrality.

Enforcement of rules and regulations for the protection of game, seal and other fisheries in Alaska, and the regulations of the international conventions relative to fisheries on the high seas.

Enforcement of the sponge fishing law.

Enforcement of laws and the administration of oaths generally in Alaska.

Enforcement of miscellaneous laws for other branches of the government:

Transporting floating court in Alaska when necessary.

Suppression of mutinies on merchant vessels.

Life saving and assistance are of great importance and the duties connected with this branch are:

Saving life and property upon the high seas and along the coasts of the United States.

Assistance to vessels in distress.

Flood relief on the western rivers.

Destruction and removal of wrecks, derelicts, or other dangers to navigation.

International service of ice observation and ice patrol in the North Atlantic Ocean.

Extending medical and surgical aid to United States vessels engaged in deep sea fishing.

Assisting other branches of the government in the performance of duties assigned.

Transporting government agents.

Caring for and transporting shipwrecked and destitute persons in Alaska elsewhere.

Rendering medical, dental, and general welfare service to natives in Alaska.

Carrying the United States mails.

Collecting statistics regarding loss of life and property on vessels.

The Life Saving Service was amalgamated in 1915 with the Revenue Cutter Service as one division called the Coast Guard. In the early 1870's, the Life Saving Service planned and inaugurated the beach patrol, an institution of a distinct American origin.[1]

These stations constituted the Life Saving Service of the United States, which long ago won its supremacy over all kindred institutions of the world. Its achievements and successes at shipwreck, many of them as brilliant as human effort can make them, have earned the praise of the civilized world. It brought to the Coast Guard in 1915 a record of 177,286 lives saved from the perils of the sea, from 1871 to 1914, inclusive.[2]

As an example of this great humanitarian work, it is recorded that for a five-year period ending 30 June, 1928, the number of lives saved or persons rescued from peril by the Coast Guard totalled 15,279. The lives saved and vessels assisted made a grand total of 12,370. The heroism and daring incident to these rescues comprise the lion's share of the proud traditions of the Coast Guard.

> But the men that sail the ocean
> In a wormy, rotten craft,
> When the sea ahead is mountains
> With a hell-blown gale baft;
> When the mainmast cracks and topples,
> And she's lurching in the trough,
> Them's the guys that greets the cutter
> With the smiles that won't come off.[3]

[1] Centuries ago, China organized the first humane society with the mission of saving life from the perils of the sea. In 1824, the Royal National Institution for the preservation of life from shipwreck was founded, an institution which has added lasting luster to the world's life saving annals.

[2] Oliver M. Maxam, "The Life Saving Stations of the United States Coast Guard," U. S. Naval Institute PROCEEDINGS, May, 1929 (p. 377).

[3] Arthur Somers Roche, *The Coast Guard Cutter.*

THE MISSION OF THE UNITED STATES COAST GUARD ACADEMY

To graduate young men with sound bodies, stout hearts, and alert minds, with a liking for the sea and its lore, and with that high sense of honor, loyalty, and obedience which goes with trained initiative and leadership; well grounded in seamanship, the sciences, and the amenities, and strong in the resolve to be worthy of the traditions of commissioned officers in the United States Coast Guard in the service of their country and humanity.

In the accomplishment of that mission, the Coast Guard produces the officers who lead the men that man the ships which must be ever ready to take the sea in all weather. Succor to mariners in distress when gales are strong, waves mountainous, and the seamanship hazardous is rarely accomplished with other than "sound bodies, stout hearts, and alert minds." The Navy knows and the Navy is ever proud of the splendid work of the Coast Guard.

THE UNITED STATES MARINE CORPS

Semper Fidelis

"When they aren't fighting, they're working."

GENERAL BEN H. FULLER, U.S.M.C.

Marines have been landing as sea soldiers from ships of war on foreign shores since the dawn of recorded history, for it is written that the marines of Phoenicia, Egypt, Greece, Carthage, and Rome had similar duties to the marines of the day, in that they were the soldiers on board fighting ships and were usually the "spear head" in landing operations. Although the Royal British Marines were organized in 1664, some of their forefathers may have been forced by Roman marines to serve under the eagle of Julius Caesar before the Christian Era. British-American colonial marines (Lawrence Washington, brother of George Washington, was one) served under Admiral "Grog" Vernon, Royal Navy, at Carthagena and in Cuba in 1741. A marine was closely associated with the first battle of the Revolution, for when Major Pitcairn, Royal British Marines, cried out, "Desperse you rebels," there followed immediately the "shot heard around the world."

It was on October 5, 1775, that the Continental Congress first referred to "marines." Because of the thousands of marines then serving on armed vessels of the states as well as on privateers, Congress created an *organization* or corps of marines. After the war of the Revolution, the Army, Navy, and the Corps of Marines were, due to reasons of national economy, completely disbanded and discharged from all duties. Congress authorized a number of marines as part of the complement of every vessel ordered to be constructed during the period of 1794-98. It was on 11 July, 1798, that John Adams and Congress created officially the modern organization known as the United States Marine Corps. The headquarters was moved in 1800 from Philadelphia to Washington.

The Marine Corps has always been a military and administrative organization which, with the exception of services rendered by the Navy such as medical and dental assistance, and the Judge Advocate General's Department, the administration has been complete in itself. The Major General Commandant is assisted in carrying on the administrative work of the Marine Corps by three staff officers—the Adjutant and Inspector, the Quartermaster, and the Paymaster.

Those officers are under the immediate jurisdiction of the Major General Commandant who is also aided in co-ordinating all activities by a general officer who carries the title of Assistant to the Commandant.

General Ben H. Fuller wrote:

The Marine Corps is an element or unit of the naval service and normally subject to the laws and regulations established for the government of the Navy, but Marine Corps Headquarters is not an intimate part of the Navy Department in the same sense as the Bureau of Navigation, or bureaus of the Navy Department. The Marine Corps is a military organization (composed of soldiers trained to the ways of the sea) adapted to naval conditions. The Corps is always available for immediate use at the direction of the Secretary of the Navy acting for the President.

The marines have participated in all the wars of their country
—the Revolution (1775-83), French Naval War (1798-1801),
war with Algiers (1815), war with West Indian Pirates (1818-
30), war with Florida Indians (1835-42), Mexican War (1846-
48), Civil War (1861-65), war with Spain (1898), Chinese
Boxer War (1900), Philippine Insurrection (1899-1904), and
World War (1917-18).

The Marine Corps has also served directly under the Army.
This authority is set forth in the Revised Statutes wherein it
provides that

the Marine Corps shall at all times be subject to the laws and regulations established for the government of the Navy, except when
detached for service with the Army by orders of the President; and
when so detached they shall be subject to the rules and articles of
war prescribed for the government of the Army.

In this statute, the Marine Corps had units at the Battle of
Princeton in the Revolution; the Battle of Bladensburg and
Battle of New Orleans in the Second War with Great Britain;
in the Florida Indian Wars of 1836-37, when the Commandant
of Marines commanded the "Fighting Brigade" of the Army
of the South; at the capture of the forts of Vera Cruz, the heights
of Chapultepec, and Mexico City in the Mexican War; in the
Army of Cuban Pacification, 1906-09; in Mexico in 1914; and
with the American Expeditionary Forces in France, Belgium,
Luxemburg, and Germany. The work of 7,500 leathernecks at
a place called Belleau Woods in France will be remembered as
long as there is a United States Marine Corps. The title of
"devil dogs" remains an appellation of proud tradition.

To enumerate the minor wars and landings of the marines
throughout their history is already the subject of books. The
international police duties; the rendering of aid at earthquakes,
fires, and other catastrophes; the supervision of elections in Central America; the administration of foreign states; and the guard-
ing of United States mail has demonstrated the versatility and
the efficiency of this alert combatant organization. In addition,
the United States Marine Corps is probably the most completely

prepared of any similar organization in the world, in respect to plans and state of readiness for landing operations. In other words, they are specialists in amphibian warfare, initial seizures, and defense of advanced bases.

It is difficult for one not a member of the Marine Corps to understand all the subtle factors that make for their high *esprit de corps.* Some of these factors are tersely expressed by one of their outstanding warriors, General John A. Lejeune.

The willing, thorough-giving, and practical devotion of the marine to the cause of his Navy, and of his country, is perpetuated in his motto *Semper Fidelis,* and represents his most sacred tradition. We have always appreciated the superior importance of personnel over material. That famed *esprit de corps* attributed to the marines is but an evidence of the constantly increasing recognition of the importance of personnel over the material, more especially that quality of personnel animated by a general spirit of faith in, and loyalty to, the organization and its purposes. No improvement in its material can outdistance in importance such a quality.

It was this superb quality of marine personnel that gave to the marines in the World War their punch and drive. The marines had luck in the World War, for they were placed on the front at critical times and in critical places. Military historians say that, when the American 18th Division, the American 2d Division, and the Moroccan 18th Division attacked south of Soissons on July eighteenth the war was on that day lost to the Central Empires. It was the luck of the marines to get the chances, but success was attained by cold discipline, expert rifle and bayonet tactics, and the will to win, in short, high standards of training and unsurpassed *esprit de corps.* The marines are justly proud that their name is written on the battle flags of the American 2d Division.

Great traditions exact a price—*lives and self-sacrifice.* The casualties of the Marine Brigade in France were over 150 per cent.

Such things carry little meaning except to men who can remember the dreadful wheat field to the west of Belleau Woods, and shrapnel-flailed slopes between Blanc Mont and St. Etienne, and the line of dead engineers on the path between the heights of the Meuse near Pouilly and the place where the bridge was the last night of the war.

For the rest there is transmitted a certain old blood-stained glory, peculiarly of the marines and of the United States Naval Service. That was the Marine Brigade.[1]

With the Marines who have fought their "country's battles on the land as on the sea," there is marked emphasis on the individual training of men with particular stress on the development of initiative. Officers and men are instructed now to "fill the shoes" of their seniors if that be necessary. This means that the noncommissioned officers of the U.S. Marine Corps probably have the highest grane of intelligence and the superlative military *savoir faire* of any comparable organization in the world.

While many of its leaders had much to do with directing its destiny, its outstanding *esprit de corps* has grown up and been maintained largely through the efforts of its rank and file. While the noncommissioned of the organization are not as frequently mentioned as the commissioned officers, large credit must be given them for helping to maintain its efficiency and fighting spirit, especially in times of great stress.[2]

In no service have splendid traditions, heroic exploits, and tales of high adventure been more generally known by a service and more jealously guarded. You may "tell it to the Marines"; but when it comes time *to do,* you may be assured that it will be in conformance with the words of the laconic message scrawled by Captain Myers at the Boxer Siege in Peking—*"We will do our best."*

[1] Major John W. Thomason, Jr., U.S.M.C. "The Marine Brigade," U. S. Naval Institute PROCEEDINGS, November, 1928 (p. 968).
[2] Lieut. Col. Clyde H. Metcalf, U.S.M.C., *A History of the United States Marine Corps*, 1939, preface.

APPENDIX B

NOTES ON PRECEDENCE

Precedence in Official Washington

THE United States government has never promulgated an official table of precedence, although there is a division of Protocol of the Department of State that arranges details of seniority relative to conferences, official receptions for foreign officials, etc., and that also acts in an advisory capacity for general precedence and official ceremonies. Custom, tradition, the relative importance of certain offices, seniority in the creation of the office, together with common sense have contributed to the establishment of a generally accepted table of precedence. In a political and social system such as that of the United States, precedence is based upon the importance of the official position that has been gained by the official through election, appointment, or promotion.

The precedence issue is one which has plagued the United States ever since Thomas Jefferson, who was driven by a nebulous and contentious social complexity to write a brochure, *Rules of Etiquette*. The 1896 Act of Congress that established the line of succession from President and Vice-President through the Cabinet is to a large degree the basis of precedence for official occasions.

By a strict interpretation of this rule, the whole executive body ranks above ambassadors. There is an argument in favor of the Secretary of State ranking ambassadors,[1] but the practice of European countries has been followed, and the Secretary of State yields precedence to foreign ambassadors. Foreign ministers yield precedence to the Secretary of State.

The Speaker of the House is not included in the Presidential line of succession and would by a strict interpretation of our own law be outranked by ambassadors. The speakership has been unusually

[1] "In the monarchial countries, not only the heir apparent but all the children of the reigning sovereign, as also the brothers, nephews, and grandsons have precedence over ambassadors. . . . By a parity of reasoning, the secretary standing so near in succession to the chief magistracy, a claim might be urged for him of precedence over the ambassador."—J. W. FOSTER, *The Practice of Diplomacy*, pp. 31-32.

careful to avoid occasions where points of precedence may arise with foreign ambassadors.[1]

With the advent of Congresswomen, there arose another question of etiquette. Would these ladies rank Senators' wives, etc.? It was not until Herbert Hoover's administration that the matter was settled with the decision that Congresswomen be accorded precedence over wives of members of the House and the Senate. Mrs. Ruth Pratt (New York) was the first to receive this honor at the White House.

At this writing it is impossible to ascertain the relative precedence of the various directors and "chiefs" of the administrative structures effected by the "New Deal." Time will tell.

It is customary for naval officers on duty in Washington to leave cards at the White House, attend one of the "at homes" of the Chief of Naval Operations, as well as the annual reception given by the Secretary of the Navy. This is in addition to the calls made upon immediate superiors.

A calling convention prevails in Washington official social life for newcomers comparable to that which obtains in the capitals of Europe. It is the newcomer's place to make the initial call upon the wives of all those who rank above her husband.

Advice to Naval Officers on Duty in Washington

It is the custom for officers reporting for duty in the District of Columbia to pay calls at the residence of the officials specified below:

The President of the United States. This call should be made annually. It consists of leaving cards at the door of the White House.

The Vice-President of the United States and the Secretary of the Navy. Calls on the Vice-President and the Secretary of the Navy may be paid on the first Wednesday of any month, or on days "at home" of which notices will be found in the social columns of the local newspapers one or two days in advance.

The Assistant Secretary of the Navy, the Chief of Naval Operations, the Chief of the Bureau to which assigned, and the Officer in Charge of the office to which assigned. Owing to the large number

[1] Associated Press dispatch from Washington 4 January, 1933, reports: "The story recounted with relish over capital teacups is that dignified and formal ambassador Irwin B. Laughlin remained away from President Zamora's dinner for the diplomatic corps in protest against the Speaker of the Cortes receiving precedence over ambassadors." The Constitution of Spain provides that in the event of the death of the executive, the speaker succeeds to the presidency. It is therefore the Spanish contention that the speaker ranks as a vice-president.

of calls otherwise necessary, officers above the rank of commander only may expect return personal calls from flag officers. From time to time chiefs of bureaus and other senior officers have announced one or more days "at home" at which time calls have been made and considered as returned. With the exceptions noted above, in any exchange of personal calls the later arrival in Washington should be called upon first.

It is also the custom for an officer to make a personal call upon the Senators from his state and the Congressman from his district. The Senatorial day "at home" is Thursday; the Congressional day "at home" is Tuesday.

The uniform for official personal calls will be appropriate civilian dress, except when uniform is ordered for special occasions.

An officer making a personal call should place his address on the visiting card.

DIPLOMATIC CORPS PRECEDENCE AT WASHINGTON*

It is generally agreed that ambassadors rank all officials but the President and Vice President. The best usage holds that the ambassadors and Chief Justice of the Supreme Court are of equal rank. For this reason an ambassador or ambassadors and the Chief Justice have on few occasions been invited to the same dinner.

The ladies of social Washington, with the exception of the wives of the Vice President and the Secretary of State, make the first call on the wives of ambassadors. The wives of ambassadors receive from 4:30 until 7:00 o'clock on Fridays.

The Cabinet and their wives, with the exception of the Secretary of State and wife, make first calls on the Ministers and their wives, notwithstanding the fact that the Ministers and their wives take precedence at official functions over all of the Cabinet with the exception of the Secretary of State.

PRECEDENCE OF OFFICIALS OF U. S. GOVERNMENT

There is no official single list giving the exact precedence of Federal and State officials; or civil and diplomatic, with Army and Navy officers. The table hereunder will serve as a guide; its chief basis of authority rests upon the best accepted usages of official Washington. Precedence does not conform in all cases with that indicated by gun salutes in *Naval Regulations*.

* If any doubt exists in seating arrangement, it is suggested that unofficial opinion be requested of "Division of Protocal" of the Department of State.

(1) The President.
(2) The Vice President, when representing the President of the United States.[1]
(3) Former Presidents.
(4) Ambassadors Extraordinary and Ministers Plenipotentiary of Foreign Powers.[2]
(5) The Chief Justice.
(6) The Speaker of the House.
(7) The Secretary of State.
(8) Envoys Extraordinary and Ministers Plenipotentiary of Foreign Powers.
(9) Associate Justices of the Supreme Court.
(10) The Secretary of the Treasury.
(11) The Secretary of War.
(12) The Postmaster General.
(13) The Secretary of the Navy.
(14) The Secretary of the Interior.
(15) The Secretary of Agriculture.
(16) The Secretary of Labor.
(17) Governors of States. Note (b)
(18) Senators (by length of service). Note (a).
(19) The Director of the Budget.
(20) The General of the Armies; Admiral of the Navy.
(21) Acting Heads of Executive Departments.
(22) Former Vice Presidents of the United States.
(23) Members of the House.
(24) Charges d'affaires of Foreign Countries.
(25) The Chief of Staff of the Army, The Chief of Naval Operations, The Major General Commandant of the Marine Corps.
(26) Generals, Admirals. Note (f).
(27) Secretaries to the President.
(28) Undersecretary of State.
(29) Counselor of Department of State.
(30) Undersecretary of the Treasury.

[1] Mrs. Gann, who acted as hostess for her brother, the Honorable Charles Curtis, when he was Vice President, recently wrote in the Washington *Star:* "The Vice President represents the President in social amenities, which are necessary in official life, and the President neither makes calls nor is entertained outside the White House except when he calls upon visiting dignitaries and attends the few dinners where his presence is required by tradition."

The Vice President, when he is not officially representing the President, ranks as the Speaker of the Senate and takes precedence immediately after the Chief Justice of the Supreme Court of the United States.

[2] In Catholic countries and Catholic homes, the apostolic delegate accredited to a state has been accorded precedence over an ambassador. The title of Cardinal signifies a spiritual prince and has on occasion been accorded rank ahead of regularly accredited diplomatic corps.

(31) Solicitor General.
(32) Undersecretary of Interior.
(33) Undersecretary of Agriculture.
(34) Lieutenant Generals, Vice Admirals.
(35) Judges U. S. Circuit Court of Appeals.
(36) Judges of U. S. Court of Appeals for District of Columbia.
(37) American Ambassadors designate or on leave in the United States.
(38) The Comptroller General.
(39) Governor and Vice Governors of the Federal Reserve Board.
(40) Assistant Secretaries of Executive Departments. Note (c).
(41) Former Ambassadors of the United States.
(42) Counselors of Embassies or Legations of Foreign Powers.
(43) Major Generals, Rear Admirals.
(44) Political Advisers of the State Department.
(45) Judge and Justices of U. S. Court of Claims, Court of Custom Appeal. (and Supreme Court of D.C.)
(46) Brigadier Generals.
(47) American Envoys Extraordinary and Ministers Plenipotentiary designate or on leave in the United States.
(48) Director of the Pan American Union.
(49) Chairmen of Commissions, Directors of Boards, D.C. Commissioners, Administrators of "New Deal" Organizations, etc. Note (e).
(50) Consuls General of Foreign Powers.
(51) Senior Secretaries of Embassies or Legations of Foreign Powers. Note (d).
(52) Chiefs of Bureaus and Executive Offices; Heads of Divisions of State Department.
(53) Colonels in the Army and Captains in the Navy.
(54) Mayors. Custom has decreed that mayors of largest cities should precede (43).
(55) Consuls, in charge of Consulates of Foreign Powers.
(56) First, Second, and Third Secretaries of Embassies and Legations of Foreign Powers, according to rank.

(a) If of same length of service, by seniority of admission of their respective states to the Union.
(b) Precedence among governors is determined by the date of admission of their respective states to the Union. By Executive Order (1933) Governors of states have been accorded 19-gun salutes.
(c) Flag officers take precedence over all assistant secretaries of the Executive Departments, except over the Assistant Secretary of the Navy and Assistant Secretary of War, who outrank all military and naval officers. Hence at a function where a flag officer, the Assistant Secretary of the Navy, and the Assistant Postmaster

General would be present, the Assistant Postmaster General would outrank the flag officer because he, the Assistant Postmaster General, is senior to the Assistant Secretary of the Navy, and the Assistant Secretary of the Navy is, ex-officio, senior to the flag officer. Otherwise, if neither the Assistant Secretary of the Navy or Assistant Secretary of War were present, the flag officer would take precedence over the Assistant Postmaster General.

(d) When no Counselor of the same Legation or Embassy is present. If the Counselor is present, all Secretaries are dropped to last number. (56)

(e) The exact precedence for all Chairmen of the various Commissions and Boards cannot be determined exactly. The precedence for an individual Chairman is determined by the importance of his position; the power of the Commission in question; and the personal prestige of the gentleman concerned in relation to the same characteristics of other officials involved. The Chairman of a very important Commission or other agency may at times be assigned a precedence equal to that of Assistant Secretaries of Executive Departments.

(f) In the Army, retired officers take precedence after all active officers of the same rank.

In the Navy, retired officers take precedence with active officers of the same rank in accordance with their dates of commission in that rank.

NOTES ON WHITE HOUSE ETIQUETTE

Martha Washington, the First Lady, established with the aid of Alexander Hamilton strict rules of etiquette for the drawing-room of the President and Lady. Many of the social conventions of official Washington are derived from these original rules. They were precise and far-reaching. For example no lady was to attend a Presidential reception who was not gowned in accordance with the rules prescribed.

Mrs. James Monroe was the "First Lady of the Land" who abandoned the custom of the President's wife returning visits. It became an impossible task to return all calls.

It has been customary for the President to hold four state receptions—the first, to the diplomatic corps; second, to the judiciary; third, to the Army and Navy; fourth, to Congress. Because of the striking uniforms of the diplomatic corps and the high rank of Ambassador, this reception has been considered the most brilliant. It is referred to by some social correspondents as the "Court Society of America," for many of those of the highest social rank and distinction in the United States attend this reception.

DINNER AT THE WHITE HOUSE

Dinner guests gather in the Red Room where they are introduced to one another. Aides make known to the guests their places on the seating diagram. Dinner partners are assigned at large dinners just before the President and the First Lady enter the Red Room. They enter and greet the guests formally. The President then takes the lady who is to sit at his right and precedes all to the dining-room. The First Lady follows, as she takes the arm of the ranking man who is to sit at her right. The remainder follow by seniority. The music, "Hail to the Chief," is played during the procession. Mrs. Grover Cleveland did not observe this rule and even at state dinners invariably waited until all had left the drawing-room and then followed with her escort.[1]

At the table the general rule of honor positions is observed—senior lady to right of President, next senior to his left; senior man to right of First Lady, next senior man to her left. The system is continued, alternating men and women until juniors meet near the center of the table. At the dinner to the King and Queen of Siam, the late Chief Usher wrote,

On this occasion the State Department overruled the good American custom in favor of European court precedent, to the irritation of all of us. The King was placed at Mr. Hoover's right, the Queen at his left, with Mrs. Hoover at the right hand of the King. We felt that Mrs. Hoover was being needlessly subordinated and that the American rule was quite as good as the European. . . . Fortunately, the State Department has no authority over the menus, or we might have a lot of Asiatic or European dishes.[2]

Army and Navy officers wear full-dress uniform at all White House functions.[3] Cocked hats are usually carried and not checked with wraps. The President is addressed as "Mr. President"; the first lady, as "Mrs. ——"

As stated before, White House invitations are commands and ex-

---

[1] Irwin H. (Ike) Hoover, Chief Usher of the White House, in memoranda relating to the White House, *Saturday Evening Post* of 10 February, 1934.

[2] By permission Houghton Mifflin Co.

[3] Aiguillettes are worn on the right shoulder only by the aides (military and naval) of the President and on the left shoulder by the aides detailed to visiting sovereigns and heads of states. By present custom, aides do not wear side arms at White House functions.

cept in unusual circumstances they automatically cancel other engagements. Good form decrees that their replies should not be mailed but should be delivered in person or by messenger.

Notes on British Precedence

The elaborate and complicated system of British precedence is fixed by law and custom and regulated by the Herald's College, a corporate body originally established by Richard III. In Whitaker's *Peerage, Baronetage, Knightage, and Companionage* one reads that The rules governing arrangements of the Peerage are marked by so many complications that an expert may occasionally be perplexed.

The tables of general precedence are long and for our immediate purpose unnecessary. Nevertheless, it is of interest to note that from the sovereign to gentleman there is a fixed precedence that includes all ranks and their families. In general, "men possessing two claims to precedence, a personal one and an official one, will be ranked according to whichever of these is the higher." Foreign ambassadors rank before all except the royal family, while envoys and foreign ministers have been placed between Dukes and Marquesses.

It is a general rule that the rank of ladies is that of their husbands: if unmarried, that of their eldest brothers. The wife of an eldest son takes precedence over all the daughters, but the daughters have precedence over the wives of younger sons. It is considered by these rules that the mere official rank of the husband does not as a rule confer any dignity whatever upon his wife. There are a few exceptions to this rule, such as a Lady Mayoress (wife of the Mayor) where official duties are involved.

The titles of English peers and their wives are: Duke and Duchess, Marquess and Marchioness, Earl and Countess, Viscount and Viscountess, Baron and Baroness. If a peer has more than one hereditary title, his eldest son is given a courtesy title, one of his father's minor honours. For example, the Duke of Norfolk is also Earl of Arundel and his eldest son would be given the courtesy title of Earl of Arundel. Younger sons of Dukes and Marquesses prefix Lord to their Christian names and daughters of Dukes, Marquesses, and Earls prefix Lady to their Christian names. The younger sons of an Earl, and all children of a Viscount or Baron prefix Honourable to their names. Earl and Baron are the oldest ranks in England, but the titles Baron and Baroness are very seldom used; instead Lord and Lady are commonly employed. Lord and Lady are also general titles which may be given to any peer or peeress without discourtesy. Baronets and Knights prefix Sir to their Christian names. A Baronet's name is followed by the abbreviation Bt. The wives of Baronets and Knights are styled Lady. In case of any doubt about these titles consult Burke's *Peerage* or DeBrett's *Peerage*.

As to the proper address of letters containing the naval or military titles and other titles, the following forms should be self-explanatory: Admiral Lord ——, Rear Admiral the Earl of G ——, Captain Sir John ——, Commander the Honourable James ——.

In correspondence and on place cards at tables, it is customary among the British to place the highest decoration after the name, such as Vice-Admiral Sir John ——, R.N., K.C.B., or Lieutenant Commander Harlow Smith, D.S.O.

It is always correct and proper to refer to a military and naval officer on active duty by his official title, and use our customary "Sir" in address, irrespective of his hereditary titles.

OFFICIAL PRECEDENCE IN FRANCE

The rules of official precedence of the French Republic are based upon election, appointment, and promotion as in the United States, with the exception that there remain the titles of the monarchy and empire which are today accorded by courtesy to the holders, although it permits no precedence in the table of the officials of the republic.

These titles, such as duke, count, countess, baron, etc., are accorded as a mark of respect for family names. It is not good form to address directly any member of the nobility by the title, whether man or woman, as is customary in Germany, Belgium, and Italy. It is correct to say *Bonjour Monsieur* (or Madame) to those without titles; but in introduction or when alluding to titled folk in their presence or otherwise, the title should be used. For example, one should say to a servant at the door, *Monsieur, le baron est-il à la maison.*

The word "mon" is prefixed to Army titles but is not used by the French Navy. For example, one says, *Bonjour mon Capitaine* to an Army officer, but *Bonjour Capitaine* to a naval officer. In this connection it is considered very brusque to say *Bonjour* without madam, monsieur, or the appropriate military or naval title. The Frenchman in his superior politeness gives the tradesman and the old news vender a *Bonjour monsieur* and a *Bonjour madam.*

ORDER OF PRECEDENCE AT MEETING OF DIPLOMATS

In order to learn the fundamentals of precedence, whether sitting or standing, it is well to examine the established usage of the diplomatic body. These rules comprise the bases of all precedence and position. It took centuries of dispute to reach a general agreement, though even now there are points susceptible to dispute.

When delegates of equal rank meet at international conferences and congresses, the precedence is determined by the alphabetical order of the French names of the countries the respective delegates represent. In 1899 at the Hague Conference, the United States was listed in French, *Etats-Unis d'Amerique;* but due to a happy philological discovery, before the next Hague Conference eight years later, the United States requested that their official designation be *Amerique, Etats-Unis d'*. This change places the United States at the top of the table in the *A* column. It also gives this country the *pas* over all the other states of Central and South America.[1]

If the ceremony is one at which the diplomatic body has to take what may be termed an *active* part, its members, ranged according to the order of precedence prescribed by the *Reglement de Vienne*, are placed in the right of the center or post of honor occupied by the most eminent person present, i.e., usually the head of the state.[2] . . . .

As regards seats, the place of honor and consequently the precedence attributed to the persons forming the company—at a four-cornered table of which all four sides are occupied, or at a round or oval table, the first place is usually considered to be facing the entrance and the last place is that nearest to it. Counting from the first place, the order of seats is from right to left, and so on.

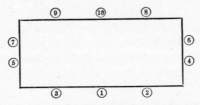

In standing, sitting, or walking, the place of honor is at the right, i.e., when the person entitled thereto stands or walks at the right. Precedence is when the person entitled goes a step before the other, who is at his left side, as in ascending a flight of stairs or entering a room.

[1] James Brown Scott, *Le Francais Langue Diplomatique*, p. 19.
[2] Sir Ernest Satow, *Diplomatic Practice*, I, p. 35.

Amongst the Turks and also at Catholic religious ceremonies, the left hand has often been regarded as the place of honor, so also among the Chinese.

In a lateral arrangement, i.e., when the persons present stand side by side in a straight line, the outside place on the right, or the central place, is the first according to circumstances. When there are only two persons, the right hand is the first (② ①) ; if there are three, the middle place is the first (③①②) ; the right hand, the second; the left hand, the third. If the number is four, the furthest to the right is the first place, the next is the second, the left of the latter is the third, and then the fourth (④ ③ ② ①).[1] Of five persons, the first is in the middle, immediately to the right is the second, to the left is the third, further to the right is the fourth, and the fifth is the furthest to the left (⑤ ③ ① ② ④). If six or more, the same principles are observed, according as the number is odd or even.[2]

Executive Order[3]

The following rules of precedence will henceforth be observed as between (1) ambassadors, ministers, and officers of the foreign service of the United States; (2) officers of the United States Army; (3) officers of the United States Navy and Marine Corps; and (4) foreign commerce officers of the United States. Previous executive orders inconsistent herewith are rescinded.

(1) In the country to which he is accredited, the chief of the diplomatic mission takes precedence over all officers of the Army, Navy, or foreign commerce service.

(2) In diplomatic missions the following ranking will be observed:

Counselors take place and precedence next in succession after the chief of mission.

Military and naval attachés take place and precedence next in succession after the counselor, or at a post where the Department of State has deemed it unnecessary to assign a counselor, after the senior first secretary. Military and naval attachés take precedence as between themselves according to their respective grades and seniority therein.

Commercial attachés rank with but after military and naval attachés.

Assistant military and naval attachés take place and precedence next after second secretaries. Assistant military and naval attachés take precedence as between themselves according to their respective grades and seniority therein.

[1] De Martens-Geffcken, *Guide Diplomatique* (1886), i, p. 131, has this order.
[2] A. Miruss, *Das Europaische Gesandtschaftsrecht* (1847).
[3] Calvin Coolidge, The White House, August 10, 1927.

Assistant commercial attachés rank with but after assistant military and naval attachés.

In the absence of the titular head of the mission, the senior diplomatic officer will act as chargé d'affaires ad interim, unless otherwise directed by the Secretary of State, and as such will take precedence over all members of the staff of the mission.

At ceremonies and receptions where the members of the mission take individual position, in the lists furnished foreign governments for inclusion in their diplomatic lists, and in the *Register* of the Department of State, place and precedence will follow the ranking indicated in the paragraphs above.

At ceremonies and receptions where diplomatic missions are present as a body, the military, naval, and commercial attachés will form distinct groups, and follow in that order the diplomatic personnel of the mission.

(3) In international conferences at which the American delegates possess plenipotentiary powers, the senior counselor of embassy or legation attached to the delegation, takes place and precedence immediately after the delegates, unless otherwise instructed by the Secretary of State.

(4) As between officers of the Departments of State and Commerce:

(*a*) The senior foreign commerce officer functioning in a consular district in which there is no diplomatic mission, shall rank with but after the senior foreign service officer functioning in that district.

(*b*) Foreign commerce officers in a consular district, other than the senior officer, shall rank with respect to the foreign service officers in the consular district other than the senior officer as follows:

1) Foreign commerce officers of Class I, with but after foreign service officers of Classes I and II;

2) Foreign commerce officers of Class II, with but after foreign service officers of Classes III and IV;

3) Foreign commerce officers of Class III, with but after foreign service officers of Classes V, VI, and VII;

4) Foreign commerce officers of Class IV, with but after foreign service officers of Classes VIII and IX, and unclassified officers of the first grade;

5) Foreign commerce officers of Class V, with but after unclassified foreign service officers of the second and third grades.

(*c*) In the absence of the foreign service officer in charge of a consular district, the foreign service officer acting shall enjoy the precedence regularly accorded the former, and in the absence of the ranking foreign commerce officer, the officer acting shall enjoy the precedence of the ranking foreign commerce officer.

(5) In the districts to which they are assigned, foreign service officers in charge of consulates general take place and precedence

immediately after brigadier generals in the Army or Marine Corps, and hold rank intermediate between rear admirals and captains in the Navy.

In the districts to which they are assigned, foreign service officers in charge of consulates take place and precedence immediately after colonels in the Army or Marine Corps and captains in the Navy.[1]

NOTE: A "diplomatic officer" includes ambassadors, ministers (whether plenipotentiary or resident), diplomatic agents, charges d'affaires, charges d'affaires ad interim, counselors of embassy or legation, and secretaries of embassy or legation. The term "diplomatic representative" is used to denote chiefs of mission only. "Foreign Service Officer" is deemed to denote permanent officers of the Foreign Service below the grade of Minister.

[1] Consular Regulations state that vice consular officers, consular assistants and consular agents rank with lieutenants in the Navy and captains in the Army. This does not appear to be authenticated by any executive order or by *Navy Regulations.*

APPENDIX C

NAVAL REGULATIONS PERTAINING TO OFFICIAL RELATIONS OF NAVAL OFFICERS WITH FOREIGN OFFICIALS, U. S. FOREIGN SERVICE OFFICIALS, AND FOREIGN STATES

Mr. Hay, Secretary of State, remarked to Mr. Roosevelt in the Cabinet Room of the White House, and in the presence of Rear Admiral Taylor, Chief of Bureau of Navigation, that *he always felt relieved when the naval officer had arrived on the scene because he always kept within the situation.*

The late Admiral H. S. Knapp, U. S. Navy, wrote in his last published article:

Surely there can be no more fundamental preparation than a knowledge of our own history and traditions, our institutions, our outlook upon the world, our time-honored policies, and evolution leading to a modification of the national viewpoint. The statement needs no elaboration to prove its truth.

Although international law, instructions, and precedents, as well as reasoned judgment based upon a study and an estimate of the situation, guide the senior naval officer present in international situations, the following regulations serve as a basis for the international dealings of the officer.

Intercourse with Foreigners

Article 717. When at a port and not informed as to the officials present whom it is usual to visit, or as to the interchange of other courtesies, the commander in chief shall send an officer of his staff to the senior representative of the United States at the port, or in the absence of any such representative, to the highest local official to inform himself.

Article 718. 1. The commander in chief shall preserve, as far as possible, the most cordial relations with the diplomatic and consular representatives of the United States in foreign countries and extend to them the honors, salutes, and other official courtesies to which they are entitled by these regulations.

2. He shall carefully and duly consider any request for service or other communications from any such representative.

3. Although due weight should be given to the opinions and advice of such representatives, a commanding officer is solely and en-

tirely responsible to his own immediate superior for all official acts in the administration of his command.

Article 719. The commander in chief shall, as a general rule, when in foreign ports, communicate with local civil officials and foreign diplomatic and consular authorities through the diplomatic or consular representative of the United States on the spot.

Article 720. In the absence of a diplomatic or consular officer of the United States at a foreign port the commander in chief, as senior officer present, has authority:

(*a*) To exercise the powers of a consul in relation to mariners of the United States. (Sec. 1433, R.S.) ;

(*b*) To communicate or remonstrate with foreign civil authorities as may be necessary;

(*c*) To urge upon citizens of the United States the necessity of abstaining from participation in political controversies or violations of the laws of neutrality.

Article 721. 1. The commander in chief shall exercise great care that all under his command scrupulously respect the territorial authority of foreign civilized nations in amity with the United States.

2. No armed force for exercise, target practice, funeral escort, or other purposes shall be landed without permission from the local authorities; nor shall large bodies of men be granted leave to visit the shore without a similar permission; nor shall men be landed to capture deserters.

3. Target practice with guns or torpedoes shall not take place without permission from the government of the country concerned within foreign territorial waters or at any point from which shots may fall or torpedoes enter therein.

Article 722. On occasions where injury to the United States or to citizens thereof is committed or threatened, in violation of the principles of international law or treaty rights, the commander in chief shall consult with the diplomatic representative or consul of the United States, and take such steps as the gravity of the case demands, reporting immediately to the Secretary of the Navy all the facts. The responsibility for any action taken by a naval force, however, rests wholly upon the commanding officer thereof.

Article 723. The use of force against a foreign and friendly state, or against anyone within the territories thereof, is illegal.

The right of self-preservation, however, is a right which belongs to states as well as to individuals, and in the case of states it includes the protection of the state, its honor, and its possessions, and the lives and property of its citizens against arbitrary violence, actual or impending, whereby the state or its citizens may suffer irreparable injury. The conditions calling for the application of the right of self-preservation cannot be defined beforehand, but must be left to the sound judgment of responsible officers, who are to perform their duties in this respect with all possible care and forbearance. In no case shall force be exercised in time of peace otherwise than as an application of the right of self-preservation as above defined. It must be used as a last resort, and then only to the extent which is absolutely necessary to accomplish the end required. It can never be exercised with a view to inflicting punishment for acts already committed.

Article 724. 1. Whenever, in the application of the above-mentioned principles, it shall become necessary to land an armed force in foreign territory on occasions of political disturbance where the local authorities are unable to give adequate protection to life and property, the assent of such authorities, or of some one of them, shall first be obtained, if it can be done without prejudice to the interests involved.

2. Due to the ease with which the Navy Department can be communicated with from all parts of the world, no commander in chief, flag officer, or commanding officer shall issue an ultimatum to the representative of any foreign government, or demand the performance of any service from any such representative that must be executed within a limited time, without first communicating with the Navy Department, except in extreme cases where such action is necessary to save life.

Article 725. The right of asylum for political or other refugees has no foundation in international law. In countries, however, where frequent insurrections occur, and constant instability of government exists, usage sanctions the granting of asylum; but even in the waters of such countries, officers should refuse all applications for asylum except when required by the interests of humanity in extreme or exceptional cases such as the pursuit of a refugee by a mob. Officers must not directly or indirectly invite refugees to accept asylum.

Article 726. So far as lies within their power, commanders in chief, division commanders, and commanding officers of ships shall protect all merchant vessels of the United States in lawful occupations, and advance the commercial interests of this country, always acting in accordance with international law and treaty obligations.

Article 727. The commander in chief shall impress upon officers and men that when in foreign ports it is their duty to avoid all possible causes of offense to the authorities or inhabitants; that due deference must be shown by them to the local laws, customs, ceremonies, and regulations; and that in all dealings with foreigners moderation and courtesy should be displayed, and that a feeling of good will and mutual respect should be cultivated.

APPENDIX D

ADMIRALITY FLEET ORDER 202/27*

Toasts at Official Dinners—Procedure when Foreign Officers Are Present

(M.—28.1.1927)

Whenever foreign officers or officials are entertained on board His Majesty's ships on occasions when it is customary for toasts to be exchanged, the following procedure, which is in consonance with the generally accepted international custom, is to be strictly observed:

1. The British officer acting as host will propose as the first toast the health of the Head of the State (Sovereign or President) of the country to which the visitors belong.

2. After this has been honoured, the senior officer of the foreign guests will propose the health of His Majesty King George V [George VI].

3. When more than one nation is represented amongst the guests, the host will propose a collective toast of the heads of the several states represented, naming them in the order of the rank and seniority of their respective representative officers present.

4. To this collective toast the senior and highest in rank of the foreign officers present will respond on behalf of all the foreign guests by proposing the health of His Majesty George V [George VI].

5. This procedure should be arranged beforehand between the British officer who is the host and his foreign guests.

6. The first toast should always be proposed in English, but, if possible, it should also be repeated in French, or in the language of the visitors.

7. Any subsequent toast may follow as the occasion demands.

* By courtesy of Vice Admiral Sir Charles Little, K.C.B., R.N.

APPENDIX E

REGULATIONS OF DIPLOMATIC AND CONSULAR OFFICERS PERTAINING TO CONTACT WITH OFFICERS OF THE NAVY

INSTRUCTIONS TO DIPLOMATIC OFFICERS

Attachés. An attaché is not recognized under the law as a diplomatic officer (R.S., sec. 1674, par. 5). Should it come to the knowledge of a diplomatic representative that any person is representing himself as an attaché or styling himself a secretary of the mission without warrant, it will be his duty to report the fact to the Department of State and to make it known informally to the government to which he is accredited.[1]

Ceremonial Representation. A military, naval, or commercial attaché forms a part of the official staff of a mission, and should be present at all ceremonies and official functions where his attendance is desired by the chief of mission.[1]

Visits of American Naval Units. Upon the arrival of an American ship of war or squadron in a foreign port where there are diplomatic officers of the United States, the following procedure in regard to visits of ceremony will be observed:

(*a*) A flag officer will pay the first visit to a diplomatic officer of or above the rank of chargé d'affaires.

(*b*) A commanding officer will pay the first visit to a diplomatic officer of or above the rank of chargé d'affaires.

(*c*) Official visits shall be returned within twenty-four hours.

(*d*) The senior officer present will if necessary arrange to furnish a suitable boat to enable a diplomatic representative to pay official visits afloat.[1]

Salutes. An ambassador is entitled once while a naval force or vessel is in port to a salute of 19 guns; an envoy extraordinary and minister plenipotentiary to a salute of 15 guns; a minister resident to a salute of 13 guns; and a chargé d'affaires to a salute of 11 guns. The salute is usually fired while the diplomatic representative is being conveyed from the vessel to the shore. He will stand and face the vessel, and at the end of the salute acknowledge it by raising his hat.[1]

Social Attentions to Naval Officers. Though diplomatic officers are expected to use their official position to advance the interests of the Navy, it may be remarked that their salaries are not established on a scale to require social attentions to the officers which call for the expenditure of money, unless they see fit to give them. The fact that

[1] Executive order of 8 March, 1927.

such attentions have been given, or are supposed to be required, will not justify a diplomatic officer in asking increased compensation.[1]

Grade of Diplomatic Representatives. The diplomatic representatives of the United States are as follows:

(*a*) Ambassadors extraordinary and plenipotentiary and special commissioners, with the rank of ambassadors extraordinary and plenipotentiary.

(*b*) Envoys extraordinary and ministers plenipotentiary and special commissioners, with the rank of envoys extraordinary and ministers plenipotentiary.

(*c*) Ministers resident. These grades of representatives are accredited by the President.

(*d*) Chargés d'affaires commissioned by the President as such and accredited by the Secretary of State to the Minister for Foreign Affairs of the government to which they are sent.

In the absence from the country to which he is accredited, or in the event of the death or disability of the chief of mission, the counselor or ranking diplomatic secretary, as the case may be, acts *ex officio* as chargé d'affaires ad interim without special instructions or credentials to that end. If there should be no counselor or diplomatic secretary at the mission the Secretary of State may designate any competent person to act ad interim, in which case he is specifically accredited by letter to the Minister for Foreign Affairs.

When the office of consul general is added to that of envoy extraordinary and minister plenipotentiary, minister resident, chargé d'affaires, or secretary of embassy or legation, the diplomatic rank is regarded as superior to and independent of the consular rank. The officer will follow the consular regulations in regard to his consular duties and official accounts, keeping correspondence in one capacity separate from correspondence in the other.[1]

Within the discretion of the President, any foreign service officer may be assigned to act as commissioner, chargé d'affaires, minister resident, or diplomatic agent for such period as the public interest may require without loss of grade, class, or salary, provided that no such officer shall receive more than one salary (Act of Feb. 23, 1931, sec. 24). With the exception of commissioner, these appointments are subject to confirmation by the Senate.[2]

Rules of Congress of Vienna. For the sake of convenience and uniformity in determining the relative rank and precedence of diplomatic representatives, the Department of State has adopted and prescribed the seven rules of the Congress of Vienna, found in the protocol of the session of March 9, 1815, and the supplementary or eighth rule of the Congress of Aix-la-Chapelle of November 21, 1818. They are as follows:

"In order to prevent the inconveniences which have frequently occurred, and which might again arise, from claims of precedence

---

[1] Executive order of 8 March, 1927.   [2] Executive order of 8 June, 1931.

among different diplomatic agents, the plenipotentiaries of the powers who signed the Treaty of Paris have agreed on the following articles, and they think it their duty to invite the plenipotentiaries of other crowned heads to adopt the same regulations:

"Article 1. Diplomatic agents are divided into three classes: that of ambassadors, legates, or nuncios; that of envoys, ministers, or other persons accredited to sovereigns; that of chargés d'affaires accredited to ministers for foreign affairs.

"Article 2. Ambassadors, legates, or nuncios only have the representative character.

"Article 3. Diplomatic agents on an extraordinary mission have not, on that account, any superiority of rank.

"Article 4. Diplomatic agents shall take precedence in their respective classes according to the date of the official notification of their arrival. The present regulation shall not cause any innovation with regard to the representative of the Pope.

"Article 5. A uniform mode shall be determined in each state for the reception of diplomatic agents of each class.

"Article 6. Relations of consanguinity or of family alliance between courts confer no precedence on their diplomatic agents. The same rule also applies to political alliances.

"Article 7. In acts or treaties between several powers which grant alternate precedence, the order which is to be observed in the signatures shall be decided by lot between the ministers.

"Article 8. It is agreed that ministers resident accredited to them shall form with respect to their precedence, an intermediate class between ministers of the second class and chargés d'affaires."

Papers Furnished to the Diplomatic Representative. After filing the prescribed oath in the Department of State and receiving his commission, the following papers will be furnished to a newly appointed diplomatic representative:

(a) A sealed letter of credence signed by the President and addressed to the head of the state to which the representative is sent. In the case of a commissioned chargé d'affaires or diplomatic agent, the letter of credence will be addressed by the Secretary of State to the Minister for Foreign Affairs.

(b) An open office copy of the letter of credence.

(c) Diplomatic passports for himself, his family, and suite.

(d) A copy of the *Register* of the Department of State.

(e) A copy of the *Instructions to Diplomatic Officers of the United States,* with any circular instructions modifying them.

CONSULAR REGULATIONS

Commanders of Squadrons. When a naval squadron of the United States visits a foreign port where there is a consular officer, it is the duty of the commander of the squadron to send a boat ashore, with an officer on board, who shall call upon the consular officer, notify him of the arrival of the squadron, and tender him a passage to the flagship at such time as he may select. It is the duty of the consular officer to accept the invitation and visit the flagship as early as convenient, which must be within a period not exceeding twenty-four hours, and to tender his official services to the commander.[1]

Note 1. Official calls. The *Navy Regulations of the United States* prescribe the following etiquette for naval officers, and consular officers will also be guided thereby:

"(*a*) A flag officer or commodore will receive the first visit from consular officers.

"(*b*) A commanding officer of the rank of captain shall pay the first visit to a consul general and will receive the first visit from other consular officers. A commanding officer below the rank of captain shall pay the first visit to a consul general and to a consul in charge of a consulate.

"(*c*) Official visits shall be returned within twenty-four hours."

Commanders of Ships of War. When a ship of war of the United States visits a foreign port where there is a consular officer, it is the duty of the commander thereof, if not a flag officer, to pay the first visit in person to a consul general, and to tender him passage to his ship. If the commander be a flag officer, or if the consular officer be of lower grade than a consul general, it is the duty of the commander to send a boat ashore, with an officer on board, to visit the consular officer and tender him a passage to the ship at such time as he may select. It is the duty of the consular officer to accept the invitation to visit the commander or return his visit, as circumstances may require, within a period not exceeding twenty-four hours, and to tender to him his official services.[1]

Salutes. A consul general is entitled once while a naval force or vessel is in port to a salute of 11 guns; a consul to a salute of 7 guns; and a vice consul, or consular agent, when he is the only representative of the United States at the post, to a salute of 5 guns. The salute may be fired either while the consular officer is on board (which is unusual), or while he is being conveyed from the vessel to the shore. In the latter case, he will stand and face the vessel, and at the end of the salute acknowledge it by raising his hat.[1]

Social Attention to Naval Officers. Though consular officers are expected to use their official position to advance the interests of the Navy, it may be remarked that their salaries are not established on a scale to require social attentions to the officers which call for the expenditure of money, unless they see fit to give them. The fact that such attentions have been given, or are supposed to be required, will not justify a consul in asking increased compensation.

[1] Executive order of 6 September, 1923.

When Naval Force May Be Asked.[1] The Navy is an independent branch of the service, not subject to the orders of the Department of State, and its officers have fixed duties prescribed for them; consuls will, therefore, be careful to ask for the presence of a naval force at their ports only when public exigencies absolutely require it, and will then give the officers in command the reasons in full for the request and leave with them the responsibility of action. If the request is addressed to the Department of State, the reasons should likewise be fully stated for its information.

[1] The American minister in foreign countries is sometimes called upon to act in concert with a commander of our naval forces. While in cases of emergency or threatened danger to American interests the naval officer is instructed to put himself in communication with the diplomatic representative of the country, he does not thereby come under his orders. The naval officer receives his instructions only through the Secretary of the Navy. While there should exist a good understanding and harmony of action, both occupy a position independent of each other.

JOHN W. FOSTER, *Practice of Diplomacy.*

APPENDIX F
ARMY REGULATIONS, CUSTOMS, AND COURTESIES

"A little experience of Army life will convince anyone that the Service is among the remaining strongholds of good manners. . . . And where in contemporary civil life will you find a profession in which a man can be fired from his job 'for conduct unbecoming a gentleman?' "

HOFFMAN NICKERSON[1]

"Here die I, Richard Grenville, with a joyful and quiet mind, for that I have ended my life as a true soldier ought to do that hath fought for his country, queen, religion, and honor. Whereby my soul most joyfully departeth out of this body, and shall always leave behind it an everlasting fame of a valiant and true soldier, that has done his duty as he was bound to do."

Last words of Sir Richard Grenville, prisoner of the Spanish after the sea action of August, 1591.

"Major, tell my father I died with my face to the enemy."[2]

I. E. AVERY

"We proudly trace the traditions of our service directly back to the Order of Knighthood, which for centuries furnished the brain and spirit and sinew to European armies, and indelibly stamped its impress upon our profession."

BRIGADIER GENERAL LINCOLN C. ANDREWS, U. S. ARMY

The United States Army officer has with justifiable pride maintained the honor, the integrity, and the gentility that is ever implied by "soldier and gentleman." As with all military and naval services that are worthy of the name, the traditions of yesterday influence the services of today. The devotion to cause of Washington, the incomparable leadership of Andrew Jackson, the gentility of Lee, and dogged perseverance of Grant, the religious cast and military genius of Stonewall Jackson constitute splendid traits that have been seldom equaled in the military history of any state.

[1] "Officer and Gentleman," *American Mercury.*
[2] A blood-stained note addressed to Major Samuel Tate, found clasped in the hand of Colonel Isaac Erwin Avery of 6th Regiment, North Carolina Confederate Troops. The paper is now on exhibition at State Museum, Raleigh, North Carolina. Avery, who commanded Hoke's Brigade, was killed on evening of second day at Gettysburg. The Colonel wrote this last message with his left hand because his right arm was paralyzed by the fatal wound.

Moreover, it is the rule that the great generals have been great gentlemen. For some its development commenced in childhood; for others it was developed through a conscientious observance of regulations, customs, and courtesies of the Army service tempered by sound character with a sense of the value of tradition and example to *ésprit de corps*. Greatness is reflected in defeat as well as in victory, at death as well as on the heights of success. The inner man was reflected when the wounded Sydney passed his cup of water to the dying soldier on the battlefield, when Grant in recognition of a gallant and brave foe displayed a magnanimous spirit towards Lee at Appomattox.

Wherever subject matter in this work touches upon manners, social usages, and courtesies it is generally true, whether the courtesies be military, naval, or civil, that they may be epitomized by the expression of thoughtfulness and respect for others. In fact thought of others in all strata of humanity reflects one of mankind's most appreciated attributes, but when that consideration is expressed by the vehicle of best usage, it reflects the gentleman in an exalted sense of the word.

West Point has been concerned in laying the foundation stones of good usage by a definite course for all cadets. The Superintendent of West Point kindly furnished, on request of the Superintendent of the Naval Academy, an outline of the course, in order that pertinent material could be used in a series of lectures at the Postgraduate School on "customs, usage, and traditions." The West Point course requires the embryo Army officers to learn what is meant by good usage, and standardizes the outstanding courtesies expected of the Army officer. Extracts of *Army Regulations* pertinent to the course are also included. West Point considers that a course of this description, properly imparted to cadets, will help to mold the representative young men into "soldiers and gentlemen."

In substance, the social usage of the Army is identical with that of the Navy. For these reasons there are set forth extracts from the West Point course—a consensus of opinion of good usage. There are, of course, departures that result from the differences in the organization and life of the respective services.

The West Pointer is taught:[1]

The relationship between an officer and his men must be given careful thought and study. Our *Army Regulations* and customs of the

[1] Quoted by permission of the Superintendent of the U. S. Military Academy.

service forbid undue familiarity between the two. This is not due to any difference in birth or social status but is countenanced solely to maintain discipline. There is an old saying which is especially applicable to the military service and that is "familiarity breeds contempt." Any officer who ignores the distinction which prevails in the Army between himself and his men will be a failure as a commander. Soldiers understand the necessity for the relation which exists between an officer and his men and have only contempt for one who oversteps the bounds.

Remember in all of your dealing with subordinates to avoid language or remarks which lessen self-respect. Employ a tone of voice and a manner such as you would ordinarily employ in a conversation with another.

Set a high standard as a gentleman and a soldier and your men will recognize in you a leader whom they will gladly follow.

Military Courtesy

(1) Courtesy among military men is indispensable to discipline; respect to superiors will not be confined to obedience on duty, but will extend to all occasions. (*A.R.*, 600-10).

(2) *Saluting.* The salute is rendered by the junior whenever he meets a person entitled to it. Those entitled to the salute are your superiors in military rank among the officers of the regular Army, Navy, Marine Corps, and of the National Guard and Reserves when in uniform. It is also customary to salute officers of friendly powers when in uniform.

Saluting distance is that distance at which recognition is easy. Usually it does not exceed thirty paces. One always salutes before the person to be saluted approaches closer than six paces. This gives him time to return the salute.

A salute is always returned by all officers present entitled to it unless they are in a formation when the senior only returns all salutes. A person returning a salute should be just as careful and precise in his manner of saluting as the person saluting.

In civilian clothes, a soldier salutes an officer when he recognizes him, even if both soldier and officer are dressed in civilian clothes.

Covered or uncovered salutes are exchanged in the same manner.

The salute is rendered but once if the senior remains in the immediate vicinity and no conversation takes place. If a conversation has taken place, the junior again salutes the senior in taking his leave or when the senior leaves.

In making reports the person rendering the report salutes regardless of rank. An example of this is the case of a company commander rendering a report to the adjutant or to the officer of the day.

A group of soldiers on the approach of an officer is called to attention by the first person noticing him.

The salute is rendered at the quick time. If a person is running, before saluting he comes down to the quick time. Likewise a mounted person does not salute at the trot or gallop. He always comes down to the walk before saluting.

When reporting to an officer in his office a junior leaves his headdress outside, unless under arms, knocks and enters when told to do so. Upon entering he marches up not closer than two paces from the officer's desk, halts, salutes, and says, "Sir, ... reports to . . . .," using names and ranks. When the business is completed, the junior steps back one step, halts, salutes, executes about face, and withdraws.

One always uncovers on entering a room where a senior is present unless under arms.

The driver of a horse drawn vehicle not in motion salutes unless it is necessary for him to use both hands to control his team. He does not salute if the vehicle is in motion.

The driver of a motor vehicle salutes unless the vehicle is in motion. Others riding in a motor car (and the driver, if the car is not in motion) salute without rising from their seats. The officer or noncommissioned officer in charge of a detail riding in a truck salutes for the entire party.

When the National Anthem is played or "to the color" sounded, at the first note all dismounted officers and men present but not in formation stand at attention facing the music and salute, except that at "escort of the color" or at "retreat" they face toward the color or flag. The salute is held until the last note of the music. Those mounted halt and salute mounted. Vehicles in motion are brought to a halt. Occupants of vehicles except the driver dismount and salute. Drivers of vehicles sit at attention.

The same marks of respect are shown toward the National Anthem of any other country when played upon official occasions.

If in uniform, covered or uncovered, face the flag and render the military salute. If in civilian clothes, stand facing the flag, remove the headdress, if covered, and hold it over the left breast.

Women present should also be instructed to rise and face the flag.

(3) *When Not to Salute.* Salutes are not rendered by individuals in the following cases.

In ranks.—The officer or noncomissioned offier in command renders or receives the salute for the entire organization. A soldier in ranks and not at attention comes to attention when addressed by an officer.

At mess.—When an officer enters the messroom or tent, the first person to perceive him calls "attention" whereupon all present stop eating, but remain seated. All remain seated at attention until the officer leaves the room or directs otherwise. An individual addressed rises and stands at attention.

Details at work do not salute. The officer or noncomissioned officer in charge, if not actively engaged at the time, salutes or acknowledges salutes for the entire party.

When actually engaged at games such as baseball, tennis, or golf, one does not salute. In a squad room or tent, individuals rise and stand at attention when an officer enters. If more than one person is present the first to perceive the officer calls "attention."

When standing to horse or leading a horse, one does not salute.

In theaters or other places of public assemblage, or in a public conveyance, salutes are not exchanged.

(4) *Other Personal Courtesies.* Except in the field under campaign or simulated campaign conditions, a mounted junior always dismounts before speaking to or replying to a dismounted senior. This should always be done even by officers of very little difference in rank. When accompanying a senior, the junior always walks or rides on his left except that an enlisted man accompanying an officer mounted rides one horse's length behind him.

Officers enter automobiles and small boats in inverse order of rank and leave in order of rank. In other words, the senior enters an automobile or small boat last and leaves it first. Juniors although entering the automobile first, take their appropriate seat in the car. The senior is always on the right.

In general, juniors habitually give the same precedence to and show the same deference towards their seniors that any courteous person does to his elders.

(5) *Calls of Courtesy (A.R., 605-125).* "The interchange of visits of courtesy between officers is of great importance and the well-established customs of the Army in this respect will be scrupulously adhered to. Failure to pay the civilities customary in official and polite society is to the prejudice of the best interests of the Service."

Calls should be paid promptly and should be brief.

An officer reporting to a new post reports to the post headquarters on his arrival. He calls upon the commanding officer in his office the day he arrives. He calls on the commanding officer at his quarters within twenty-four hours after his arrival.

He pays similar calls on his immediate commanding officer and on the commanding officer of his regiment, coast defense, separate battalion, or similar organization when such officers live on or near his station.

When in Washington, an officer calls on the Chief of Staff. If not assigned to duty in the War Department, it is sufficient to sign the officers' register in the Adjutant General's office. He then calls on the chief of his branch in his office.

(6) *Official Visits to War Vessels.* A vessel of war will be approached and boarded by commissioned officers and visitors in their company, by the starboard side and gangway; the port gangway will be used by all other persons. The commanding officer of the ship may change this rule, if expedient.

In entering a boat, the junior goes first and other officers follow in order of rank; in leaving a boat, the senior goes first.

A landing over another boat will not be made without permission, and permission to do so will not be asked if it can be avoided.

Boats will always haul clear of a ship's gangway while waiting and, when about to leave a ship's side, will endeavor to give way in ample time to clear the gangway for other boats approaching.

An officer paying a boarding visit to a vessel of war or transport is met at the gangway by the officer of the deck.

The salutes to be exchanged upon boarding and leaving a vessel of war are prescribed in the following paragraph from the *United States Navy Regulations,* to which all members of the Army visiting a vessel of war will conform.

"All officers and men, whenever reaching the quarter-deck, either from a boat, from a gangway, from the shore, or from another part of the ship, shall stop at the top of the gangway or upon arriving upon the quarter-deck, face the colors, and render the salute, after which the officer of the deck shall be saluted. In leaving the quarter-deck, the same salutes shall be rendered in inverse order. The officer of the deck shall return both salutes in each case, and shall require that they be properly made.

"The commanding officer shall clearly define the limits of the quarter-deck; it shall embrace so much of the main or other appropriate deck as may be necessary for the proper conduct of official and ceremonial functions. When the quarter-deck so designated is forward and at a considerable distance from the colors the salute to the colors prescribed in the preceding paragraph will not be rendered by officers and men except when leaving or coming aboard the ship.

"The salute to the national colors to be made by officers and enlisted men with no arms in their hands shall be the hand salute, the headdress not to be removed."

All officers in the party salute the colors, but only the senior render or return the salutes, other than that to the colors, given at the gangway of a naval vessel.

Customs of the Service
I. Definition

1. Customs of the service comprise the unwritten law for the social and official conduct of the Army of the United States. To render a custom valid and to qualify it for incorporation in this unwritten law, the following qualities are considered requisite: (1) Habitual or long-established custom; (2) Continuance without interruption; (3) Acceptance without dispute; (4) Reasonableness; (5) Exactitude; (6) Compulsory compliance; (7) Consistency with other customs.

2. The following compilation includes the most important customs of the service.

II. Titles

(1) *Regular Army*

    (a) Lieutenants. All lieutenants shall be addressed by other commissioned officers as "mister," except in official communications and except when speaking of them or making reference to them in the presence of enlisted men. When speaking directly to them or when introducing them, lieutenants are called "mister"; when speaking of them and when making reference to them to enlisted men, they are called "lieutenant"; enlisted men always address lieutenants as "lieutenant." During and since the World War, this tradition has been to a certain extent ignored in some quarters because of the fact that large numbers of persons entered the service at that time to whom old customs of the Army were unknown.

(b) Captain and Above. Officers with the grade of captain and above are referred to both officially and socially by their titles. In conversation and in non-official correspondence brigadier generals, major generals, lieutenant generals, and generals are referred to and addressed as "general." Lieutenant colonels under the same conditions are referred to and addressed as "colonel."

(c) Address between Senior and Junior. Senior officers frequently address juniors as "Smith" or "Jones," but this address does not give the junior the privilege of addressing the senior in any other way than by his proper title. A certain amount of familiarity is necessary between seniors and juniors in social intercourse, but young officers should be exceedingly careful to show proper respect to their seniors at all times.

(d) Address between Officers of Same Grade. Officers of the same grade, except where there is considerable difference in age or dates of commission, generally address one another by their surnames.

(e) Medical Corps. Officers of the Medical Corps of the grade of captain and above are addressed by their military titles (captain, major, etc.). Lieutenants are addressed as "doctor."

(f) Chaplains are addressed as "chaplain" regardless of their rank.

(g) Cadets of the United States Military Academy are addressed as "mister" socially and in conversation, and as "cadet" officially and in written communications.

(h) Title of Temporary Rank. Officers who have held temporary commissions of grades higher than those they have in the regular army are sometimes addressed socially by the titles of their former temporary rank. For instance, a captain who held the commission of lieutenant colonel during the World War is sometimes addressed socially as "colonel." The custom of thus addressing officers is quite prevalent among civilians but such practice in the regular Army is infrequent.

(i) Warrant officers are addressed as "mister."

(j) Enlisted Men. Non-commissioned officers are addressed by their titles. Officers address them as "sergeant," "corporal," etc. Officers address privates as "Smith," or "Jones." Master sergeants, technical sergeants, staff sergeants, etc., are addressed simply as "sergeant."

(2) *National Guard*

National Guard and Reserve Officers on active military duty follow the customs of the regular Army in the matter of titles and address. Both National Guard and Reserve Officers when not on duty are most frequently addressed as "mister."

(3) *Navy*

In the Navy officers with the rank of commander and above in both line and staff are addressed socially by their titles, whereas those with the rank of lieutenant commander and below are addressed as "mister."

Any officer in command of a ship, whatever its size or class, while exercising such command is addressed as "captain."

In speaking to or introducing captains of the Navy, it is customary to add after the name, "of the Navy," in order to indicate that the officer belongs to the Navy and not to the Army, Marine Corps, or National Guard. The reason for this practice is that the grade of captain in the Navy corresponds to our grade of colonel in the Army.

III. Calls

For all posts in the United States, calling hours are from 8:00 to 9:00 in the evening. It is permissible to call on Sunday afternoon between three and five o'clock. This practice differs from the custom of civil life where calls are usually made in the afternoon.

An officer arriving at a post at which he expects to remain longer than twenty-four hours should call on the post commander. If assigned to duty there, he should call on all of his intermediate commanders. These calls should be made immediately after the call on the post commander and should be at the office of those concerned. If unable to wear uniform, an explanation should be made for appearing in civilian clothes.

The official visit to the post and intermediate commanders should be repeated at their residences within twenty-four hours after arrival. If the commander is married and his wife is present on the post, it is the custom for the officer making the visit to be accompanied by his wife. These calls should be formal and should ordinarily last no longer than ten minutes.

It is not necessary for the new arrival to make other calls until the officers of the battalion, regiment, or garrison have called on him.

It is customary for officers to call on a new arrival as soon as he is situated so that callers can be received comfortably and without embarrassment. If the newcomer is married and his family is present, ladies call with their husbands.

Calls should be returned promptly, within one week or ten days.

While the house guest of a brother officer, the newcomer should make every effort to have his own quarters ready for occupancy as soon as possible. Within a week after moving into his own quarters, the officer should call on his former host and hostess.

After receiving an invitation to dinner or a private party, it is absolutely necessary to call upon the hostess within one week after the event. This call should be made whether one attends the function or not.

When the commanding officer has guests visiting him, it is customary and proper to call upon them.

When an officer leaves his station to be permanently away, or on leave for a considerable period, he should call upon his commanding officers.

If obliged to leave hurriedly after being a guest at a garrison and having been extended the privilege of the officers' club, put your card, with the initials *p.p.c.* (*pour prendre congé*) therein, on the club bulletin board. Mail cards to those friends you are unable to call upon.

It is customary for all officers of a unit or garrison to call upon the commanding officer on New Year's Day.

Calling Cards. In the service as in civil life do not neglect to observe social conventions in the use of visiting cards. At receptions, teas, or similar functions, it is customary to leave a card for each person in whose name the invitation is extended, and for the guest of honor if there be one.

In regard to the number of cards to leave, the rule is simple. A bachelor or a married officer not accompanied by his wife, leaves one card for the officer called upon and one for each of the adult members of the officer's household. When an officer is accompanied by his wife or his mother or both, the ladies leave one card for each of the adult ladies of the household in addition to those left by the officer himself.

IV. Social Functions

Whenever guests are taken to a post dance, reception, or other function, they should be introduced to the members of the garrison. Nothing makes a guest, particularly a civilian, more discomfited or ill at ease than to be a member of a party, none of whom is known to him. Be sure to introduce the guest to your friends. It is your duty to devote yourself to your guests and to make sure that they are enjoying themselves. The gentlemanly thing to do, if some one is seen who has apparently been forgotten, is to go to him, introduce yourself, and make him acquainted with other members of the garrison. At small posts this impolite neglect will without doubt be the exception rather than the rule, but at large posts such neglects are apt to occur.

It is customary for officers of all grades to dance or to chat with the wives of the senior officers of the unit.

A member of a dinner party which later in the evening attends a post hop or other dance must not fail to dance with the hostess and the guest of honor. It is essential that everyone in the party pay special attention to the hostess and her guest and also to other members of that party.

Invitations to dinners and private functions, when accepted, constitute social obligations. By all means return these social obligations, but do so in a manner suited to your means. In the Army everyone knows the amount of everyone else's pay and due consideration is shown.

Officers should not discuss official subjects at social functions. Garrison disputes must be avoided.

V. Messes

The officers' mess is important as a meeting place of bachelor officers, and customs of the Service have laid down some very strict laws regarding it. These laws vary at different posts and at different messes. However, in general, an officer should never attend a meal unless properly dressed. Before leaving the table one should always ask to be excused. The senior officer at the table is the president of the mess and is due consideration as such.

Usually the evening week-day meal and the Sunday midday meal are formal. It is customary in some messes that at these meals no one sits down until the senior officer of the mess arrives. No one leaves the table or asks to be excused until the senior officer present has finished his meal, and left the table, or has stated that the meal is finished and everyone is at liberty to leave. If a member of the mess arrives late, he should express his apologies to the president of the mess and request permission to sit down.

Discussions of orders of the commanding officer are out of order. The mentioning of ladies' names as a conversational topic is customarily forbidden.

It is customary for officers of an organization and sometimes their families also to eat certain meals in the mess of their organization. For example, the captain and lieutenants of a troop eat Christmas dinner with the men of the troop in the troop mess hall.

VI. General Rules

Distinguished visitors, either military or civilian, are generally honored by appropriate receptions, either by the commander or by the officers of the garrison. Although such gatherings are primarily social, they have nevertheless an official aspect. Attendance at these functions should be regarded as obligatory and absence therefrom should occur only for those reasons which would necessitate absence from a military formation.

On Christmas Day the band generally gives a short concert in front of the officers' quarters. Be sure to thank the band leader for this courtesy.

When the commanding officer says "I desire" or "I wish" rather than "I direct you to do so-and-so," this wish or desire has all the authority of a direct order.

The junior is on the left of the senior when walking, riding, or driving. He should open doors for the senior and go through the opening last.

When mounted, the junior brings his horse to the walk before saluting a dismounted senior. When mounted, the junior dismounts before addressing or replying to a dismounted senior. When both senior and the junior are mounted, the junior salutes while his horse is at the gait of the senior's mount or at a slower gait.

Avoid the impolite practice of approaching an officer senior to you whom you know or remember well and of expecting him to remember your name and where he has known you before. When you speak to an officer, introduce yourself by name and refresh his memory regarding where he has known you.

SOCIAL CUSTOMS

Introduction. The chapters on "Military Courtesy" and "Customs of the Service" have dealt with those requirements of correct behavior which are more or less peculiar to military men and which have become obligatory in the service as the result either of regulation or tradition. These regulations and traditions are necessarily limited in scope and their observance, while of the first importance, is by no means sufficient. In all official and social contacts not so regulated, whether within the Service or among civilians, the Army officer is expected, of his own initiative, to observe the highest standards of gentlemanly conduct.

Gentlemanly conduct arises in the first instance from innate qualities and in the second from a knowledge of social customs.

Social customs are the forms, fashions, and manners observed in the society of educated and cultivated people. They constitute a code of behavior in the development of which it has been the purpose to foster beauty, grace, and courtesy while eliminating whatever is coarse or offensive. At the same time social customs are intensely practical. They aim to facilitate life, to get things done quickly, to smooth the course of friendly gatherings, and to eliminate friction in our daily contacts with one another.

A knowledge of social customs comes inevitably with experience. To depend entirely on experience is, however, a slow and costly procedure.[1]

On arrival in a strange community, always inquire what are the customs but great care should be exercised in selecting an authorita-

[1] The West Point *Manual* states: "These discussions must be regarded as elemental. The student should not consider himself qualified until he has had recourse to other and more comprehensive works on the subject." It is regretted that space prevents the inclusion of all the West Point discussions.

tive source for this information. One should never permit himself to adopt a standard which his instincts tell him is lower than it should be.

Acknowledging Courtesies. A gentleman renders appropriate acknowledgment for every courtesy extended to him, and for every kind, generous, or helpful act of which he is the beneficiary. It is rude to accept the hospitality of one's friends without expressing appreciation and it is both rude and selfish not to attempt to reciprocate. In a few of the routine events of social life, such as dinners and formal calls, the exchange is usually *quid pro quo.* In the majority of cases, however, there can be no value relationship between the courtesy received and that offered in return. People in moderate circumstances are not expected to return on anything suggesting a money basis the entertainment extended to them by wealthy friends and acquaintances. Nevertheless, within the limit of their resources, they must discharge the obligations they have accepted. The essential requirement on the part of every gentleman is a sense of appreciation so sincere and so responsive as to make it impossible for him to permit any generous act to go unrecognized. As to just what form the acknowledgment should take depends on all related circumstances. As a general rule, obligations of the sort contemplated may be satisfied by personal thanks, by calling or mailing cards, by writing a letter of appreciation, by sending an inexpensive gift, or by offering in return the same or a similar courtesy or one which, even though of an entirely different nature, is equally enjoyable.

If an invitation is declined it is imperative to state some reason. It is exceedingly rude to decline without offering an excuse.

Dinner invitations should be answered at once. To delay even for a day is impolite and inconsiderate of the hostess. Under no circumstances should a dinner invitation be answered *conditionally* nor should you ask the hostess if you can give a reply later. You must give a definite acceptance or refusal at once.

Having accepted a dinner invitation, nothing but the most compelling emergency should prevent your attendance. To break a dinner engagement simply for your personal convenience is an unforgivable breach of etiquette.

Whenever an invitation of any sort calls for a response (R.s.v.p.) it should be answered at once.

Engaging and intelligent conversation requires among other things a broad contact with literature and a familiarity with current events. The officer should, whenever possible, devote a certain amount of time each day to reading and study. Likewise he should cultivate an interest in national and world affairs as well as in the happenings of merely local import. While specialization is the order of the day, every officer should strive to maintain a broad point of view and a lively sympathy and interest in human affairs and activities the world over.

Making Introductions.

(*a*) *Names.* Always enunciate the names of both persons clearly and distinctly. In introducing close relatives, it is desirable to state the relationship. On the other hand, it is not necessary to give the name unless it differs from one's own. Examples: "I want you to meet my mother"; and "May I introduce my sister (cousin), Mrs. _____."

(*b*) *Precedence.* As a general rule, gentlemen are introduced *to* ladies. However, there are a few cases where this procedure is reversed. For example, ladies are introduced to the President of the United States and to cardinals. In addition, it is usually proper and desirable to introduce very young ladies to gentlemen who are of advanced years or who combine moderate age with rank or title of considerable importance.

A single lady is introduced to a married lady unless there is marked difference in their ages in which case the younger is introduced to the older. In introducing two married ladies or two single ladies, if no other basis of precedence exists, it is courteous to introduce the one with whom you are better acquainted to the other. The same rule may be followed with propriety among officers of the same grade or in introducing civilian gentlemen of equal rank. In the government service and in official and diplomatic life, ladies have the same relative rank as their husbands. When there is no appreciable difference in age or rank between two persons, the question of priority is ignored.

(*c*) *Permission to Introduce.* Except at small social gatherings where all guests have been invited personally, one should ask permission of a young unmarried lady before introducing another man to her.

(*d*) *Procedure.* An introduction, however quickly over, should be made the occasion of some little formality. This is particularly true if one of the persons has the claim of age or rank. The person making the introduction should assume a dignified attitude, as should the persons being introduced. If the persons to be introduced are some little distance from one another, the junior should be brought to the senior; never the reverse. Never escort a lady around a room to meet an assembly of people.

(*e*) *Use of Titles.* Officers of the Army or Marine Corps of the grade of captain and above, and officers of the Navy of the grade of lieutenant commander and above are always addressed and introduced by their titles. The commander of any vessel in the Navy is addressed and introduced as captain. A captain of the Navy should be introduced as "captain so-and-so of the Navy," to distinguish him from captains of the Army and Marine Corps. Officers of junior rank in all services are usually addressed as "mister." However, in recent years, it is the generally accepted practice to introduce such an officer by his title, and this is especially desirable if he be in civilian dress.

APPENDIX G
REGULATIONS AND INSTRUCTIONS FOR BOARDING OFFICERS

"U. S. Navy Regulations"

In Peace

"The senior officer in port, whatever may be his rank, shall, upon the arrival of a foreign ship of war, send an officer to such ship to offer the customary courtesies. In case two or more ships of the same nation arrive in company, then the visit shall be made to the senior ship only" 345 (a).

"When such a visit is made to a ship of the Navy, an officer shall be sent to return it at once." 345 (b).

"The guard ship of the senior division shall send an officer to board incoming men-of-war, except flagships and vessels attached to the fleet. Flagships shall be boarded by a line officer on the staff of the commander in chief or the senior flag officer present" 357 (1).

"The guard ship of the senior division present shall also send an officer or competent chief petty officer to board all merchant vessels or yachts flying American colors found in or arriving at foreign ports; also all vessels which are probably carrying mail for the fleet. If no flag officer be present, this boarding visit shall be made by the guard ship of the day" 357 (2).

"The following summary of information in regard to merchant ships or yachts shall be obtained by boarding officers, and boarding books must conform thereto:

(*a*) Name, nationality, and kind of vessel.

(*b*) Name of owner (if a yacht) and whether or not he is on board, the name of the master, and the number of crew.

(*c*) Tonnage and cargo.

(*d*) Place from, time out, and kind of passage.

(*e*) Probable date of departure from port and port then bound for.

(*f*) Any casualties, extraordinary events on the passage, general route taken; ships, fog, ice, etc., encountered.

(*g*) General remarks.

In case of a man-of-war, substitute in (*b*) 'Name and rank of the commanding officer, and, if a flagship, of the flag officer,' and omit (c).

In case of a merchant vessel, the fact of her carrying mail, with the destination of such mail, shall be entered under 'General remarks' " 357 (3).

"The date and place at which the boarding visit was made shall be noted in every case and the signature and rank of the boarding officer appended" 357 (4).

"Immediately after boarding a vessel, the boarding officer shall report on board the flagship of the commander in chief or the ship of the senior officer present, and there enter in the boarding book a full record of the visit, and shall sign his name and rank to the same" 357 (5).

NOTE.—Under no conditions should a boarding officer display a boarding book or write therein when on board a foreign man-of-war. Etiquette requires that information be gained without too much apparent catechizing. This is an old established custom.

"In boarding arriving vessels, care shall be taken not to violate the rules of the port, and in case they are subject to quarantine, the boarding officer shall, if possible, obtain the information required without going alongside.

"Vessels at sea coming from a suspected port not having a clean bill of health, or otherwise liable to quarantine, shall not be boarded unless it be absolutely necessary, and the fact of such communication, when it occurs, shall be reported on arrival in port to the health officer."

In War

Boarding Officers' Duties When the United States Is at War, and the Right of Visit and Search Is Exercised. "It is doubtful that all articles of 'Instructions for the Navy of the United States Governing Maritime Warfare,' issued June, 1917, would be adhered to by the government of the United States in a future war. Nevertheless, there is at this time no reason to think that the boarding officer's method of exercise of visit and search would be materially changed from established law and custom. Therefore, Sec. VI of the 'Instructions' of June, 1917, relating thereto are quoted hereunder.

Visit and Search, Where and When Exercised. "42. The belligerent right of visit and search, subject to exemptions mentioned in Sec.

VII (Limitations on Visit and Search) may be exercised outside of neutral jurisdiction upon private vessels after the beginning of war in order to determine their nationality, the port of destination and departure, the character of their cargo, the nature of their employment, or other facts which bear on their relation to the war."

Method of Exercise. "43. The right should be exercised with tact and consideration, and in strict conformity with treaty provisions, where they exist.

"44. Subject to any special treaty provisions the following procedure is directed: Before summoning a vessel to lie to, a ship of war must hoist her own national flag. The summons shall be made by firing a blank charge (*coup de semonce*), by other international signal, or by both. The summoned vessel, if a neutral, is bound to stop and lie to, and she should also display her colors; if an enemy vessel, she is not so bound, and may legally even resist by force, but she thereby assumes all risks of resulting damage.

"45. If the summoned vessel resists or takes to flight, she may be pursued and brought to, by forcible measures, if necessary.

"46. When the summoned vessel has brought to, the ship of war shall send a boat with an officer to conduct the visit and search. If practicable, a second officer should accompany the officer charged with the examination. There may be arms in the boat, but the boat's crew shall not have any on their persons. The officer (or officers), wearing side arms, may be accompanied on board by not more than two unarmed men of the boat's crew.

"47. The boarding officer shall first examine the ship's papers in order to ascertain her nationality, ports of departure and destination, character of cargo, and other facts deemed essential. If the papers furnish conclusive evidence of the innocent character of vessel, cargo, and voyage, the vessel shall be released; if they furnish probable cause for capture, she shall be seized and sent in for adjudication.

"48. If the papers do not furnish conclusive evidence of the innocent character of the vessel, the cargo, and voyage, or probable cause for capture, the boarding officer shall continue the examination by questioning the personnel or by searching the vessel or by examining her cargo. If such further examination furnishes satisfactory evidence of innocency, the vessel shall be released; otherwise she shall be seized and sent in for adjudication.

"49. The boarding officer must record the facts concerning the visit and search upon the log book of the vessel visited, including the date when and the position where the visit occurred. This entry in the log must be made whether the vessel is held or not."

Papers. "50. The papers which will generally be found on board a private vessel are:

(1) The certificate of registry or nationality.

(2) A certified bill of sale, or certificate thereof duly authenticated, in the absence of certificate of registry or nationality, or in the case of a vessel which has recently been transferred from enemy to neutral ownership.

(3) The crew list.

(4) The passenger list.

(5) The log book.

(6) The bill of health.

(7) The clearance papers.

(8) The charter party, if chartered.

(9) Invoices or manifests of cargo.

(10) Bills of lading.

"The evidence furnished by the papers against a vessel is conclusive. Regularity of papers and evidence of the innocence of cargo or destination furnished by them are not necessarily conclusive and, if doubt exists, a search of the ship or cargo should be made to establish the facts. If a vessel has deviated far from her direct course, this, if not satisfactorily explained, is a suspicious circumstance warranting search, however favorable the character of the papers."

APPENDIX H
SOCIAL FORMS AFLOAT AND ASHORE
FORMAL INVITATIONS

Reception

The Commander-in-Chief
and Officers of the United States Fleet
request the pleasure of your company
at a reception
to be held on board the U.S.S. *West Virginia*
on Saturday afternoon, the twenty-fourth of June,
from four until six o'clock

Boats leave from
Pier 14.

The Wardroom Officers of the U.S.S. *Tennessee*
request the pleasure of
Major and Mrs. James McDonald, Jr's.,
company at dinner
on Saturday, the twenty-fourth of June,
at seven o'clock

Ship's boat will leave from
Dowley's Landing at six-thirty

A Collective Invitation Used by Military and Naval Service

The Executive Officer and the Wardroom Officers
of the U.S.S. *Memphis* request the pleasure of the
company of the Executive Officer and seven Wardroom
Officers of H.M.S. *Nelson* at dinner, on board,
at half past seven on
Monday evening, the tenth of
February

Reply

Commander Hyde-Smith, Lieutenant Commander A, Lieutenant
Commander B, Lieutenant Commander C, Lieutenant D, Lieuten-

ant E, Sub-Lieutenant F, Sub-Lieutenant G, Paymaster Commander H accept with pleasure the kind invitation of the Executive Officer and Wardroom Officers of the U.S.S. *Memphis* for dinner on board at half past seven o'clock on Monday evening, the tenth of February.

Form Invitation Useful Aboard

The following form, printed or preferably engraved, has been found very satisfactory for invitations to social affairs aboard ship. Further information such as boats for guests, "Please reply to flag lieutenant," etc., may be written in the lower right- and left-hand corners. "R.s.v.p." or, in its place, "Please reply to—" is usually placed in the lower left corner.

THE COMMANDER

BATTLESHIP DIVISIONS, BATTLE FLEET

requests the pleasure of

company at

on board the Flagship *West Virginia*

on

at   o'clock

Replies to Wedding Invitations and Receptions

There is a difference between a wedding invitation and one that also includes the reception. To the wedding invitation alone no reply is necessary should the invited attend. If unable to attend, then two visiting cards should be sent. On the other hand, if invited to wedding and reception, one accepts or declines by formal reply, "kind invitation to the wedding and reception of their . . . ."

Boat Card

The following is the suggested wording for cards to enclose with invitations for fleet receptions, large dances, etc. Such cards minimize "gate crashing," and at the same time tend to allay any anxiety of guests as to boats and parking facilities.

Please present this card

at Fifth Street Naval Landing, San Pedro,

on Saturday, the twenty-third of January

The Naval Patrol

Kindly Pass One   Will Make Necessary

Parking Arrangements

A Reply to an Informal Collective Invitation

Dear Commander Cunningham:

Will you please accept, on behalf of myself and Officers, our sincere thanks for your kind invitation to dinner on Wednesday evening.

I enclose herewith a list of the Officers who will come, with their rank and respective seniority.

I should be very grateful to you, if you would let me know what dress should be worn.

With kindest regards, I am,

Yours sincerely

A Formal At-Home Invitation

Rear Admiral and Mrs. George Davis Smith

At Home

Wednesday Afternoon, June twenty-first

from four to six

Eleven Dewey Road

A Formal Invitation to a Reception Given in Someone's Honor

To Meet

Vice Admiral Sir William Gordon, Royal Navy

Rear Admiral Charles G. Delp

requests the pleasure of your company

on board the U.S.S. *New Mexico*

on Tuesday afternoon, the twentieth of June

from four until seven o'clock

Boats leave from

. . . .   R.s.v.p.

In honour of

Vice-Admiral The Hon. R. A. R. Plunkett-Ernle-Erle-Drax,

C.B., D.S.O., R.N.

Mrs. Drax

and

Officers of H.M.S. *Norfolk* and *Danae*

Admiral and Mrs. William Harrison Standley

At Home

on Thursday, November the ninth

from five until seven o'clock

Chief of Naval Operations House

Observatory Circle

Wedding Invitation

Lieutenant Colonel and Mrs. James Edmund Clive

request the honor of your presence

at the marriage of their daughter

Marcia Anne

to

Allen James Davenport

Ensign, United States Navy

on Tuesday evening, the twenty-sixth of May

Nineteen hundred and thirty-four

at eight o'clock

Lindsey Chapel, Emmanuel Church

Boston, Massachusetts

A Form Used by the U. S. Naval Forces in Europe

Vice-Admiral Roger Welles

the Captain and Officers

of the U.S.S. *Memphis*

request the pleasure of your company at a reception

on board the U.S.S. *Memphis*

on Saturday, August twenty-first

from five until seven o'clock

Please present this card
to Boat Officer

NOTE: In a large port, and where many guests are expected, it is preferable to inclose a small card with the invitation. The card should designate the boat landing, and should also state the request that the card be presented to Boat Officer.

Invitation to a Luncheon Given in Someone's Honor

Mrs. Ridgley would be glad if Mrs. Sampson would take luncheon with her quite informally, at half after twelve o'clock, on Monday,

June the twenty-fifth at the College Club, 33 Chestnut Avenue, to meet Miss Rollins.

Haddon Apartments

June 23, 1933

Acceptance

Mrs. Sampson accepts with pleasure Mrs. Ridgley's kind invitation to meet Miss Rollins at luncheon at half after twelve o'clock, on Monday, June twenty-fifth, at The College Club.

326 West 65th Street

June 23, 1933

The following invitation is a model of that in general use by the United States Diplomatic Service in Europe. The acceptance should be written in French

Seal of Department of State

Le Ministre des États-Unis d'Amérique

et Madame Bliss prient

Commander and Mrs. Wilson

de leur faire l'honneur de venir passer la soirée

chez eux, le mardi, 14 septembre, a 9½ heures

R.s.v.p.   On Dansera

NOTE: An invitation should be replied to in the language of the invitation if that language is French. French still remains the language of etiquette and diplomacy, although English was used as a parallel text in the Treaty of Versailles, The Kellogg Pact, and subsequent treaties.

Acceptance in French

Commander et Mrs. Wilson se feront un grand plaisir de se rendre à l'obligeante invitation de M. le Ministre des États-Unis et Madame Bliss de venir passer la soirée chez eux, le mardi, 14 septembre, a 9½ heures.

CORRESPONDENCE

Invitations

1. Le commandant et les officiers du cuirassé "Bayard" prient les officiers du croiseur "Chester" de leur faire l'honneur de passer l'après-midi du 15 courant à bord du cuirassé "Bayard."

On dansera de 2ʰ jusqu' à 5ʰ.

Date.

Invitations Acceptées

2. Le capitaine de vaisseau N. accepte avec mille remercîments, l'aimable invitation du commandant du croiseur "Choiseul" pour lundi soir, 2 avril.

Date.

3. Le commandant et les officiers du cuirassé "Florida" se font un honneur d'accepter, avec bien des remercîments, l'aimable invitation du colonel N. et des officiers du 75ᵉ régiment d'infanterie de ligne.
Date.

4. Le capitaine de vaisseau N., commandant du croiseur "New Orleans," a l'honneur d'accepter l'aimable invitation à dîner de Son Excellence le Gouverneur, pour samedi, 20 février, à 8 heures.
Date.

5. Chère madame,
C'est avec mille remercîments et un bien grand plaisir que nous acceptons, mon ami N. et moi, votre gracieuse invitation à dîner.
Veuillez agréer, chère madame, l'expression de tout mon respect.
Date.   N. N.

Regrets

6. Les officiers du croiseur "Detroit" ont l'honneur de présenter leurs sincères remercîments aux officiers du cuirassé "Marceau" pour leur aimable invitation, et regrettent bien de ne pouvoir l'accepter, étant déjà engagés pour l'après-midi du 15 courant.
Date.

Social Notes

Informal Invitation

265 Southsea Boulevard
June twenty-sixth

My dear Mrs. Greenwood,
Will you and Commander Greenwood give us the pleasure of dining with us on Thursday, June the twenty-eighth, at eight o'clock?
We shall be very glad if you are able to come.
Sincerely yours,

Anne M. Johnson

Informal Acceptance

4516 Elmwood Ave.,
June the twenty-seventh

My dear Mrs. Johnson,
Commander Greenwood and I are delighted to accept your very kind invitation to dine with you on Thursday, June the twenty-eighth, at eight o'clock.
We appreciate your kind thought of us.
Sincerely yours,

Mary Greenwood

Informal Regret

My dear Mrs. Johnson,

Commander Greenwood and I regret exceedingly that we shall be unable to dine with you on Thursday, June the twenty-eighth, as unfortunately we have a previous engagement for that evening.

Yours sincerely,

Mary Greenwood

Visiting Card Invitation

It is the general custom in the United States that with the exception of invitations to dinners, luncheons, house parties, and other formal affairs, visiting cards are used for invitations to affairs of semi-formal and informal nature. A lady may use her visiting cards for invitations to bridge, informal dances, teas, and teas to meet guests.

Replies to visiting card invitations are formally worded, and in the third person throughout.

Monday, June 26

Bridge at two o'clock

MRS. JOHN SPENCER DAVIS

R.S.V.P.

To meet

Mrs. Donald Green

MRS. ROBERT DEW

Four to six o'clock

Saturday, June the tenth

Informal Regret for an At Home

15 February, 1933.

(1) Dear Lady Cunningham

(2) My dear Mrs. Johnson

I am sorry that my tour of duty will prevent my being present at your At Home on Saturday afternoon next, but if you will allow me I will take another opportunity of calling upon you.

(1) Believe me, dear Lady Cunningham,

Faithfully yours,

. . . .

or

(2) With kindest regards, I am,

Yours sincerely,

. . . .

Address such as

Lady Cunningham

. . . .

. . . .

Receipt of Cards to Clubs

The Captain and Officers of the U.S.S. *Texas* present their sincere thanks to the President and Committee of the Yacht Club for their kindness in extending to them the privilege of temporary membership during their stay in Santa Barbara.

February 4, 1933.

NOTE: These official letters do not relieve the captain and officers who have frequented the club of the amenity of leaving their personal visiting cards at the club for the President and the members.

Place Cards, Menus, and Music Programs

Place cards are used for the convenience of guests and hosts at formal and official luncheons and dinners. The cards should be placed at the proper places in conformance with a seating diagram that has been made out with due regard to precedence. Where precedence is not a point (but be sure it is not), then seat with attention to the congeniality and personality of the guests sitting in proximity to one another.

Good usage decrees that plain white cards may be used. The cards may have embossed or stamped in the upper left corner the flag of the Admiral, the seal of the ship, or insignia of the organization. The names of the guests may be written neatly on the place cards, although on very formal occasions they are printed or embossed on the cards.

It is also customary to have printed menus for official luncheons and dinners. If not practicable to print menus they may be typewritten on light cardboard. One menu for two guests should be sufficient, although on extraordinary occasions it is often desirable to have one for each guest in the event that autographs are desired.

At military and naval formal dinners when music is played during the meal it is customary to have a few programs of the music to be rendered made out for the convenience of the guests. There have been times when without the program it was very difficult to recognize the selections played.

At a dinner given on board the R.N. *Amerigo Vespucci,* 14 August, 1933, by the Italian Admiral commanding the Training Squadron, good taste with practicality was demonstrated by using an attractive combination place card, menu, and music program.

The combination was in the form of a folder with the Admiral's flag, and the division and ship embossed on the outer cover. On the outer cover there was a rectangular indentation wherein the guest's name could be inscribed. The folder held an insert. On the front of the insert was a photograph of the *Amerigo Vespucci* under full sail. The insert opened to the menu and facing it was the musical program.

Whenever it is expected that considerable entertaining will be done by a ship, there should be a recheck of the following:

Wardroom Calling Cards

Formal Blank Invitations

Place Cards

Stock Cards for printing menus, programs, etc.

A die with flag seal, ship seal, or organization insignia.

Standing committees should be detailed when on foreign duty to make wardroom calls. It is customary to make the details with due regard to the proficiency in foreign languages of the members of the committee. For example No. 1 Committee for French men-of-war; No. 2 for German men-of-war; No. 3 for Spanish men-of-war.

APPENDIX I
NAVAL WEDDINGS

If the officer is married in dress uniform with officers attending as ushers, etc., the following points may be useful:

1. In honor of the bride on the "day of days" insist that all the officers of the wedding party wear full dress uniform (epaulettes and cocked hat) with sword. In summer, and depending on the latitude, white full dress.

2. By all means have a rehearsal, if only to get an "estimate of the situation."

3. Ushers should carry cocked hats while escorting guests to their seats. It is well to insure that one officer takes charge as head usher in order that he may be free to escort distinguished and elderly guests as well as to co-ordinate the duties of the ushers. There are usually six ushers, although four or two may function.

4. The ancient and traditional ceremony of the bride and groom walking under the arched swords of the officer ushers is always expected. The practice of drawing swords at the altar or in the chancel of the church is entirely wrong. Because of the old law of right of sanctuary and refuge, as well as the very nature of a church, it is considered a flagrant breach of military etiquette to draw a sword in church. The "arch" should be made outside the church if possible but, if inclement weather or street traffic should preclude this, then the crossing of swords may take place in the vestibule near the door. Civilian ushers line up with naval ushers. The senior usher should give the order "Draw swords."

5. It is expected that the best man, ushers, and bridesmaids will take places in the receiving line if a reception is held.

6. At a convenient time the bridegroom should present his sword to the bride in order that she may carry out the traditional custom of cutting the wedding cake. The wedding party is expected to assist at this ceremony.

7. It is well to remember that officers are on dress parade, and many civilians gain their impression of the officer personnel by the bearing, poise, and conduct of its representatives at weddings.

APPENDIX J
OFFICIAL CORRESPONDENCE

OFFICIAL USAGE[1]

The President of the United States.

Address:
> The President,
> The White House.
> *or*
> The President,
> Washington, D.C.

Salutation:
> Sir:
> *or*
> To the President:
> *or*
> Dear Mr. President:

Complimentary close:
> Your obedient servant, (old form)
> *or*
> Respectfully submitted,
> *or*
> Yours respectfully,
> *or*
> Faithfully yours, (informal)

The Vice President of the United States.

Address:
> The Vice President,
> The United States Senate.
> *or*
> The Honorable
> The Vice President of the United States,
> *or*
> The Honorable John N. Garner,
> Vice President of the United States,
> Washington, D.C.

[1] The author acknowledges his indebtedness to the Macmillan Company for authority to use the general format and usage found in *The Secretary's Handbook*, by Taintor and Munro. Proper names have been changed to conform to the incumbents of certain offices at the time of writing.

Salutation: My dear Mr. Vice President:
or
Sir:

Complimentary close: I have the honor to be, Sir, (old form)
                                Your obedient servant,
or
Yours respectfully,
or
Very truly yours,

Speaker of the House of Representatives.

Address: The Honorable
                                The Speaker of the House of Repre-
                                   sentatives,
or
The Honorable Henry T. Rainey,
                                Speaker of the House of Representa-
                                 tives,
                                 Washington, D.C.

Salutation: Sir:
or
My dear Mr. Speaker:
or
Dear Mr. Rainey: (informal)

Complimentary close: Very truly yours,

Cabinet Officers.

Address: The Honorable
                                The Secretary of State,
                                Washington, D.C.
or
The Honorable Cordell Hull,
                                Secretary of State,
                                Washington, D.C.

Salutation: My dear Mr. Secretary:
or
Sir:
or
Dear Sir:

Complimentary close: Very truly yours,

Chief Justice of the Supreme Court.

Address:	The Chief Justice of the Supreme Court, Washington, D.C.
	or
	The Honorable Charles Evans Hughes, Chief Justice of the Supreme Court, Washington, D.C.
Salutation:	My dear Mr. Chief Justice:
	or
	My dear Mr. Hughes: (informal)
Complimentary close:	Very truly yours,

Associate Justice of the Supreme Court.

Address:	The Honorable Willis Van Devanter, Associate Justice of the Supreme Court, Washington, D.C.
Salutation:	My dear Mr. Justice:
	or
	My dear Justice Van Devanter:
Complimentary close:	Very truly yours,

Governor.

Address:	The Honorable The Governor of Maryland, Annapolis, Maryland,
	or
	The Honorable Albert C. Ritchie, Governor of Maryland.
Salutation:	Sir:
	or
	Dear Sir:
	or
	Dear Governor Ritchie: (informal)
Complimentary close:	Very truly yours,

Attorney General.

Address:	The Honorable The Attorney General of the United States, Washington, D.C.

or

The Honorable Homer S. Cummings,
   The Attorney General

Salutation: My dear Mr. Attorney General:
                        or

                        Sir:
                        or

                        Dear Sir:

Complimentary close: Very truly yours,

Under Secretary of State.

Address: The Under Secretary of State,
                        Washington, D.C.
                        or

                        The Honorable Wiliam Phillips,
                        Under Secretary of State,
                        Washington, D.C.

Salutation: Sir:
                        or

                        Dear Sir:
                        or

                        Dear Mr. Phillips: (informal)

Complimentary close: Very truly yours,

Assistant Secretary of Navy.

Address: The Assistant Secretary of the Navy,
                        Washington, D.C.
                        or

                        The Honorable Henry L. Roosevelt,
                        Assistant Secretary of the Navy,
                        Washington, D.C.

Salutation: Sir:
                        or

                        Dear Mr. Roosevelt: (informal)

Complimentary close: Very truly yours,

Senator.

Address: The Honorable Carter Glass,
                        The United States Senate,
                        Washington, D.C.

Salutation: Dear Sir:
                                       or
                               My dear Senator Glass:
Complimentary close: Very truly yours,

Representative.
   Address: The Honorable Carl Vinson.
                                  The House of Representatives,
                                     Washington, D.C.
   Salutation: Sir:
                                       or
                               Dear Sir:
                                       or
                               My dear Congressman:
   Complimentary close: Very truly yours,

Commissioner.
   Address: The Honorable ....,
                                  Commissioner of the Bureau of Edu-
                                     cation,
                                     Washington, D.C.
   Salutation: Sir:
                                       or
                               Dear Sir:
   Complimentary close: Very truly yours,

State Senator.
   Address: The Honorable Hugh Lyttle,
                                  The State Senate,
                                     Albany, New York.
                                       or
                               Senator Lyttle,
                                  The State Capitol,
                                     Albany, New York.
   Salutation: Dear Sir:
                                       or
                               Dear Senator Lyttle: (informal)
   Complimentary close: Very truly yours,

Member of Assembly or Legislature.

Address:	The Honorable A. I. Flynn,
	Member of Assembly,
	Albany, N.Y.
	or
	Assemblyman Flynn,
	The State Capitol,
	Albany, New York.
Salutation:	Sir:
	or
	Dear Sir:
	or
	Dear Mr. Flynn: (informal)
Complimentary close:	Very truly yours,

Mayor.

Address:	The Honorable James M. Curley,
	Mayor of the City of Boston,
	City Hall, Boston, Mass.
	or
	The Mayor of the City of Boston,
	City Hall, Boston, Mass.
Salutation:	Sir:
	or
	My dear Mr. Mayor:
	Dear Mayor Curley: (informal)
Complimentary close:	Yours respectfully,
	or
	Very truly yours,

Foreign Ambassador.

Address:	His Excellency,
	Katsuji Debuchi,
	Ambassador of Japan,
	Washington, D.C.
Salutation:	Excellency:
	or
	Your Excellency:
	or
	Sir:

Complimentary close: Accept, Excellency, the renewed assurance of my highest consideration,

British Ambassador.

Address: His Excellency,
. The Ambassador of Great Britain.
or
His Excellency,
Sir Ronald Lindsay, K.C.B.,
Ambassador of Great Britain.

Salutation: Excellency:
or
Sir:

Complimentary close: I have the honor to be,
With the highest consideration,
Your Excellency's most obedient servant,

Ministers from Foreign Countries.

Address: His Excellency,
The Honorable ....
Minister of ....
or
Envoy Extraordinary and Minister Plenipotentiary from ....
or
Mr. .... (followed by the official title)

Salutation: Sir:
or
My dear Mr. Minister:

Complimentary close: Same as Ambassador's.

American Ambassador.

Address: His Excellency,
The American Ambassador,
London, England.
or
The Honorable Robert Worth Bingham,
American Ambassador,
London, England.

Salutation:	Dear Mr. Ambassador:
	or
	Your Excellency:
	or
	Sir:
Complimentary close:	I have the honor to be, Sir,
	Your obedient servant,
	or
	Very truly yours,

Chargé d'Affaires.

Address:	Count Jean de Voudrey
	Charge d'Affaires,
	Luxemburg.
Salutation:	Dear Sir:
	or
	Sir:
Complimentary close:	Accept, Sir, the renewed assurance of my
	high consideration,

Consul.

Address:	To the American Consul at Shanghai,
	or
	Edwin S. Cunningham, Esq.,
	American Consul at Shanghai.
Salutation:	Dear Sir:
Complimentary close:	Very truly yours,

*Correct Usage in Addressing in Correspondence Members
of Royalty and of the Nobility of Great Britain*

King.

Address:	The King's Most Excellent (or Gracious)
	Majesty,
Salutation:	Sire:
	or
	May it please your Majesty:
Complimentary close:	I have the honor to remain
	Your Majesty's most obedient servant,

Queen.

Address:	The Queen's Most Excellent (or Gra-
	cious) Majesty,
Salutation:	Madam:

or

May it please your Majesty:

Complimentary close: Same as King's.

Prince.

Address: His Royal Highness the Prince of Wales,
            His Royal Highness Prince George,

Salutation: Sir:

or

May it please your Royal Highness:

Complimentary close: I remain, Sir, with the greatest respect
                        Your Royal Highness' most dutiful and
                        obedient servant,

Princess.

Address: Her Royal Highness the Princess Mary,

Salutation: Madam:

Complimentary close: Similar to Prince's.

Higher Titles Have Been Omitted

Baronet.

Address: Sir George Robinson, Bt. or Bart.,

Salutation: Sir: (formal)
            Dear Sir George: (informal)

Complimentary close: Believe me, dear Sir George, faithfully
                        yours,

Wife of Baronet.

Address: Lady Robinson:

Salutation: Madam: (formal)
            Dear Lady Robinson: (informal)

Complimentary close: Similar to Baronet's.

Knight.

Address: Sir William ...., K.C.M.G.,

Salutation: Sir: (formal)
            Dear Sir William: (informal)

Complimentary close: Believe me, dear Sir William, faithfully
                        yours,

Knight's Wife.

Address: Lady ...., (family name)

Salutation: Madam: (formal)
            Dear Lady ....: (informal)

Complimentary close: Similar to Knight's.

Correct Ecclesiastical Usage for Officials of Catholic Church

The Pope.

Address:
His Holiness, Pope Pius XII,
or
His Holiness, the Pope,

Salutation:
Your Holiness:
or
Most Holy Father:

Complimentary close:
Your dutiful son or daughter,
or
Respectfully yours,

Cardinal.

Address:
His Eminence Cardinal . . . .

Salutation:
Your Eminence:

Complimentary close:
Respectfully yours,

If also an *Archbishop.*
His Eminence the Cardinal Archbishop
. . . . ,
or
His Eminence Cardinal . . . . ,
Archbishop of . . . . ,

Archbishop.

Address:
His Excellency, the Archbishop of. . . . . . ,
or
The Most Reverend Archbishop of. . . . . ,

Salutation:
Your Excellency:
or
Most Reverend Archbishop:
or
Dear Archbishop . . . . : (informal)

Complimentary close:
Respectfully yours,

Bishop.

Address:
The Bishop of . . . . ,
The Most Reverend . . . . D.D.
or
The Most Reverend Bishop . . . . . . ,

Salutation:
Your Excellency:
or
Dear Bishop . . . . : (informal)

Complimentary close:
Respectfully yours,

Priest.

Address:	Rev. Father Jones,
	or
	Rev. J. B. Jones,
Salutation:	Dear Father Jones:
	or
	Reverend and Dear Father:
	or
	Dear Father:
Complimentary close:	Respectfully yours,
	or
	Very truly yours,
	or
	Sincerely yours,

Correct Ecclesiastical Usage for Protestant Clergy in America
Protestant Episcopal Bishop.

Address:	To the Right Reverend William T. Manning,
	Bishop of New York,
Salutation:	Right Reverend and Dear Sir: (formal)
	or
	Dear Bishop Manning: (informal)
	or
	My dear Bishop ....: (informal)
Complimentary close:	Sincerely yours,

Dean.

Address:	Dean ....,
	or
	The Very Rev. Dean ....,
Salutation:	Very Reverend Sir: (formal)
	Dear Dean ....: (informal)
Complimentary close:	Yours respectfully,
	or
	Sincerely yours,
	or
	Cordially yours, (informal)

Methodist Bishop.

Address:	Reverend Bishop ....,
Salutation:	Dear Bishop ....,
	or
	My dear Bishop ....,
	or
	Dear Sir:
Complimentary close:	Sincerely yours,
	or
	Respectfully yours,

Other Clergymen.

Address:	The Reverend James M. Rogers,
	or
	Rev. James M. Rogers,
	or
	Rev. Dr. James M. Rogers, (if entitled to a degree)
	or
	Rev. J. M. Rogers, D.D.
Salutation:	Dear Sir: *or* My dear Sir:
	or
	Dear Mr. Rogers: (informal)
	or
	Dear Dr. Rogers: (if entitled to a degree)
Complimentary close:	Yours respectfully,
	or
	Yours sincerely,

Jewish Rabbi.

Address:	Rabbi Stephen Wise,
	or
	Rev. Stephen Wise,
Salutation:	Dear Sir:
	or
	Dear Dr. Wise:
Complimentary close:	Yours respectfully,

Superior of a Sisterhood.

Address:	Reverend Mother M. (followed by initials designating order, if desired)

or
Reverend Mother Superior (without initials of order)

Salutation: Reverend Mother:
Dear Reverend Mother: (informal)
or
My dear Reverend Mother: (name added if desired)

Complimentary close: Yours respectfully,

Member of a Sisterhood.

Address: Sister Mary Angela, (followed by initials of order, if desired)
or
Sister Mary Angela, O.S.D. (Order of St. Dominic)

Salutation: Dear Sister *or* My dear Sister:
or
Dear Sister Angela:
or
My dear Sister Angela:

Complimentary close: Yours sincerely,

President of a University.

Address: Nicholas Murray Butler, LL.D.
President of Columbia University,
or
President Nicholas Murray Butler,
Columbia University, New York.
or
President Butler,

Salutation: Dear Sir:
or
Dear President Butler:

Complimentary close: Sincerely yours,
or
Very truly yours,

College or University Professor.

Address: Professor Victor J. West,
Stanford University, Palo Alto

or

Victor J. West, Ph.D.,
Professor of English

Salutation: Dear Sir:

or

Dear Professor West: (informal)

Complimentary close: Sincerely yours,

or

Very truly yours.

College or University Instructor.

Address: Robert Blake, Esq.

or

Robert Blake, Ph.D. (if entitled to the degree)

or

Dr. Robert Blake.

Salutation: Dear Mr. *or* Dr. Blake:

Complimentary close: Sincerely yours,

Salutations for Semi-Official Letters and Other Correspondence Where the Naval Form it Not Used

Dear Sir:
Dear Madam:
Gentlemen:
Mesdames:
My dear Mrs. Brown, (formal American usage)
Dear Mrs. Brown, (informal American usage)

Correct Forms for Complimentary Close of Official Letters Not in Naval Form

Very truly yours,	Faithfully yours,
Yours truly,	Sincerely yours,
Respectfully yours,	Yours sincerely,

General Rules for Inside Address

Business letter: The name and the address of the receiver is placed at the left top of the page before the salutation.

Official letter: The best current usage dictates that the inside address be placed on the lower left side beneath the letter.

Personal and friendly letters: The inside address is usually omitted.

The American Use of Honorable and Esquire

Honorable. By custom and usage, the title *honorable* is used in addressing correspondence and communications to the following officials: governors, cabinet officers, senators, congressmen, American ambassadors, American ministers, the secretary to the President, assistant secretaries of the executive departments, judges (not of the Supreme Court), heads of independent boards and commissions.

Esquire. The title *esquire* should be used in addressing the following officials: chief clerks and chiefs of bureaus of the executive department, commissioners of the District of Columbia, mayors of cities, American diplomatic officers below the grade of minister, American consular officers.

APPENDIX K
A NOTE ON THE MUCH-QUOTED LETTER OF JOHN PAUL JONES ON THE QUALIFICATIONS OF A NAVAL OFFICER

The letter so frequently quoted and ascribed to John Paul Jones is given below. Recent research has disclosed that this letter as commonly printed, was not written by Jones, but was a composite letter of collected phrases and clauses of Jones's, published for the first time by Augustus C. Buell in his work, *Paul Jones, Founder of the American Navy.*

Without entering into details of the literary argument, the facts of which have been adequately and conclusively covered by Mr. L. H. Bolander, an Assistant Librarian at the Naval Academy,[1] it will suffice to set forth the first paragraph of Jones's letter and Mr. Buell's version of it.

The following quotation is from a letter, a copy of which was made by Jones's secretary, and may be found in the Library of Congress. It is part of an open letter to the Marine Committee, dated 21 January, 1777.

None other than a Gentleman, as well as a Seaman, both in theory and practice is qualified to support the character of a Commissioned Officer in the Navy, nor is any man fit to command a Ship of War who is not also capable of communicating his Ideas on Paper in Language that becomes his Rank.

Please note the first two paragraphs of the letter as interpreted by Mr. Buell. There is no proof that John Paul Jones ever wrote the letter; but as Mr. Bolander states, "That he truly was the author of such phrases is beyond doubt."[1]

In short, Mr. Buell drafted a letter that covered many of Jones's suggestions and opinions; and, although this literary sharpness is not condoned, the Buell letter of Jones is quoted as the essence of that brave, dashing officer's code. For there are a variety of influences that have shaped our naval tradition, yet none have been of greater importance than the life and writings of the "Founder of the American Navy."

[1] L. H. Bolander, "Two Notes on John Paul Jones," Naval Institute PROCEEDINGS, LIV, No. 305.

QUALIFICATIONS OF THE NAVAL OFFICER

*A Collection from Jones's Reports and Letters in Modern
Version as Arranged by A. C. Buell*

It is by no means enough that an officer of the navy should be a capable mariner. He must be that, of course, but also a great deal more. He should be as well a gentleman of liberal education, refined manners, punctilious courtesy, and the nicest sense of personal honour.

He should not only be able to express himself clearly and with force in his own language both with tongue and pen, but he should also be versed in French and Spanish—for an American officer particularly the former—for our relations with France must necessarily soon become exceedingly close in view of the mutual hostility of the two countries towards Great Britain.

The naval officer should be familiar with the principles of International Law, and the general practice of Admiralty Jurisprudence, because such knowledge may often, when cruising at a distance from home, be necessary to protect his flag from insult or his crew from imposition or injury in foreign ports.

He should also be conversant with the usages of diplomacy, and capable of maintaining, if called upon, a dignified and judicious diplomatic correspondence; because it often happens that sudden emergencies in foreign waters make him the diplomatic as well as the military representative of his country, and in such cases he may have to act without opportunity of consulting his civic or ministerial superiors at home, and such action may easily involve the portentious issue of peace or war between great powers. These are general qualifications, and the nearer the officer approaches the full possession of them the more likely he will be to serve his country well and win fame and honours for himself.

Coming now to view the naval officer aboard ship and in relation to those under his command, he should be the soul of tact, patience, justice, firmness, and charity. No meritorious act of a subordinate should escape his attention or be left to pass without its reward, even if the reward be only one word of approval. Conversely, he should not be blind to a single fault in any subordinate, though, at the same time, he should be quick and unfailing to distinguish error from malice, thoughtlessness from incompetency, and well-meant short-coming from heedless or stupid blunder. As he should be universal and impartial in his rewards and approval of merit, so should he be judicial and unbending in his punishment or reproof of misconduct.

In his intercourse with subordinates he should ever maintain the attitude of the Commander, but that need by no means prevent him from the amenities of cordiality or the cultivation of good cheer within proper limits. Every Commanding Officer should hold with his subordinates such relations as will make them constantly anxious to receive invitations to sit at his mess-table, and his bearing towards them should be such as to encourage them to express their feelings to him with freedom and to ask his views without reserve.

It is always for the best interests of the Service that a cordial interchange of sentiments and civilities should subsist between superior and subordinate officers aboard ship. Therefore, it is the worst of policy in superiors to behave towards their subordinates with indiscriminate hauteur, as if the latter were of a lower species. Men of liberal minds, themselves accustomed to command, can ill brook being thus set at naught by others who, from temporary authority, may claim a monopoly of time and sense for the time being. If such men experience rude, ungentle treatment from their superiors, it will create such heartburnings and resentments as are nowise consonant with that cheerful ardour and ambitious spirit that ought ever to be characteristic of officers of all grades. In one word, every Commander should keep constantly before him the great truth, that to be well obeyed he must be perfectly esteemed.

But it is not alone with subordinate officers that a Commander has to deal. Behind them, and the foundation of all, is the crew. To his men, the Commanding Officer should be Prophet, Priest, and King. His authority when off shore being necessarily absolute, the crew should be as one man impressed that the Captain, like the Sovereign, "can do no wrong."

This is the most delicate of all the Commanding Officer's obligations. No rule can be set for meeting it. It must ever be a question of tact and perception of human nature on the spot and to suit the occasion. If an officer fails in this, he cannot make up for such failure by severity, austerity, or cruelty. Use force and apply restraint or punishment as he may, he will always have a sullen crew and an unhappy ship. But force must be used sometimes for the ends of discipline. On such occasions the quality of the Commander will be most sorely tried. . . .

When a Commander has, by tact, patience, justice, and firmness, each exercised in its proper turn, produced such an impression upon those under his orders in a ship of war, he has only to await the appearance of his enemy's top-sails upon the horizon. He can never tell when that moment may come. But when it does come, he may be sure of victory over an equal or somewhat superior force, or honourable defeat by one greatly superior. Or, in rare cases, sometimes justifiable, he may challenge the devotion of his followers to sink with him alongside the more powerful foe, and all go down together with the unstricken flag of their country still waving defiantly over them in their ocean sepulchre.

No such achievements are possible to an unhappy ship with a sullen crew.

All these considerations pertain to the naval officer afloat. But part, and often an important part, of his career must be in port or on duty ashore. Here he must be of affable temper and a master of civilities. He must meet and mix with his inferiors of rank in society ashore, and on such occasions he must have tact to be easy and gracious with them, particularly when ladies are present; at the same time without the least air of patronage or affected condescension, though constantly preserving the distinction of rank. . . .

APPENDIX L
UNIFORM AND PAY OF THE FIRST OFFICERS OF THE NAVY

The uniform of the officers of the Navy is thus described in a resolution to the Marine Committee:

IN MARINE COMMITTEE

PHILADELPHIA, September 5, 1776.

Resolved, That the uniform of the Officers in the Navy of the United States be as follows:

Captains. Blue cloth with red lapels, slash cuff, stand-up collar, flat yellow buttons, blue britches, red waistcoat with narrow lace.

Lieutenants. Blue with red lapels, a round cuff faced, stand-up collar, yellow buttons, blue britches, red waistcoat plain.

Masters. Blue with lapels, round cuff, blue britches, and red waistcoat.

Midshipmen. Blue lapeled coat, a round cuff, faced with red, stand-cup collar, with red at the button and button hole, blue britches, and red waistcoat.

Extract from the Minutes,

JOHN BROWN, *Secretary.*

Uniform of the Marine Officers

A green coat faced with white, round cuff, slash'd sleeves and pockets, with buttons round the cuff, silver epaulette on the right shoulder, skirts turned back, buttons to suit the facings.

White waistcoat and britches edged with green, black gaiters and garters, green shirts for the men if they can be procured.

This original uniform order did not meet with the satisfaction of the majority of the naval captains at Boston. In March, 1777, they proposed more elaborate uniforms.[1] For example,

Gold epaulettes on the right shoulder, the figure of a rattlesnake embroidered on the straps of the epaulettes, with the motto, "Don't tread on me." The waistcoat trimmed with gold lace. . . .

John Paul Jones evidently adopted the uniform he had previously desired and recommended, for John Adams who had gone to

---

[1] This memorandum may be found among the Paul Jones's Manuscript, in the Congressional Library, signed by Captains John Manley, Hector McNeil, Dudley Saltonstall, E. Hinman, Joseph Olney, John Roche, and John Paul Jones, and by Captain McNeil for Captain William Thompson, and by Captain Olney for Captain Abraham Whipple.

Lorient, France, in the *Alliance* with Captain Landais, writes in his diary from that point, May, 1779:

After dinner walked out with Captains Jones and Landais to see Jones's marines dressed in the English uniforms, red and white. A number of very active and clever sergeants and corporals are employed to teach them the exercise and manoeuvres and marches, &c., after which Jones came on board our ship. Jones has art and secrecy, and aspires very high. You see the character of the man in his uniform, and that of his officers and marines, *variant from the uniform established by Congress*—golden button-holes for himself, two epaulettes; marines in red and white instead of green. Eccentricities and irregularities are to be expected from him—they are in his character, they are visible in his eyes. His voice is soft and still and small, his eye has keenness and wildness and softness in it.

The monthly pay of all officers and men in the American Navy in 1776, from the date of the new commission under the free and independent states of America was as follows:

Rank	Of Ships of 20 Guns	Of Ships 10 to 20 Guns
Captain	$60	$48
Lieutenant	30	24
Master	30	24
———— Mate	15	15
Boatswain	15	13
———— Mate	9½	9
Gunner	15	13
———— Mate	9½	9
Surgeon	25	21⅔
———— Mate	15	13⅓
Carpenter	15	13
———— Mate	9½	9
Cooper	9	9
Midshipman	12	12
Armourer	9	9
Sailmaker	10	10
———— Mate	8⅓	8⅓
Yeoman	8½	8½
Quartermaster	9	8½
Cook	9	8½
Cockswain	9	9
Captain's clerk	15	12
Steward	10	10
Chaplain	20	
Yeoman of powder-room	9½	9

Master-at-arms 10
Seaman 8   9
    That the pay of the officers in such vessels be—   8
    That vessels under ten guns be commanded by lieutenants:
Lieutenant, commanding 30
Mate 15
Boatswain 12
Gunner 12
Carpenter 12

APPENDIX M

THE YACHT ENSIGN

There are quoted hereunder extracts of the opinion of the Judge Advocate General of the Navy at the direction of the Secretary of the Navy on the questions,

as to whether a ship of the Navy should dip her ensign in return for such dip by a yacht flying the yacht ensign and, secondly, whether the yacht ensign might properly be made the object of a hand salute rendered on boarding or leaving the yacht.

With reference to the legal status of the yacht ensign attention is invited to the Act of August 7, 1848 (46 U.S.C. 109), which provides:

"All licensed yachts shall use a signal of the form, size, and colors prescribed by the Secretary of the Navy; and the owners thereof shall at all times permit the naval architects in the employ of the United States to examine the copy the models of such yachts (Revised Statutes 4215)."

This office knows of no other law or regulation pertaining to the legal status of this flag.

Soon after the passage of the above Act, the Secretary of the Navy, by virtue of the authority delegated to him in the Act, requested the New York Yacht Club to submit a proposed design. The design of the present flag was submitted, and on February 21, 1849, was approved by the Navy Department.

Article 341 *Navy Regulations*, 1920, provides: "When any vessel salutes a ship of the Navy by dipping her national ensign, it shall be returned dip for dip. . . ."

The following is quoted from a letter addressed to the Secretary of State by the Secretary of the Navy on January 17, 1931:

"The following is in answer to the questions of the Minister of Sweden, as contained in the copy of his letter enclosed in your letter FA811.015/122 of the Secretary of the Navy of January 12, 1931.

"(a) The United States has no naval or merchant flag. All government vessels fly the national flag. They may carry other flags but they are in addition to and not instead of the national flag.

"(b) There is but one class of vessels coming under the laws of the United States, namely yachts, which do not fly the national ensign, and they fly the yacht ensign instead of the national flag."

If Article 341 *Navy Regulations* is strictly construed, a ship of the Navy returns a dip only when saluted by a vessel dipping her national ensign. In this connection it is noted that the law authorizing the yacht ensign refers to it as a signal. It does not appear that authority was delegated to the Secretary of the Navy to prescribe a national flag for yachts. However, there is no provision in the law that such signal shall not be flown in lieu of the national ensign as in the case of the flag or pennant of the Merchant Marine Naval Reserve (34 U.S.C. 805). Since the only law pertaining to the yacht ensign is the Act of August 7, 1848 (46 U.S.C. 109), this office is of the opinion that the letter from the Secretary of the Navy to the Secretary of State, quoted in paragraph above, is conclusive as to its use. For the same reason the honors, salutes and ceremonies to be accorded the yacht ensign should be based on a consideration of custom and usage. Legal questions are not involved.

The Judge Advocate General believes it is customary for naval vessels to return the dip of a licensed yacht flying the yacht ensign. The routine of the New York Yacht Club incorporates this custom and provides that vessels of the United States and foreign navies shall be saluted. This appears to be a good custom. The law authorizing yacht ensigns does not conflict with the custom of the sea in returning dip for dip and, under the decision of the Secretary of the Navy, this ensign should be used on licensed yachts instead of the national flag.

The routine of the New York Yacht Club also provides for saluting the quarter-deck when coming on board or leaving a yacht. There does not appear to be any legal objection to such custom. In view of the history of this salute as a personal recognition to the seat of authority, the Judge Advocate General believes such custom is a proper one.

Accordingly, this office is of the opinion that a ship of the Navy should return a dip made by a yacht flying the yacht ensign and that the yacht ensign may properly be made the object of a hand salute to be rendered on boarding or leaving a yacht.

W. B. Woodson

March 2, 1939
APPROVED:
Charles Edison
Acting Secretary of the Navy.

"THE LAWS OF THE NAVY"

Now these are laws of the Navy,
  Unwritten and varied they be;
And he that is wise will observe them,
  Going down in his ship to the sea;
As naught may outrun the destroyer,
  Even so with the law and its grip,
For the strength of the ship is the Service,
  And the strength of the Service, the ship.

Take heed what ye say of your seniors,
  Be your words spoken softly or plain,
Lest a bird of the air tell the matter,
  And so ye shall hear it again.

If ye labour from morn until even'
  And meet with reproof for your toil,
It is well—that the guns be humbled,
  The compressor must check the recoil.

On the strength of one link in the cable,
  Dependeth the might of the chain.
Who knows when thou mayest be tested?
  So live that thou bearest the strain!

When the ship that is tired returneth,
  With the signs of the sea showing plain,
Men place her in dock for a season,
  And her speed she reneweth again.
So shall thou, lest perchance thou grow weary
  In the uttermost parts of the sea,
Pray for leave, for the good of the Service,
  As much and as oft as may be.

Count not upon certain promotion,
  But rather to gain it aspire;
Though the sight-line end on the target,
  There cometh, perchance, a miss-fire.

If ye win through an Arctic ice floe,
 Unmentioned at home in the Press,
Heed it not, no man seeth the piston,
 But it driveth the ship none the less.

Can'st follow the track of the dolphin
 Or tell where the sea swallows roam;
Where leviathan taketh his pastime;
 What ocean he calleth his home?
Even so with the words of thy seniors,
 And the orders those words shall convey.
Every law is as naught beside this one—
 "Thou shalt not criticise, but obey!"
Saith the wise, "How may I know their purpose?"
 Then acts without wherefore or why.
Stays the fool but one moment to question,
 And the chance of his life passeth by.

Do they growl? It is well: be thou silent,
 So that work goeth forward amain;
Lo, the gun throws her shot to a hair's breath
 And shouteth, yet none shall complain.
Do they growl and the work be retarded?
 It is ill, speak, whatever their rank;
The half-loaded gun also shouteth,
 But can she pierce armor with blank?

Doth the funnels make war with the paintwork?
 Do the decks to the cannon complain?
Nay, they know that some soap or a scraper
 Unites them as brothers again.
So ye, being Heads of Departments,
 Do your growl with a smile on your lip,
Lest ye strive and in anger be parted,
 And lessen the might of your ship.

Dost think, in a moment of anger,
 'Tis well with thy seniors to fight?
They prosper, who burn in the morning,
 The letters they wrote over-night;

For some there be, shelved and forgotten,
　　With nothing to thank for their fate,
Save that (on a half-sheet of foolscap),
　　Which a fool "Had the honor to state—."

Dost deem that thy vessel needs gilding,
　　And the dockyard forbear to supply;
Place thy hand in thy pocket and gild her,
　　There be those who have risen thereby.

If the fairway be crowded with shipping,
　　Beating homeward the harbour to win,
It is meet that, lest any should suffer,
　　The steamers pass cautiously in;
So thou, when thou nearest promotion,
　　And the peak that is gilded is nigh,
Give heed to thy words and thine actions,
　　Lest others be wearied thereby.
It is ill for the winners to worry,
　　Take thy fate as it comes with a smile,
And when thou art safe in the harbour
　　They will envy, but may not revile.

Uncharted the rocks that surround thee,
　　Take heed that the channels thou learn,
Lest thy name serve to buoy for another
　　That shoal, the Courts-Martial Return.
Though Armour, the belt that protects her,
　　The ship bears the scar on her side;
It is well if the court acquit thee;
　　It were best hadst thou never been tried.

Now these are laws of the Navy,
　　Unwritten and varied they be;
And he that is wise will observe them,
　　Going down in his ship to the sea.
As the wave rises clear to the hawse pipe,
　　Washes aft, and is lost in the wake,
So shall ye drop astern, all unheeded,
　　Such time as the law ye forsake.

Now these are the Laws of the Navy
  And many and mighty are they.
But the hull and the deck and the keel
  And the truck of the law is—OBEY

—*By* Captain Hopwood, R.N.

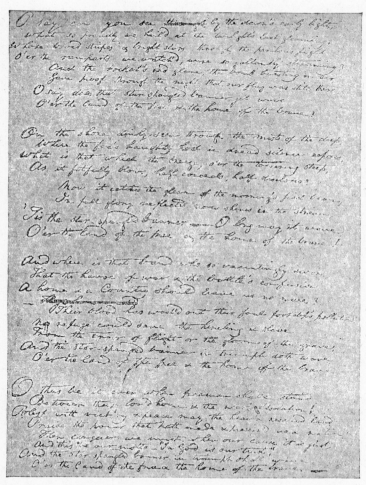

The original manuscript of the final text of the "Star-Spangled Banner,"
in the handwriting of Francis Scott Key (see Naval Institute Proceedings, June, 1927).

The Star-Spangled Banner

proof through the night that our Flag was still there. Oh, say, does that Star-Span-gled Ban-ner yet wave, O'er the land of the free, and the home of the brave?

2 On the shore dimly seen through the mists of the deep,
   Where the foe's haughty host in dread silence reposes,
   What is that which the breeze, o'er the towering steep,
   As it fitfully blows, half conceals, half discloses?
   Now it catches the gleam of the morning's first beam,
   In full glory reflected, now shines on the stream;
   And the Star-Spangled Banner, Oh, long may it wave,
   O'er the land of the free, and the home of the brave!

3 And where is that band who so vauntingly swore,
   That the havoc of war and the battle's confusion,
   A home and a country shall leave us no more?
   Their blood has wash'd out their foul footsteps' pollution!
   No refuge could save the hireling and slave,
   From the terror of flight, or the gloom of the grave;
   And the Star-Spangled Banner, in triumph doth wave,
   O'er the land of the free, and the home of the brave!

4 O thus be it e'er when freemen shall stand,
   Between their lov'd home, and the war's desolation;
   Blest with vict'ry and peace, may the Heav'n rescued land,
   Praise the Pow'r that hath made and preserved us a nation.
   Then conquer we must, for our cause it is just,
   And this be our motto: "In God is our trust!"
   And the Star-Spangled Banner, in triumph shall wave,
   O'er the land of the free, and the home of the brave!

Anchor's Aweigh

Music by
CHAS. A ZIMMERMAN

1. Stand Na - vy down the field, Sails set to the sky, . . . We'll nev - er change our course, So Ar - my you steer shy - y - y - y. Roll up the score, Na - vy, An - - chor's A - weigh, . . . Sail Na - vy down the field And sink the Ar - my, sink the Ar - my Grey. . . .

2 Get under way, Navy,
  Decks cleared for the fray,
We'll hoist true Navy Blue
  So Army down your Grey-y-y-y.
Full speed ahead, Navy;
  Army heave to,
Furl Black and Grey and Gold
And hoist the Navy, hoist the Navy Blue.

3 Blue of the Seven Seas,
  Gold of God's great sun—
Let these our colors be
  Till all of time be done-n-n-ne,
By Severn shore we learn
  Navy's stern call:
Faith, courage, service true
  With honor over, honor over all.

The Marine's Hymn

1. From the Halls of Mon-te-zu — ma To the shores of Trip-o-li . We fight our coun-try's bat — tles On the land as on the sea . . . First to fight for right and free — dom And to keep our hon-or clean . . We are proud to claim the ti — tle Of U-nit-ed States Ma-rine. . .

2 Our flag's unfurl'd to ev'ry breeze,
  From dawn to setting sun,
We have fought in ev'ry clime and place
  Where we could take a gun;
In the snow of far off northern lands,
  And in sunny tropic scenes,
You will find us always on the job—
  The United States Marines.

3 Here's health to you and to our corps,
  Which we are proud to serve;
In many a strife we've fought for life,
  And never lost our nerve.
If the Army and the Navy
  Ever look on Heaven's scenes,
They will find the streets are guarded
  By United States Marines.

BIBLIOGRAPHY

List of Titles of Books Used as Source Material

"Many things contained in this book are no other than collections of other authors, and my labor is no more therein than theirs who gather a variety of flowers out of several gardens to compose one sightly garland."

SIR WM. MONSON (1703)

SOCIOLOGICAL AND PSYCHOLOGICAL CONSIDERATION OF CUSTOMS, TRADITIONS, AND USAGE

Ellis, Havelock, *The Dance of Life,* Boston and New York: Houghton Mifflin Co., 1924.

Ludovici, Anthony M. *A Defence of Aristocracy,* London: Constable and Co., Ltd., 1933.

Rapport, Dr. Angelo S., *Superstitions of Sailors,* London: Stanley Paul Co., Ltd., 1928.

Spencer, Herbert, *Principles of Sociology,* 3 vols. Part 4, "Ceremonial Institutions," New York: 1880.

Veblen, Thorstein, *The Theory of the Leisure Class,* New York: 1899.

SEA LORE, CUSTOMS, TRADITIONS, USAGE, MEMOIRS, AND NAVAL HISTORY

Alden, Carroll Storrs, and Earle, Ralph, Captain, U.S.N., *Makers of Naval Tradition,* Boston: Ginn and Co., 1925.

Allen, G. W., *Our Naval War with France,* Boston: Houghton Mifflin Co., 1909.

Ammen, Daniel, Rear Admiral, U.S.N., *Old Navy and the New,* Philadelphia: J. W. Lippincott Co., 1891.

Arnold-Forster, D., Rear Admiral, R.N., *The Ways of the Navy,* London and Melbourne: Ward, Loch and Co., 1932.

Barney, Mary, *A Biographical Memoir of the Late Commodore Barney,* Boston: 1832.

Beckett, W. N. T., Commander, R.N., *A Few Naval Customs, Expressions, Traditions, and Superstitions,* 2d ed., Portsmouth, England: Gieves, Ltd.

Brown, Abel, *The Naval Monument,* Boston: Phillips Sampson and Co., 1816.

Clark, George R., Rear Admiral, (Ret.), U.S.N., Stevens, W. O.,

Alden, Carroll S., Krafft, Herman F., *A Short History of the United States Navy,* rev. ed., Philadelphia and London: J. B. Lippincott and Co., 1927.

Chatterton, E. Keble, *Sailing the Seas,* London: Chapman and Hall, 1931.

Coggeshall, George, *History of American Privateers and Letters of Marque,* New York.

Conrad, Joseph, *The Mirror of the Sea: Memories and Impressions,* Garden City, New York: Doubleday Page & Co., 1921.

Cooper, J. Fenimore, *The History of the Navy of the United States,* 2 vols., Philadelphia: Lea and Blanchard, 1839.

Duncan, Robert B., *Brave Deeds of American Sailors,* Philadelphia: George W. Jacobs & Co., 1912.

Field, C., Colonel, R.M.L.I., *Old Times Afloat: A Naval Anthology,* London: Andrew Melrose, Ltd., 1932.

Gleaves, Albert, Lieutenant Commander, U.S.N., *James Lawrence, Captain, United States Navy, Commander of the "Chesapeake,"* New York: G. P. Putnam's Sons, 1904.

Green, Fitzhugh, Lieutenant Commander, U.S.N., *Our Naval Heritage,* New York and London: The Century Co., 1925.

Hall, Basil, Captain, R.N., *Fragments of Voyages and Travels,* new ed., London: Edward Mixon, 1846.

Jones, C. C., *Life of Commodore Tatnall,* Savannah: 1878.

Jones, George, *Sketches of Naval Life: A Series of Letters From the "Brandywine" and "Constitution" Frigates,* New Haven: 1829.

Kimball, H., *The Naval Temple: Complete History of the Battles Fought by the Navy of the United States,* Boston: 1816.

DeKoven, Mrs. Reginald, *Life and Letters of John Paul Jones,* 2 vols., Charles Scribner's Sons, 1913.

Lowry, R. G., Lieut. Commander, R.N., *The Origin of Some Naval Terms and Customs,* London: Sampson Low, Marston & Co., Ltd.

Mackenzie, A. S., *Life of Stephen Decatur,* Boston: Chas. C. Little and Jas. Brown, 1846.

Mahan, A. T., Captain, U.S.N., *Types of Naval Officers: Drawn from History of the British Navy,* Boston: Little, Brown and Co., 1918.

Masefield, John, *Sea Life in Nelson's Time,* New York: Macmillan Co., 1925.

Monson, Sir William, *Naval Tracts,* 6 books written in 1703.

Montgomery, James Eglington, of the Admiral's Staff, *Our Admiral's Flag Abroad: The Cruise of Admiral D. G. Farragut,* New York: G. P. Putnam's Sons, 1869.

Morris, Charles, Commodore, U.S.N., *The Autobiography of Commodore Morris,* U. S. Naval Institute PROCEEDINGS.

Paullin, C. O., *The Navy of the American Revolution,* New York.

Porter, D. D., *Memoirs of Commodore David Porter.*

Puckle, Bertram S., *Funeral Customs: Their Origin and Development,* New York: Frederick A. Stokes, 1926.

Robinson, Charles N., Commander, R.N., *The British Tar in Fact and Fiction,* New York: Harper and Bros., 1909.

Robinson, William Morrison, *The Confederate Privateers,* New Haven: Yale University Press, 1928.

Rogers, Stanley, *Sea Lore,* New York: Thomas Y. Crowell Co.

Russel, Phillip, *John Paul Jones, Man of Action.*

Sayer, Edmund S., *Ships of Other Days* (limited ed.) Nice, France: Imprimerie Gastaud, 1930.

Sherburne, J. H., *Life and Character of the Chevalier John Paul Jones* (First Naval Seniority Lists, Uniforms and Pay of Officers and Men, etc.) .

Snow, Elliot, Rear Admiral (C.C.) , U.S.N., (Ret.) , *Life in a Man-of-War: or Scenes in "Old Ironsides" during Her Cruise in the Pacific,* Boston and New York: Houghton Mifflin Co., Cambridge: Riverside Press, 1929.

Snow, Elliot, Rear Admiral (C.C.) , U.S.N. (Ret.) , and Gosnell, A. H., Lieutenant Commander, U.S.N.R., *"On the Decks of "Old Ironsides,"* New York: Macmillan Co., 1932.

Stewart, C. W., editor. *John Paul Jones Commemoration at Annapolis . . . 1906,* Washington: Government Printing Office, 1907.

Swan, Oliver G. (edited by) , *Deep Water Days* (A collection) , Philadelphia: McCrae, Smith Co., 1929.

Ward, Edward W., *The Wooden World* (First published London, 1707) , Society for Nautical Research, 41 Westcombe Park Road, London, S.E. 3, Edwin Chappell, 1929.

Wells, Gerard, Rear Admiral, R.N., *Naval Customs and Traditions,* London: Philip Alan, 1930.

Yexley, Lionel, *Our Fighting Sea Men,* London: Stanley Paul & Co., 1911.

MARINE ENCYCLOPEDIAS; NAUTICAL DICTIONARIES OF WORDS, PHRASES AND EXPRESSIONS; ROUTINE BOOKS, ORDER BOOKS, AND NAVAL REGULATIONS

A Naval Encyclopedia, a Dictionary of Nautical Words and Phrases, Biographical Notices, and Records of Naval Officers, prepared by officers of the Navy, Philadelphia: L. R. Hammersly and Co., 1881.

Ansted, A., *A Dictionary of Sea Terms.* Brown, Son and Ferguson, Ltd., 1933.

Belknap, Reginald R., Captain, U.S.N., *Routine Book,* Annapolis, Md.: U. S. Naval Institute.

Blunt, Edmund H., *Theory and Practice of Seamanship . . . .* with Rules, Regulations, and Instructions for the Naval Service, New York: 1824.

Bradford, Gershom, *A Glossary of Sea Terms,* New York: Yachting, Inc., 1927.

Cowan, Frank, *A Dictionary of the Proverbs and Proverbial Phrases of the English Language Relating to the Sea,* Greensburgh, Pennsylvania: Olivier Publishing House, 1894.

Falconer's Marine Dictionary, rev. by Dr. Wm. Burney, London: 1815.

Neeser, Robert Wilden, *Statistical and Chronological History of the United States Navy* (2 vols.), New York: The Macmillan Co., 1909.

Plunkett, Honorable R., Commander, R.N., *Modern Officer of the Watch,* 5th ed., London: John Hogg, 1913.

Smith, Logan Pearsall, *Words and Idioms. Studies in the English Language,* 4th ed., London: Constable and Co., 1933.

Smyth, W. H., Vice-Admiral, R.N., *Sailor's Word Book: An Alphabetical Digest of Nautical Terms,* London: Blackie and Sons, 1867.

Regulations of the Colonial and United States Navy

(1) *Rules for the Regulation of the Navy of the United Colonies; Pay Tables; Articles of Enlistment and Distribution of Prize Money.* Philadelphia: 23 November, 1775. Text appears in Way & Gideon editions of journals of American Congress vol. I, p. 185-391 (Con-

gressional library book No. Z2:7:1) , and in Journals of Continental Congress, edited from original records.

(2) *Naval Regulations* (1802) , reprint 1809; these are entitled *Naval Regulations Issued by Command of the President of the United States of America,* and are signed "by command, Rt. Smith, secretary" and dated 25 January, 1802.

(3) *Naval Regulations* (1814) .

(4) "American State Papers," *Naval Affairs,* vol. I, 1794-1825, p. 512 *Rules, Regulations, and Instructions for the Naval Service.* President Monroe to the House of Representatives, 20 April, 1818. Prepared by Board of Navy Commissioners in obedience to act of Congress 7 February, 1815 entitled "an act to alter and amend the several acts for establishing a Navy Department, by adding thereto a board of commissioners."

(5) *Report on the Rules for the Naval Service.* 29 December, 1819, Sec't. Smith Thompson, *Senate document No. 15,* 16th Cong., 1st Session, vol. 1, "showing wherein the rules, regulations, and instructions adopted by the naval service are at variance with the existing laws, and suggesting amendment of the laws so as to make them conform."

(6) *Rules and Regulations of the Naval Service.* Sec't. Smith Thompson, 11 January, 1821, *Senate Document No. 65,* 16th Cong., 2d. Session, vol. 2, "the rules and regulations for the naval service prepared and reported under the authority of an act of Congress of 7 February, 1815, with a schedule of alterations and additions as have been deemed necessary."

(7) *The Rules of the Navy Department Regulating the Civil Administration of the Navy,* city of Washington, printed at the Globe office, by F. P. Blair. This was called the "Red Book" and was published in 1832; the *Rules, Regulations,* etc., of 1818 was called the "Blue Book" and was effective in 1832 for the military administration as distinguished from the civil.

(8) *Rules and Regulations Prepared by the Board of Revision for the Government of the Navy, 23 December, 1833.* House of Representatives *Executive Document No. 20 and 375,* 23d Cong., 1st Session, serial No. 254 and 258.

(9) *Book of Regulations for Use of Commanders, Pursers, and Recruiting Officers* (1838) .

(10) *Financial Regulations for Naval Officers* (1838) .

(11) *General Regulations for Navy and Marine Corps,* published

in Washington, by J. and G. S. Gideon, 1841. These were prepared in obedience to joint resolution of Congress of 24 May, 1842, 72d Con., 3d Session, *House Document 148*, serial No. 421. Poore's reference on this is "Jan. 13, 1843, copy of proposed new regulations," Sec't. A. P. Upshur, in response to House of Representatives resolution.

(12) *Regulations, Circulars, Orders and Decisions for Guide of Officers of Navy* (1851). In 1853 the *Orders and Instructions* for the Navy were declared not legal by the Attorney General and were withdrawn. Poore refers to 1851 amendments necessary due to abolishing of flogging in the Navy.

(13) *Regulations of Navy* (1863).

(14) *Regulations for Government of Navy* (1865), 344 pages.

(15) *Regulations for Government of Navy* (1869), various amendments and additions were issued.

(16) *Regulations for Government of Navy* (1870), various amendments and additions were issued.

(17) *Regulations for Government of Navy* (1876), various amendments and additions were issued.

(18) *Regulations for Government of Navy* (1893), various amendments and additions were issued.

(19) *Regulations for Government of Navy* (1896), various amendments and additions were issued.

(20) *Regulations for Government of Navy* (1900), various amendments and additions were issued.

(21) *Regulations for Government of Navy* (1909), various amendments and additions were issued.

The above references are listed in *Check list of U. S. Public Documents, 1789-1909* and *Poore's Index to U. S. Publications,* as well as appearing in original and state papers indicated.

(22) *U. S. Navy Regulations* (1913), various amendments and additions.

(23) *U. S. Navy Regulations* (1920), various amendments and additions, which is effective at this writing.

WAR OF 1812

Abbot, Willis J., *Blue Jackets of 1812: A History of the Naval Battles of the Second War with Great Britain,* New York: Dodd, Mead and Co., 1887.

Frost, Holloway H., Commander, U.S.N., *We Build a Navy*, Annapolis: U. S. Naval Institute, 1929.

James, Wm., *Naval Occurrences of the Late War between Great Britain and the United States of America*, London: 1817.

Roosevelt, Theodore, *Naval War of 1812*, New York: G. P. Putnam's Sons, 1882.

Biographies and Autobiographies of officers listed under "Naval History."

FLAGS, HERALDRY, AND ARMS

Boutell, *Manual of Heraldry*, London and New York: Frederick Warne and Co., Ltd., 1931.

Preble, George Henry, Rear Admiral, U.S.N., *History of the Flag of the United States of America: Symbols, Standards, Banners, and Flags of Ancient and Modern Nations*, Boston: H. Williams and Co., 1880.

————, *Origin and History of American Flag*, 2 vols., Philadelphia: Nicholas L. Brown, 1907.

Johnson, Willis F., *The National Flag: a History*, Cambridge, Mass.: Houghton Mifflin Co., 1930.

Smith, Colonel Nicholas, *Our Nation's Flag: In History and Incident*, Milwaukee: The Young Churchman Co., 1908.

Spanish Franciscan, *Book of Knowledge of All Kingdoms, Lands, and Lordships That Are in the World, and the Arms and Devices of Each Land*, etc., London: Old ed., Printed for the Hakluyt Society, 1912.

The Flag Code adopted at the National Flag Conference, June 14-15, 1923, as revised and endorsed at the Second National Flag Conference, May 15, 1924.

SOCIAL CUSTOMS, CONVENTIONS, PRECEDENCE, ETIQUETTE, AND SOCIAL CORRESPONDENCE

Armiger, *Titles, A Guide to the Right Use of British Titles and Honours*, London: A. and C. Black, Ltd.

Burke's *Peerage, Baronetage, and Knightage.*

Castiglione, Count Baldesar, *The Book of the Courtier* (Latest of more than 140 editions), New York: Charles Scribner's Sons, 1903.

Foster, John W., *The Practice of Diplomacy*, Boston and New York: Houghton Mifflin Co., 1906.

Greever, Garland, and Jones, Easley S., *The Century Handbook of Writing*, New York: The Century Co., 1933.

Meyers, Elizabeth, *The Social Letter*, New York: Brentano's, 1918.

Post, Emily, *Etiquette*, New York.

Regulations of the Navy, Army, and Foreign Service.

Reserve Officers' Manual, United States Navy, Government Printing Office, 1932.

Satow, Sir Ernest Mason, *A Guide to Diplomatic Practices*, New York: Longmans, Green and Co., 1917.

Taintor, Sarah Augusta, and Monro, Kate M., *The Secretary's Handbook: A Manual of Correct Usage*, New York: Macmillan Co., 1929.

West Point Monograph, *Military Discipline, Courtesies, and Customs of the Service*, West Point: 1930.

Whitaker's *Peerage, Baronetage, Knightage, and Companionage*, 1933.

SHIPS AND NAVAL PRINTS, SEA PAINTINGS, ETC.

Chatterton, E. Keble, *Old Sea Paintings*, New York: Dodd Mead and Co., 1928.

Chatterton, E. Keble, *Old Ship Prints*, New York: Dodd Mead and Co., 1927.

Colasanti, J. M., *Our Navy and Defenders*, Portsmouth, Virginia: 1905-1906.

Culver, Henry B., text, drawn by Gordon Grant, *The Book of Old Ships*. Doubleday, Page and Co., Garden City, New York: 1924.

Laughton, L. G. Carr, *Old Ship Figure-Heads and Sterns*, New York: Minton Balch and Co., 1925. Printed in Great Britain.

Walton, William, and others, *The Army and Navy of the United States* 1776-1890, Philadelphia: George Barrie, 1890.

Zogbaum, Rufus Fairchild, *All Hands*, New York and London: Harper and Bros., 1897.

MISCELLANEOUS

Barnes, Captain Wm., *When Ships Were Ships*, Albert and Charles Boni, New York, 1930.

Richmond, Sir Herbert, Vice-Admiral, R.N., *Command and Discipline*, London: Edward Stanton, 1927.

Smith, C. Fox. *Anchor Lane*, London: Methuen and Co., Ltd., 1933.

Van Denburgh, Elizabeth Douglas, *My Voyage in the United States Frigate "Congress,"* New York: Desmond Fitzgerald, Inc., 1913.

Willis, G. H. A., Paymaster Captain, C.B., R.N., *The Royal Navy As I Saw It,* London: John Murray, 1927.

Yacht Club of New York, *Club Book of By-Laws, Racing Rules, and Yacht Routine,* 1932.

I gratefully acknowledge the information that I have derived from the Naval Institute PROCEEDINGS issued for over sixty years. Those who care to pursue further a study of our vanishing history and traditions will find in the Naval Institute PROCEEDINGS a rich store-house of naval lore and history.

INDEX

NOTE.—"Nautical Words and Expressions," Chap. IX, are not indexed but are arranged alphabetically in that chapter. Ships and titles of books are italicized.